MACMILLAN ANTHOLOGIES OF ENGLISH LITERATURE

General Editors:
A. Norman Jeffares, formerly Professor of English, University of Stirling
Michael Alexander, Berry Professor of English Literature, University of St Andrews

MACMILLAN ANTHOLOGIES
OF ENGLISH LITERATURE

Volume 1 THE MIDDLE AGES (700–1550)
Michael Alexander and Felicity Riddy

Volume 2 THE RENAISSANCE (1550–1660)
Gordon Campbell

Volume 3 THE RESTORATION AND
EIGHTEENTH CENTURY (1660–1798)
Ian McGowan

Volume 4 THE NINETEENTH CENTURY (1798–1900)
Brian Martin

Volume 5 THE TWENTIETH CENTURY (1900–present)
Neil McEwan

MACMILLAN ANTHOLOGIES
OF ENGLISH LITERATURE

THE RENAISSANCE (1550–1660)

Edited by
Gordon Campbell

M
MACMILLAN

First published 1989

Published by
MACMILLAN EDUCATION LTD
Houndmills, Basingstoke, Hampshire RG21 2XS
and London
Companies and representatives
throughout the world

Typeset by Wessex Typesetters
(Division of The Eastern Press Ltd)
Frome, Somerset

Printed in Hong Kong

British Library Cataloguing in Publication Data
The Renaissance: (1550–1660).—(Macmillan
anthologies of English literature; V.2)
I. Campbell, Gordon
820.8′′003
ISBN 0–333–39265–5
ISBN 0–333–46475–3 Pbk

Contents

General Introduction

There can often be a gulf between the restricted reading required by a school, college or university syllabus and the great expanse of English literature which is there to be explored and enjoyed. There are two effective ways of bridging that gulf. One is to be aware of how authors relate or have related to their contemporary situations and their contemporaries, how they accept, develop or react against what has been written by their predecessors or older contemporaries, how, in short, they fit into the long history of English literature. Good histories of literature – and there is a welcome increase of interest in them – serve to place authors in their context, as well as giving a panoptic view of their careers.

The second way is to sample their work, to discover the kind or kinds of writing they have produced. Here is where the anthology contributes to an enjoyment of reading. It conveys the flavour of an author as nothing but reading that author can. And when an author is compared to his or her fellow writers – a thing a good anthology facilitates – the reader gains several extra dimensions, not least an insight into what thoughts, what fears, what delights have occupied writers at different times. To gain such insights is to see, among other things, the relevance of past authors to the present, to the reader. Reading an anthology shows something of the vast range of our literature, its variety of form and outlook, of mood and expression, from black despair to ecstatic happiness; it is an expansive experience widening our horizons, enhancing specialised study, but also conveying its own particular pleasures, the joy of finding familiar pieces among unfamiliar, of reacting to fresh stimuli, of reaching new conclusions about authors, in short, of making literature a part of oneself.

Anthologies also play a part in the life of a literature. If we are the beneficiaries of our literary inheritance, we are also trustees for it, and the maintenance of the inheritance for future generations requires new selections of properly edited texts. The Macmillan Literary Anthologies, which have followed on from the Macmillan Histories of Literature, are designed to present these texts with the essential pertinent information. The selection made of poetry, prose and plays has been wide and inclusive, authors appear in the order of their dates of birth, texts – with the exception of the Middle English section – are largely modernised and footnotes are kept to a minimum. A broadly representative policy has been the aim of the general editors, who have maintained a similar format and proportion in each volume, though the medieval volume has required more annotation.

ANJ
MJA

Introduction: The English Renaissance

The period of English literature covered by this volume is known to students of literature as the Renaissance, and to students of history as the Early Modern period. These phrases are not merely descriptive, for each term represents an ideological construction of the past. The idea of a renaissance, or rebirth, implies a preceding period of decadence, a period which separates the time of renewal from the exemplary values and achievements of a still earlier period. According to this model, which was invented by the humanist writers of the late fifteenth and early sixteenth centuries, the exemplary period was that of classical antiquity, the civilisations of ancient Greece and Rome. The period of decadence was the Middle Ages, which was seen as a time in which the values of antiquity were corrupted. The Renaissance, however, was regarded as a time when the decadence of the Middle Ages was rejected in favour of a revival of the ideals of the ancient world. The upheaval of the Reformation created an ecclesiastical model parallel to the cultural notion of the Renaissance, for the new Protestant church was seen as recovering the purity of the early church from the corruption and superstition of the Middle Ages. The historians' term 'Early Modern' is an attempt to avoid the cultural bias of the term 'Renaissance', but is nonetheless built on the idea of a medieval period followed by a modern period, in the early stages of which are to be found the roots of the present.

The notion of a medieval period of darkness and ignorance stretching from the fall of Rome (or, in the ecclesiastical model, from the official adoption of Christianity as the state religion in the fourth century) to the sixteenth century will seem ridiculous to anyone familiar with the accomplishments of medieval literature, or to anyone who has visited the magnificent cathedrals of the period. The idea of a Renaissance which supersedes the accomplishments of a millenium may seem untenable to the twentieth-century student of sixteenth- and seventeenth-century literature, but because the model was taken seriously at the time, the modern student of Renaissance literature must take it seriously. According to this model the history of English (and European) culture may be traced to ancient Rome and thence to its roots in ancient Greece, rather than to our barbarian ancestors. The consequences of this view of our cultural history are not only reflected in the literature included in this volume, but continue to be felt in English education up to the present time. The ancient language which has traditionally been taught in English schools is not the Old English of our ancestors but rather the Latin of ancient Rome and the Greek of ancient Athens. The humanists of the Renaissance championed the fiction of a cultural past which linked us to two remote Mediterranean countries and ignored the continuity of English cultural history.

This theory of cultural descent was sufficiently powerful to create a literature which reflected its tenets, and in due course theory became fact, for Renaissance literature increasingly came to be based on classical rather than English models. The plays of Shakespeare and his contemporaries, for example, owe comparatively little to the lively tradition of English medieval drama. Instead they are constructed on the model of the five-act play, a form borrowed from the plays of ancient Rome. Similarly, the fact that many Renaissance plays are described on their title-pages as comedies or tragedies testifies to the power of these ancient categories to shape the controlling ideas of the drama of the period. The influence of Roman plays even extends to the values celebrated in Renaissance drama. When Romeo and Juliet commit suicide at the end of Shakespeare's tragedy, for example, the audience did not assume that the lovers had committed a sin which condemned them to eternal torment, despite the fact that the Elizabethan church condemned suicide in these terms; in Shakespearean tragedy the audience is invited to see suicide as a noble act, and this attitude derives from the values of ancient Rome rather than those of Elizabethan England.

The self-conscious influence of the literature and values of the ancient world can be felt throughout the literature of the English Renaissance. The pervasive mythological imagery of the period, for example, is not drawn from the ancient religions of England, but rather from the religions of ancient Greece and Rome. This classical mythology was so powerful a resource for Renaissance writers that it was often used as a code for speaking about the Christian faith. The 'all-judging Jove' of Milton's *Lycidas*, for example, is a thinly disguised all-judging Jehovah. Similarly, the writers of the Renaissance often chose to cast their works in forms borrowed from classical literature. It would not have been surprising if English Renaissance literature had been largely written in Latin that ancient forms such as epic, pastoral and satire would have been adopted; what is remarkable is that a vernacular language, in this case English, should be turned to the service of these forms. Education in this period, both in the schools and in the universities, was conducted wholly through the medium of Latin. The writers which this educational system produced retained the ancient forms with which they were so familiar, but used them as vessels in which to establish English as a literary language capable of supporting a literature as great as the literature of Greece and Rome. This sense of the competition between English literature and the literature of the ancient world accounts in large measure for the classical texture of so much English Renaissance literature.

The appropriation of an ancient and remote literary tradition as the basis of a new national literature does not of course produce a replica of that ancient literature. Once a literature is freed from the constraints of a classical language, it gradually moves away from its classical base. In drama, for example, early tragedies such as Kyd's *Spanish Tragedy* are markedly Senecan in tone and effect. As English tragedy developed from its neo-classical beginnings, however, it gradually evolved into a form that was only vestigially classical. Characters slowly became more introspective than their counterparts in classical plays; there is, for example, no character as self-questioning as Hamlet in ancient drama. Similarly, the classical ghosts which thump across the stages of early Renaissance plays increasingly become a psychological rather than a physical presence on the stage, and the notion of tragedy involving the demise of a single character slowly evolves into the pervasive corruption of tragedies of late Renaissance dramatists such as Webster.

Renaissance writers turned the vernacular languages to the service of classical forms, but it was of course impossible to ignore the indigenous literary traditions which were already built into those languages. Ironically, it was the common Latin culture of Renaissance Europe which fostered a mutual awareness of the establishment of various vernacular literatures. For English writers the central model was often the literature of Italy, though Italian influences were often mediated through France and the Low Countries, and arrived in England wholly transformed. The gap between the precepts of Machiavelli and the figure of Machiavel on the English stage, for example, can in some measure be explained by reference to the popular image of Machiavelli in France. Of the great Italian writers, Dante had surprisingly little influence on the literature of the English Renaissance. The fountainhead of European and English literature of the Renaissance was not Dante, but Petrarch, for it was Petrarch and his successors who established the language of love which was inherited by the Renaissance, and which sharply distinguishes the love poetry of the Renaissance from its counterparts in the ancient world. Indeed, it could be argued that Petrarch was responsible for the idea of romantic love which was celebrated in Renaissance poetry and has become an integral part of the western cultural tradition. An emotion which began as a literary attitude in Petrarchan poetry has become a real emotion in modern western culture; in the western world people now fall in love, and marry for love, and this convention separates us from cultures which have not been influenced by this tradition, and therefore encourage marriage by arrangement.

The central theme of English Renaissance literature is love, but that emotion is neither the literary attitude of the Petrarchans nor the emotion which modern students of Renaissance literature may experience in their private lives and may therefore be tempted to impose on Renaissance literature. This literature is not receptive to such an imposition, because it is poised on the point at which poets were struggling to reconcile the artificial Petrarchan language of love which they had inherited with the real erotic impulses which prompted their poetry. The love celebrated in the sonnets and comedies of the period has its origins in a Petrarchan tradition which in turn derived from the courtly poetry of Provence and the literary traditions of the twelfth-century Renaissance in France. From the cult of the Virgin Mary the Petrarchans adopted the veneration of the lady as a figure of spotless purity and virtue; from the neo-Platonic tradition they adopted the idea of love as an ennobling emotion which raised the mind above mere physical attraction. In the closing years of the sixteenth century a third influence, that of Ovidian eroticism, began to colour the literature of love, and poets such as Sir Philip Sidney began to describe their love in frankly voluptuous conceits. In poets such as John Donne this erotic strain co-exists with the tradition of idealising the woman. In the comedies of the English Renaissance love is an emotion (like tragic emotion) experienced only by the upper classes; this convention reflects the origins of romantic love in the courtly love of the Petrarchans. When working-class characters such as shepherds fall in love in English comedies, their emotions are an object of mirth. When love appears in the tragedies of the period, it becomes a destructive force, just as it had been in the tragedies of classical antiquity. In Shakespeare's tragedies hardened generals such as Othello and Antony are destroyed by the intensity of their love. In Milton's *Paradise Lost*, an epic in which the fall of humankind is presented as a tragedy, the fall of Adam is occasioned by his excessive love of Eve.

The discrepancy between the presentation of love in Renaissance literature and the modern sense of the nature of that emotion is a useful reminder of the gap in values which must be overcome if that literature is properly to be understood. The same may be said of the chief characteristic of Renaissance literature, that of decorum. In the twentieth century we are inclined to value sincerity and naturalness, but these are not values which are celebrated in Renaissance literature. Pastoral poems, in which the poet pretends to be a shepherd, seem to the modern reader artificial. In 'The Passionate Shepherd to his Love', for example, Marlowe speaks with a voice so innocent that we have difficulty reconciling it with the voice of Marlowe the radical playwright. But decorum demands that the voice of the pastoral poet be pure and guileless, and that his love reflect the values of a golden age of eternal summer in which shepherds are freed from the tending of sheep in order to concentrate on the composition of love-songs. Part of the genius of Marlowe's poem is his ability to extirpate utterly the sordidness of the world in which he lived, and instead to present himself as the purest of lovers. The 'Passionate Shepherd' is not extending an invitation to cohabit outside the confines of marriage, but rather to enter into a world in which love is uncontaminated by any worldly or moral concerns.

Similar notions of decorum also govern the comedies and tragedies of the period. Shakespeare's comedies, for example, are not naturalistic and psychologically-plausible accounts of courtship, but rather dramatic expositions of the notion that love can conquer all obstacles. The values which they celebrate are not our values, nor are they necessarily Shakespeare's values: they are the values of the genre, in this case comedy. In the comic view of the world, the most vital characters are female, and Shakespeare's comedies accordingly have at their centres heroines whose intelligence and vitality is unmatched by the comparatively dim-witted men with whom they are paired at the end of each play. The fact that women dominate these plays, and that the plays celebrate female values, does not make Shakespeare a feminist, but simply a writer of dramatic comedy. When he turns to tragedy his apparent values shift to meet the constraints of decorum in that genre. Tragedy is a male genre; except in the case of tragedies of love, in which a woman must of necessity assume a crucial part, tragedies are dominated by male characters. They also celebrate male values such as strength of character and soundness of judgement; tragic heroes who fail to live up to these standards inevitably fall. The demands of decorum could make Marlowe and Shakespeare celebrants of love when they were writing pastoral or comedy, and exponents of masculine military virtues when they were writing tragedy.

For many modern readers the aspect of Renaissance literature which alienates more than any other is the pervasive presence of religion. In the case of allusions to the gods of ancient Greece and Rome, the twentieth-century reader is likely to be merely puzzled, but such puzzles can usually be resolved by reference to the explanatory footnotes which gloss such references in volumes like this one. Allusions to Christianity constitute a more difficult problem, for the modern secular reader is tempted to see Renaissance literature as representative of our superstitious past, and the modern religious reader is likely to think many of the Christian allusions blasphemous. In Donne's sonnet 'Batter my heart', for example, the poet assumes the voice of a Petrarchan lady, God is described as a male Petrarchan lover, and Satan is portrayed as the despised other man in an adulterous Petrarchan triangle. The poem ends with a plea on the part of the lady to be ravished by God. Such an analogy, though common in early literature, would no longer be considered in many Christian circles as an appropriate way of describing the nature of the relationship between a believer and her god. What must be appreciated is that in the early seventeenth century Christians were so soaked in the traditions of neo-platonism that they assumed that the love of man and woman was an earthly reflection of the love of God and his believers for each other. This analogy even extended to the sexual aspect of human love, so that, for example, the ecstasy of joining God in the moment of death is assumed to be analogous to human sexual ecstasy; this analogy often manifests itself in the infamous pun on 'die', which in some contexts refers to both physical death and sexual consummation. Such analogies now seem strange and strained, but it must be appreciated that they permeate Renaissance literature. In Ben

Jonson's poem on the death of his first son, Jonson proposes an analogy between the creation of a child and the creation of a poem. Again, the analogy may seem to the modern reader to skate on the edge of blasphemy, but to Renaissance poets such analogies were commonplace; they inhabited a world which was deemed in all respects to reflect the divine order of things.

The preoccupation with analogies between earthly affairs and God's relationship to his creation is a marked characteristic of the religious writing of the period. The other striking feature is a preoccupation with death which may seem to the modern reader excessively morbid. Daily life, however, was more often marred by death than is the case now. Pregnancy was often a death sentence for the mother, and most infants died young. The plague regularly cut swathes through the population; violent deaths and public judicial executions were commonplace. It is now possible for an individual to live for many years without experiencing the death of a close contemporary or a member of his family; such was not the case in the Renaissance, and the regular encounters with death which were a common feature of life encouraged a more pressing awareness of mortality than is now the case. This awareness manifested itself not only in memorial poems, but also in literature not directly concerned with death. Shakespeare's sonnets, or Ralegh's lyrics, for example, are often preoccupied with the classical notion of time as a force which devours beauty and life itself. Many lyrics of the period expound the theme of *carpe diem*, a Latin phrase which literally means 'seize the day'. *Carpe diem* poems encourage the snatching of the pleasures of the moment. Herrick's 'Gather ye rosebuds while ye may' and Marvell's 'To his Coy Mistress' are both centred on the *carpe diem* motif, as is Feste's 'O mistress mine' in *Twelfth Night*:

> What is love? 'Tis not hereafter;
> Present mirth hath present laughter,
>   What's to come is still unsure.
> In delay there lies no plenty –
> Then come kiss me, sweet and twenty,
>   Youth's a stuff will not endure.

The notion that love can offer solace in the face of the uncertainties of life is a central concern of Renaissance literature. Happily it is one of the threads which connects the literature of the Renaissance to our own time. The modern reader of Renaissance literature retains an awareness of the historical distance between our own time and the Renaissance, but the stronger impression is of a continuity which enables us to read and study that literature with an immediacy which affords enormous pleasure.

GC

Note on Annotation and Glossing

An asterisk * at the end of a word indicates that such words are glossed in the margin.

A dagger † at the end of a word or phrase indicates that the word or phrase is annotated, or given a longer gloss, at the foot of the page.

Note on Dates

Where dates appear at the end of extracts, that on the left denotes the date of composition, that on the right, the date of publication.

King Henry VIII

1491–1547

Henry was born at Greenwich, the son of Henry VII and Elizabeth of York. He received a rigorous education (his tutors included the poet John Skelton), and became an accomplished scholar, musician, linguist and poet. His elder brother died in 1502, and he succeeded to the throne of England on the death of his father in 1509; he became 'supreme head' of the English church (in place of the Pope) in 1534, and King of Ireland in 1540.

Henry published theological treatises in both English and Latin; for one of these he earned the papal title 'Defender of the Faith'. He composed masses (in five parts), motets, songs and instrumental music.

PASTIME WITH GOOD COMPANY

Pastime with good company
I love and shall until I die.
Grutch* who list,† but none deny, — grumble
So God be pleased, thus live will I.
For my pastance,* — recreation
Hunt sing and dance,
My heart is set;
All goodly sport
For my comfort,
Who shall me let?* — obstruct

Youth must have some dalliance,
Of good or ill some pastance;
Company methinks them best,
All thoughts and fancies to digest.
For idleness,
Is chief mistress
Of vices all;
Then who can say
But mirth and play
Is best of all?

who list whoever wants to

Company with honesty
Is virtue, vices to flee;
Company is good and ill,
But every man hath his free will.
The best ensue,
The worst eschew;
My mind shall be,
Virtue to use,
Vice to refuse,
Thus shall I use me.

Sir Thomas Wyatt

1503–42

Thomas Wyatt was born in Kent. He was educated privately, but may have attended the University of Cambridge. He was given his first appointment at the court of Henry VIII at the age of thirteen and was later appointed to various diplomatic posts which took him to France, Italy, Spain and Flanders; he was knighted in 1535. His early marriage collapsed, apparently because of the adultery of his wife, and there is considerable evidence that he became the lover of Anne Boleyn. He apparently confessed this relationship to the king, but although he was imprisoned in the Tower of London, he escaped the mass execution of her supposed lovers, whom he commemorated in the elegy 'In mourning wise'. He died of a fever in October 1542 while engaged on a diplomatic errand for the king.

Wyatt's mission to the papal court in 1527 seems to have stimulated an interest in Petrarch, and many of Wyatt's finest poems are translations or imitations of Petrarch's sonnets. Similarly, his *The Quiet of Mind* is a translation (from a French version) of an essay by Plutarch, the most popular Greek author of the Renaissance. Wyatt's poems have been the subject of fierce critical debate in recent years. The authorship of many poems traditionally attributed to him is far from certain, as is the relationship between the poems and various incidents in Wyatt's life. The metrical irregularity of Wyatt's poems has in the past been censured, but it is now recognised that the rough rhythms of his verse derive from an earlier English tradition, and cannot be expected to conform to the more rigid pattern of iambic pentameter which became established after his death.

THE LONG LOVE†

The long love that in my thought doth harbour
And in mine heart doth keep his residence,
Into my face presseth with bold pretence,
And therein campeth, spreading his banner.
She that me learneth* to love and suffer — teaches me
And will* that my trust and lust's negligence — wishes
Be reined by reason, shame and reverence,
With his hardiness taketh displeasure.
Wherewithal unto the heart's forest he fleeth,
Leaving his enterprise with pain and cry,
And there him hideth, and not appeareth.
What may I do, when my master feareth,
But in the field with him to live and die?
For good is the life ending faithfully.

1557

WHOSO LIST TO HUNT†

Whoso list* to hunt: I know where is an hind.* — wishes; female deer
But as for me, alas I may no more:
The vain travail hath wearied me so sore,
I am of them that farthest cometh behind.
Yet may I by no means my wearied mind
Draw from the deer, but as she fleeth afore
Fainting I follow. I leave off therefore,
Sithens* in a net I seek to hold the wind. — since
Who list her hunt, I put him out of doubt,
As well as I may spend his time in vain,
And graven with diamonds in letters plain
There is written her fair neck round about:
'*Noli me tangere*,† for Caesar's I am,
And wild for to hold, though I seem tame.'

1527

The long love this sonnet is a translation of Petrarch's *Amor, che nel penser* (*Canzoniere* 140); Surrey's 'Love that doth reign' translates the same sonnet

Whoso list to hunt this sonnet, an adaptation of a sonnet by Petrarch, probably refers to Henry VIII's success in courting Anne Boleyn, with whom Wyatt was in love

noli me tangere (Latin) 'do not touch me'; the line is a partial translation of 'noli me tangere quia Caesaris sum', which was inscribed on the collars of Caesar's deer; the fact that 'noli me tangere' is left untranslated recalls the use of the phrase (in the Vulgate) by Jesus to Mary Magdalene after the resurrection (John 20.17). *Caesar* probably represents Henry VIII

FAREWELL LOVE

Farewell Love, and all thy laws for ever!
Thy baited hooks shall tangle me no more:
Senec† and Plato† call me from thy lore,
To perfect wealth my wit for to endeavour.
In blind error when I did persever,
Thy sharp repulse, that pricketh aye so sore,
Hath taught me to set in trifles no store,
And 'scape forth, since liberty is liever.* — more precious
Therefore farewell! Go trouble younger hearts,
And in me claim no more authority;
With idle youth go use thy property,* — the bow
And thereon spend thy many brittle darts:
For hitherto though I have lost all my time,
Me lusteth* no longer rotten boughs to climb. — I want

1557

MY GALLEY CHARGÈD†

My galley chargèd with forgetfulness
Through sharp seas in winter nights doth pass
'Tween rock and rock, and eke* mine enemy alas, — also
That is my lord,† steereth with cruelness,
And every oar a thought in readiness,
As though that death were light in such a case.
An endless wind doth tear the sail apace,
Of forcèd sighs and trusty fearfulness;
A rain of tears, a cloud of dark disdain
Hath done the wearied cords great hinderance,
Wreathèd with error, and eke with ignorance.
The stars† be hid that led me to this pain,
Drowned is reason that should me comfort,
And I remain despairing of the port.

1557

Senec, Plato Seneca, the Roman Stoic philosopher (*c.* 4 BC–AD 65), and Plato, the ancient Greek philosopher (*c.* 429–347 BC)
My galley chargèd this sonnet is a translation of Petrarch's *Passa la nave mia* (*Canzoniere* 189)
lord Cupid, god of love
stars the lady's eyes

YOU THAT IN LOVE

You that in love find luck and abundance
And live in lust and joyful jollity,
Arise for shame, do away your sluggardy!
Arise I say, do May some observance!
Let me in bed lie dreaming in mischance,
Let me remember the haps* most unhappy mishaps
That me betide in May† most commonly,
As one whom love list little to advance.
Sepham† said true that my nativity
Mischanced was with the ruler of the May:†
He guessed I prove of that the verity,†
In May my wealth* and eke* my life I say well-being also
Have stood so oft in such perplexity.
Rejoice! Let me dream of your felicity.
1538 1557

RESOUND MY VOICE

Resound my voice, ye woods that hear me plain,
Both hills and vales causing reflection;* echo
And rivers eke record* ye of my pain, also retell
Which hath ye oft forced by compassion
As judges to hear mine exclamation,
Among whom pity I find doth remain:
Where I it seek alas there is disdain.

Oft ye rivers, to hear my woeful sound
Have stopped your course; and plainly to express
Many a tear, by moisture of the ground
The earth hath wept, to hear my heaviness,
Which causeless to suffer without redress
The hugy oaks have roarèd in the wind,
Each thing me thought complaining in their kind.

May the month associated with lovers
Sepham Edward Sepham, an Oxford don who cast Wyatt's horoscope
ruler of the May Venus
prove . . . verity experience the truth of that

Why then alas doth not she on me rue?* take pity
Or is her heart so hard that no pity
May in it sink, my joy for to renew?
O stony heart, how hath this joinèd thee,
So cruel that art, cloaked with beauty?
No grace to me from thee there may proceed
But as rewarded death for to be my meed.* recompense

1557

THEY FLEE FROM ME

They flee from me, that sometime did me seek
With naked foot stalking in my chamber.
I have seen them gentle, tame, and meek
That now are wild, and do not remember
That sometime they put themself in danger
To take bread at my hand; and now they range,
Busily seeking with a continual change.

Thankèd be fortune it hath been otherwise
Twenty times better, but once in special,
In thin array after a pleasant guise
When her loose gown from her shoulders did fall,
And she me caught in her arms long and small,* slender
Therewithal sweetly did me kiss,
And softly said, 'Dear heart, how like you this?'

It was no dream: I lay broad waking.
But all is turned through my gentleness
Into a strange fashion of forsaking,
And I have leave to go of her goodness,
And she also to use newfangleness.* fickleness
And since that I so kindly am served,
I would fain know what she hath deserved.

1557

LIKE AS THE SWAN

Like as the swan towards her death
Doth strain her voice with doleful note,
Right so sing I with waste of breath:
I die! I die! and you regard it not.

I shall enforce my fainting breath
That all that hears this deadly note
Shall know that you doth cause my death:
I die! I die! and you regard it not.

Your unkindness hath sworn my death,
And changèd hath my pleasant note
To painful sighs that stops my breath:
I die! I die! and you regard it not.

Consumeth my life, faileth my breath:
Your fault is forger of this note.
Melting in tears, a cruel death
I die! I die! and you regard it not.

My faith with me after my death
Buried shall be, and to this note
I do bequeath my weary breath,
To cry: 'I died! and you regard it not!'

IN ETERNUM

In eternum† I was once determed* — determined
For to have loved, and my mind affirmed
That with my heart it should be confirmed* — strengthened
In eternum.

Forthwith I found the thing that I might like,
And sought with love to warm her heart alike,
For as me thought I should not see the like
In eternum.

---

in eternum (Renaissance Latin) 'forever'

To trace this dance I put myself in press;* exerted myself
Vain hope did lead, and bade I should not cease
To serve, to suffer, and still* to hold my peace always
In eternum.

With this first rule I furthered me apace,
That as me thought my truth had taken place
With full assurance to stand in her grace
In eternum.

It was not long ere I by proof had found
That feeble building is on feeble ground,
For in her heart this word did never sound –
In eternum.

In eternum then from my heart I kest* cast
That I had first determed for the best:
Now in the place another thought doth rest
In eternum.

WHAT MEANETH THIS?

What meaneth this? When I lie alone
I toss, I turn, I sigh, I groan,
My bed me seems as hard as stone:
What meaneth this?

I sigh, I plain* continually, lament
The clothes that on my bed do lie
Always methink they lie awry:
What meaneth this?

In slumbers oft for fear I quake,
For heat and cold I burn and shake,
For lack of sleep my head doth ache:
What meaneth this?

Amornings then when I do rise,
I turn unto my wonted guise,
All day after muse and devise:†
What meaneth this?

And if perchance by me there pass
She unto whom I sue for grace,
The cold blood forsaketh my face:
What meaneth this?

But if I sit near her by,
With loud voice my heart doth cry,
And yet my mouth is dumb and dry:
What meaneth this?

To ask for help no heart I have,
My tongue doth fail* what I should crave, lacks
Yet inwardly I rage and rave:
What meaneth this?

Thus have I passed many a year
And many a day, though nought appear
But most of that that most I fear:
What meaneth this?

IN MOURNING WISE†

In mourning wise since daily I increase,†
Thus should I cloak the cause of all my grief;
So pensive mind with tongue to hold his peace
My reason sayeth there can be no relief:
Wherefore give ear, I humbly you require,
The affect* to know that thus doth make me moan. passion
The cause is great of all my doleful cheer
For those that were, and now be dead and gone.

muse and devise ponder and surmise
In mourning wise this elegy commemorates the five men who were executed as Anne Boleyn's lovers: her brother Lord Rochford, the courtiers Henry Norris, Francis Weston and William Brereton, and the court musician Mark Smeaton
In mourning . . . increase since I daily become more adept in mourning

What though to death desert* be now their call, deserved
As by their faults it doth appear right plain?
Of force I must lament that such a fall
Should light on those so wealthily did reign,
Though some perchance will say, of cruel heart,
A traitor's death why should we thus bemoan?
But I alas, set this offence apart,
Must needs bewail the death of some be gone.

As for them all I do not thus lament,
But as of right my reason doth me bind;
But as the most* doth all their deaths repent, greatest
Even so do I by force of mourning mind.
Some say, 'Rochford, haddest thou been not so proud,
For thy great wit each man would thee bemoan,
Since as it is so, many cry aloud
"It is great loss that thou art dead and gone".'

Ah! Norris, Norris, my tears begin to run
To think what hap did thee so lead or guide
Whereby thou hast both thee and thine undone
That is bewailed in court of every side;
In place also where thou hast never been
Both man and child doth piteously thee moan.
They say, 'Alas, thou art far overseen
By thine offences to be thus dead and gone.'

Ah! Weston, Weston, that pleasant was and young,
In active things who might with thee compare?
All words accept that thou diddest speak with tongue,
So well esteemed with each where thou diddest fare.
And we that now in court doth lead our life
Most part in mind doth thee lament and moan;
But that thy faults we daily hear so rife,
All we should weep that thou art dead and gone.

Brereton farewell, as one that least I knew.
Great was thy love with divers as I hear,
But common voice doth not so sore thee rue
As other twain that doth before appear;
But yet no doubt but thy friends thee lament
And other hear their piteous cry and moan.
So doth each heart for thee likewise relent
That thou givest cause thus to be dead and gone.

Ah! Mark, what moan should I for thee make more,
Since that thy death thou hast deservèd best,†
Save only that mine eye is forcèd sore
With piteous plaint to moan thee with the rest?
A time thou haddest above thy poor degree,
The fall whereof thy friends may well bemoan:
A rotten twig upon so high a tree
Hath slipped thy hold, and thou art dead and gone.

And thus farewell each one in hearty wise!
The axe is home, your heads be in the street;
The trickling tears doth fall so from my eyes
I scarce may write, my paper is so wet.
But what can hope when death hath played his part,
Though nature's course will thus lament and moan?
Leave sobs therefore, and every Christian heart
Pray for the souls of those be dead and gone.
1536

From SATIRE I

[*Mine own John Poyntz*]

My Poyntz,† I cannot frame my tune to feign,
To cloak the truth for praise without desert
Of them that list all vice for to retain.
I cannot honour them that sets their part
With Venus† and Bacchus† all their life long,
Nor hold my peace of them although I smart.
I cannot crouch nor kneel, to do so great a wrong
To worship them like God on earth alone
That are as wolves these seely* lambs among. innocent
I cannot with my word complain and moan
And suffer nought, nor smart without complaint,
Nor turn* the word that from my mouth is gone. recall

deservèd best Smeaton had confessed under torture

Poyntz John Poyntz was a courtier at the court of Henry VIII; Wyatt's poem explains to Poyntz why he has withdrawn from the court

Venus goddess of love

Bacchus god of wine and revelry

I cannot speak and look like a saint,
Use wiles for wit,† and make deceit a pleasure,
And call craft counsel, for profit still to paint.* flatter
I cannot wrest the law to fill the coffer,
With innocent blood to feed myself fat,
And do most hurt where most help I offer.
1541 1557

WHEN FIRST MINE EYES

When first mine eyes did view and mark
Thy fair beauty to behold,
And when mine ears listened to hark
The pleasant words that thou me told,
I would as then I had been free
From ears to hear and eyes to see.

And when my lips gan* first to move, began
Whereby my heart to thee was known,
And when my tongue did talk of love
To thee that hast true love down thrown,
I would my lips and tongue also
Had then been dumb, no deal to go.†

And when my hands have handled aught
That thee hath kept in memory,
And when my feet have gone and sought
To find and get thy company,
I would each hand a foot had been
And I each foot a hand had seen.

And when in mind I did consent
To follow this my fancy's will,
And when my heart did first relent
To taste such bait, my life to spill,
I would my heart had been as thine
Or else thy heart had been as mine.
1557

use wiles for wit substitute deceit for intelligence

no . . . go not to move at all

Henry Howard, Earl of Surrey

1517?–47

Henry Howard was the eldest son of Thomas Howard, Earl of Surrey. When Thomas Howard became Duke of Norfolk in 1524, Henry Howard assumed the courtesy title of Earl of Surrey. At the age of thirteen Surrey entered the household of the Duke of Richmond (the illegitimate son of Henry VIII), where he was educated. In 1532 he married Lady Frances de Vere, and in the same year travelled (with Thomas Wyatt) to France as an attendant of Henry VIII and Anne Boleyn (who was his cousin); he remained at the French court for more than a year. He took up a military career which culminated in his appointment in 1545 as commander at Boulogne, with the title of Lieutenant-General of the King on Sea and Land. Surrey fell from favour in 1546, when he was charged with placing the arms of Edward the Confessor in the first quarter of his shield, an heraldic impropriety which was absurdly deemed to constitute a claim to the throne. His request for trial by combat was refused, and he was tried in Guildhall on 13 January 1547; he was beheaded on Tower Hill on 19 January, a victim of court politics.

In common with Wyatt, many of Surrey's finest poems are translations. His translation of two books of Virgil's *Aeneid* (II and IV) into unrhymed iambic pentameter introduced blank verse into the English literary tradition. Again like Wyatt, he translated and imitated sonnets by Petrarch. The rhyme scheme which he invented for his sonnets became the dominant English form, which was later used by Shakespeare. His name has been linked with that of Wyatt since their poems were published together in *Tottel's Miscellany* (1557). The two poets have much in common, but the metrical regularity and emotional serenity of Surrey's poems contrasts sharply with the tumultuousness of Wyatt's verse.

THE SOOTE SEASON[†]

The soote* season, that bud and bloom forth brings   sweet
With green hath clad the hill and eke* the vale;   also
The nightingale with feathers new she sings;
And turtle to her make* hath told her tale.   mate
Summer is come, for every spray now springs;
The hart hath hung his old head on the pale;*   fence
The buck in brake his winter coat he flings;
The fishes flete* with new repairèd scale;   swim
The adder all her slough away she slings;
The swift swallow pursueth the flies small;
The busy bee her honey now she mings;[†]
Winter is worn that was the flowers' bale.[†]
And thus I see among these pleasant things
Each care decays, and yet my sorrow springs.

1557

SET ME WHERE AS THE SUN[†]

Set me where as the sun doth parch the green,
Or where his beams may not dissolve the ice;
In temperate heat where he is felt and seen;
With proud people, in presence sad* and wise;   serious
Set me in base, or yet in high degree,
In the long night, or in the shortest day,
In clear weather, or where mists thickest be,
In lost youth, or when my hairs be grey;
Set me in earth, in heaven, or yet in hell,
In hill, in dale, or in the foaming flood;
Thrall,* or at large, alive where so I dwell,   captive
Sick, or in health, in ill fame or in good:
Yours will I be, and with that only thought
Comfort myself when that my hope is nought.

1557

The soote season this sonnet is a translation of Petrarch's *Zefiro torna* (*Canzoniere* 310)
mings produces by mixing
bale cause of harm

Set me where as the sun this sonnet is a translation of Petrarch's *Pommi ove 'l sole* (*Canzoniere* 145)

LOVE THAT DOTH REIGN†

Love that doth reign and live within my thought,
And built his seat within my captive breast,
Clad in the arms wherein with me he fought,
Oft in my face he doth his banner rest.
But she that taught me love and suffer pain,
My doubtful hope and eke my hot desire
With shamefast look to shadow and refrain,
Her smiling grace converteth straight to ire.
And coward love then to the heart apace
Taketh his flight, where he doth lurk and plain
His purpose lost, and dare not show his face.
For my lord's* guilt thus faultless bide I pain; i.e. love
Yet from my lord shall not my foot remove.
Sweet is the death that taketh end by love.

1557

FROM TUSCAN CAME†

From Tuscan came my lady's worthy race;
Fair Florence was sometime her ancient seat;†
The western isle,* whose pleasant shore doth face Ireland
Wild Cambria's* cliffs, did give her lively heat. Wales
Fostered she was with milk of Irish breast;
Her sire an earl,† her dame of prince's† blood;
From tender years in Britain she doth rest,
With a king's child,† where she tastes ghostly* food. spiritual

Love that doth reign this sonnet is a translation of Petrarch's *Amor, che nel penser* (*Canzoniere* 140), which was translated by Wyatt as 'The long love'

From Tuscan came the sonnet is addressed to Lady Elizabeth Fitzgerald, who is lightly disguised as 'Geraldine'

Fair Florence . . . seat the Fitzgeralds traced their ancestry to the Geraldi of Florence

earl Gerald Fitzgerald, ninth Earl of Kildare

prince Lady Elizabeth's mother was a first cousin to Henry VIII

king's child Princess Mary

Hunsdon† did first present her to my eyen:* — eyes
Bright is her hue, and Geraldine she hight:* — is called
Hampton† me taught to wish her first for mine,
And Windsor,† alas, doth chase me from her sight.
Beauty of kind, her virtues from above;
Happy is he that may obtain her love.
1537 1557

WYATT RESTETH HERE

Wyatt resteth here, that quick* could never rest; — living
Whose heavenly gifts increasèd by disdain,
And virtue sank the deeper in his breast:
Such profit he by envy could obtain.

A head, where wisdom mysteries did frame;
Whose hammers beat still in that lively brain
As on a stithe,* where that some work of fame — anvil
Was daily wrought to turn to Britain's gain.

A visage stern and mild; where both did grow
Vice to contemn, in virtue to rejoice;
Amid great storms whom grace assurèd so
To live upright and smile at fortune's choice.

A hand that taught what might be said in rhyme;
That reft Chaucer the glory of his wit;
A mark* the which, unparfited for time,† — target
Some may approach, but never none shall hit.

A tongue that served in foreign realms his king;
Whose courteous talk in virtue did enflame
Each noble heart; a worthy guide to bring
Our English youth by travail unto fame.

Hunsdon a Norfolk estate (now Hunstanton Hall) which belonged to Surrey's father

Hampton, Windsor Hampton Court Palace and Windsor Castle were both royal residences

unparfited for time incomplete for want of time (i.e. death)

An eye, whose judgment none affect* could blind, no emotion
Friends to allure, and foes to reconcile;
Whose piercing look did represent a mind
With virtue fraught, reposèd, void of guile.

A heart, where dread was never so impressed
To hide the thought that might the truth advance;
In neither fortune loft, nor yet repressed,
To swell in wealth, or yield unto mischance.

A valiant corse,* where force and beauty met; body
Happy, alas too happy, but for foes:
Livèd and ran the race that nature set;
Of manhood's shape, where she the mould did lose.

But to the heavens that simple soul is fled,
Which left with such as covet Christ to know
Witness† of faith that never shall be dead;
Sent for our health, but not receivèd so.

Thus, for our guilt, this jewel have we lost.
The earth his bones, the heavens possess his ghost.

1557

MARTIAL, THE THINGS FOR TO ATTAIN†

Martial, the things for to attain
The happy life be these, I find:
The riches left,* not got with pain; inherited
The fruitful ground; the quiet mind:
The equal friend; no grudge nor strife;
No charge* of rule nor governance; responsibility
Without disease the healthful life;
The household of continuance;†

---

witness refers to Wyatt's paraphrase of the penitential psalms

Martial, the things for to attain a translation of *Vitam quae faciunt beatiorem* by the Roman poet Martial

continuance ancient and enduring

The mean diet, no delicate fare;
Wisdom joined with simplicity;
The night dischargèd of all care,
Where wine may bear no sovereignty;
The chaste wife wise, without debate;
Such sleeps as may beguile the night;
Contented with thy own estate,
Neither wish death nor fear his might.

From AENEID,† Book II

And now we gan* draw near unto the gate, began to
Right well escaped the danger, as methought,
When that at hand a sound of feet we heard.
My father then, gazing throughout the dark,
Crièd on me, 'Flee, son! They are at hand.'
With that bright shields and sheen* armours I saw. shining
But then I know not what unfriendly god
My troubled wit from me bereft for fear;
For while I ran by the most secret streets,
Eschewing still the common haunted track,
From me caitiff,* alas, bereavèd was wretch
Creüsa then, my spouse, I wot* not how, know
Whether by fate, or missing of the way,
Or that she was by weariness retained.
But never sith* these eyes might her behold, since
Not did I yet perceive that she was lost,
Nor never backward turnèd I my mind,
Till we came to the hill where as there stood
The old temple dedicate to Ceres.†
And when that we were there assembled all,
She was only away, deceiving us,
Her spouse, her son, and all her company.
What god or man did I not then accuse,
Near wood for ire? Or what more cruel chance
Did hap to me in all Troy's overthrow?

Aeneid in this passage from the end of Book II of Surrey's translation of Virgil's *Aeneid*, Aeneas describes his flight from Troy with his aged father Anchises, his small son Ascanius and a few companions; his wife Creüsa had died in the confusion of their escape

Ceres the goddess of agriculture

Ascanius to my feres I then betook,†
With Anchises, and eke* the Trojan gods, also
And left them hid within a valley deep.
And to the town I gan me hie† again,
Clad in bright arms, and bent for to renew
Adventures past, to search throughout the town,
And yield my head to perils once again.
    And first the walls and dark entry I sought
Of the same gate where as I issued out,
Holding backwards the steps where we had come,
In the dark night, looking all round about.
In every place the ugsome* sights I saw, horrible
The silence self of night aghast my sprite.* spirit
From hence again I passed unto our house,
If she by chance had been returnèd home.
The Greeks were there, and had it all beset:* surrounded
The wasting fire blown up by drift of wind
Above the roofs; the blazing flame sprang up,
The sound whereof with fury pierced the skies.
To Priam's† palace and the castle then
I made; and there at Juno's† sanctuary,
In the void porches, Phoenix,* Ulysses* eke, Greek warriors
Stern guardians stood, watching of the spoil.
The riches here were set, reft from the brent* burnt
Temples of Troy; the tables of the gods,
The vessels eke that were of massy* gold, solid
And vestures spoiled, were gathered all in heap.
The children orderly, and mothers pale for fright,
Long rangèd on a row stood round about.
    So bold was I to show my voice that night,
With clepes* and cries to fill the streets throughout, shouts
With Creüsa's name in sorrow, with vain tears,
And oftensithes* the same for to repeat. often
The town restless with fury as I sought,
Th'unlucky figure of Creüsa's ghost,
Of stature more than wont, stood fore mine eyes.
Abashèd then I woxe.* Therewith my hair waxed
Gan start right up, my voice stuck in my throat.
When with such words she gan my heart remove:

to my feres . . . betook committed into the care of my companions
gan me hie began to hurry
Priam King of Troy
Juno goddess of women, Jupiter's consort

'What helps to yield unto such furious rage,
Sweet spouse?' quod she. 'Without will of the gods
This chancèd not; nor lawful was for thee
To lead away Creüsa hence with thee:
The king of the high heaven suffreth it not.
A long exile thou art assigned to bear,
Long to furrow large space of stormy seas:
So shalt thou reach at last Hesperian land,
Where Lydian Tiber with his gentle stream
Mildly doth flow along the fruitful fields.†
There mirthful wealth, there kingdom is for thee,
There a king's child† prepared to be thy make.* mate
For thy beloved Creüsa stint thy tears:
For now I shall not see the proud abodes
Of Myrmidons,† nor yet of Dolopes;†
Nor I, a Trojan lady and the wife
Unto the son of Venus the goddess,†
Shall go a slave to serve the Greekish dames.
Me here the god's great mother holds.
And now farewell, and keep in father's breast
The tender love of thy young son and mine.'
This having said, she left me all in tears,
And minding much to speak; but she was gone,
And subtly fled into the weightless air.
Thrice raught† with my arms t'accoll† her neck,
Thrice did my hands vain hold th'image† escape
Like nimble winds, and like the flying dream.
So night spent out, return I to my feres;
And there wand'ring I find together swarmed
A new number of mates, mothers and men,
A rout exiled, a wretched multitude,
From eachwhere flocked together, pressed to pass,
With heart and goods, to whatsoever land
By sliding seas me listed* them to lead. I wished

So shalt thou . . . fruitful fields refers to the future site of Rome
king's child Lavinia, daughter of Latinus, King of Laurentum in Latium; in *Aeneid VII* Aeneas lands in Latium and is received by King Latinus, who gives him his daughter Lavinia in marriage
Myrmidons, Dolopes tribes from Thessaly who fought on the side of the Greeks in the Trojan War
the son . . . the goddess Aeneas was the son of the mortal Anchises and the goddess Venus
raught reached out
t'accoll to embrace
image the accent falls on the second syllable

And now rose Lucifer† above the ridge
Of lusty† Ide,† and brought the dawning light.
The Greeks held th'entries of the gates beset;
Of help there was no hope. Then gave I place,
Took up my sire,* and hasted to the hill. Anchises

1538 1557

Lucifer the planet Venus
lusty means 'pleasant', but may be a misprint (for 'lofty')
Ide Ida, a mountain near Troy

Queen Elizabeth I

1533–1603

Elizabeth, daughter of Henry VIII and Anne Boleyn, was Queen of England and Ireland from 1558 to 1603. Her tutors included the humanist scholar Roger Ascham, with whom she studied Latin and Greek; as a child she spoke and composed in these languages, and in French and Italian; she later added Spanish to her linguistic arsenal. As an adult she continued to write poetry; she also translated Boethius, Horace and Plutarch. Only a handful of her poems survives, and some of these are of doubtful authenticity.

WHEN I WAS FAIR AND YOUNG

When I was fair and young, and favour gracèd me,
Of many was I sought, their mistress for to be;
But I did scorn them all, and answered them therefore,
'Go, go, go, seek some otherwhere,
Importune me no more'.

How many weeping eyes I made to pine with woe,
How many sighing hearts I have no skill to show;
Yet I the prouder grew, and answered them therefore,
'Go, go, go, seek some otherwhere,
Importune me no more'.

Thus spake fair Venus' son,† that proud victorious boy,
And said 'Fine dame, since that you be so coy,
I will so pluck your plumes that you will say no more,
'Go, go, go, seek some otherwhere,
Importune me no more'.

When he had spake these words, such change grew in my breast
That neither night nor day since that I could take any rest;
Then lo I did repent that I had said before,
'Go, go, go, seek some otherwhere,
Importune me no more'.

1589

Venus' son: Cupid, the god of love, was often represented as a boy

The Mirror for Magistrates

The Mirror for Magistrates is a collection of tragedies by various authors. The tragedies take the form of monologues by historical figures who describe their downfalls. The first edition of 1559 was organised by George Ferrers, an official at the court of Henry VIII, and William Baldwin, an obscure figure who had connections with Oxford and with the Inns of Court. Subsequent editions were enlarged by various compilers between 1563 and 1609. The tragedy of Richard Earl of Cambridge was contributed by Baldwin. Shakespeare drew on this account to dramatise the fall of the Earl of Cambridge in *Henry V* II.2.

From RICHARD EARL OF CAMBRIDGE

How Richard Earl of Cambridge intending the King's death was put to death at Southampton

Haste maketh waste, hath commonly been said,
And secret mischief seld* hath lucky speed;*   seldom   success
A murdering mind with proper peise* is weighed,   weight
All this is true, I find it in my creed.
And therefore Baldwin warn all states* take heed,   noblemen
How they conspire any other to betrap,
Lest mischief meant light in the miner's lap.†

For I Lord Richard, heir Plantagenet,
Was Earl of Cambridge, and right fortunate,
If I had had the grace my wit to set
To have content me with mine own estate.
But o false honours, breeders of debate,
The love of you our lewd hearts doth allure
To lose ourselves by seeking you unsure.

Lest mischief . . . lap Lest intended mischief alight in the lap of the underminer (i.e. traitor)

Because my brother* Edmund Mortimer,† brother-in-law
Whose elder sister† was my wedded wife,
I mean that Edmund that was prisoner
In Wales so long, through Owen's† busy strife,
Because I say, that after Edmund's life,
His rights and titles must by law be mine
(For he ne had, nor could increase his line)†

Because the right of realm and crown was ours,
I searchèd means to help him thereunto.
And where the Henries† held it by their powers
I sought a shift* their tenures† to undo, plan
Which being force, sith* force or sleight must do, since
I void of might, because their power was strong
Set privy sleight against their open wrong.

But sith the deaths of most part of my kin
Did dash my hope, throughout the father's days†
I let it slip, and thought it best begin
When as the son should dread least such assays.* attempts
For force through speed, sleight speedeth through delays†
And seld doth treason time so fitly find
As when all dangers must be out of mind.

Wherefore while Henry of that name the fifth
Prepared his army to go conquer France,
Lord Scrope† and I thought to attempt a drift
To put him down my brother to advance.
But were it God's will, my luck, or his good chance,
The king wist* wholly whereabout we went, knew
The night before the king to shipward bent.

Edmund Mortimer Edmund Mortimer, fifth Earl of March (1391–1425) was descended from the third son of Edward III, and therefore thought that he had a better claim to the throne than did Henry IV, who was descended from the fourth son

elder sister Richard's wife was Anne Mortimer, sister of Edmund

Owen Owen Glendower (who appears in Shakespeare's *Henry IV Part One*), led the Welsh rebellion against Henry IV; he captured and imprisoned Sir Edmund Mortimer (uncle of the Mortimer of line 15), who became Glendower's adherent and married his daughter. The confusion of the two Edmund Mortimers also occurs in Holinshed and Shakespeare

(For he . . . his line) For he neither had children, nor could he have any

the Henries Henry IV and Henry V

tenures tenures of the throne

the father's days the reign of Henry IV

For force . . . delays Just as force is assisted by speed, so deception is helped by delays

Lord Scrope Henry Scrope, third Baron Scrope of Masham (who appears in Shakespeare's *Henry V*), was a fellow-conspirator of the Earl of Cambridge, and was executed with him

Then were we straight as traitors apprehended,
Our purpose spied, the cause thereof was hid,
And therefore lo a false cause we pretended
Wherethrough my brother was from danger rid.
We said from hire of the French king's coin, we did
Behight* to kill the king; and thus with shame — promise
We stained ourselves, to save our friend from blame.

When we had thus confessed so foul a treason,
That we deserved, we suffered by the law.†
See Baldwin see, and note (as it is reason)
How wicked deeds, to woeful ends do draw,
All force doth fail, no craft* is worth a straw — power
To attain things lost, and therefore let them go,
For might ruleth right, and will though God say no.

1559

suffered . . . law Lord Scrope and the Earl of Cambridge were beheaded on 5 August 1415 for conspiracy against the king

Arthur Golding

1536?–1605?

Arthur Golding was born in London, the son of a court official. He was educated at Queens' College, Cambridge, but left without a degree. He inherited large estates, and assumed the career of a translator. He translated many classical works (from Latin) and theological treatises (from French and Latin). His most famous work is his translation of Ovid's *Metamorphoses*. The story of Pyramus and Thisbe is taken from Book IV of Golding's translation. Shakespeare drew on this version for the plot of *Romeo and Juliet*, and dramatised the same story in the play within the play at the end of *A Midsummer Night's Dream*.

From METAMORPHOSES

[*Pyramus and Thisbe*]

Within the town† (of whose huge walls so monstrous high and thick,
The fame is given Semiramis† for making them of brick)
Dwelt hard together two young folk in houses joined so near
That under all one roof well nigh both twain conveyèd were.
The name of him was Pyramus, and Thisbe called was she.
So fair a man in all the East was none alive as he,
Nor near a woman, maid nor wife in beauty like to her.
This neighbourhood bred acquaintance first, this neighbourhood first
  did stir
The secret sparks, this neighbourhood first an entrance in did show,
For love to come to that to which it afterward did grow.
And if that rite had taken place they had been man and wife,
But still their parents went about to let† which (for their life)
They could not let, for both their hearts with equal flame did burn.
No man was privy to their thoughts, and for to serve their turn

town Babylon
Semiramis an Assyrian princess to whom many ancient structures (including the walls of Babylon) were attributed
let prevent

Instead of talk they usèd signs. The closelier they suppressed
The fire of love, the fiercer still it ragèd in their breast.
The wall that parted house from house had riven therein a cranny
Which shrunk at making of the wall. This fault not marked of any
Of many hundred years before (what doth not love espy?)
These lovers first of all found out, and made a way thereby
To talk together secretly, and through the same did go
Their loving whisperings very light and safely to and fro.
Now as at one side Pyramus, and Thisbe on the t'other
Stood often drawing one of them the pleasant breath from other:
'O thou envious wall', they said, 'why lettest thou lovers thus?
What matter were it if that thou permitted both of us
In arms each other to embrace? Or if thou think that this
Were overmuch, yet mightest thou at least make room to kiss.
And yet thou shalt not find us churls, we think, ourselves in debt
For this same piece of courtesy, in vouching safe to let
Our sayings to our friendly ears thus freely come and go'.
Thus having where they stood in vain complainèd of their woe,
When night drew near, they bade adieu and each gave kisses sweet
Unto the parget† on their side, the which did never meet.
Next morning with her cheerful light had driven the stars aside
And Phoebus† with his burning beams the dewy grass had dried,
These lovers at their wonted place by foreappointment met.
Where after much complaint and moan they covenanted to get
Away from such as watchèd them, and in the evening late
To steal out of their fathers' house and eke† the city gate.
And to th'intent that in the fields they strayed not up and down
They did agree at Ninus' tomb† to meet without the town,
And tarry underneath a tree that by the same did grow
Which was a fair high mulberry with fruit as white as snow,
Hard by a cool and trickling spring. This bargain pleased them both
And so daylight (which to their thought away but slowly goeth)
Did in the ocean fall to rest, and night from thence doth rise.
As soon as darkness once was come, straight Thisbe did devise
A shift to wind her† out of doors, that none that were within
Perceivèd her; and muffling her with clothes about her chin,
That no man might discern her face, to Ninus' tomb she came
Unto the tree, and sat her down there underneath the same.

parget plaster
Phoebus epithet of Apollo as god of the sun
eke also
Ninus' tomb Semiramis erected a vast tomb for her husband King Ninus outside the walls of Babylon
shift to wind her device to enable her to escape

Love made her bold. But see the chance, there comes besmeared with blood
About the chaps† a lioness all foaming from the wood
From slaughter lately made of kine† to staunch her bloody thirst
With water of the foresaid spring. Whom Thisbe spying first
Afar by moonlight, thereupon with fearful steps gan† fly,
And in a dark and irksome cave did hide herself thereby.
And as she fled away for haste she let her mantle fall
The which for fear she left behind, not looking back at all.
Now when the cruel lioness her thirst had staunchèd well
In going to the wood she found the slender weed† that fell
From Thisbe, which with bloody teeth in pieces she did tear.
The night was somewhat further spent ere Pyramus came there
Who seeing in the subtle† sand the print of lion's paw,
Waxed pale for fear. But when also the bloody cloak he saw
All rent and torn, 'one night', he said, 'shall lovers two confound,
Of which long life deservèd she of all that live on ground.
My soul deserves of this mischance the peril for to bear.
I, wretch, have been the death of thee, which to this place of fear
Did cause thee in the night to come, and came not here before.
My wicked limbs and wretched guts with cruel teeth therefore
Devour ye, o ye lions all that in this rock doth dwell.
But cowards use to wish for death'.† The slender weed that fell
From Thisbe up he takes, and straight doth bear it to the tree
Which was appointed erst the place of meeting for to be.
And when he had bewept and kissed the garment which he knew,
Receive thou my blood too (quoth he) and there withall he drew
His sword, the which among his guts he thrust, and by and by
Did draw it from the bleeding wound beginning for to die,
And cast himself upon his back, the blood did spin on high
As when a conduit pipe is cracked, the water bursting out
Doth shoot itself a great way off and pierce the air about.
The leaves that were upon the tree besprinkled with his blood
Were dièd black; the root also bestainèd as it stood
A deep dark purple colour straight from berries cast.
Anon scarce ridded of her fear with which she was aghast,
For doubt of disappointing him comes Thisbe forth in haste,
And for her lover looks about, rejoicing for to tell
How hardly she had scaped† that night the danger that befell.

chaps jaws
kine cattle
gan began to
weed article of clothing
subtle finely particled
But cowards . . . death cowards merely wish for death, but brave men bring it upon themselves
scaped escaped

And as she knew right well the place and fashion† of the tree
As which she saw so late before, even so when she did see
The colour of the berries turned, she was uncertain whether
It were the tree at which they both agreed to meet together.
While in this doubtful stound† she stood, she cast her eye aside
And there beweltered in his blood her lover she espied
Lie sprawling with his dying limbs, at which she started back,
And looked as pale as any box,† a shuddering through her strack,†
Even like the sea which suddenly with whizzing noise doth move,
When with little blast of wind it is but touched above.
But when approaching nearer him she knew it was her love,
She beat her breast, she shriekèd out, she tore her golden hairs,
And taking him between her arms did wash his wounds with tears,
She meynt† her weeping with his blood, and kissing all his face
Which now became as cold as ice, she cried in woeful case
'Alas what chance, my Pyramus, hath parted thee and me?
Make answer o my Pyramus, it is thy Thisbe, even she
Whom thou dost love most heartily, that speaketh unto thee.
Give ear and raise thy heavy head'. He hearing Thisbe's name,
Lift up his dying eyes and having seen her closed the same.
But when she knew her mantle there and saw his scabbard lie
Without the sword, 'unhappy man thy love hath made thee die;
Thy love', she said, 'hath made thee slay thyself. This hand of mine
Is strong enough to do the like. My love no less than thine
Shall give me force to work my wound. I will pursue the dead.
And wretched woman as I am, it shall of me be said.
That like as of thy death I was the only cause and blame,
So am I thy companion eke and partner in the same,
For death which only could alas asunder part us twain,
Shall never so dissever us but we will meet again.
And you the parents of us both, most wretched folk alive,
Let this request that I shall make in both our names belive†
Entreat you to permit that we whom chaste and steadfast love
And whom even death hath joined in one, may as it doth behoove
In one grave be together laid. And thou unhappy tree
Which shroudest now the corpse of one, and shall anon through me
Shroud two, of this same slaughter hold the sicker† signs for aye,†
Black be the colour of thy fruit and mourning like alway,
Such as the murder of us twain may evermore bewray'.†

fashion shape
stound stupor
box boxwood
strack struck
meynt mixed
belive eagerly
sicker certain
for aye forever
bewray reveal

This said, she took the sword yet warm with slaughter of her love,
And setting it beneath her breast, did to her heart it shove.
Her prayer with the gods and with their parents took effect.
For when the fruit is throughly[†] ripe, the berry is bespecked
With colour tending to a black.[†] And that which after fire
Remained, rested in one tomb as Thisbe did desire.

1565

throughly thoroughly

tending . . . black dark purple, like blood

George Gascoigne

1539?–77

George Gascoigne was the son of Sir John Gascoigne, a Justice of the Peace and Member of Parliament who lived in Bedfordshire. He may have studied at Trinity College, Cambridge, and in 1555 he entered Gray's Inn to study law. He entered Parliament in 1557, and then took up the life of a courtier. He returned to Gray's Inn in 1565, and then retired to Bedfordshire as a farmer. In 1570 he was imprisoned for debt. From 1572 to 1574 he was a soldier in Holland, and was imprisoned by the Spanish for four months. In 1576 he entered government service, and was sent to France and Holland to monitor events there. In the final year of his life he enjoyed both prosperity and royal patronage.

Gascoigne was one of the most versatile and innovative writers of his time. He wrote the first account of English versification (*Certain Notes of Instruction Concerning the Making of Verse or Rhyme in English*) and the first prose comedy (*Supposes*). His poems, translations and treatises range from the devotional to the obscene, from the bitterly satirical to the obsequiously celebratory. His finest work, *The Adventures of Master F.J.*, is a prose romance which exists in two different versions. The 1573 version is a bawdy tale set in England; the 1575 version, which pretends to be a translation of an Italian source, is comparatively bland, and is set in Italy. The extract from the novel printed here is taken from the earlier version.

From A HUNDRED SUNDRY FLOWERS

Of all the birds[†]

Of all the birds that I do know,
Phillip[†] my sparrow hath no peer:
For sit she high or sit she low,
Be she far off or be she near,
There is no bird so fair, so fine,
Nor yet so fresh as this of mine.

Come in a morning merrily
When Phillip hath been lately fed,
Or in an evening soberly,
When Phillip list* to go to bed: wishes
It is a heaven to hear my Phip,
How she can chirp with cherry lip.

She never wanders far abroad,
But is on hand when I do call:
If I command she lays on load,
With lips, with teeth, with tongue and all.
She chants, she chirps, she makes such cheer,
That I believe she hath no peer.

And yet besides all this good sport,
My Phillip can both sing and dance:
With new-found toys of sundry sort,
My Phillip can both prick* and prance: compose music
And if you say but fend cut[†] Phip,
Lord how the peat[†] will turn and skip.

Her feathers are so fresh of hue,
And so well prunèd every day:
She lacks none oil, I warrant you,
To trim her tail both trick and gay.
And though her tongue be somewhat wide,
Her tongue is sweet and short beside,

Of all the birds the editor of the 1573 edition of *A Hundred Sundry Flowers*, from which these poems are taken, said in a headnote to this poem that Gascoigne 'wrote (at his friend's request) in praise of a gentlewoman, whose name was Phillip, as followeth'

Phillip the standard name for a sparrow

fend cut a defensive stroke in fencing

peat a term of endearment for a lively young woman

And for the rest I dare compare.
She is both tender, sweet and soft:
She never lacketh dainty fare,
But is well fed and feedeth oft:
For if my Phip have lust to eat,
I warrant you Phip lacks no meat.

And then if that her meat be good,
And such as like do love alway:
She will lay lips thereon by-the-rood,
And see that none be cast away:
For when she once hath felt a fit,
Phillip will cry still, yit, yit, yit.

And to tell truth he were to blame,
Which had so fine a bird as she,
To make him all this goodly game,
Without suspect of jealousy:
He were a churl and knew no good
Would see her faint for lack of food.

Wherefore I sing and ever shall,
To praise as I have often proved,
There is no bird amongst them all,
So worthy for to be belov'd.
Let others praise what bird they will,
Sweet Phillip shall be my bird still.

Si fortunatus infelix†

1573

If any flower†

If any flower that here is grown,
Or any herb may ease your pain,
Take and account it as your own,
But recompense the like again:
For some and some is honest play,
And so my wife taught me to say.

si . . . infelix prosperous yet unhappy
If any flower this poem appears in a section of *A Hundred Sundry Flowers* entitled 'Gascoigne's Gardenings', and is said by the 1573 editor to be one of his 'toys in rhyme' composed in the course of a walk in a garden

If here to walk you take delight,
Why come, and welcome when you will:
If I bid you sup here this night,
Bid me another time, and still
Think some and some is honest play,
For so my wife taught me to say.

Thus if you sup or dine with me,
If you walk here, or sit at ease,
If you desire the thing you see,
And have the same your mind to please,
Think some and some is honest play,
And so my wife taught me to say.

1573

From *A Discourse of the Adventures Passed by Master F.J.*†

Suppertime came and passed over, and not long after came the handmaid of the Lady Elinor into the great chamber, desiring F.J. to repair unto their mistress, the which he willingly accomplished: and being now entered into her chamber, he might perceive his mistress in her night's attire, preparing herself towards bed, to whom F.J. said: 'Why how now Mistress? I had thought this night to have seen you dance (at least or at last) amongst us?' 'By my troth good servant,' quod she, 'I adventured so soon unto the great chamber yesternight, that I find myself somewhat sickly disposed and therefore do strain courtesy (as you see) to go the sooner to my bed this night: but before I sleep,' quod she, 'I am to charge you with a matter of weight,' and taking him apart from the rest, declared that (as that present night) she would talk with him more at large in the gallery adjoining to her chamber. Hereupon F.J. discreetly dissimulating his joy, took his leave and retired into the great chamber, where he had not long continued before the Lord of the castle commanded a torch to light him to his lodging, whereas as he prepared himself and went to bed, commanding his servant also to go to his rest. And when he thought his servant, as the rest of the household be safe, he arose again, and taking his nightgown, did under the same convey his naked sword, and so walked to the gallery, where he found

The Adventures of Master F.J. in the 1573 version of the novella, which appeared in *A Hundred Sundry Flowers* under the title 'A Discourse of the Adventures Passed by Master F.J.'), 'F.J.' is identified only by his initials although the narrator, who calls himself 'G.T.', guesses that the initials might stand for 'Freeman Jones'. Elinor and Frances are the daughters of a lord whom F.J. is visiting

his good mistress walking in her nightgown and attending his coming. The moon was now at the full, the skies clear, and the weather temperate, by reason whereof he might the more plainly, and with the greater contentation behold his long desired joys, and spreading his arms abroad to embrace his loving mistress, he said: 'Oh my dear lady when shall I be able with the least desert to countervail[†] the least part of this your bountiful goodness?' The dame (whether it were of fear indeed, or that the wiliness of womanhood had taught her to cover her conceits[†] with some fine dissimulation) start back from the knight, and shrieking (but softly) said unto him, 'Alas servant what have I deserved, that you come against me with naked sword as against an open enemy.' F.J. perceiving her intent excused himself, declaring that he brought the same for their defence, and not to offend her in any wise. The lady being therewith somewhat appeased, they began with more comfortable gesture to expel the dread of the said late affright, and sithence[†] to become bolder of behaviour, more familiar in speech, and most kind in accomplishing of common comfort. But why hold I so long discourse in describing the joys which (for lack of like experience) I cannot set out to the full? Were it not that I know to whom I write, I would the more beware what I write. F.J. was a man, and neither of us are senseless, and therefore I should slander him (over and besides a greater obloquy to the whole genealogy of Aeneas)[†] if I should imagine that of tender heart he would forbear to express her more tender limbs against the hard floor. Suffice that of her courteous nature she was content to accept boards for a bed of down, mats for cameric[†] sheets, and the nightgown of F.J. for a counterpoint[†] to cover them, and thus with calm content, instead of quiet sleep, they beguiled the night, until the proudest star began to abandon the firmament, when F.J. and his mistress, were constrained also to abandon their delights, and with ten thousand sweet kisses and straight embracings, did frame themselves to play loth to depart. Well, remedy was there none, but Dame Elinor must return unto her chamber, and F.J. must also convey himself (as closely as might be) into his chamber, the which was hard to do, the day being so far sprung, and he having a large base court to pass over before he could recover his stairfoot door. And though he were not much perceived, yet the Lady Frances being no less desirous to see an issue to these enterprises, than F.J. was to cover them in secrecy, did watch, and even at the entering of his chamber door, perceived the point of his naked sword glistering under the skirt of his nightgown:

countervail reciprocate
conceits thoughts
sithence subsequently
genealogy of Aeneas as this version of the story is set in England, the reference is to the descent of the British from Brutus, great-grandson of Aeneas
cameric cambric, i.e. fine white linen
counterpoint a quilted bedcover

whereat she smiled and said to herself, this gear goeth well about. Well, F.J. having now recovered his chamber, he went to bed, and there let him sleep, as his mistress did on that other side. Although the Lady Frances being throughly tickled now in all the veins, could not enjoy such quiet rest, but arising, took another gentlewoman of the house with her, and walked into the park to take the fresh air of the morning. They had not long walked there, but they returned, and though F.J. had not yet slept sufficiently, for one who had so far travailed in the night past, yet they went into his chamber to raise him, and coming to his bedside, found him fast on sleep. 'Alas,' quod that other gentlewoman, 'it were pity to wake him.' 'Even so it were,' quod Dame Frances, 'but we will take away somewhat of his, whereby he may perceive that we were here,' and looking about his chamber, his naked sword presented itself into the hands of Dame Frances, who took it with her, and softly shutting his chamber door again, went down the stairs and recovered her own lodging, in good order and unperceived of anybody, saving only that other gentlewoman which accompanied her. At the last F.J. awaked, and apparelling himself, walked out also to take the air, and being thoroughly recomforted as well with remembrance of his joys forepassed, as also with the pleasant harmony which the birds made on every side, and the fragrant smell of the redolent flowers and blossoms which budded on every branch, he did in these delights compile these verses following.

The occasion (as I have heard him rehearse) was by encounter that he had with his lady by light of the moon: and forasmuch, as the moon in midst of their delights did vanish away, or was overspread with a cloud, thereupon he took the subject of his theme. And thus it ensueth, called 'A Moonshine Banquet'.

G.T.

Dame Cynthia† herself (that shines so bright,
And deigneth not to leave her lofty place:
But only then, when Phoebus† shows his face
Which is her brother born and tends her light,)
Disdained not yet to do my lady right:
To prove that in such heavenly wights* as she, persons
It fitteth best that right and reason be
For when she spied my lady's golden rays,
Into the clouds,
Her head she shrouds,
And shamed to shine where she her beams displays.

Cynthia goddess of the moon
Phoebus epithet of Apollo as sun-god; twin brother of Phoebe (i.e. Cynthia)

Good reason yet, that to my simple skill,
I should the name of Cynthia adore:
By whose high help, I might behold the more
My lady's lovely looks at mine own will,
With deep content, to gare,† and gaze my fill:
Of courtesy and not of dark disdain,
Dame Cynthia disclosed my lady plain.
She did but lend her light (as for a light)
With friendly grace,
To show her face,
That else would show and shine in her despite.†

Dan† Phoebus he with many a lowering look,
Had her beheld of yore in angry wise:
And when he could none other mean devise
To stain her name, this deep deceit he took
To be the bait that best might hide his hook:
Into her eyes his parching beams he cast,
To scorch their skins, that gazed in her full fast:
Whereby when many a man was sunburnt so
They thought my Queen,
The sun had been
With scalding flames, which wrought them all their woe.

And thus when many a look had looked so long,
As that their eyes were dim and dazzled both:
Some fainting hearts that were both lewd and loth
To look again from whence the error sprung,
Gan close their eye from fear of further wrong:
And some again once drawn into the maze,
Gan lewdly blame the beams of beauty's blaze:
But I with deep foresight did soon espy.
How Phoebus meant,
By false intent,
To slander to her name with cruelty.

gare experience a fit of passion
in her despite to her disadvantage
Dan a title (like 'Sir')

Wherefore at better leisure thought I best,
To try the treason of his treachery:
And to exalt my lady's dignity
When Phoebus fled and drew him down to rest
Amid the waves that walter* in the west, roll
I gan behold this lovely lady's face,
Whereon Dame Nature spent her gifts of grace:
And found therein no parching heat at all,
But such bright hue,
As might renew,
An angel's joys in reign celestial.

The courteous moon that wished to do me good,
Did shine to show my dame more perfectly,
But when she saw her passing jollity,
The moon for shame, did blush as red as blood,
And shrunk aside and kept her horns in hood:
So that now when Dame Cynthia was gone,
I might enjoy my lady's looks alone,
Yet honoured still the moon with true intent:
Who taught us skill,
To work our will,
And gave us place, till all the night was spent.

F.J.

This ballade, or howsoever I shall term it, percase† you will not like, and yet in my judgement it hath great good store of deep invention, and for the order of the verse, it is not common, I have not heard many of like proportion, some will account it but a diddledum:† but whoso hath heard F.J. sing it to the lute, by a note of his own device, I suppose he would esteem it a pleasant diddledum, and for my part, if I were not partial, I would say more in commendation of it than now I mean to do, leaving it to you and like judgements.

1573

percase perhaps

diddledum trifle

Nicholas Breton
1545?–1626

Nicholas Breton was born into an eminent family in Essex; his father died when he was young, and his mother then married the poet George Gascoigne. Details of Breton's life are obscure, but he was probably educated at Oriel College, Oxford, after which he settled in London as a writer. His publications include twenty-two volumes of poetry, twenty-two books in prose, and various poems in anthologies. He wrote satire, romance and religious verse, but his finest poems are pastoral lyrics.

SHALL WE GO DANCE THE HAY

Shall we go dance the hay,† the hay?
Never pipe could ever play
Better shepherd's roundelay.†

Shall we go sing the song, the song?
Never love did ever wrong,
Fair maids, hold hands all along.

Shall we go learn to woo, to woo?
Never thought came ever to,
Better dead could better do.

Shall we go learn to kiss, to kiss?
Never heart could ever miss
Comfort, where true meaning is.

Thus at base† they run, they run,
When the sport was scarce begun.
But I waked, and all was done.

1600

hay a country dance with a serpentine movement
roundelay a kind of round dance
base a game in which each of two sides occupies a base from which the players run

Edmund Spenser

1552?–99

Spenser was born in London, and in 1561 entered Merchant Taylors' School, where his fellow pupils included Lancelot Andrewes, Thomas Kyd and Thomas Lodge. While still at school he published translations of Petrarch (from Marot's French version) and Du Bellay. He studied at Pembroke Hall, Cambridge, and in 1579 entered the household of the Earl of Leicester, where he became a friend of Sir Philip Sidney, to whom he dedicated *The Shepherd's Calender*; in the same year he began to write *The Fairy Queen*. In 1580 Spenser moved to Ireland, initially as private secretary to Lord Grey, the Lord Deputy of Ireland. After Grey's departure Spenser remained in government service in various parts of Ireland. In 1588 he bought Kilcolman (a large estate in County Cork), where he established a small English colony and became a friend of his neighbour Sir Walter Ralegh. Books I to III of *The Fairy Queen* were published in 1590, and books IV to VI were added in 1596. In 1594 Spenser married Elizabeth Boyle; their courtship is celebrated in the *Amoretti* sonnets, and their wedding in *Epithalamion*. Two years later Spenser, the most humane of poets, published the distinctly inhumane *View of the Present State of Ireland*, a prose treatise in which Spenser defends the atrocities of Lord Grey; the tract is deeply rooted in English contempt for the Irish people.

Many of Spenser's works are lost, but those which remain are sufficient to establish him as the greatest English poet of his century. His vast epic romance, *The Fairy Queen*, of which six books and a fragment survive, is an allegorical narrative which extols various virtues (the six surviving books deal with holiness, temperance, chastity, friendship, justice and courtesy); Spenser identifies the Fairy Queen with Queen Elizabeth, to whom the poem is dedicated.

Spenser's poems have traditionally been presented in an unmodernised form; this practice has made him an unnecessarily difficult poet, and has reduced the popularity of his poetry. The selection printed here disregards this convention by printing the poems in a modernised form, although the archaic words which are a feature of his style have been retained.

From THE FAIRY QUEEN, Book II, canto xii, stanzas 42–87

[*The Bower of Bliss*]

42 Thence passing forth, they shortly do arrive
Whereas* the Bower of Bliss was situate— where
A place picked out by choice of best alive
That nature's work by art can imitate;
In which whatever in this worldly state
Is sweet and pleasing unto living sense,
Or that may daintest fantasy aggrate,* please
Was pourèd forth with plentiful dispense†
And made there to abound with lavish affluence.

43 Goodly it was enclosèd round about,
As well their entered guests to keep within
As those unruly beasts to hold without;
Yet was the fence thereof but weak and thin.
Nought feared their† force that fortilage* to win fortress
But wisdom's power and temperance's might,
By which the mightest things efforcèd been.†
And eke* the gate was wrought of substance light, also
Rather for pleasure than for battery or fight.

44 It framèd was of precious ivory,
That seemed a work of admirable wit;* skill
And therein all the famous history
Of Jason† and Medea† was ywrit* written
Her mighty charms, her furious loving fit,
His goodly conquest of the golden fleece,
His falsèd* faith, and love too lightly flit,* broken abandoned
The wondered* Argo,† which in venturous* wonderful adventurous
piece* episode
First through the Euxine† seas bore all the flower of Greece.

dispense the act of dispensing liberally
their possibly a misprint for 'they'
efforcèd been are forced open
Jason . . . Creüsa (15 lines) the Greek hero *Jason* sailed in the *Argo* to Colchis, on the Black (*Euxine*) Sea in search of the golden fleece; he was assisted by the sorcery of the king's daughter, *Medea*, whom he later abandoned for *Creüsa*

45 Ye might have seen the frothy billows fry* — foam
Under the ship, as thorough them she went,
That seemed the waves were into ivory
Or ivory into the waves were sent;
And otherwhere* the snowy substance sprent* — elsewhere — sprinkled
With vermeil, like the boy's† blood therein shed,
A piteous spectacle did represent:
And otherwhiles with gold besprinkelèd,
It seemed th' enchanted flame† which did Creüsa† wed.

46 All this and more might in that goodly gate
Be read, that ever open stood to all
Which thither came. But in the porch there sate
A comely personage of stature tall
And semblance pleasing, more than natural,
That travellers to him seemed to entice.
His looser garment to the ground did fall,
And flew about his heels in wanton wise,
Not fit for speedy pace or manly exercise.

47 They in that place him Genius† did call –
Not that celestial power to whom the care
Of life and generation of all
That lives pertains in charge particular,
Who wondrous things concerning our welfare
And strange phantoms doth let us oft foresee,
And oft of secret ill bids us beware;
That is our self, whom though we do not see,
Yet each doth in himself it well perceive to be.

48 Therefore a god him sage antiquity
Did wisely make, and good Agdistes† call.
But this same was to that quite contrary:
The foe of life, that good envies to all,
That secretly doth us procure to fall
Through guileful semblants which he makes us see.
He of this garden had the governal,* — management
And pleasure's porter was devised to be,
Holding a staff in hand for more formality.

boy Apsyrtus, Medea's brother, whom she killed and threw into the sea bit by bit to delay her father's pursuit

enchanted flame Medea's wedding present to Creüsa was an enchanted wedding gown which burst into flames and killed her

Genius this evil *Genius* is opposed to a good genius, *Agdistes*, who is described from 47.2 to 48.2

49 With divers flowers he daintily was decked
And strowèd round about, and by his side
A mighty mazer* bowl of wine was set, maple
As if it had to him been sacrified;
Wherewith all new-come guests he gratified.
So did he eke Sir Guyon passing by,
But he his idle courtesy defied,
And overthrew his bowl disdainfully,
And broke his staff with which he charmèd semblants sly.†

50 Thus being entered, they behold around
A large and spacious plain, on every side
Strewèd with pleasance,* whose fair grassy ground pleasure-gardens
Mantled with green and goodly beautified
With all the ornaments of Flora's† pride,
Wherewith her mother Art – as half in scorn
Of niggard Nature – like a pompous bride
Did deck her and too lavishly adorn,
When forth from virgin bower she comes in th' early morn.

51 Thereto the heavens always jovial†
Looked on them lovely,* still in steadfast state; lovingly
Ne suffered storm nor frost on them to fall,
Their tender buds or leaves to violate,
Nor scorching heat nor cold intemperate
T' afflict the creatures which therein did dwell;
But the mild air with season moderate
Gently attempered,† and disposed so well
That still it breathed forth sweet spirit and wholesome smell.

charmèd semblants sly conjured up false appearances
Flora goddess of flowers
jovial under the influence of Jove, i.e. joyous
attempered i.e. modified its temperature

52 More sweet and wholesome than the pleasant hill
Of Rhodope,† on which the nymph that bore
A giant babe herself for grief did kill;
Or the Thessalian Tempe,† where of yore
Fair Daphne† Phoebus'† heart with love did gore;
Or Ida,† where the gods loved to repair
Whenever they their heavenly bowers forlore;* departed
Or sweet Parnass,† the haunt of muses fair;
Or Eden self, if aught with Eden mote* compare. might

53 Much wondered Guyon† at the fair aspect
Of that sweet place, yet suffered no delight
To sink into his sense nor mind affect,
But passèd forth and looked still forward right,†
Bridling his will and mastering his might,
Till that he came unto another gate –
No gate, but like one, being goodly dight* adorned
With boughs and branches which did broad dilate
Their clasping arms in wanton wreathings intricate.

54 So fashionèd a porch with rare device,
Arched overhead with an embracing vine
Whose bunches hanging down seemed to entice
All passersby to taste their luscious wine,
And did themselves into their hands incline,
As freely offering to be gatherèd –
Some deep empurpled as the hyacint,* sapphire
Some as the rubine* laughing sweetly red, ruby
Some like fair emeralds, not yet well ripenèd.

Rhodope the mountain in Thrace where Orpheus sang (hence 'pleasant') and the name of the nymph who gave birth to a 'giant babe' by Neptune and (in another version of the story) was transformed into the mountain
Tempe the valley in Thessaly to which *Daphne* fled to escape the amorous *Phoebus*, and where she was transformed into a laurel
Ida the mountain where the three goddesses appeared for the judgement of Paris, and from which the gods watched the Trojan War
Parnass Mount Parnassus was sacred to Apollo and the muses
Guyon the champion of temperance, protagonist of Book II
forward right directly ahead

55 And them amongst, some were of burnished gold,
So made by art to beautify the rest,
Which did themselves amongst the leaves enfold
As lurking from the view of covetous guest,
That the weak boughs, with so rich load oppressed,
Did bow adown, as over-burdenèd.
Under that porch a comely dame did rest,
Clad in fair weeds,* but foul disorderèd, clothes
And garments loose, that seemed unmeet for womanhead.

56 In her left hand a cup of gold she held,
And with her right the riper fruit did reach,
Whose sappy liquor, that with fullness swelled,
Into her cup she scruzed* with dainty breach* squeezed crushing
Of her fine fingers, without foul impeach,†
That so fair wine press made the wine more sweet.
Thereof she used to give to drink to each
Whom passing by she happenèd to meet.
It was her guise* all strangers goodly so to greet. habit

57 So she to Guyon offered it to taste,
Who taking it out of her tender hand,
The cup to ground did violently cast,
That all in pieces it was broken found,
And with the liquor stainèd all the land.
Whereat Excess exceedingly was wroth,
Yet n'ot* the same amend, ne yet withstand, could not
But suffered him to pass, all were she loath –
Who nought regarding her displeasure forward goeth.

58 There the most dainty paradise on ground
Itself doth offer to his sober eye,
In which all pleasures plenteously abound
And none does other's happiness envy –
The painted flowers, the trees upshooting high,
The dales for shade, the hills for breathing space,
The trembling groves, the crystal* running by. clear stream
And that which all fair works doth most aggrace,* enhance
The art which all that wrought, appearèd in no place.

foul impeach unpleasant hindrance

59 One would have thought – so cunningly the rude
And scornèd parts were mingled with the fine –
That nature had for wantonness* ensued* — playfulness — imitated
Art, and that art at nature did repine.* — complain
So striving each th' other to undermine,
Each did the other's work more beautify;
So differing both in wills, agreed in fine;* — in the end
So all agreed through sweet diversity
This garden to adorn with all variety.

60 And in the midst of all, a fountain stood,
Of richest substance that on earth might be,
So pure and shiny that the silver flood
Through every channel running one might see.
Most goodly it with curious imagery
Was overwrought,† and shapes of naked boys,
Of which some seemed with lively jollity
To fly about, playing their wanton toys,* — amorous games
Whilst others did themselves embay* in liquid joys. — bathe

61 And over all, of purest gold was spread
A trail of ivy in his native hue;
For the rich metal was so colourèd
That wight who did not well-avised it view
Would surely deem it to be ivy true.
Low his lascivious arms adown did creep,
That themselves dipping in the silver dew,
Their fleecy flowers they tenderly did steep,
Which drops of crystal seemed for wantonness to weep.

62 Infinite streams continually did well
Out of this fountain, sweet and fair to see,
The which into an ample laver† fell,
And shortly grew to so great quantity
That like a little lake it seemed to be;
Whose depth exceeded not three cubits† height,
That through the waves one might the bottom see,
All paved beneath with jasper shining bright,
That seemed the fountain in that sea did sail upright.

overwrought wrought all over
laver the basin of the fountain
three cubits about $1\frac{1}{2}$ metres

63 And all the margent* round about was set — border
With shady laurel trees, thence to defend* — fend off
The sunny beams which on the billows beat,
And those which therein bathèd mote offend.
As Guyon happened by the same to wend,
Two naked damsels he therein espied,
Which therein bathing seemèd to contend
And wrestle wantonly, ne cared to hide
Their dainty parts from view of any which them eyed.

64 Sometimes the one would lift the other quite
Above the waters, and then down again
Her plunge, as over-masterèd by might,
Where both awhile would coverèd remain,
And each the other from to rise restrain;
The whiles their snowy limbs, as through a veil
So through the crystal waves, appearèd plain;
Then suddenly both would themselves unheal,* — uncover
And th' amorous sweet spoils to greedy eyes reveal.

65 As that fair star,† the messenger of morn,
His dewy face out of the sea doth rear,
Or as the Cyprian† goddess, newly born
Of th' ocean's fruitful froth, did first appear,
Such seemèd they, and so their yellow hair
Crystalline humour* droppèd down apace. — clear water
Whom such when Guyon saw, he drew him near,
And somewhat gan relent his earnest pace,
His stubborn breast gan secret pleasance to embrace.

66 The wanton maidens him espying, stood
Gazing awhile at his unwonted guise;
Then th' one herself low duckèd in the flood,
Abashed that her a stranger did avise;* — view
But th' other rather higher did arise,
And her two lily paps aloft displayed,
And all that might his melting heart entice
To her delights she unto him bewrayed.* — displayed
The rest hid underneath, him more desirous made.

fair star the planet Venus
Cyprian the goddess Venus rose out of the sea near Cyprus

67 With that, the other likewise up arose,
And her fair locks, which formerly were bound
Up in one knot, she low adown did loose;
Which flowing long and thick, her clothed around,
And th' ivory in golden mantle gowned,
So that fair spectacle from him was reft;* stolen
Yet that which reft it no less fair was found.
So hid in locks and waves from looker's theft,
Nought but her lovely face she for his looking left.

68 Withal† she laughèd, and she blushed withal,†
That blushing to her laughter gave more grace,
And laughter to her blushing, as did fall.
Now when they spied the knight to slack his pace
Them to behold, and in his sparkling face
The secret signs of kindled lust appear,
Their wanton merriments they did increase,
And to him beckoned to approach more near,
And showed him many sights that courage† cold could rear.* arouse

69 On which when gazing him the palmer† saw,
Her much rebuked those wandering eyes of his,
And, counselled well, him forward thence did draw.
Now are they come nigh to the Bower of Bliss –
Of her fond favourites so named amiss –
When thus the palmer: 'Now, sir, well avise,
For here the end of all our travel is;
Here wons* Acrasia,† whom we must surprise, dwells
Else she will slip away and all our drift despise.'†

70 Eftsoons† they heard a most melodious sound
Of all that mote delight a dainty ear,
Such as at once might not on living ground,
Save in this paradise, be heard elsewhere.
Right hard it was for wight† which did it hear
To read* what manner music that mote be, discern
For all that pleasing is to living ear
Was there consorted in one harmony –
Birds, voices, instruments, winds, waters, all agree.

withal . . . withal at that . . . because of that
courage sexual desire
palmer Guyon's companion is a palmer, i.e. pilgrim
Acrasia means 'intemperance' in Renaissance Latin
our drift despise spoil our plans
eftsoons soon after
wight human being

71 The joyous birds, shrouded in cheerful shade,
Their notes unto the voice attempered* sweet; attuned
Th' angelical soft trembling voices made
To th' instruments divine respondence meet;†
The silver sounding instruments did meet
With the base murmur of the water's fall;
The water's fall with difference discrete,†
Now soft, now loud, unto the wind did call;
The gentle warbling wind low answerèd to all.

72 There, whence that music seemèd heard to be,
Was the fair witch herself now solacing
With a new lover, whom through sorcery
And witchcraft she from far did thither bring.
There she had him now laid aslumbering
In secret shade, after long wanton joys;
Whilst round about them pleasantly did sing
Many fair ladies and lascivious boys,
That ever mixed their song with light licentious toys.

73 And all that while, right over him she hung,
With her false eyes fast fixèd in his sight,
As seeking medicine whence she was stung,
Or greedily depasturing* delight; consuming
And oft inclining down with kisses light,
For fear of waking him, his lips bedewed,
And through his humid eyes did suck his sprite,* spirit
Quite molten into lust and pleasure lewd;
Wherewith she sighèd soft, as if his case she rued.

74 The whiles someone did chant this lovely lay:†
'Ah see, who so fair thing dost fain* to see, delight
In springing flower the image of thy day;
Ah see the virgin rose, how sweetly she
Doth first peep forth with bashful modesty,
That fairer seems the less ye see her may;
Lo see soon after, how more bold and free
Her barèd bosom she doth broad display;
Lo see soon after, how she fades and falls away.

respondence meet fitting response
difference discrete distinct variation
lovely lay song of love

75 'So passeth in the passing of a day
Of mortal life the leaf, the bud, the flower,
Ne more doth flourish after first decay,
That erst was sought to deck both bed and bower
Of many a lady, and many a paramour.
Gather, therefore, the rose whilst yet is prime,
For soon comes age, that will her pride deflower.
Gather the rose of love whilst yet is time,
Whilst loving thou mayst lovèd be with equal crime.'

76 He ceased, and then gan all the choir of birds
Their diverse notes t' attune unto his lay,
As in approvance of his pleasing words.
The constant pair heard all that he did say,
Yet swervèd not, but kept their forward way
Through many covert groves and thickets close,
In which they creeping did at last display* discover
That wanton lady with her lover loose,
Whose sleepy head she in her lap did soft dispose.* lay down

77 Upon a bed of roses she was laid,
As faint through heat, or dight to pleasant sin,†
And was arrayed, or rather disarrayed,
All in a veil of silk and silver thin
That hid no whit her alabaster skin,
But rather showed more white, if more might be.
More subtle web Arachne† can not spin,
Nor the fine nets† which oft we woven see
Of scorchèd dew do not in th' air more lightly flee.

78 Her snowy breast was bare to ready spoil
Of hungry eyes, which n'ot* therewith be filled; could not
And yet through languor of her late sweet toil,
Few drops more clear than nectar forth distilled,
That like pure orient pearls adown it trilled;
And her fair eyes, sweet smiling in delight,
Moistened their fiery beams, with which she thrilled* penetrated
Frail hearts, yet quenchèd* not; like starry light, killed
Which sparkling on the silent waves does seem more bright.

dight . . . sin prepared for sensual sin
Arachne Lydian maiden who defeated the goddess Athena in a tapestry-weaving contest, whereupon Athena turned her into a spider; her name means 'spider' in Greek
fine nets the gossamer on which the dew has been dried by the sun

79 The young man sleeping by her seemed to be
Some goodly swain of honourable place,* rank
That certes* it great pity was to see assuredly
Him his nobility so foul deface.
A sweet regard* and amiable grace, demeanour
Mixèd with manly sternness, did appear
Yet sleeping† in his well-proportioned face,
And on his tender lips the downy hair
Did now but freshly spring, and silken blossoms bear.

80 His warlike arms, the idle instruments
Of sleeping praise, were hung upon a tree,
And his brave shield, full of old monuments,
Was foully rased,* that none the signs might see. erased
Ne for them, ne for honour carèd he,
Ne aught that did to his advancement tend,
But in lewd loves and wasteful luxury* licentiousness
His days, his goods, his body he did spend.
O horrible enchantment, that him so did blend.* blind

81 The noble elf and careful palmer drew
So nigh them, minding nought but lustful game,
That sudden forth they on them rushed, and threw
A subtle† net, which only for the same
The skilful palmer formally† did frame.
So held them under fast, the whiles the rest
Fled all away for fear of fouler shame.
The fair enchantress, so unwares oppressed†
Tried all her arts and all her sleights thence out to wrest.

82 And eke her lover strove. But all in vain,
For that same net so cunningly was wound* woven
That neither guile nor force might it distrain.†
They took them both, and both them strongly bound
In captive bands, which there they ready found.
But her in chains of adamant he tied,
For nothing else might keep her safe and sound;
But Verdant† – so he hight† – he soon untied,
And counsel sage instead thereof to him applied.

yet sleeping even while he slept
subtle finely woven
formally for that particular purpose
unawares oppressed taken by surprise
distrain tear apart
Verdant means 'giver of spring'
hight was called

83 But all those pleasant bowers and palace brave* splendid
Guyon broke down with rigour* pitiless; violence
Ne aught their goodly workmanship might save
Them from the tempest of his wrathfulness,
But that their bliss he turned to balefulness.
Their groves he felled, their gardens did deface,
Their arbors spoil,* their cabinets† suppress,† destroyed
Their banquet houses burn, their buildings raze,
And of the fairest late, now made the foulest place.

84 Then led they her away, and eke that knight
They with them led, both sorrowful and sad;
The way they came, the same returned they right,
Till they arrivèd where they lately had
Charmed those wild beasts that raged with fury mad.
Which now awaking, fierce at them gan fly,
As in their mistress' rescue, whom they led;
But them the palmer soon did pacify.
Then Guyon asked what meant those beasts which there did lie.

85 Said he, 'These seeming beasts are men indeed,
Whom this enchantress hath transformèd thus –
Whilom* her lovers which her lusts did feed, formerly
Now turnèd into figures hideous,
According to their minds like* monstruous.' correspondingly
'Sad end,' quoth he, 'of life intemperate,
And mournful meed of joys delicious.†
But, palmer, if it mote thee so aggrate,* please
Let them returnèd be unto their former state.'

86 Straightway he with his virtuous staff them struck,
And straight of beasts they comely men became;
Yet being men they did unmanly look,
And starèd ghastly, some for inward shame
And some for wrath to see their captive dame.
But one above the rest in special,
That had an hog been late, hight Grill† by name,
Repinèd* greatly and did him miscall* sorrowed revile
That had from hoggish form him brought to natural.

cabinets garden-houses
suppress tear down
meed . . . delicious reward of voluptuous joys
Grill according to the ancient philosopher and biographer Plutarch (*c.* AD 50–*c.* 125), *Grill* was the companion of Odysseus who was transformed into a pig (his name means 'pig' in Greek) and refused to be changed back to his human shape

87 Said Guyon, 'See the mind of beastly man
That hath so soon forgot the excellence
Of his creation, when he life began,
That now he chooseth, with vile difference,* preference
To be a beast and lack intelligence.'
To whom the palmer thus: 'The dunghill kind
Delights in filth and foul incontinence:
Let Grill be Grill, and have his hoggish mind.
But let us hence depart, whilst weather serves and wind.'

1590

From THE FAIRY QUEEN, Book III, canto vi, stanzas 30–50

[*The Garden of Adonis*]

30 In that same garden all the goodly flowers,
Wherewith dame Nature doth her beautify,
And decks the garlands of her paramours
Are fetched: there is the first seminary
Of all things that are born to live and die
According to their kinds. Long work it were,
Here to account* the endless progeny describe
Of all the weeds* that bud and blossom there; plants
But so much as doth need, must needs be counted* here. recounted

31 It sited* was in fruitful soil of old, situated
And girt in with two walls on either side;
The one of iron, the other of bright gold,
That none might through break, nor overstride.
And double gates it had, which opened wide,
By which both in and out men moten* pass; might
Th'one faire and fresh, the other old and dried:
Old Genius† the porter of them was,
Old Genius, the which a double nature has.

Genius god of generation, the opposite of the evil Genius of the Bower of Bliss (II.xii.47–8)

32 He letteth in, he letteth out to wend,
All that to come into the world desire;
A thousand thousand naked babes† attend
About him day and night, which do require* request
That he with fleshly weeds* would them attire: clothes
Such as him list, such as eternal fate
Ordained hath, he clothes with sinful mire,
And sendeth forth to live in mortal state,
Till they again return back by the hinder gate.

33 After that they again returnèd been,
They in that Garden planted be again;
And grow afresh, as they had never seen
Fleshly corruption, nor mortal pain.
Some thousand years so doen they there remain;
And then of him are clad with other hue,†
Or sent into the changeful world again,
Till thither they return, where first they grew:
So like a wheel around they run from old to new.

34 Ne needs there gardener to set, or sow,
To plant or prune: for of their own accord
All things, as they created were, do grow,
And yet remember well the mighty word,
Which first was spoken by th'almighty lord,
That bade them to increase and multiply.
Ne do they need with water of the ford,* stream
Or of the clouds to moisten their roots dry;
For in themselves eternal moisture they imply.* contain

35 Infinite shapes of creatures there are bred,
And uncouth* forms, which none yet ever knew, unusual
And every sort is in a sundry* bed distinctive
Set by itself, and ranked in comely row.
Some fit for reasonable souls† t'endue,†
Some made for beasts, some made for birds to wear,
And all the thankful spawn of fishes' hue
In endless ranks along enrangèd were,
That seemed the ocean could not contain them there.

naked babes pre-existent souls awaiting the clothing of flesh
hue shape (i.e. in a purified form)
reasonable souls souls with reason, i.e. human beings
t'endue to dress themselves with

36 Daily they grow, and daily forth are sent
Into the world, it to replenish more;
Yet is the stock† not lessenèd, nor spent,
But still remains in everlasting store,
As first it was created as of yore.
For in the wide womb of the world there lies,
In hateful darkness and in deep horror,
An huge eternal chaos, which supplies
The substances of nature's fruitful progenies.

37 All things from thence do their first being fetch,
And borrow matter, whereof they are made,
Which when as form and feature it does catch,* assume
Becomes a body, and doth then invade* enter
The state of life, out of the grisly shade.
That substance* is eterne, and bideth so, matter
Ne when the life decays, and form does fade,
Doth it consume† and into nothing go,
But changèd is, and often altered to and fro.

38 The substance is not changed, nor alterèd,
But th'only† form and outward fashion;†
For every substance is conditionèd†
To change her hue, and sundry forms to don,
Meet for her temper and complexion:†
For forms are variable and decay,
By course of kind,† and by occasion;* necessity
And that fair flower of beauty fades away,
As doth the lily fresh before the sunny ray.

stock the primeval matter which becomes the material counterpart to the forms in the garden
doth it consume i.e. 'is it consumed'
th'only i.e. 'only the'
fashion appearance (trisyllabic, like *complexion* and *occasion*.
is conditionèd has the potential
meet for . . . complexion appropriate to her temperament and to the elements which make up her nature
by course of kind in the course of nature

39 Great enemy to it, and to all the rest,
That in the Garden of Adonis† springs,
Is wicked Time, who with his scythe addressed,* equipped
Does mow the flowering herbs and goodly things,
And all their glory to the ground down flings,
Where they do wither, and are foully marred:
He flies about, and with his flaggy* wings drooping
Beats down both leaves and buds without regard,
Ne ever pity may relent† his malice hard.

40 Yet pity often did the gods relent,
To see so fair things marred, and spoilèd quite:
And their great mother Venus did lament
The loss of her dear brood, her dear delight;
Her heart was pierced with pity at the sight,
When walking through the Garden, them she spied,†
Ye n'ot she† find redress for such despite.
For all that lives, is subject to that law:
All things decay in time, and to their end do draw.

41 But were it not, that Time their troubler is,
All that in this delightful Garden grows,
Should happy be, and have immortal bliss:
For here all plenty, and all pleasure flows,
And sweet love gentle fits† amongst them throws,
Without fell* rancour, or fond* jealousy; fierce foolish
Frankly† each paramour his leman* knows,† lover
Each bird his mate, ne any does envy
Their goodly merriment, and gay felicity.

Garden of Adonis in learned discourse the phrase referred to a fecund paradise frequented by Adonis, who was originally a Phoenician god of renascent nature, and in Greek mythology was the youth loved by Aphrodite
ne ever . . . relent nor will pity ever have reason to relent
spied Spenser's original word was presumably *saw* (to rhyme with *law*)
n'ot she she could not
fits fits of passion
frankly freely and openly
knows has sexual relations with

42 There is continual spring, and harvest* there autumn
Continual, both meeting at one time:
For both the boughs do laughing blossoms bear,
And with fresh colours deck the wanton prime* spring
And eke at once the heavy trees they climb,
Which seem to labour under their fruits' load:
The whiles the joyous birds make their pastime
Amongst the shady leaves their sweet abode,
And their sweet loves without suspicion tell abroad.

43 Right in the middest of that paradise,
There stood a stately mount, on whose round top
A gloomy grove of myrtle trees did rise,
Whose shady boughs sharp steel did never lop,
Nor wicked beasts their tender buds did crop,
But like a garland compassèd the height
And from their fruitful sides sweet gum did drop,
That all the ground with precious dew bedight* adorned
Threw forth most dainty odours, and most sweet delight.

44 And in the thickest covert of that shade,
There was a pleasant arbour, not by art
But of the trees' own inclination† made,
Which knitting their rank* branches part to part, dense
With wanton† ivy twine entrailled athwart,
And eglantine, and caprifoil* among, honeysuckle
Fashioned above within their inmost part,
That neither Phoebus'† beams could through them throng,
Nor Aeölus'† sharp blast could work them any wrong.

---

inclination means both 'angle' and 'willingness'
wanton growing luxuriantly
Phoebus god of the sun
Aeölus Greek god of the winds

45† And all about grew every sort of flower,
To which sad lovers were transformed of yore;
Fresh Hyacinthus† Phoebus' paramour,
Foolish Narcisse,† that likes the watery shore,
Sad Amaranthus,† made a flower but late,
Sad Amaranthus, in whose purple gore
Me seems I see Amintas'† wretched fate,
To whom sweet poets' verse have given endless date.

46 There went fair Venus often to enjoy
Her dear Adonis' joyous company,†
And reap sweet pleasure of the wanton boy;
There yet, some say, in secret does he lie,
Lapped in flowers and precious spicery,
By her hid from the world, and from the skill†
Of Stygian gods,† which do her love envy;
But she herself, whenever that she will,
Possesseth him, and of his sweetness† takes her fill.†

47 And sooth it seems they say:† for he may not
For ever die, and ever buried be
In baleful night, where all things are forgot;
All* be he subject to mortality, although
Yet in eterne in mutability,
And by succession made perpetual,
Transformèd oft, and changèd diversely:
For him the father of all forms they call;
Therefore needs mote* he live, that living gives to all. must

stanza 45 is missing a line; in the 1609 edition a truncated line ('And dearest love') was added between lines 3 and 4.

Hyacinthus When Phoebus' discus was blown aside by the wind it struck and killed Hyacinthus, the boy whom the god loved; Phoebus made the hyacinth spring from the boy's blood

Narcisse in Greek mythology Narcissus fell in love with his own reflection in the water, died of this insatiable love, and was transformed into the flower which bears his name

Amaranthus a purple flower regarded by the Christians of late antiquity as a symbol of immortality; in Greek it means 'unfading'

Amintas a reference to *Aminta*, a play by the Italian poet Tasso (1544–95) which Spenser might have read in Thomas Watson's Latin version; the eponymous hero dies of grief for his lover, and is transformed into an amaranthus

company as a sexual partner

skill / Of Stygian gods the Styx was a river in the underworld, the gods of which had the 'skill' of death

sweetness by confusion with a similar word 'Adonis' was said to mean 'sweetness' in Greek

takes her fill used in the sexual sense, of impregnation

sooth . . . say it seems that they speak the truth

48 There now he liveth in eternal bliss,
Joying[†] his goddess, and of her enjoyed:
Ne feareth he henceforth that foe of his,
Which with his cruel tusk him deadly cloyed:* gored
For that wild boar, the which him once annoyed,* injured
She firmly hath emprisonèd for ay,
That her sweet love his malice mote avoid,
In a strong rocky cave, which is they say,
Hewn underneath that mount, that none him loosen may.

49 There now he lives in everlasting joy,
With many of the gods in company,
Which thither haunt, and with the wingèd boy
Sporting himself in safe felicity:
Who when he hath with spoils and cruelty
Ransacked the world, and in the woeful hearts
Of many wretches set his triumphs high,
Thither resorts, and laying his sad darts
Aside, with fair Adonis plays his wanton parts.

50[†] And his true love Psyche with him plays,[†]
Fair Psyche to him lately reconciled,
After long troubles and unmeet upbrays,* upbraids
With which his mother Venus her reviled,
And eke himself her cruelty exiled:
But now in steadfast love and happy state
She with him lives, and hath him borne a child,
Pleasure,[†] that doth both gods and men aggrate,* please
Pleasure, the daughter of Cupid and Psyche late.

1590

Joying giving joy to
stanza 50 the story of Cupid and Psyche is contained in *The Golden Ass*, a novel by Apuleius, a second-century Roman writer. When Psyche attempted to see the face of Cupid, her nocturnal lover, he abandoned her. After undergoing trials imposed by Venus, Psyche was reunited with Cupid in heaven. Renaissance commentators interpreted the fable as an allegory of the struggles of the human soul, the Greek word for which is *psyche*
plays enjoys sexual pleasures
Pleasure sexual pleasure, and (in the allegorical tradition) the pleasure of the soul perpetuating itself

From AMORETTI

Sonnet 75

One day I wrote her name upon the strand,
But came the waves and washèd it away;
Again I wrote it with a second hand,
But came the tide, and made my pains his prey.
'Vain man', said she, 'that dost in vain assay,*   attempt
A mortal thing so to immortalise,
For I myself shall like to this decay,
And eke* my name be wipèd out likewise'.   also
'Not so', quod* I, 'let baser things devise*   said   plan
To die in dust, but you shall live by fame;
My verse your virtues rare shall eternise,
And in the heavens write your glorious name.
Where whenas death shall all the world subdue,
Our love shall live, and later life renew'.

1595

EPITHALAMION†

Ye learnèd sisters,† which have oftentimes
Been to me aiding,† others to adorn,†
Whom ye thought worthy of your graceful rhymes,†
That* even the greatest did not greatly scorn   so that
To hear their names sung in your simple lays,
But joyèd* in their praise –   rejoiced
And when ye list your own mishaps to mourn,†
Which death, or love, or fortune's wreck† did raze,*   destroy
Your string could soon to sadder tenor* turn,   tone
And teach the woods and waters to lament
Your doleful dreariment* –   grief

Epithalamion a Greek word meaning 'upon the bridal chamber'; in the Renaissance the Latin form of the word (epithalamium) referred to a popular genre which celebrated the marriages of gods and mythologised national heroes. Spenser's use of the Greek form indicates that his is a personal poem in celebration of real people

learnèd sisters the nine muses, Greek goddesses who inspire the creative arts and intellectual pursuits

Been to me aiding helped me

others to adorn Spenser is here referring to his poems in praise of Queen Elizabeth (*The Fairy Queen*), Sir Philip Sidney (*Astrophel* and *The Ruins of Time*), and Sir Walter Ralegh (*Colin Clout*)

graceful rhymes poems conferred by the grace of the muses

And when . . . mourn a reference to Spenser's *Tears of the Muses*

wreck the action of destroying

Now lay those sorrowful complaints aside,
And having all your heads with garland crowned,
Help me mine own love's praises to resound.
Ne* let the same of any be envied;† — nor
So Orpheus† did for his own bride,
So I unto myself alone will sing.
The woods shall to me answer, and my echo ring.

Early, before the world's light-giving lamp
His golden beam upon the hills doth spread,
Having dispersed the night's uncheerful damp,
Do ye awake, and with fresh lustihead* — vigour
Go to the bower* of my beloved love, — bedroom
My truest turtledove.
Bid her awake, for Hymen† is awake
And long since ready forth his masque* to move, — procession
With his bright tead† that flames with many a flake,* — spark
And many a bachelor to wait on him
In their fresh garments trim.
Bid her awake, therefore, and soon her dight;* — dress herself
For lo, the wishèd day is come at last
That shall for all the pains and sorrows past
Pay to her usury of long delight.
And whilst she doth her dight,
Do ye to her of joy and solace sing,
That all the woods may answer, and your echo ring.

Bring with you all the nymphs that you can hear,†
Both of the rivers and the forests green
And of the sea that neighbours to her near,
All with gay garlands goodly well beseen.†
And let them also with them bring in hand
Another gay garland
For my fair love, of lilies and of roses,
Bound truelove†-wise with a blue silk riband.
And let them make great store of bridal posies,
And let them eke* bring store of other flowers — also
To deck the bridal bowers.

of any be envied by any be begrudged
Orpheus the beauty of the song of the mythical Greek musician Orpheus enabled him to rescue his wife Eurydice from the underworld
Hymen the god of the marriage festival
tead Hymen's torch, the bright burning of which was a good omen
you can hear can hear you
well beseen beautifully displayed
truelove a symbolic ornamental knot of two intertwined loops

And let the ground whereas* her foot shall tread, where
For fear the stones her tender foot should wrong,
Be strewed with fragrant flowers all along,
And diapered† like the discoloured mead.†
Which done, do at her chamber door await.
For she will waken straight.* at once
The whiles* do ye this song unto her sing; while
The woods shall to you answer, and your echo ring.

Ye nymphs of Mulla,† which with careful heed
The silver scaly trouts do tend full well,
And greedy pikes which use therein to feed –
Those trouts and pikes all others do excel –
And ye likewise which keep the rushy lake,†
Where none do fishes take:
Bind up the locks the which hang scattered light,
And in his waters which your mirror make,
Behold your faces as the crystal bright,
That when you come whereas my love doth lie,
No blemish she may spy.
And eke ye lightfoot maids† which keep the deer
That on the hoary mountain use to tower,†
And the wild wolves which seek them to devour
With your steel darts do chase from coming near,
Be also present here
To help to deck her and to help to sing,
That all the woods may answer, and your echo ring.

Wake now, my love, awake, for it is time.
The rosy morn† long since left Tithon's† bed,
All ready to her silver coach to climb,
And Phoebus† gins* to show his glorious head. begins
Hark how the cheerful birds do chant their lays
And carol of love's praise –

diapered ornately patterned
discoloured mead variegated meadow
Mulla Spenser's name for the river Awbeg, which passed close to his estate in County Cork, Ireland
rushy lake a small lake (still choked with reeds) beside Spenser's castle
maids the nymphs of Diana, virgin goddess of the hunt
use to tower are accustomed to climb
rosy morn . . . Tithon Aurora (or Eos), goddess of the dawn, was married to the aged human Tithonus
Phoebus god of the sun

The merry lark her mattins† sings aloft,
The thrush replies, the mavis* descant† plays, — song-thrush
The ouzel† shrills, the ruddock† warbles soft –
So goodly all agree with sweet concent* — harmony
To this day's merriment.
Ah my dear love, why do ye sleep thus long,
When meeter were† that ye should now awake
T' await the coming of your joyous make,* — mate
And hearken to the birds' love-learnèd song
The dewy leaves among.
For they of joy and pleasance to you sing,
That all the woods them answer, and their echo ring.

My love is now awake out of her dreams,
And her fair eyes like stars that dimmèd were
With darksome cloud now show their goodly beams,
More bright than Hesperus's† head doth rear* — hold high
Come now ye damsels,* daughters of delight, — bridesmaids
Help quickly her to dight;
But first come ye, fair Hours† which were begot
In Jove's sweet paradise of* Day and Night, — by
Which do the seasons of the year allot,
And all that ever in this world is fair
Do make and still* repair. — always
And ye three handmaids of the Cyprian queen,†
The which do still adorn her beauty's pride,
Help to adorn my beautifullest bride;
And as ye her array, still throw between* — at intervals
Some graces to be seen,
And as ye use† to Venus, to her sing,
The whiles the woods shall answer, and your echo ring.

---

mattins morning song of birds
descant musical accompaniment sung above the main theme
ouzel blackbird; the European blackbird is a songbird
ruddock the European robin
meeter were would be more fitting
Hesperus the evening star
Hours in ancient Greek literature the Hours, goddesses of the seasons of fertility, are often present at weddings; their father was Jove, god of the radiant sky (hence 'day'), and their mother Themis, blindfolded (hence 'night'?) goddess of justice
three . . . queen the three Graces, goddesses personifying grace, charm and beauty, often present at weddings in ancient literature; attendants of Venus, who rose out of the sea near Cyprus, and called 'the Cyprian' by Homer
use are accustomed to do

Now is my love all ready forth to come.
Let all the virgins* therefore well await;   bridesmaids
And ye fresh boys that tend upon her groom,†
Prepare yourselves; for he is coming straight.
Set all your things in seemly good array,
Fit for so joyful day,
The joyfullest day that ever sun did see.
Fair sun, show forth thy favourable ray,
And let thy lifeful heat not fervent* be,   too hot
For fear of burning her sunshiny* face,   sunny
Her beauty to disgrace.*   disfigure
O fairest Phoebus, father† of the muse,
If ever I did honour thee aright,
Or sing the thing that mote* thy mind delight,   might
Do not thy servant's simple boon* refuse,   prayerful request
But let this day, let this one day be mine –
Let all the rest be thine.
Then I thy sovereign praises loud will sing,
That all the woods shall answer, and their echo ring.

Hark how the minstrels gin to shrill aloud
Their merry music that resounds from far,
The pipe,† the tabor,† and the trembling crowd,†
That well agree withouten breach or jar.†
But most of all the damsels do delight
When they their timbrels* smite,   tambourines
And thereunto do dance and carol† sweet,
That all the senses they do ravish quite,
The whiles the boys run up and down the street
Crying aloud with strong confusèd* noise,   blended
As if it were one voice.

---

tend . . . groom attend her bridegroom
father Phoebus was not the father of the muses, but he was 'Musagetes', leader of the muses
pipe, tabor a three-holed pipe (which could be played with one hand) and tabor (a small drum) were played by one performer, usually a peasant
crowd the crwth, an ancient Celtic bowed instrument
breach or jar break or discord
carol sing joyful songs

Hymen io Hymen,† *Hymen* they do shout,
That even to the heavens their shouting shrill
Doth reach, and all the firmament doth fill;
To which the people standing all about,
As in approvance do thereto applaud,
And loud advance her laud.†
And evermore they *Hymen*, *Hymen* sing,
That all the woods them answer, and their echo ring.

Lo where she comes along with portly* pace, dignified
Like Phoebe† from her chamber of the east
Arising forth to run her mighty race,
Clad all in white, that seems* a virgin best. is appropriate to
So well it her beseems that ye would ween* think
Some angel she had been.
Her long loose yellow locks like golden wire,
Sprinkled with pearl, and purling flowers† atween,
Do like a golden mantel her attire,
And being crownèd with a garland green,
Seem like some maiden queen.
Her modest eyes, abashèd to behold
So many gazers as on her do stare,
Upon the lowly ground affixèd are;
Ne dare lift up her countenance too bold,
But blush to hear her praises sung so loud,
So far from being proud.
Nath'less* do ye still loud her praises sing, nevertheless
That all the woods may answer, and your echo ring.

Tell me, ye merchants' daughters, did ye see
So fair a creature in your town before,
So sweet, so lovely, and so mild as she,
Adorned with beauty's grace and virtue's store?* treasure
Her goodly eyes like sapphires shining bright,
Her forehead ivory white,
Her cheeks like apples which the sun hath rudded,* reddened
Her lips like cherries, charming men to bite,
Her breast like to a bowl of cream uncrudded,†
Her paps like lilies budded,

Hymen io Hymen a ritual cry to Hymen (see note to l. 25); 'io' is a Greek and Latin word which proclaims joy (like hurrah!)
advance her laud extol her praises
Phoebe title of Diana (l. 67) as moon-goddess
purling flowers embroidered flowers edged with gold threads
uncrudded uncurdled, i.e. fresh

Her snowy neck like to a marble tower,
And all her body like a palace fair,
Ascending up with many a stately stair
To honour's seat and chastity's sweet bower.†
Why stand ye still, ye virgins, in amaze
Upon her so to gaze,
Whiles ye forget your former lay* to sing, — song
To which the woods did answer, and your echo ring?

But if ye saw that which no eyes can see,
The inward beauty of her lively sprite,* — living spirit
Garnished with heavenly gifts of high degree,
Much more then would ye wonder at that sight
And stand astonished like to those which read* — saw
Medusa's mazeful head.†
There dwells sweet love and constant chastity,
Unspotted faith and comely womanhead,
Regard of honour and mild modesty.
There virtue reigns as queen in royal throne
And giveth laws alone,
The which the base affections† do obey,
And yield their services unto her will;
Ne thought of thing uncomely ever may
Thereto approach to tempt her mind to ill.
Had ye once seen these her celestial treasures
And unrevealèd pleasures,
Then would ye wonder and her praises sing,
That all the woods should answer, and your echo ring.

Open the temple gates unto my love.
Open them wide that she may enter in,
And all the posts* adorn as doth behoove,* — door-posts; is fitting
And all the pillars deck with garlands trim,
For to receive this saint† with honour due
That cometh in to you.
With trembling steps and humble reverence
She cometh in, before th' Almighty's view.
Of her ye virgins learn obedience –

honour's seat . . . bower i.e. the head; honour and chastity are states of mind

Medusa's . . . head the head of the gorgon (female monster) Medusa was covered with snakes; those who saw it were turned to stone. *Mazeful* refers both to the tangle of snakes and to the stupefying effect on their beholders

base affections lower emotions, i.e. the passions

saint a person who leads a holy life

When so ye come into those holy places,
To humble your proud faces.
Bring her up to th' high altar, that she may
The sacred ceremonies there partake,
The which do endless matrimony make;
And let the roaring organs† loudly play
The praises of the Lord in lively notes,
The whiles with hollow throats
The choristers the joyous anthem sing,
That all the woods may answer, and their echo ring.

Behold whiles she before the altar stands,
Hearing the holy priest that to her speaks
And blesseth her with his two happy hands,†
How the red roses flush up in her cheeks
And the pure snow with goodly vermeil* stain — bright red
Like crimson dyed in grain;* — fast dyed
That even th' angels, which continually
About the sacred altar do remain,
Forget their service and about her fly,
Oft peeping in her face, that seems more fair
The more they on it stare.
But her sad* eyes still fastened on the ground — steadfast
Are governèd with goodly modesty,
That suffers not one look to glance awry
Which may let in a little thought unsound.* — sinful
Why blush ye, love, to give to me your hand,
The pledge of all our band?†
Sing ye sweet angels, *Alleluia*† sing,
That all the woods may answer, and your echo ring.

Now all is done. Bring home the bride again,
Bring home the triumph of our victory,
Bring home with you the glory of her gain,†
With joyance bring her and with jollity.
Never had man more joyful day than this
Whom heaven would heap with bliss.

---

roaring organs when the crescendo pedal is pressed all the stops are gradually brought into action; by the time the bride reaches the altar it may be said to 'roar'
happy hands the priest's hands impart future happiness
band bond of marriage
Alleluia the Latin form of a Hebrew compound meaning 'praise Jehovah', here referring to a song of praise to God
her gain having gained her

Make feast therefore now all this livelong day;
This day forever to me holy is.
Pour out the wine without restraint or stay,
Pour not by cups, but by the belly* full,   wine-skin
Pour out to all that wull;*   want it
And sprinkle† all the posts and walls with wine,
That they may sweat and drunken be withal.*   as well
Crown ye god Bacchus* with a coronal,*   god of wine   garland
And Hymen also crown with wreaths of vine,
And let the Graces dance unto the rest –
For they can do it best –
The whiles the maidens do their carol sing,
To which the woods shall answer, and their echo ring.

Ring ye the bells, ye young men of the town,
And leave your wonted* labours for this day.   customary
This day is holy; do ye write it down,
That ye forever it remember may.
This day† the sun is in his chiefest height,
With Barnaby† the bright,
From whence declining daily by degrees
He somewhat loseth of his heat and light,
When once the Crab behind his back† he sees.
But for this time it ill ordainèd was
To choose the longest day in all the year
And shortest night, when longest fitter were;
Yet never day so long but late* would pass.   at last
Ring ye the bells to make it wear away,
And bonfires make all day,
And dance about them, and about them sing,
That all the woods may answer, and your echo ring.

sprinkle in classical epithalamia the place in which the wedding feast was held was said to be sprinkled with nectar
this day 11 June, on the Julian Calendar then in use in Protestant states (which nominally included Ireland), was the summer solstice
Barnaby 11 June is the feast day of the apostle Barnabas; it is bright because of the solstice
Crab . . . back the astrological sign Cancer, which the sun sees *behind his back*, i.e. on the side of the sun opposite the earth, when it leaves Gemini; in the Julian calendar this happens on 12 June

Ah when will this long weary day have end,
And lend me leave to come unto my love?
How slowly do the hours their numbers spend!* waste away
How slowly does sad time his feathers move!
Haste thee, O fairest planet,† to thy home
Within the western foam;
Thy tirèd steeds long since have need of rest.
Long though it be, at last I see it gloom,* darken
And the bright evening star* with golden crest Hesperus
Appear out of the east.†
Fair child of beauty, glorious lamp of love,
That all the host of heaven* in ranks dost lead the stars
And guidest lovers through the nightès dread,
How cheerfully thou lookest from above
And seemst to laugh atween thy twinkling light,
As* joying in the sight as if
Of these glad many which for joy do sing,
That all the woods them answer, and their echo ring.

Now cease, ye damsels, your delights forepast;* past
Enough is it that all the day was yours.
Now day is done, and night is nighing fast;
Now bring the bride into the bridal bowers.
Now night is come, now soon her disarray,* undress her
And in her bed her lay.
Lay her in lilies and in violets,
And silken curtains over her display,* spread out
And odoured sheets, and Arras* coverlets. a rich tapestry
Behold how goodly my fair love does lie
In proud humility;
Like unto Maia† whenas Jove her took* ravished
In Tempe,† lying on the flowery grass
Twixt sleep and wake, after she weary was
With bathing in the Acidalian brook.†

fairest planet the sun, a planet in Ptolemaic cosmology
Appear . . . east Hesperus does *appear*, i.e. rise heliacally, but Spenser errs in making it appear in the east
Maia a shy Arcadian nymph, on whom Jove fathered Mercury
Tempe . . . Acidalian brook in classical sources Maia was not associated with Tempe (a valley close to Mount Olympus described by ancient poets as the most delightful place on earth) or with the Acidalian brook (a stream in Boeotia at the font of which the Graces were said to bathe); the latter is, however, associated with Venus, one of whose surnames is Acidalia

Now it is night, ye damsels may be gone
And leave my love alone,
And leave likewise your former lay to sing;
The woods no more shall answer, nor your echo ring.

Now welcome Night, thou night so long expected,
That long days' labour† dost at last defray,* pay back
And all my cares, which cruel love collected,
Hast summed in one and cancellèd for aye;* for ever
Spread thy broad wing over my love and me,
That no man may us see,
And in thy sable mantle us enwrap,
From fear of peril and foul horror free.
Let no false treason seek us to entrap,
Nor any dread disquiet once annoy
The safety of our joy;
But let the night be calm and quietsome,
Without tempestuous storms or sad affray;* dark fear
Like as when Jove† with fair Alcmena† lay,
When he begot the great Tirynthian groom†,
Or like as when he with thyself† did lie,
And begot Majesty.
And let the maids and young men cease to sing;
Ne let the woods them answer, nor their echo ring.

Let no lamenting cries nor doleful tears
Be heard all night within, nor yet without;
Ne let false whispers, breeding hidden fears,
Break gentle sleep with misconceivèd doubt.* unfounded fear
Let no deluding dreams nor dreadful sights
Make sudden sad affrights;
Ne let house fires nor lightning's helpless harms,
Ne let the Puck† nor other evil sprites,
Ne let mischievous witches with their charms,
Ne let hobgoblins'* names whose sense we see not, mischievous elves
Fray* us with things that be not. frighten

labour preparations for the wedding
Jove . . . Tirynthian groom Jove assumed the form of Amphitryon in order to seduce Amphitryon's wife Alcmena, on whom he fathered Hercules, who is here called Tirynthian because he was born in Tiryns, and groom because he later cleansed the Augean stables
thyself Night; the myth is Spenser's invention
Puck a malevolent spirit until transformed by Shakespeare

Let not the screech owl nor the stork be heard,
Nor the night raven that still deadly yells,
Nor damnèd ghosts called up with mighty spells,
Nor grisly vultures† make us once afeared;
Ne let th' unpleasant choir of frogs still croaking
Make us to wish their choking.
Let none of these their dreary accents sing;
Ne let the woods them answer, nor their echo ring.

But let still* silence true night watches keep, always
That sacred peace may in assurance reign,
And timely sleep, when it is time to sleep,
May pour his limbs forth on your pleasant plain.
The whiles an hundred little wingèd loves,
Like divers-feathered doves,
Shall fly and flutter round about your bed,
And in the secret dark that none reproves
Their pretty stealths shall work, and snares shall spread
To filch away sweet snatches of delight,
Concealed through covert night.
Ye sons of Venus,† play your sports* at will; amorous games
For greedy Pleasure, careless of your toys,* amorous games
Thinks more upon her paradise of joys
Than what ye do, albe it good or ill.
All night therefore attend* your merry play, indulge in
For it will soon be day;
Now none doth hinder you, that say* or sing, speak
Ne will the woods now answer, nor your echo ring.

Who is the same which at my window peeps,
Or whose is that fair face that shines so bright?
Is it not Cynthia,† she that never sleeps,
But walks about high heaven all the night?
O fairest goddess, do thou not envy
My love with me to spy;

vultures vultures fed on bodies (sometimes human) left outside

sons of Venus 'little wingèd loves' of line 357; Cupid, the god of Love, was the son of Venus

Cynthia another name for Diana/Phoebe, the moon goddess, who was born on Mount Cynthus

For thou likewise didst love, though now unthought,
And for a fleece of wool, which privily
The Latmian shepherd† once unto thee brought,
His pleasures with thee wrought.
Therefore to us be favourable† now;
And sith of women's labours† thou hast charge,
And generation goodly† dost enlarge,
Incline thy will t' effect our wishful vow,
And the chaste womb inform with timely seed,
That may our comfort breed.
Till which, we cease our hopeful hap† to sing,
Ne let the woods us answer, nor our echo ring.

And thou, great Juno,† which with awful* might   awesome
The laws of wedlock still dost patronize,
And the religion* of the faith first plight*   sanctity   pledged
With sacred rites hast taught to solemnize,
And eke for comfort often callèd art
Of* women in their smart*   by   labour pains
Eternally bind thou this lovely band,†
And all thy blessings unto us impart.
And thou, glad Genius,† in whose gentle hand
The bridal bower and genial* bed remain   marital
Without blemish or stain,
And the sweet pleasures of their loves' delight
With secret aid dost succour and supply,
Till they bring forth the fruitful progeny –
Send us the timely fruit of this same night.
And thou, fair Hebe,† and thou, Hymen free,
Grant that it may so be.
Till which, we cease your further praise to sing,
Ne any woods shall answer, nor your echo ring.

Latmian shepherd Endymion fell in love with the moon, and fell asleep on Mount Latmos. Spenser conflates Endymion with Pan, who seduced the moon *for a fleece of wool*

favourable in the East (notably at Ephesus) Cynthia was venerated as a fertility goddess; her favour is the gift of children

labours the pains of childbirth. Cynthia was identified with Lucina, the goddess of midwives

goodly of handsome appearance

our hopeful hap the happening for which we hope

Juno sister and wife of Jove; as Juno Jugalis she was goddess of marriage

band bond of marriage

Genius in Roman religion each woman had a protective spirit called a Juno, and each man had a Genius. Spenser endows his Genius with a role in marriage comparable to Juno's

Hebe daughter of Jove and Juno, goddess of youth

And ye high heavens, the temple of the gods,
In which a thousand torches flaming bright
Do burn, that to us wretched earthly clods
In dreadful darkness lend desirèd light;
And all ye powers which in the same remain –
More than we men can feign* – imagine
Pour out your blessing on us plenteously,
And happy influence† upon us rain,
That we may raise a large posterity,†
Which from the earth – which they may* long possess may they
With lasting happiness –
Up to your haughty palaces may mount,
And for the guerdon* of their glorious merit reward
May heavenly tabernacles there inherit,
Of blessed saints for to increase the count.
So let us rest, sweet love, in hope of this,
And cease till then our timely joys to sing.
The woods no more us answer, nor our echo ring.

Song made in lieu of many ornaments,
With which my love should duly have been decked,
Which cutting off through hasty accidents,†
Ye would not stay your due time to expect,* await
But promised both to recompense –
Be unto her a goodly ornament,
And for short time† an endless monument.

1595

influence used in the astrological sense of stellar influence
raise . . . posterity create many descendants
Which . . . accidents which having been truncated by accidental circumstances occasioned by haste
short time the time till the end of the world, so termed because time is shorter than eternity

Sir Walter Ralegh
1554?–1618

Walter Ralegh (who spelt his surname as 'Ralegh' rather than 'Raleigh' and as an adult pronounced it as 'Rahley') was born in Devon. After a year at Oriel College, Oxford, he went to France for four years, serving in the Huguenot army. He returned to London, where he seems to have studied law at the Middle Temple, and then resumed his military career. In 1580 he sailed for Ireland, where he supervised the massacre of 600 Spanish and Italian mercenaries who had surrendered at Smerwick. He enjoyed the favour of Queen Elizabeth throughout the 1580s, and was knighted in 1584, but in 1594 fell from royal grace and was briefly imprisoned when the Queen discovered that Ralegh had been having an affair with one of her maids of honour (whom he subsequently married). In 1595 he sailed for Guiana (now Venezuela) in search of the mythical wealth of El Dorado, and subsequently led successful military expeditions to Cadiz and the Azores. On the accession of James I in 1603 Ralegh was stripped of his offices and imprisoned in the Tower of London: he was charged with treason, condemned and then reprieved, but was kept in the Tower (in a flat with his wife and a son who was born there) until 1616, during which time he wrote his vast *History of the World*. He was released in order to undertake another expedition to search for gold in Guiana. The expedition was a disaster, and when Ralegh returned to England the charge of treason was renewed; he was beheaded on 29 October 1618.

Much of Ralegh's poetry is lost, and the small corpus which survives contains many poems of doubtful authenticity. His poems are often deeply pessimistic, the creations of a man who was at once highly intelligent and resigned to defeat. In his prose works Ralegh shows an extraordinary command of both narrative and description, but he is at his best in long passages of reflection, which are often elegiac in tone.

A FAREWELL TO FALSE LOVE

Farewell false Love, the oracle of lies,
A mortal foe and enemy to rest:
An envious boy, from whom all cares arise,
A bastard vile, a beast with rage possessed,
A way of error, a temple full of treason,
In all effects contrary unto reason:

A poisoned serpent covered all with flowers,
Mother of sighs and murderer of repose,
A sea of sorrows from whence are drawn such showers
As moisture lends to every grief that grows,
A school of guile, a net of deep deceit,
A gilded hook that holds a poisoned bait;

A fortress foiled, which reason did defend,
A Siren song, a fever of the mind,
A maze wherein affection finds no end,
A ranging cloud that runs before the wind,
A substance like the shadow of the sun,
A goal of grief for which the wisest run;

A quenchless fire, a nurse of trembling fear,
A path that leads to peril and mishap,
A true retreat of sorrow and despair,
An idle boy that sleeps in pleasure's lap,
A deep mistrust of that which certain seems,
A hope of that which reason doubtful deems.

Sith,* then, thy trains* my younger years betrayed, since consequences
And for my faith ingratitude I find,
And sith repentance hath my wrongs bewrayed,* betrayed
Whose course was ever contrary to kind,
False Love, Desire, and Beauty frail, adieu –
Dead is the root whence all these fancies grew.

1588

A VISION UPON THIS CONCEIT OF 'THE FAIRY QUEEN'†

Methought I saw the grave where Laura† lay,
Within that Temple,† where the vestal flame
Was wont to burn, and passing by that way,
To see that buried dust of living fame,
Whose tomb fair love, and fairer virtue kept,
All suddenly I saw the Fairy Queen:
At whose approach the soul of Petrarch wept,
And from thenceforth those graces were not seen.
For they this Queen attended, in whose stead
Oblivion laid him down on Laura's hearse:
Hereat the hardest stones were seen to bleed,
And groans of buried ghosts the heavens did pierce.
  Where Homer's spright* did tremble all for grief, spirit
  And cursèd th' access of that celestial thief.

1590

THE NYMPH'S REPLY TO THE SHEPHERD†

If all the world and love were young,
And truth in every shepherd's tongue,
These pretty pleasures might me move,
To live with thee and be thy love.

Time drives the flocks from field to fold,
When rivers rage, and rocks grow cold,
And Philomel† becometh dumb,
The rest complains of cares to come.

A Vision upon this Conceit of 'The Fairy Queen' this poem was printed in the first edition of Spenser's *The Fairy Queen*
conceit the poem which Spenser has 'conceived'
Laura the woman celebrated by the Italian poet Petrarch (1304–74) in his poems
Temple the temple of Vesta (Roman goddess of the fire burning on the hearth) in Rome contained the 'hearth fire' of the Roman state, which was tended by priestesses called vestal virgins
The Nymph's Reply to the Shepherd this poem is a response to Marlowe's 'The Passionate Shepherd to his Love'
Philomel the nightingale; but 'becometh dumb' also recalls the myth of Philomena, whose brother-in-law cut out her tongue so that she would not reveal the fact that he had raped her

The flowers do fade, and wanton fields,
To wayward winter reckoning yields,
A honey tongue, a heart of gall,
Is fancy's spring, but sorrow's fall.

Thy gowns, thy shoes, thy beds of roses,
Thy cap, thy kirtle, and thy poesies,
Soon break, soon wither, soon forgotten,
In folly ripe, in reason rotten.

Thy belt of straw and ivy buds,
Thy coral clasps and amber studs,
All these in me no means can move,
To come to thee, and be thy love.

But could youth last, and love still breed,
Had joys no date, nor age no need,
Then these delights my mind might move,
To live with thee, and be thy love.

1600

SIR WALTER RALEGH TO QUEEN ELIZABETH

Our passions are most like to floods and streams,
The shallow murmur, but the deep are dumb.
So, when affections yield discourse, it seems
The bottom is but shallow whence they come.
They that are rich in words must needs discover
That they are poor in that which makes a lover.

1655

AS YOU CAME FROM THE HOLY LAND†

As you came from the holy land
Of Walsingham,†
Met you not with my true love
By the way as you came?

How shall I know your true love
That have met many one,
As I went to the holy land
That have come, that have gone?

She is neither white nor brown
But as the heavens fair,
There is none hath a form so divine
In the earth or the air.

Such as one did I meet, good sir,
Such an angelic face,
Who like a queen, like a nymph, did appear
By her gait, by her grace.

She hath left me here all alone,
All alone as unknown,
Who sometimes did me lead with herself,
And me loved as her own.

What's the cause that she leaves you alone,
And a new way doth take,
Who loved you once as her own
And her joy did you make?

I have loved her all my youth,
But now am old, as you see;
Love likes not the falling fruit
From the withered tree.

As you came from the Holy Land the metre and rhyme-scheme suggest that the poem was composed as a ballad

Walsingham the shrine of Our Lady of Walsingham (in Norfolk) was the principal place of Marian pilgrimage in England

Know that love is a careless child
And forgets promise past,
He is blind, he is deaf when he list,* wishes to be
And in faith never fast.

His desire is a dureless* content transient
And a trustless joy,
He is won with a world of despair
And is lost with a toy.

Of womenkind such indeed is the love,
Or the word Love abused,
Under which many childish desires
And conceits* are excused. fantasies

But true love is a durable fire,
In the mind ever burning,
Never sick, never old, never dead,
From itself never turning.

1631

SIR WALTER RALEGH TO HIS SON

Three things there be that prosper up apace
And flourish, whilst they grow asunder far,
But on a day they meet all in one place,
And when they meet they one another mar;
And they be these – the wood, the weed, the wag.
The wood is that which makes the gallow tree,
The weed is that which strings the hangman's bag,
The wag, my pretty knave, betokeneth thee.
Mark well, dear boy: whilst these assemble not,
Green springs the tree, hemp grows, the wag is wild;
But when they meet, it makes the timber rot,
It frets the halter, and it chokes the child.
Then bless thee, and beware, and let us pray
We part not with thee at this meeting day.

EVEN SUCH IS TIME†

Even such is Time, which takes in trust
Our youth, our joys, and all we have,
And pays us but with age and dust;
Who in the dark and silent grave,
When we have wandered all our ways,
Shuts up the story of our days.
But from which earth and grave and dust
The Lord shall raise me up, I trust.
1618 1618

From THE DISCOVERY OF GUIANA†

[*El Dorado*]

This Martinez was he that christened the city of Manoa, by the name of El Dorado,† and as Berrio informed me upon this occasion. Those Guianians and also the borderers, and all other in that tract which I have seen are marvellous great drunkards, in which vice I think no nation can compare with them: and at the times of their solemn feasts when the Emperor carouseth with his Captains, tributaries, and governors, the manner is thus. All those that pledge him are first stripped naked, and their bodies anointed all over with a kind of white Balsamum (by them called Curcai) of which there is great plenty and yet very dear amongst them, and it is of all other the most precious, whereof we have had good experience: when they are anointed all over, certain servants of the Emperor having prepared gold made into fine powder blow it through hollow canes upon their naked bodies, until they be all shining from the foot to the head, and in this sort they sit drinking by twenties and hundreds and continue in drunkenness sometimes six or seven days together: the same is also confirmed by a letter written into Spain which was intercepted, which master Robert Dudley† told me he had seen. Upon this sight, the Images of gold in their Temples, the plate, armours, and shields of gold which they use in the wars, he called it El Dorado.

Even such is Time contemporary sources claim that Ralegh wrote this poem in the Tower the night before he was executed

The Discovery of Guiana Ralegh's 'Guiana' is part of modern Venezuela

El Dorado (Spanish) 'the gilded man', i.e. the mythical Emperor of Manoa; also the name of this city

Robert Dudley the naval commander Sir Robert Dudley (1574–1649) had explored Guiana in 1594

[*Lagartos*]

On both sides of this river, we passed the most beautiful country that ever mine eyes beheld: and whereas all that we had seen before was nothing but woods, prickles, bushes, and thorns, here we beheld plains of twenty miles in length, the grasses short and green, and in divers parts groves of trees by themselves, as if they had been by all the art and labour in the world so made of purpose: and still as we rowed, the Deer came down feeding by the water's side, as if they had been used to a keeper's call. Upon this river there were great store of fowl, and of many sorts: we saw in it divers sorts of strange fishes, and of marvellous bigness, but for Lagartos† it exceeded, for there were thousands of those ugly serpents, and the people call it for the abundance of them the river of Lagartos, in their language. I had a Negro a very proper young fellow, that leaping out of the Galley to swim in the mouth of this river, was in all our sights taken and devoured with one of those Lagartos.

1595–6 1596

From THE HISTORY OF THE WORLD chapter 6.12

[*History and Death*]

By this which we have already set down, is seen the beginning and end of the three first monarchies of the world; whereof the founders and erectors thought, that they could never have ended. That of Rome which made the fourth, was also at this time almost at the highest. We have left it flourishing in the middle of the field; having rooted up, or cut down, all that kept it from the eyes and admiration of the world. But after some continuance, it shall begin to lose the beauty it had; the storms of ambition shall beat her great boughs and branches one against another; her leaves shall fall off, her limbs wither, and a rabble of barbarous nations enter the field, and cut her down.

Now these great kings, and conquering nations, have been the subject of those ancient Histories, which have been preserved, and yet remain among us; and withal of so many tragical poets, as in the persons of powerful princes and other mighty men have complained against infidelity, time, destiny, and most of all against the variable success of

Lagartos in Latin American Spanish, a collective term for crocodiles and alligators

worldly things, and instability of fortune. To these undertakings the greatest lords of the world have been stirred up, rather by the desire of fame, which plougheth up the air, and soweth in the wind; than by the affection of bearing rule, which draweth after it so much vexation, and so many cares. And that this is true, the good advice of Cineas[†] to Pyrrhus[†] proves. And certainly, as fame hath often been dangerous to the living, so is it to the dead of no use at all; because separate from knowledge. Which were it otherwise, and the extreme ill bargain of buying this lasting discourse, understood by them which are dissolved; they themselves would then rather have wished, to have stolen out of the world without noise; than to be put in mind, that they have purchased the report of their actions in the world, by rapine, oppression and cruelty, by giving in spoil the innocent and labouring soul to the idle and insolent, and by having emptied the cities of the world of their ancient inhabitants, and filled them again with so many and so variable sorts of sorrows.

Since the fall of the Roman Empire (omitting that of the Germans, which had neither greatness nor continuance) there hath been no state fearful[†] in the East, but that of the Turk,[†] nor in the West any prince that hath spread his wings far over his nest, but the Spaniard; who since the time that Ferdinand[†] expelled the Moors out of Granada, have made many attempts to make themselves masters of all Europe. And it is true, that by the treasures of both Indies, and by the many kingdoms which they possess in Europe, they are at this day the most powerful. But as the Turk is now counterpoised by the Persian, so instead of so many millions as have been spent by the English, French, and Netherlands in a defensive war, and in diversions against them, it is easy to demonstrate, that with the charge of two hundred thousand pound continued but for two years or three at the most, they may not only be persuaded to live in peace, but all their swelling and overflowing streams may be brought back into their natural channels and old banks. These two nations, I say, are at this day the most eminent, and to be regarded; the one seeking to root out the Christian Religion altogether, the other the truth and sincere profession thereof, the one to join all Europe to Asia, the other the rest of all Europe to Spain.

For the rest, if we seek a reason of the succession and continuance of this boundless ambition in mortal men, we may add to that which hath been already said; That the kings and princes of the world have always

Cineas a Thessalian diplomat who advised King *Pyrrhus* of Epirus that war with Rome was a battle with a hydra

fearful causing fear

Turk in 1453 Constantinople had fallen to the Ottoman Turks, who in the sixteenth century had expanded into the Balkans and North Africa

Ferdinand King Ferdinand the Catholic (1452–1516) had expelled the Moors from Granada in 1492

laid before them, the actions, but not the ends, of those great ones which preceded them. They are always transported with the glory of the one, but they never mind the misery of the other, till they find the experience in themselves. They neglect the advice of God, while they enjoy life, or hope it; but they follow the counsel of Death, upon his first approach. It is he that puts into man all the wisdom of the world, without speaking a word; which God with all the words of his Law, promises, or threats, doth not infuse. Death which hateth and destroyeth man, is believed; God, which hath made him and loves him, is always deferred: *I have considered* (saith Solomon†) *all the works that are under the Sun, and behold, all is vanity and vexation of spirit*: but who believes it, till Death tells it us? It was Death, which opening the conscience of Charles the fifth,† made him enjoin his son Philip† to restore Navarre; and King Francis† the first of France, to command that justice should be done upon the murderers of the Protestants in Merindol† and Cabrières,† which till then he neglected. It is therefore Death alone that can suddenly make man to know himself. He tells the proud and insolent, that they are but abjects, and humbles them at the instant; makes them cry, complain, and repent, yea, even to hate their forepassed happiness. He takes the account of the rich, and proves him a beggar; a naked beggar, which hath interest in nothing, but in the gravel that fills his mouth. He holds a glass before the eyes of the most beautiful, and makes them see therein, their deformity and rottenness; and they acknowledge it.

O eloquent, just and mighty Death! whom none could advise, thou hast persuaded; that none hath dared, thou has done; and whom all the world hath flattered, thou only hath cast out of the world and despised: thou hast drawn together all the far stretched greatness, all the pride, cruelty, and ambition of man, and covered it all over with these two narrow words, *Hic jacet*.†

1603–14 — 1614

Solomon King Solomon, in Ecclesiastes 1.14
Charles Charles V (1500–58), the Holy Roman Emperor, whose grandfather Ferdinand the Catholic had annexed the Spanish part of the Pyrenean kingdom of Navarre in 1516
Philip Philip II (1527–98), King of Spain
Francis Francis I (1494–1547), King of France
Mérindol, Cabrières villages in Provence where in 1545 the Vaudois, who were thought by the English to be Protestants, were massacred as heretics
Hic jacet 'Here lies', the opening words on Latin tombstone inscriptions

LETTER TO SIR ROBERT CECIL: JULY 1592†

I pray be a mean† to her Majesty for the signing of the bills for the guards' coats, which are to be made now for the progress,† and which the Clerk of the Check† hath importuned me to write for.

My heart was never broken till this day, that I hear the Queen goes away so far off – whom I have followed so many years with so great love and desire, in so many journeys, and am now left behind her, in a dark prison all alone. While she was yet near at hand, that I might hear of her once in two or three days, my sorrows were the less: but even now my heart is cast into the depth of all misery. I that was wont to behold her riding like Alexander,† hunting like Diana,† walking like Venus,† the gentle wind blowing her fair hair about her pure cheeks, like a nymph; sometime sitting in the shade like a Goddess; sometime singing like an angel; sometime playing like Orpheus.† Behold the sorrow of this world! Once amiss, hath bereaved me of all. O Glory, that only shineth in misfortune, what is become of thy assurance? All wounds have scars, but that of fantasy; all affections their relenting, but that of womankind. Who is the judge of friendship, but adversity? Or when is grace witnessed, but in offences? There were no divinity, but by reason of compassion; for revenges are brutish and mortal. All those times past – the loves, the sithes,† the sorrows, the desires, can they not weigh down one frail misfortune? Cannot one drop of gall be hidden in so great heaps of sweetness? I may then conclude, *Spes et fortuna, valete* [farewell hope and good fortune]. She is gone, in whom I trusted, and of me hath not one thought of mercy, nor any respect of that that was. Do with me now, therefore, what you list.† I am more weary of life than they are desirous I should perish; which if it had been for her, as it is by her, I had been too happily born.

Yours, not worthy any name or title,

W.R.

1592

Letter to Sir Robert Cecil Ralegh wrote this letter in 1592, on hearing that Queen Elizabeth was going on progress; he was describing a queen who was almost 60 years old. Sir Robert Cecil (1563?–1612), later Earl of Salisbury and Viscount Cranborne, was a statesman who held various high offices under Queen Elizabeth and King James

mean intermediary

progress the state journey of a monarch

Clerk of the Check an officer in the royal household in charge of servants and household guards; Ralegh was the honorary Captain of the Guard

Alexander Alexander the Great (356–323 BC), the Greek general, was often portrayed riding his horse Bucephalus

Diana Roman goddess of the hunt

Venus Roman goddess of love and beauty; in paintings such as Botticelli's 'Birth of Venus' the wind blows her blonde hair

Orpheus legendary Greek musician, often portrayed playing a lyre

sithes sighs

list wish

Richard Hooker

1554?–1600

Richard Hooker was born in Exeter, and was educated at the local grammar school. Through the influence of Bishop Jewel he was able to enter Corpus Christi College, Oxford, where he was eventually elected to a Fellowship and appointed deputy to the Professor of Hebrew. He resigned his Fellowship on his marriage in 1584, and became a parish priest in Buckinghamshire. The following year he was appointed Master of the Temple, the title enjoyed by the senior priest of the Temple church, which was used by members of the legal societies known as the Inner and Middle Temple. Hooker became involved in a violent theological controversy with the Afternoon-Reader, the Calvinist Walter Travers; 'the pulpit', in the words of Thomas Fuller, 'spake pure Canterbury in the morning and Geneva in the afternoon'. The dispute finally died down, but Hooker decided to undertake a scholarly investigation of the principles of the Church of England. He retired to a living near Canterbury, and there wrote *The Laws of Ecclesiastical Polity.*

The Laws of Ecclesiastical Polity is an enormous treatise devoted to the question of church government. Puritans argued that the hierarchical government of the church, particularly the system of bishops and archbishops, was unbiblical and should therefore be dismantled. Hooker chose to defend this system, and argued that his Puritan opponents were mistaken in their mechanical reliance on the Bible as their sole authority. He argued that the Bible should not be the only guide, but should be considered alongside 'natural law', which he considered to be the expression of God's reason. He argued that ecclesiastical government, civil government and even the Bible should be interpreted in the light of this law of nature.

From THE LAWS OF ECCLESIASTICAL POLITY

From Preface

Think not that ye[†] read the words of one who bendeth himself as an adversary against the truth which ye have already embraced; but the words of one who desireth even to embrace together with you the self-same truth, if it be the truth; and for that cause (for no other, God he knoweth) hath undertaken the burdensome labour of this painful kind of conference. For the plainer access whereunto, let it be lawful for me to rip up to the very bottom, how and by whom your discipline was planted, at such time as this age we live in began to make first trial thereof.

A founder[†] it had, whom, for mine own part, I think incomparably the wisest man that ever the French church did enjoy, since the hour it enjoyed him. His bringing up was in the study of the civil law. Divine knowledge he gathered, not by hearing or reading so much, as by teaching others. For, though thousands were debtors to him, as touching knowledge in that kind; yet he to none but only to God, the author of that most blessed fountain, the Book of Life, and of the admirable dexterity of wit, together with the helps of other learning which were his guides: till being occasioned to leave France, he fell at the length upon Geneva; which city the bishop[†] and clergy thereof had a little before (as some do affirm) forsaken, being of likelihood frighted with the people's sudden attempt for abolishment of popish religion: the event of which enterprise they thought it not safe for themselves to wait for in that place. At the coming of Calvin thither, the form of their civil regiment was popular, as it continueth at this day: neither king, nor duke, nor nobleman of any authority or power over them, but officers chosen by the people yearly out of themselves, to order all things with public consent. For spiritual government, they had no laws at all agreed upon, but did what the pastors of their souls by persuasion could win them unto. Calvin, being admitted one of their preachers, and a divinity reader amongst them, considered how dangerous it was that the whole estate of that church should hang still on so slender a thread as the liking of an ignorant multitude is, if it have power to change whatsoever

ye the preface is addressed 'to them that seek (as they term it) the reformation of the laws and orders ecclesiastical in the Church of England', that is to the English Calvinists

founder John Calvin (1509–64), the French leader of the reformation in Geneva

bishop Pierre de la Baume, the last bishop to be recognised in Geneva, left for France in July 1533; Calvin arrived the following month

itself listeth. Wherefore taking unto him two† of the other ministers for more countenance of the action, (albeit the rest were all against it,) they moved, and in the end persuaded with much ado, the people to bind themselves by solemn oath, first never to admit the Papacy amongst them again; and secondly, to live in obedience unto such orders concerning the exercise of their religion, and the form of their ecclesiastical government, as those their true and faithful ministers of God's word had agreeably to scripture set down for that end and purpose.

[2.] When these things began to be put in ure,† the people also (what causes moving them thereunto, themselves best know) began to repent them of that they had done, and irefully to champ upon the bit they had taken into their mouths; the rather, for that they grew by means of this innovation into dislike with some churches near about them, the benefit of whose good friendship their state could not well lack.

It was the manner of those times (whether through men's desire to enjoy alone the glory of their own enterprises, or else because the quickness of their occasions required present despatch; so it was) that every particular church did that within itself, which some few of their own thought good, by whom the rest were all directed. Such number of churches then being, though free within themselves, yet small, common conference beforehand might have eased them of much after trouble. But a greater inconvenience it bred, that every later endeavoured to be certain degrees more removed from conformity with the church of Rome, than the rest before had been: whereupon grew marvellous great dissimilitudes, and by reason thereof, jealousies, heart-burnings, jars and discords amongst them. Which, notwithstanding, might have easily been prevented, if the orders, which each church did think fit and convenient for itself, had not so peremptorily been established under that high commanding form, which tendered them unto the people, as things everlastingly required by the law of that Lord of lords, against whose statutes there is no exception to be taken. For by this mean it came to pass, that one church could not but accuse and condemn another of disobedience to the will of Christ, in those things where manifest difference was between them: whereas the selfsame orders allowed, but yet established in more wary and suspense manner, as being to stand in force till God should give the opportunity of some general conference what might be best for every of them afterwards to do; this I say had both prevented all occasion of just dislike which others might take, and reserved a greater liberty unto the authors

two Guillaume Farel, the French Protestant reformer who had persuaded Calvin to stay in Geneva, and Augustin Courauld, the former monk whose age and blindness enhanced the visionary quality of his preaching

in ure into practice

themselves of entering into farther consultation afterwards. Which though never so necessary they could not easily now admit, without some fear of derogation from their credit: and therefore that which once they had done, they became for ever after resolute to maintain.

Calvin therefore and the other two his associates, stiffly refusing to administer the holy Communion to such as would not quietly, without contradiction and murmur, submit themselves unto the orders which their solemn oath had bound them to obey, were in that quarrel banished† the town.

1593

banished Calvin and Farel went to Basel, after which Calvin became minister at Strasbourg and Farel at Neuchâtel; Courauld became pastor at Orbe, where he died in 1538

John Lyly
1554?–1606

John Lyly was born in Kent, and educated at Magdalen College, Oxford, and at Cambridge. He settled in London and assumed a literary career as a pamphleteer and court playwright. He served as a Member of Parliament from 1598 to 1601. His best-known work is *Euphues*, a prose romance published in two parts (*Euphues: The Anatomy of Wit*, 1578, and *Euphues and his England*, 1580). *Euphues* is chiefly remarkable for its extraordinary style, the chief characteristic of which is the extensive use of balanced antitheses. The extract printed below is taken from 'A Cooling Card for Philautus', a letter of advice to lovers in *Euphues: The Anatomy of Wit*.

From EUPHUES: THE ANATOMY OF WIT

[*A Cooling Card for Philautus*]

But at the first the ox wieldeth not the yoke, nor the colt the snaffle, nor the lover good counsel; yet time causeth the one to bend his neck, the other to open his mouth, and should enforce the third to yield his right to reason. Lay before thine eyes the slights and deceits of thy lady, her snatching in jest and keeping in earnest, her perjury, her impiety, the countenance she showeth to thee of course,[†] the love she beareth to others of zeal, her open malice, her dissembled mischief. O, I would in repeating their vices thou couldest be as eloquent as in remembering them thou oughtest to be penitent. Be she never so comely, call her counterfeit; be she never so straight, think her crooked; and wrest all parts of her body to the worst, be she never so worthy. If she be well set[†] then call her a boss,[†] if slender a hazel twig, if nut-brown as black as a coal, if well-coloured a painted wall; if she be pleasant then is she a wanton, if sullen a clown,[†] if honest then is she coy, if impudent a harlot. Search every vein and sinew of their disposition; if she have no sight in descant[†] desire her to chant it, if no cunning to dance request

of course habitually
well set solidly formed
boss an insulting term for a fat woman
clown an ill-bred person
sight in descant skill in singing

her to trip it, if no skill in music proffer her the lute, if an ill gait then walk with her, if rude† in speech talk with her; if she be gag-toothed† tell her some merry jest to make her laugh, if pink-eyed some doleful history to cause her weep: in the one her grinning will show her deformed, in the other her whining like a pig half roasted.

It is a world† to see how commonly we are blinded with the collusions of women, and more enticed by their ornaments being artificial than their proportion being natural. I loathe almost to think on their ointments and apothecary drugs, the sleeking of their faces and all their slibber-sauces† which bring queasiness to the stomach and disquiet to the mind. Take from them their periwigs, their paintings, their jewels, their rolls,† their bolsterings,† and thou shalt soon perceive that a woman is the least part of herself. When they be once robbed of their robes then will they appear so odious, so ugly, so monstrous that thou wilt rather think them serpents than saints, and so like hags that thou wilt fear rather to be enchanted than enamoured. Look in their closets and there shalt thou find an apothecary's shop of sweet confections, a surgeon's box of sundry salves, a pedlar's pack of new fangles. Besides all this, their shadows, their spots, their lawns, their lyfkies,† their ruffs, their rings show them rather cardinals' courtesans than modest matrons, and more carnally affected than moved in conscience. If every one of these things severally be not of force to move thee yet all of them jointly should mortify thee.

Moreover, to make thee the more stronger to strive against these sirens† and more subtle to deceive these tame serpents, my counsel is that thou have more strings to thy bow than one. It is safe riding at two anchors, a fire divided in twain burneth slower, a fountain running into many rivers is of less force, the mind enamoured on two women is less affected with desire and less infected with despair, one love expelleth another and the remembrance of the latter quencheth the concupiscence of the first.

1578

rude unskilled
gag-toothed having a projecting tooth
world marvel
slibber-sauces a repulsive compound used as a cosmetic
rolls pads forming part of a woman's head-dress
bolsterings pads used to bolster a dress
lyfkies bodices
sirens in Greek mythology, creatures whose bewitching song lured sailors to their deaths

Sir Philip Sidney

1554–86

Philip Sidney was born at Penshurst Place, in Kent. In 1564 he entered Shrewsbury School, on the same day as Fulke Greville, who was to become his lifelong friend. Four years later he proceeded to Christ Church, Oxford, but did not take a degree. In 1572 he travelled to France with the Earl of Lincoln, and he subsequently toured the courts of Europe until 1575. Thereafter he assumed the role of a courtier, living at the London home of his uncle the Earl of Leicester. In 1580 he unwisely wrote to the queen opposing her proposed marriage to the brother of the French king, and he was obliged to withdraw for a time from the court. He was knighted in 1583 for reasons of court protocol. In November 1585 he joined Leicester's expedition to the Low Countries. He was wounded in a minor skirmish near Zutphen in September 1586, and three weeks later died of his wounds.

Sidney's greatest works were written during the last seven years of his short life. He wrote a treatise on English poetry, variously known as *An Apology for Poetry* and *The Defence of Poesy*; its grace and eloquence make it by far the best English example of a genre which had found distinguished exponents on the continent. Sidney's prose romance, the *Arcadia*, is one of the liveliest (and funniest) books of the English Renaissance; it exists in two versions, known as the *Old Arcadia* (which was finished by 1581) and the *New Arcadia* (a radical but incomplete revision undertaken about three years later). Sidney's sonnet sequence, *Astrophil and Stella*, was written in 1582. 'Stella' represents Lady Penelope Rich, a married woman of whom Sidney was enamoured. The exact nature of their relationship, and the extent to which it is mirrored in the sonnet sequence, remain problematical.

From AN APOLOGY FOR POETRY

[*The Golden World of Poetry*]

There is no art delivered to mankind that hath not the works of Nature† for his principal object, without which they could not consist, and on which they so depend, as they become actors and players, as it were, of what Nature will have set forth. So doth the astronomer look upon the stars, and, by that he seeth, setteth down what order Nature hath taken therein. So do the geometrician and arithmetician in their diverse sorts of quantities. So doth the musician in times tell you which by nature agree, which not. The natural philosopher thereon† hath his name, and the moral philosopher standeth upon† the natural virtues, vices, and passions of man; and 'follow Nature' (saith he) 'therein, and thou shalt not err'.† The lawyer saith what men have determined;† the historian what men have done. The grammarian speaketh only of the rules of speech; and the rhetorician and logician, considering what in Nature will soonest prove and persuade, thereon give artificial rules, which still are compassed within the circle of a question† according to the proposed matter. The physician weigheth the nature of a man's body, and the nature of things helpful or hurtful unto it. And the metaphysic, though it be in the second and abstract notions†, and therefore be counted supernatural,† yet doth he indeed build upon the depth of Nature.

Only the poet, disdaining to be tied to any such subjection, lifted up with the vigour of his own invention, doth grow in effect into another nature, in making things either better than Nature bringeth forth, or, quite anew, forms such as never were in Nature, as the Heroes, Demigods, Cyclops, Chimeras, Furies,† and such like: so as he goeth hand in hand with Nature, not enclosed within the narrow warrant of her gifts, but freely ranging only within the zodiac† of his own wit.

Nature never set forth the earth in so rich tapestry as divers poets have done; neither with pleasant rivers, fruitful trees, sweet-smelling

---

Nature the created world
thereon for that reason
standeth upon is concerned with
'follow . . . err' a Stoic aphorism the meaning of which varied with interpretation of the word 'nature'
determined refers to legal decisions
compassed . . . question i.e. their enquiries are limited by the questions which they ask
second . . . notions first notions deal with the nature of objects, second notions with modes of comprehension of objects
supernatural i.e. at one remove from nature
Heroes . . . Furies in Attic Greek heroes were a race between gods and men; demigods had one divine and one mortal parent; Cyclopes were giants with only one eye, in the middle of the forehead; the chimera resembled a lion at the front, a goat in the middle, and a dragon at the rear; the Furies, goddesses of vengeance, were represented as women with serpents in their hair
zodiac just as nature was confined within the celestial zodiac, so poetry is confined within the zodiac of man's intellect (*wit*)

flowers, nor whatsoever else may make the too much loved earth more lovely. Her world is brazen,† the poets only deliver a golden.†

But let those things alone, and go to man – for whom as the other things are, so it seemeth in him her uttermost cunning is employed – and know whether she have brought forth so true a lover as Theagenes,† so constant a friend as Pylades,† so valiant a man as Orlando,† so right a prince as Xenophon's Cyrus,† so excellent a man every way as Virgil's Aeneas. Neither let this be jestingly conceived, because the works of the one† be essential,† the other in imitation or fiction; for any understanding knoweth the skill of the artificer standeth in that *Idea* or fore-conceit of the work, and not in the work itself. And that the poet hath that *Idea* is manifest, by delivering them forth in such excellency as he hath imagined them. Which delivering forth also is not wholly imaginative,† as we are wont to say by them that build castles in the air; but so far substantially it worketh, not only to make a Cyrus, which had been but a particular excellency as Nature might have done, but to bestow a Cyrus upon the world to make many Cyruses, if they will learn aright why and how that maker† made him.

Neither let it be deemed too saucy a comparison to balance the highest point of man's wit with the efficacy of Nature; but rather give right honour to the heavenly Maker of that maker, who having made man to His own likeness, set him beyond and over all the works of that second† nature: which in nothing he† showeth so much as in Poetry, when with the force of a divine breath he bringeth things forth far surpassing her† doings, with no small argument to the incredulous of that first accursed fall of Adam: since our erected wit maketh us know what perfection is, and yet our infected will keepeth us from reaching unto it. But these arguments will by few be understood, and by fewer granted. Thus much (I hope) will be given me, that the Greeks with some probability of reason gave him the name above all names of learning.

brazen . . . golden refers to the traditional idea that the first age of man was the golden age of perfection and immortality, which was followed by progressive decline into the ages of silver, brass and (the present age) iron
Theagenes Chariclea's lover in the Greek romance *Aethiopica*, by the fourth-century bishop Heliodorus
Pylades the faithful friend of Orestes in various Greek tragedies
Orlando Roland, Charlemain's paladin, was (as Orlando) the hero of epics by Pulci, Boiardo and Ariosto
Xenophon's Cyrus refers to *Cyropaedia*, a historical novel by the soldier Xenophon; its model hero is Cyrus the Elder, founder of the Achaemenid Persian Empire
the one nature
be essential are real
not wholly imaginative i.e. not existing only as an image in the mind
maker poet, i.e. Xenophon
second nature creates, but was itself created by God, and is therefore secondary
he man
her nature

Now let us go to a more ordinary opening† of him, that the truth may be more palpable: and so I hope, though we get not so unmatched a praise as the etymology of his names will grant, yet his very description, which no man will deny, shall not justly be barred from a principal commendation.

Poesy therefore is an art of imitation, for so Aristotle termeth it in his word *mimesis*, that is to say, a representing, counterfeiting, or figuring forth – to speak metaphorically, a speaking picture – with this end, to teach and delight.

1595

From ASTROPHIL AND STELLA

1

Loving in truth, and fain in verse my love to show,
That she (dear she) might take some pleasure of my pain:
Pleasure might cause her read, reading might make her know,
Knowledge might pity win, and pity grace obtain,
  I sought fit words to paint the blackest face of woe,
Studying inventions fine, her wits to entertain:
Oft turning others' leaves, to see if thence would flow
Some fresh and fruitful showers upon my sun-burned† brain.
  But words came halting forth, wanting Invention's stay,
Invention, Nature's child, fled step-dame Study's blows,
And others' feet still seemed but strangers in my way.
Thus great with child to speak, and helpless in my throes,
  Biting my truant pen, beating myself for spite,
  'Fool,' said my Muse to me, 'look in thy heart† and write.'

opening exposition
sun-burned by the flames of love
in thy heart i.e. at the image of Stella in my heart

2

Not at first sight, nor with a dribbèd† shot
  Love gave the wound, which while I breathe will bleed:
  But known worth did in mine† of time proceed,
Till by degrees it had full conquest got.
I saw and liked, I liked but loved not,
  I loved, but straight did not what Love decreed:
  At length to Love's decrees, I forced, agreed,
Yet with repining at so partial† lot.
  Now even that footstep† of lost liberty
Is gone, and now like slave-born Muscovite,†
I call it praise to suffer tyranny;
And now employ the remnant of my wit,
  To make myself believe that all is well,
  While with a feeling skill I paint my hell.

31

With how sad steps, o Moon, thou climb'st the skies,
  How silently, and with how wan a face,
  What, may it be that even in heavenly place
That busy archer† his sharp arrows tries?
Sure, if that long with Love acquainted eyes
  Can judge of Love, thou feel'st a lover's case;
  I read it in thy looks, thy languished grace,
To me that feel the like, thy state descries.
  Then ev'n of fellowship, o Moon, tell me
Is constant Love deemed there but want of wit?
Are Beauties there as proud as here they be?
Do they above love to be loved, and yet
  Those lovers scorn whom that† Love doth possess?
  Do they call virtue there ungratefulness?†

dribbèd random
mine a tunnel containing explosives under the wall of a city under seige
partial one-sided (i.e. favouring the lady)
footstep footprint
slave-born Muscovite citizens of the Russian Empire (Muscovy) were popularly believed to enjoy their enslavement by the czars
archer Cupid
whom that whom
Do they . . . ungratefulness? i.e. 'do they call ungratefulness a virtue there?'

39

Come sleep, o sleep, the certain knot of peace,
The baiting† place of wit, the balm of woe,
The poor man's wealth, the prisoner's release,
Th'indifferent judge between the high and low;
  With shield of proof shield me from out the prease†
Of those fierce darts, despair at me doth throw:
O make in me those civil wars to cease;
I will good tribute pay if thou do so.
  Take thou of me smooth pillows, sweetest bed,
A chamber deaf to noise, and blind to light:
A rosy garland,† and a weary head:
And if these things, as being thine by right,
  Move not thy heavy grace, thou shalt in me,
  Livelier then elsewhere, Stella's image see.

54

Because I breathe not love to every one,
  Nor do not use set colours for to wear,†
  Nor nourish special locks of vowèd hair,
Nor give each speech a full point† of a groan,
The courtly nymphs, acquainted with the moan
  Of them, who in their lips Love's standard bear;
  'What he?' say they of me, 'now I dare swear,
He cannot love: no, no, let him alone.'
  And think so still, so Stella know my mind,
Profess indeed I do not Cupid's art;
But you fair maids, at length this true shall find,
That his right badge is but worn in the heart:
  Dumb swans, not chattering pies,† do lovers prove,
  They love indeed, who quake to say they love.

baiting resting
prease crowd
rosy garland i.e. a garland of silence; the rose was associated with the god of silence
do not . . . wear i.e. am not in the habit of wearing a lady's colours
point measure (a musical term)
pies magpies

71

Who will in fairest book of Nature know,
How Virtue may best lodged in beauty be,
Let him but learn of Love to read in thee,
Stella, those fair lines, which true goodness show.
There shall he find all vices' overthrow,
Not by rude force, but sweetest sovereignty
Of reason, from whose light those night-birds† fly;
That inward sun in thine eyes shineth so.
And not content to be Perfection's heir
Thyself, dost strive all minds that way to move,
Who mark in thee what is in thee most fair.
So while thy beauty draws the heart to love,
As fast thy virtue bends that love to good:
'But ah,' Desire still cries, 'give me some food.'

74

I never drank of Aganippe† well,
Nor ever did in shade of Tempe† sit:
And Muses scorn with vulgar brains to dwell,
Poor layman I, for sacred rites unfit.
Some do I hear of Poets' fury tell,
But (God wot) wot not what they mean by it:
And this I swear by blackest brook of hell,†
I am no pick-purse of another's wit.
How falls it then, that with so smooth an ease
My thoughts I speak, and what I speak doth flow
In verse, and that my verse best wits doth please?
Guess we the cause: 'What, is it thus?' Fie no:
'Or so?' Much less: 'How then?' Sure thus it is:
My lips are sweet, inspired with Stella's kiss.

night-birds traditional emblems of the vices
Aganippe a fountain at the foot of Mount Helicon sacred to the muses
Tempe the valley in Thessaly into which Apollo pursued Daphne, who was turned into a laurel tree
brook of hell the Styx, by which the gods swore their most solemn oaths which if broken caused the loss of immortality

79

Sweet kiss, thy sweets I fain would sweetly indite,[†]
  Which even of sweetness sweetest sweetener art:
  Pleasingest consort,[†] where each sense holds a part,
Which, coupling doves, guides Venus' chariot right.[†]
Best charge, and bravest retreat in Cupid's fight,
  A double key, which opens to the heart,
  Most rich,[†] when most his riches[†] it impart:
Nest of young joys, schoolmaster of delight,
  Teaching the mean,[†] at once to take and give
The friendly fray, where blows both wound and heal,
The pretty death,[†] while each in other live.
Poor hope's first wealth, hostage of promised weal,[†]
  Breakfast of love, but lo, lo, where she is,
  Cease we to praise, now pray we for a kiss.

1582 1591

From CERTAIN SONNETS

32

Leave me o Love, which reachest but to dust,
And thou my mind aspire to higher things:
Grow rich in that which never taketh rust:
Whatever fades, but fading pleasure brings.

Draw in thy beams, and humble all thy might,
To that sweet yoke, where lasting freedoms be:
Which breaks the clouds and opens forth the light,
That doth both shine and give us sight to see.

O take fast hold, let that light be thy guide,
In this small course which birth draws out to death,
And think how evil becometh him to slide,
Who seeketh heaven, and comes of heavenly breath.
  Then farewell world, thy uttermost I see,
  Eternal Love maintain thy life in me.

1598

indite put into words
consort a company of musicians playing together
doves . . . right the chariot of Venus was traditionally drawn by doves
rich, riches plays on the name of Lady Penelope Rich, the model for Stella
mean means
pretty death sexual detumescence
weal good fortune

From THE COUNTESS OF PEMBROKE'S ARCADIA, Book II, Chapter 25

[*A Skirmish*]

They† were overtaken by an unruly sort of clowns† and other rebels which, like a violent flood, were carried they themselves knew not whither. But as soon as they came within perfect discerning these ladies, like enraged beasts, without respect of their estates or pity of their sex, they began to run against them, as right villains thinking ability to do hurt to be a great advancement; yet so many as they were, so many almost were their minds,† all knit together only in madness. Some cried 'Take'; some 'Kill'; some, 'Save'; but even they that cried 'Save' ran for company with them that meant to kill. Everyone commanded; none obeyed; he only seemed chief captain that was most rageful.

Zelmane, whose virtuous courage was ever awake, drew out her sword, which upon those ill-armed churls giving as many wounds as blows, and as many deaths almost as wounds, lightning courage and thundering smart upon them, kept them at a bay, while the two ladies got themselves into the lodge, out of the which Basilius (having put on an armour long untried) came to prove his authority among his subjects, or at least to adventure his life with his dear mistress to whom he brought a shield, while the ladies trembling attended the issue of this dangerous adventure. But Zelmane made them perceive the odds between an eagle and a kite, with such a nimble steadiness and such an assured nimbleness that while one was running back for fear, his fellow had her sword in his guts.

And by and by was both her heart and help well increased by the coming in of Dorus† who, having been making of hurdles† for his master's sheep, heard the horrible cries of this mad multitude; and having straight represented before the eyes of his careful love the peril wherein the soul of his soul might be, he went to Pamela's† lodge, but found her in a cave hard by, with Mopsa† and Dametas,† who at that time would not have opened the entry to his father. And therefore leaving them there as in a place safe, both for being strong and unknown, he ran as the noise guided him. But when he saw his friend in such danger among them, anger and contempt (asking no counsel but of

They Philoclea, younger daughter of Basilius (king of Arcadia), and Zelmane, a Paphlagonian princess
clowns rustics
so many . . . their minds Sidney's version of the Latin tag *tot homines, quot sententiae*
Dorus the assumed name of Musidorus, a Thessalian prince who is disguised as a shepherd
hurdles pens
Pamela elder daughter of Basilius
Mopsa and Dametas Dametas is a shepherd who looks after the daughters of Basilius; Mopsa is his daughter

courage) made him run among them with no other weapon but his sheep-hook, and with that overthrowing one of the villains, took away a two-hand sword from him, and withal helped him from ever being ashamed of losing it.† Then lifting up his brave head, and flashing terror into their faces, he made arms and legs go complain to the earth how evil their masters had kept them. Yet the multitude still growing and the very killing wearying them, fearing lest in long fight they should be conquered with conquering, they drew back toward the lodge; but drew back in such sort that still their terror went forward; like a valiant mastiff, whom when his master pulls back by the tail from the bear with whom he hath already interchanged a hateful embracement, though his pace be backward, his gesture is forward, his teeth and eyes threatening more in the retiring than they did in the advancing: so guided they themselves homeward, never stepping step backward but that they proved themselves masters of the ground where they stepped.

Yet among the rebels there was a dapper fellow, a tailor by occupation who, fetching his courage only from their going back, began to bow his knees, and very fencer-like to draw near to Zelmane. But as he came within her distance, turning his sword very nicely about his crown, Basilius, with a side blow, strake off his nose. He (being a suitor to a seamster's daughter, and therefore not a little grieved for such a disgrace) stooped down, because he had heard that if it were fresh put to, it would cleave on again. But as his hand was on the ground to bring his nose to his head, Zelmane with a blow sent his head to his nose. That saw a butcher, a butcherly chuff† indeed (who that day was sworn brother to him in a cup of wine) and lifted up a great lever, calling Zelmane all the vile names of a butcherly eloquence. But she, letting slip the blow of the lever, hit him so surely upon the side of the face that she left nothing but the nether jaw, where the tongue still wagged, as willing to say more if his master's remembrance had served. 'O,' said a miller that was half drunk, 'see the luck of a good-fellow,' and with that word ran with a pitchfork at Dorus; but the nimbleness of the wine carried his head so fast that it made it over-run his feet, so that he fell withal just between the legs of Dorus, who, setting his foot on his neck (though he offered two milch kine† and four fat hogs for his life) thrust his sword quite through from one ear to the other; which took it very unkindly, to feel such news before they heard of them, instead of hearing, to be put to such feeling. But Dorus, leaving the miller to vomit his soul out in wine and blood, with his two-hand sword strake off another quite by the waist who the night before had dreamed he was grown a couple, and, interpreting it that he should be married, had

helped . . . losing it i.e. killed him
chuff rascal
milch kine dairy cows

bragged of his dream that morning among his neighbours. But that blow astonished quite a poor painter who stood by with a pike in his hands. This painter was to counterfeit the skirmish between the Centaurs and Lapithes,† and had been very desirous to see some notable wounds, to be able the more lively to express them; and this morning, being carried by the stream of this company, the foolish fellow was even delighted to see the effect of blows. But this last, happening near him, so amazed him that he stood stock still, while Dorus, with a turn of his sword, strake off both his hands. And so the painter returned well skilled in wounds, but with never a hand to perform his skill.

1583–4 1590

Centaurs and Lapithes at the wedding of the king of the Lapithae (warlike Thessalians), the Centaurs (horses with men's heads) attempted to abduct the bride, and a drunken battle ensued

Sir Fulke Greville (Lord Brooke)

1554–1628

Fulke Greville was born in Warwickshire, the son of an eminent landowner. He was educated at Shrewsbury School, where he was an exact contemporary of Philip Sidney, and attended Jesus College, Cambridge. In 1577 he went to court, where he quickly became a favourite of the queen. On the accession of James I he was knighted, and in 1621 he was raised to the peerage and granted Warwick Castle; seven years later he was murdered there by a servant.

Greville's poems, his two Senecan tragedies, and even his prose life of Sidney are preoccupied with philosophical and political themes; he was by nature an intellectual rather than a poet, and even the lyrical poems in *Caelica* are more memorable for their fluidity of thought than for their poetic qualities.

From CAELICA

1

Love, the delight of all well-thinking minds,
Delight, the fruit of virtue dearly loved,
Virtue, the highest good that reason finds,
Reason, the fire wherein men's thoughts be proved,
Are from the world by Nature's power bereft,
And in one creature, for her glory, left.

Beauty her cover is, the eye's true pleasure;
In honour's fame she lives, the ear's sweet music;
Excess of wonder grows from her true measure;
Her worth is passion's wound and passion's physic;
From her true heart clear springs of wisdom flow,
Which imaged in her words and deeds men know.

Time fain would stay, that she might never leave her,
Place doth rejoice that she must needs contain her,
Death craves of heaven that she might not bereave her,
The heavens know their own and do maintain her;
Delight, love, reason, virtue let it be
To set all women light but only she.

81

Under a throne† I saw a virgin† sit,
The red and white rose quartered in her face;†
Star of the north, and for true guards† to it,
Princes, church, states, all pointing out her grace.
The homage done her was not born of wit:
Wisdom admired, zeal took ambition's place,
State in her eyes taught order how to fit,
And fix confusion's unobserving race.
Fortune can here claim nothing truly great,
But that this princely creature is her seat.

84

Farewell sweet boy,* complain not of my truth; Cupid
Thy mother loved thee not with more devotion;
For to thy boy's play I gave all my youth,
Young master, I did hope for your promotion.
While some sought honours, princes' thoughts observing,
Many wooed fame, the child of pain and anguish,
Others judged inward good a chief deserving,
I in thy wanton visions joyed to languish.
I bowed not to thy image for succession,
Nor bound thy bow to shoot reformèd kindness,
Thy plays of hope and fear were my confession,
The spectacles to my life was thy blindness;
But Cupid now farewell, I will go play me
With thoughts that please me less, and less betray me.

1633

throne the canopy of a throne
virgin Queen Elizabeth I
The red . . . face i.e. her face is an heraldic emblem of her descent from Henry VII (a Lancastrian, hence the red rose) and Elizabeth of York (a Yorkist, hence the white rose)
guards refers to two stars close to the Pole Star in Ursa Minor

AN EPITAPH UPON THE RIGHT HONOURABLE SIR PHILIP SIDNEY†

Silence augmenteth grief, writing increaseth rage,
Staled are my thoughts, which loved and lost the wonder of our age;
Yet quickened now with fire, though dead with frost ere now,
Enraged I write I know not what; dead, quick,* I know not how. alive

Hard-hearted minds relent and rigour's tears abound,
And envy strangely rues his end, in whom no fault was found.
Knowledge her light hath lost, valour hath slain her knight,
Sidney is dead, dead is my friend, dead is the world's delight.

Place, pensive, wails his fall whose presence was her pride;
Time crieth out, 'My ebb is come; his life was my spring tide.'
Fame mourns in that she lost the ground of her reports;
Each living wight* laments his lack, and all in sundry sorts. person

He was (woe worth that word!) to each well-thinking mind
A spotless friend, a matchless man, whose virtue ever shined;
Declaring in his thoughts, his life, and that he writ,
Highest conceits, longest foresights, and deepest works of wit.

He, only like himself, was second unto none,
Whose death (though life) we rue, and wrong, and all in vain do moan;
Their loss, not him, wail they that fill the world with cries,
Death slew not him, but he made death his ladder to the skies.

Now sink of sorrow I who live – the more the wrong!
Who wishing death, whom death denies, whose thread is all too long;
Who tied to wretched life, who looks for no relief,
Must spend my ever dying days in never ending grief.

Heart's ease and only I, like parallels, run on,
Whose equal length keep equal breadth and never meet in one;
Yet for not wronging him, my thoughts, my sorrow's cell,
Shall not run out, though leak they will for liking him so well.

An Epitaph upon the Right Honourable Sir Philip Sidney this poem is sometimes attributed to Greville, but its authorship is uncertain

Farewell to you, my hopes, my wonted waking dreams,
Farewell, sometimes enjoyèd joy, eclipsèd are thy beams.
Farewell, self-pleasing thoughts which quietness brings forth,
And farewell, friendship's sacred league, uniting minds of worth.

And farewell, merry heart, the gift of guiltless minds,
And all sports which for life's restore variety assigns;
Let all that sweet is, void; in me no mirth may dwell:
Philip, the cause of all this woe, my life's content, farewell!

Now rhyme, the son of rage, which art no kin to skill,
And endless grief, which deads my life, yet knows not how to kill,
Go, seek that hapless tomb, which if ye hap to find
Salute the stones that keep the limbs that held so good a mind.

1593

From LIFE OF SIR PHILIP SIDNEY

[*The Character of Sidney*]

Indeed he was a true model of worth; a man fit for conquest, plantation, reformation, or what action soever is greatest and hardest amongst men: withall, such a lover of mankind and goodness, that whosoever had any real parts in him found comfort, participation, and protection to the uttermost of his power; like Zephyrus† he giving life where he blew. The universities abroad and at home accounted him a general Maecenas† of learning, dedicated their books to him, and communicated every invention, or improvement of knowledge with him. Soldiers honoured him and were so honoured by him as no man thought he marched under the true banner of Mars† that had not obtained Sir Philip Sidney's approbation. Men of affairs in most parts of Christendom entertained correspondency with him. But what speak I of these, with whom his own ways and ends did concur? Since (to descend) his heart and capacity were so large that there was not a cunning painter, a skilful engineer, an excellent musician, or any other artificer of extraordinary fame, that made not himself known to this famous spirit and found him his true friend without hire and the common rendezvous of worth in his time.

Now let princes vouchsafe to consider, of what importance it is to the honour of themselves and their estates to have one man of such eminence; not only as a nourisher of virtue in their courts or service,

Zephyrus Greek personification of the west wind

Maecenas Roman patron of Virgil and Horace

Mars Roman god of war

but besides for a reformed standard, by which even the most humorous† persons could not but have a reverend ambition to be tried and approved current. This I do the more confidently affirm, because it will be confessed by all men that this one man's example and personal respect did not only encourage learning and honour in the schools, but brought the affection and true use thereof both into the court and camp. Nay more, even many gentlemen excellently learned amongst us will not deny but that they affected to row and steer their course in his wake. Besides which honour of unequal nature and education, his very ways in the world did generally add reputation to his prince and country, by restoring amongst us the ancient majesty of noble and true dealing: as a manly wisdom that can no more be weighed down by any effeminate craft than Hercules could be overcome by that contemptible army of dwarfs.† This was it which, I profess, I loved dearly in him and still shall be glad to honour in the great men of this time: I mean that his heart and tongue went both one way, and so with everyone that went with the truth, as knowing no other kindred, party, or end.

Above all, he made the religion he professed the firm basis of his life: for this was his judgement (as he often told me) that our true-heartedness to the reformed religion in the beginning, brought peace, safety, and freedom to us; concluding that the wisest and best way was that of the famous William Prince of Orange,† who never divided the consideration of estate from the cause of religion, nor gave that sound party occasion to be jealous or distracted upon any appearance of safety whatsoever; prudently resolving, that to temporize with the enemies of our faith was but (as among sea-gulls) a strife, not to keep upright, but aloft upon the top of every billow: which false-heartedness to God and man would in the end find itself forsaken of both, as Sir Philip conceived. For to this active spirit of his, all depths of the devil proved but shallow fords; he piercing into men's counsels and ends, not by their words, oaths, or compliments, all barren in that age, but by fathoming their hearts and powers by their deeds, and found no wisdom where he found no courage, nor courage without wisdom, nor either without honesty and truth. With which solid and active reaches of his, I am persuaded, he would have found or made a way through all the traverses even of the most weak and irregular times. But it pleased God in this decrepit age of the world, not to restore the image of her ancient vigour in him, otherwise than as in a lightning before death.

1604–14 1652

humorous ill-disposed
army of dwarfs after Hercules defeated Antaeus, he was attacked by dwarfs as he lay sleeping
William Prince of Orange William the Silent, founder of the Protestant Dutch Republic; Greville's point is that Sidney died for the Protestant cause championed by Prince William

Lancelot Andrewes

1555–1626

Lancelot Andrewes was born in London and educated at Merchant Taylors' School and Pembroke Hall, Cambridge. In the course of his career he became Master of Pembroke Hall (1589) and Dean of Westminster (1601), and after declining two bishoprics became Bishop of Chichester (1605), Ely (1609) and finally Winchester (1619). His learning was (rightly) legendary; he mastered fifteen languages, and possessed an unrivalled knowledge of Patristic literature. He was one of the leading translators of the Authorised Version of the Bible (1611), and was largely responsible for the translation of the Pentateuch and the historical books from Joshua to I Chronicles. His finest original composition was his incomparable manual of private devotions, which was written in Greek. His sermons are written in an ornate style, and are characterised by the rhetorical use of quotations in Greek and Latin, and by extensive word-play.

From SERMON 15 'OF THE NATIVITY'†

[*On Matthew* 2.2]

Now, to *Venimus*,† their coming it self. And it follows well. For, it is not a star only, but a lode-star; and, whither should *stella Ejus ducere*,† but *ad Eum*?† Whither lead us, but to Him, whose the star is? The star, to the star's master.

All this while we have been at *dicentes*, saying and seeing. Now we shall come to *Facientes*, see them do somewhat upon it. It is not saying, nor seeing will serve Saint James: he will call, and be still calling for *Ostende mihi*, show me thy faith by some work. And, well may he be

Sermon 15, 'Of the Nativity' this sermon was preached before King James on 25 December 1622. Its fame rests on T. S. Eliot's use of it in *Journey of the Magi*. The passage printed here expounds a phrase in Matthew 2.2, 'for we have seen his star in the East, and are come to worship him', or (in Andrewes's Latin text) 'vidimus enim stellam ejus in Oriente, et venimus adorare eum'

Venimus we have come

stella . . . ducere his star lead

ad Eum to him

allowed to call for it, this day: it is the day of *Vidimus*,† appearing, being seen. You have seen his star; let him now see your star, another while. And, so they do. Make your faith to be seen; so it is; their faith, in the steps of their faith. And, so was Abraham's first, by coming forth of his country; as, these here do, and so walk in the steps of the faith of Abraham, do his first work.

It is not commended, to stand gazing up into heaven too long, not on Christ himself ascending, much less on his star. For, they sat not still gazing on the star. Their *Vidimus* begat *Venimus*; their seeing made them come; come, a great journey. *Venimus* is soon said; but a short word; but, many a wide and weary step they made, before they could come to say *Venimus*, lo, here we are come; come, and at our journey's end. To look a little on it. In this their coming, we consider, 1. First, the distance of the place, they came from. It was not hard by, as the shepherds' (but a step to Bethlehem, over the fields): This was riding many a hundred miles, and cost them many a day's journey. 2. Secondly, we consider the way, that they came: If it be pleasant, or plain and easy: For, if it be, it is so much the better. 1. This was nothing pleasant; for, through deserts: all the way waste and desolate. 2. Nor (secondly) easy neither: For, over the rocks and craggs of both Arabies† (specially Petra†) their journey lay. 3. Yet, if safe: but, it was not; but exceeding dangerous, as lying through the middest of the black tents of Kedar,† a nation of thieves and cut-throats; to pass over the hills of robbers; infamous then, and infamous to this day. No passing, without great troop, or convoy. 4. Last, we consider the time of their coming, the season of the year. It was no summer progress. A cold coming they had of it, at this time of the year; just, the worst time of the year, to take a journey, and specially a long journey, in. The ways deep, the weather sharp, the days short, the sun farthest off *in solstitio brumali*,† the very dead of winter. *Venimus*, we are come, if that be one; *Venimus*, we are (now) come, come at this time, that (sure) is another.

All these difficulties they overcame, of a wearisome, irksome, troublesome, dangerous, unseasonable journey: and for all this, they came. And, came it cheerfully, and quickly; as appeareth, by the speed they made. It was but *Vidimus, Venimus*, with them; they saw, and they came: No sooner saw, but they set out presently. So, as upon the first appearing of the star (as it might be, last night) they knew, it was Balaam's star;† it called them away, they made ready straight to begin their journey this morning. A sign, they were highly conceited,† of his

Vidimus we have seen
both Arabies refers to the lands of a tribe in northern Arabia which the Bible associates with Kedar, and to the Nabatean territory, of which *Petra* (in Jordan) was the capital
black tents of Kedar Song of Solomon, 1.5
in . . . brumali at the winter solstice
Balaam's star Numbers 24.17
conceited convinced

birth, believed some great matter of it, that they took all these pains, made all this haste, that they might be there to worship him, with all the possible speed they could. Sorry for nothing so much, as that they could not be there soon enough, with the very first, to do it even this day, the day of his birth. All considered, there is more in *Venimus* than shows at the first sight. It was not for nothing, it was said (in the first verse) *Ecce Venerunt*;† their coming hath an *Ecce* on it: it well deserves it.

And we, what should we have done? Sure, these men of the East shall rise in judgement against the men of the West, that is, us: and their faith, against ours, in this point. With them, it was but *Vidimus, Venimus*: With us, it would have been but *Veniemus*† at most. Our fashion is, to see and see again, before we stir a foot: specially, if it be to the worship of Christ. Come such a journey, at such a time? No: but fairly have put it off to the spring of the year, till the days longer, and the ways fairer, and the weather warmer; till better travelling to Christ. Our Epiphany† would (sure) have fallen in Easter-week at the soonest.

But then, for the distance, desolateness, tediousness, and the rest, any of them were enough to mar our *Venimus* quite. It must be no great way (first) we must come: we love not that. Well fare the Shepherds yet, they come but hard by: rather like them than the Magi. Nay, not like them neither. For, with us, the nearer (lightly) the further off: our proverb is (you know) the nearer the church the further from God.

1622 1629

Ecce Venerunt behold they have come
Veniemus we shall come
Epiphany the feast celebrated on 6 January in commemoration of the visit of the Magi to the infant Jesus

George Peele

1556–96

George Peele was born in London, the son of the Clerk of Christ's Hospital. He was educated at Christ's Hospital, Broadgates Hall (now Pembroke College), Cambridge and Christ Church, Oxford. He moved to London in about 1581 and became an actor, playwright and poet. His finest plays are *The Arraignment of Paris* (1584) and *The Old Wives' Tale* (1595).

WHAT THING IS LOVE?

What thing is love? For sure love is a thing.
It is a prick, it is a sting,
It is a pretty, pretty thing;
It is a fire, it is a coal,
Whose flame creeps in at every hole;
And as my wit doth best devise,
Love's dwelling is in ladies' eyes,
From whence do glance love's piercing darts,
That make such holes into our hearts;
And all the world herein accord,
Love† is a great and mighty lord;
And when he list* to mount so high, wishes
With Venus† he in heaven doth lie,
And evermore hath been a god,
Since Mars† and she played even and odd.

1591

Love Cupid, the god of love
Venus goddess of love, mother of Cupid
Mars god of war, and lover of Venus

Chidiock Tichborne

1558?–86

Chidiock Tichborne was born into a devout Roman Catholic family in Southampton. He became involved in the Babington conspiracy to assassinate the Queen, and was accordingly hanged and disembowelled on 20 September 1586. He is said to have written 'My prime of youth', his only surviving poem, in the Tower of London the night before he was executed.

TICHBORNE'S ELEGY

Written with his own hand in the Tower before his execution

My prime of youth is but a frost of cares,
My feast of joy is but a dish of pain;
My crop of corn is but a field of tares,
And all my good is but vain hope of gain.
The day is past, and yet I saw no sun;
And now I live, and now my life is done.

My tale was heard, and yet it was not told,
My fruit is fallen, and yet my leaves are green;
My youth is spent, and yet I am not old,
I saw the world, and yet I was not seen.
My thread is cut, and yet it is not spun;[†]
And now I live, and now my life is done.

I sought my death, and found it in my womb,
I looked for life and saw it was a shade;
I trod the earth, and knew it was my tomb,
And now I die, and now I was but made.
My glass is full, and now my glass is run;
And now I live, and now my life is done.

1586 1586

thread . . . spun alludes to the Fates of classical mythology; the first spun the thread of life, the second measured it and the third cut it

20 HENDECASYLLABON[†]

T.K. in cygneam cantionem Chidiochi Tychborne[†]

Thy prime of youth is frozen with thy faults,
Thy feast of joy is finished with thy fall;
Thy crop of corn is tares availing naughts,
Thy good God knows thy hope, thy hap* and all. fate
Short were thy days, and shadowed was thy sun,
T'obscure thy light unluckily begun.

Time trieth truth, and truth hath treason tripped;
Thy faith bore fruit as thou hadst faithless been.
Thy ill-spent youth thine after-years hath nipped,
And God that saw thee hath preserved our Queen.
Her thread still holds, thine perished though unspun,
And she shall live when traitors' lives are done.

Thou soughtst thy death, and found it in desert,
Thou look'dst for life, yet lewdly forced it fade;
Thou trodst the earth, and now on earth thou art,
As men may wish thou never hadst been made.
Thy glory and thy glass are timeless run;
And this, O Tichborne, hath thy treason done.

Hendecasyllabon hendecasyllables are lines with eleven syllables (*hendeka* means 'eleven' in Greek), but as these lines have only ten syllables, the poet is probably alluding to the Hendeka, the executioners in ancient Athens; hendecasyllabon therefore means 'verses by the executioners'

T.K. . . . Tychborne T.K. on the swan song of Chidiock Tichborne

Thomas Lodge

1558–1625

Thomas Lodge was the son of the Lord Mayor of London, and was probably born in London. He was educated at Merchant Taylors' School, Trinity College, Oxford, and Lincoln's Inn. He soon abandoned law to take up a literary career in London. He published literary pamphlets, translations, plays, poems and many prose romances, the most famous of which is *Rosalind* (1590), which he wrote while on a privateering voyage to the Canaries. From 1591 and 1593 he sailed on an expedition to South America. He later became a Roman Catholic, and turned to the study of medicine; he graduated in medicine at Avignon in 1600, and two years later received an MD from Oxford. He divided the rest of his life between medical practice, literature, and travel on the continent.

LOVE IN MY BOSOM†

Love in my bosom like a bee
Doth suck his sweet;
Now with his wings he plays with me,
Now with his feet.
Within mine eyes he makes his nest,
His bed amidst my tender breast;
My kisses are his daily feast,
And yet he robs me of my rest:
Ah, wanton,† will ye?

Love in my bosom this poem appeared in Lodge's *Rosalind* (1590)

wanton an affectionate term for a spoilt child, here applied to Cupid

And if I sleep, then percheth he
With pretty flight,
And makes his pillow of my knee
The livelong night.
Strike I my lute, he tunes the string;
He music plays if so I sing;
He lends me every lovely thing;
Yet cruel he my heart doth sting:
Whist,* wanton, still ye! – Hush

Else I with roses every day
Will whip you hence,
And bind you, when you long to play,
For your offence.
I'll shut mine eyes to keep you in,
I'll make you fast it for your sin,
I'll count your power not worth a pin, –
Alas! what hereby shall I win
If he gainsay me?

What if I beat the wanton boy
With many a rod?
He will repay me with annoy,
Because a god.
Then sit thou safely on my knee,
And let thy bower my bosom be;
Lurk in mine eyes, I like of thee.
O Cupid, so thou pity me,
Spare not, but play thee!

1590

PLUCK THE FRUIT†

Pluck the fruit and taste the pleasure,
Youthful lordings, of delight;
Whilst occasion gives you seizure,* opportunity
Feed your fancies and your sight:
After death, when you are gone,
Joy and pleasure is there none.

Pluck the fruit this poem appeared in Lodge's *Robert, Second Duke of Normandy* (1591)

Here on earth no thing is stable,
Fortune's changes well are known;
Whilst as youth doth then enable,
Let your seeds of joy be sown:
After death, when you are gone,
Joy and pleasure is there none.

Feast it freely with your lovers,
Blithe and wanton sweets do fade,
Whilst that lovely Cupid hovers
Round about this lovely shade:
Sport it freely one to one,
After death is pleasure none.

Now the pleasant spring allureth,
And both place and time invites:
But, alas, what heart endureth
To disclaim his sweet delights?
After death, when we are gone,
Joy and pleasure is there none.

1591

Robert Greene

1558–92

Robert Greene was born in Norwich, and educated at St John's College, Cambridge, and Clare Hall, Cambridge. He travelled widely in Europe, and in about 1585 he settled in London, where he adopted the career of a miscellaneous writer and lived the life of a profligate drunkard. He wrote eight plays, the best-known of which is *Friar Bacon and Friar Bungay*. He also wrote several prose romances, the finest of which is *Menaphon* (1589), which contains the poem 'Weep not, my wanton'.

From MENAPHON

Weep not, my wanton

Weep not, my wanton,† smile upon my knee;
When thou art old there's grief enough for thee.
    Mother's wag, pretty boy,
    Father's sorrow, father's joy;
    When thy father first did see
    Such a boy by him and me,
    He was glad, I was woe;
    Fortune changed made him so,
    When he left his pretty boy,
    Last his sorrow, first his joy.

Weep not, my wanton, smile upon my knee;
When thou art old there's grief enough for thee.
    Streaming tears that never stint,
    Like pearl-drops from a flint,
    Fell by course from his eyes,
    That one another's place supplies;
    Thus he grieved in every part,
    Tears of blood fell from his heart,
    When he left his pretty boy,
    Father's sorrow, father's joy.

---

wanton an affectionate term for a spoilt child

Weep not, my wanton, smile upon my knee;
When thou art old there's grief enough for thee.
 The wanton smiled, father wept;
 Mother cried, baby leapt;
 More he crowed, more we cried,
 Nature could not sorrow hide.
 He must go, he must kiss
 Child and mother, baby bliss:
 For he left his pretty boy,
 Father's sorrow, father's joy.
Weep not, my wanton, smile upon my knee;
When thou art old there's grief enough for thee.

1589

George Chapman

1559?–1634

George Chapman was born in Hertfordshire, the son of a small landowner, and was probably educated at Oxford. From 1582 until at least 1591 he served as a soldier in Holland. By 1594 he had settled in London, and during the next four years wrote several long poems, including a continuation of Marlowe's *Hero and Leander*. He then became a professional playwright, composing tragedies and comedies for the public theatres and masques for the court; his plays were admired by Shakespeare (and later by T. S. Eliot, who described Chapman as 'potentially the greatest artist' of the Elizabethan dramatists). His most famous work is his translation of Homer, which was published at intervals between 1598 and 1616. Chapman's Homer is more remarkable for its vigour than for its faithfulness to Homer's Greek, and has always been admired more by poets than by classical scholars; in common with many Renaissance translators, Chapman was more concerned to recreate a great poem in English than to translate the original poem literally. Keats immortalised Chapman's translation in his sonnet 'On first looking into Chapman's Homer'. The extract printed here is taken from Chapman's translation of the *Odyssey*, Book 9, in which Odysseus blinds Polyphemus, the one-eyed Cyclops.

From ODYSSEY, Book 9

[*The Blinding of Polyphemus*]

He* took, and drunk, and vehemently joyed — *Polyphemus*
To taste the sweet cup; and again employed
My flagon's powers, entreating more, and said:
'Good guest, again afford my taste thy aid,
And let me know thy name, and quickly now,
That in thy recompense I may bestow
A hospitable gift on thy desert,
And such a one as shall rejoice thy heart.

For to the Cyclops too the gentle earth
Bears generous wine, and Jove augments her birth,
In store of such, with showers; but this rich wine
Fell from the river that is mere* divine, pure
Of nectar and ambrosia.' This again
I gave him, and again; nor could the fool abstain,
But drunk as often. When the noble juice
Had wrought upon his spirit, I then gave use
To fairer language, saying: 'Cyclop! now,
As thou demandest, I'll tell my name, do thou
Make good thy hospitable gift to me.
My name is No-Man; No-Man each degree
Of friends, as well as parents, call my name.'
He answered, as his cruel soul became:
'No-Man! I'll eat thee last of all thy friends;
And this is that in which so much amends
I vowed to thy deservings, thus shall be
My hospitable gift made good to thee.'
This said, he upwards fell, but then bent round
His fleshy neck; and Sleep, with all crowns crowned,
Subdued the savage. From his throat brake out
My wine, with man's-flesh gobbets, like a spout,
When, loaded with his cups, he lay and snored;
And then took I the club's end up, and gored
The burning coal-heap, that the point might heat;
Confirmed my fellows' minds, lest fear should let
Their vowed assay, and make them fly my aid.
Straight was the olive-lever, I had laid
Amidst the huge fire to get hardening, hot,
And glowed extremely, though 'twas green; which got
From forth the cinders, close about me stood
My hardy friends; but that which did the good
Was God's good inspiratión, that gave
A spirit beyond the spirit they used to have;
Who took the olive spar, made keen before,
And plunged it in his eye, and up I bore,
Bent to the top close, and helped pour it in,
With all my forces. And as you have seen
A ship-wright bore a naval beam, he oft
Thrusts at the auger's froofe,* works still aloft, handle
And at the shank help others, with a cord
Wound round about to make it sooner bored,
All plying the round still; so into his eye
The fiery stake we laboured to imply.* penetrate

Out gushed the blood that scalded, his eye-ball
Thrust out a flaming vapour, that scorched all
His brows and eye-lids, his eye-strings did crack,
As in the sharp and burning rafter brake.
And as a smith, to harden any tool,
Broad axe, or mattock,† in his trough doth cool
The red-hot substance, that so fervent is
It makes the cold wave straight to seethe and hiss;
So sod* and hissed his eye about the stake. seethed
He roared withal, and all his cavern brake
In claps like thunder. We did frighted fly,
Dispersed in corners. He from forth his eye
The fixéd stake plucked; after which the blood
Flowed freshly forth; and, mad, he hurled the wood
About his hovel. Out he then did cry
For other Cyclops, that in caverns by
Upon a windy promontory dwelled;
Who, hearing how impetuously he yelled,
Rushed every way about him, and inquired,
What ill afflicted him, that he expired
Such horrid clamours, and in sacred night
To break their sleeps so? Asked him, if his fright
Came from some mortal that his flocks had driven?
Or if by craft, or might, his death were given?
He answered from his den: 'By craft, nor might,
No-Man hath given me death.' They then said right.
'If no man hurt thee, and thyself alone,
That which is done to thee by Jove is done;
And what great Jove inflicts no man can fly.
Pray to thy Father yet, a Deity,
And prove, from him if thou canst help acquire.'
  Thus spake they, leaving him; when all-on-fire
My heart with joy was, that so well my wit
And name deceived him.

1614–15

mattock a tool for breaking hard ground

Francis Bacon, Lord St Albans

1561–1626

Francis Bacon was born in London, the son of Queen Elizabeth's Lord Keeper of the Great Seal (a high office of state). In 1573, at the age of twelve, he entered Trinity College, Cambridge; he left without a degree after two years, and took up the study of law at Gray's Inn. He qualified as a barrister in 1582, and two years later was elected to Parliament, in which he was to remain, representing various constituencies, for thirty-four years. He rose in the hierarchy of Gray's Inn, and was instrumental in securing the conviction of the Earl of Essex for treason. He was knighted by King James in 1603, and thereafter secured a series of important posts: Solicitor-General in 1607, Attorney-General in 1613, Lord Keeper in 1617 and Lord Chancellor in 1618. He was created Baron Verulam in 1618 and raised to Viscount St Albans in 1621. Later in 1621 he was convicted of accepting bribes in his judicial capacity, and retired to the private life of a writer.

Bacon wrote seminal treatises on the philosophy of science, including *The Advancement of Learning* (1605) and *Novum Organum* (1620; the title, borrowed from a book by Aristotle, means 'New Instrument'), and also published various collections of essays. *The Essays* deal with matters of politics, personal conduct, science and philosophy. The two essays printed below appeared in Bacon's third collection, which was published in 1625.

From THE ESSAYS

Of Death

Men fear death, as children fear to go in the dark; and as that natural fear in children is increased with tales, so is the other. Certainly the contemplation of death, as the wages of sin and passage to another world, is holy and religious, but the fear of it, as a tribute due unto nature, is weak. Yet in religious meditations there is sometimes mixture of vanity and of superstition. You shall read in some of the friars' books of mortification, that a man should think with himself what the pain is if he have but his finger's end pressed or tortured, and thereby imagine what the pains of death are, when the whole body is corrupted and dissolved; when many times death passeth with less pain than the torture of a limb, for the most vital parts are not the quickest of sense. And by him that spake† only as a philosopher and natural man, it was well said, *Pompa mortis magis terret, quam mors ipsa.*† Groans and convulsions, and a discoloured face, and friends weeping, and blacks,† and obsequies, and the like show death terrible. It is worthy the observing that there is no passion in the mind of man so weak, but it mates and masters the fear of death; and therefore death is no such terrible enemy when a man hath so many attendants about him that can win the combat of him. Revenge triumphs over death; love slights it; honour aspireth to it; grief flieth to it; fear preoccupateth† it; nay we read, after Otho the emperor† had slain himself, pity (which is the tenderest of affections) provoked many to die out of mere compassion to their sovereign, and as the truest sort of followers. Nay Seneca adds niceness† and satiety:† *Cogita quamdiu eadem feceris; mori velle, non tantum fortis, aut miser, sed etiam fastidiosus potest.*† A man would die, though he were neither valiant nor miserable, only upon a weariness to do the same thing so oft over and over. It is no less worthy to observe how little alteration in good spirits the approaches of death make, for they appear to be the same men till the last instant. Augustus Cæsar† died in a compliment: *Livia, conjugii nostri memor, vive et vale,*† Tiberius† in dissimulation, as Tacitus saith of him: *Iam Tiberium vires et corpus, non dissimulatio, deserebant,*† Vespasian† in a jest, sitting upon the stool: *Ut puto Deus fio;*† Galba† with a sentence: *Feri, si ex*

him that spake Seneca, the Roman Stoic philosopher and tragedian (*c.* 4 BC–AD 65)
Pompa . . . ipsa 'the ceremonies of death are more frightening than death itself'; a recollection of Seneca's *Epistles* (XXIV.14)
blacks mourning clothes
preoccupateth usurps (by suicide)
Otho the emperor ancient historians record that when the army of the Emperor Otho (AD 32–69) was defeated at Bedriacum (near Cremona) on 16 April 69, many of his followers followed him in committing suicide (Tacitus, *History* II.49; Plutarch, *Otho* 17)
niceness fastidiousness
satiety loss of appetite through excess
cogita . . . potest Bacon's translation of this passage from Seneca's *Epistles* (LXXVII.6) follows immediately
Augustus Caesar the first Roman emperor (63 BC–AD 14); his second wife was Livia Drusilla (58 BC–AD 29)
Livia . . . vale 'remembering our marriage, Livia, live and farewell' (Suetonius, *Octavius Augustus*, 69)
Tiberius the second Roman emperor (42 BC–37 AD)
Iam . . . deserebant 'Tiberius was losing his physical powers, but not his powers of dissimulation'; the sentence is quoted from the *Annals* (VI.50) of Tacitus (*c.* AD 56–*c.* 115), the Roman historian
Vespasian the ninth Roman emperor (AD 9–79)
Ut . . . fio 'I think that I am becoming a god' (Suetonius, *Vespasian* 23)
Galba the sixth Roman emperor (*c.* 3 BC–AD 69)

re sit populi Romani,[†] holding forth his neck; Septimius Severus[†] in despatch: *Adeste si quid mihi restat agendum*.[†] And the like. Certainly the Stoics bestowed too much cost upon death, and by their great preparations made it appear more fearful. Better saith he,[†] *qui finem vitæ extremum inter munera ponat naturæ*.[†] It is as natural to die as to be born; and to a little infant, perhaps, the one is as painful as the other. He that dies in an earnest pursuit is like one that is wounded in hot blood, who, for the time, scarce feels the hurt, and therefore a mind fixed and bent upon somewhat that is good doth avert the dolours[†] of death. But above all, believe it, the sweetest canticle is, *Nunc dimittis*;[†] when a man hath obtained worthy ends and expectations. Death hath this also, that it openeth the gate to good fame, and extinguisheth envy. *Extinctus amabitur idem*.[†]

1625

Of Love

The stage is more beholding to love than the life of man. For as to the stage, love is ever matter of comedies, and now and then of tragedies, but in life it doth much mischief, sometimes like a siren,[†] sometimes like a fury.[†] You may observe that amongst all the great and worthy persons (whereof the memory remaineth, either ancient or recent) there is not one that hath been transported to the mad degree of love, which shows that great spirits and great business do keep out this weak passion. You must except nevertheless Marcus Antonius,[†] the half-partner[†] of the empire of Rome, and Appius Claudius,[†] the decemvir[†] and lawgiver; whereof the former was indeed a voluptuous man, and

Feri . . . Romani 'do it, if it be for the people of Rome' (Tacitus, *History* I.41)
Septimus Severus Roman emperor (AD *c.* 145–211)
Adeste . . . agendum 'hurry, if there is anything else for me to do' (Dion Cassius LXXVII.17)
he the Roman satirist Juvenal (*c.* AD 60–*c.* 127)
qui . . . naturæ 'who regards the end of life as one of nature's blessings' (Juvenal, *Satires* X.358)
dolours sorrows
Nunc dimittis the song of Simeon, so named from the first two words ('now depart') in the Vulgate version of Luke 2.29–32; in the Anglican tradition it is part of Evensong
Extinctus . . . idem 'the same person [who is envied during his lifetime] will be loved when he is dead' (Horace, *Epistles* II.i.14)
siren in Greek mythology, the sirens were monsters with women's heads who lured sailors to their deaths with their beguiling songs
fury the furies were Greek avenging goddesses
Marcus Antonius Mark Antony (*c.* 83 BC–AD 31), who was *half-partner* to Octavian and Lepidus; Antony's responsibility was the eastern half of the empire, including Egypt; he is said to be 'voluptuous' because of his association with Cleopatra
Appius Claudius was chief of the ten magistrates (*decemviri*) who in 451 BC suspended the Roman constitution and prepared a new code of law. According to a late legend, he became enamoured of Verginia, who was spared his lust when she was killed by her father; this episode was said to have precipitated the overthrow of the decemvirs in 449 BC (see Livy III.33)

inordinate, but the latter was an austere and wise man; and therefore it seems (though rarely) that love can find entrance not only into an open heart, but also into a heart well fortified, if watch be not well kept. It is a poor saying of Epicurus,[†] *Satis magnum alter alteri theatrum sumus*,[†] as if man, made for the contemplation of heaven and all noble objects, should do nothing but kneel before a little idol, and make himself a subject, though not of the mouth (as beasts are), yet of the eye, which was given him for higher purposes. It is a strange thing to note the excess of this passion, and how it braves the nature and value of things, by this: that the speaking in a perpetual hyperbole is comely in nothing but in love. Neither is it merely in the phrase, for whereas it hath been well said[†] that the arch-flatterer, with whom all the petty flatterers have intelligence, is a man's self, certainly the lover is more. For there was never proud man thought so absurdly well of himself as the lover doth of the person loved; and therefore it was well said, 'That it is impossible to love and to be wise.'[†] Neither doth this weakness appear to others only, and not to the party loved, but to the loved most of all, except the love be reciproque.[†] For it is a true rule that love is ever rewarded either with the reciproque or with an inward and secret contempt. By how much the more men ought to beware of this passion, which loseth not only things but itself. As for the other losses, the poet's relation[†] doth well figure them: that he[†] that preferred Helena quitted[†] the gifts of Juno and Pallas. For whosoever esteemeth too much of amorous affection quitteth both riches and wisdom. This passion hath his floods in the very times of weakness, which are great prosperity and great adversity, though this latter hath been less observed, both which times kindle love, and make it more fervent, and therefore show it to be the child of folly. They do best who, if they cannot but admit love, yet make it keep quarter[†] and sever it wholly from their serious affairs and actions of life, for if it check[†] once with business, it troubleth men's fortunes, and maketh men that they can no ways be true to their own ends. I know not how, but martial men are given to love; I think it is but as they are given to wine, for perils commonly ask to be paid in pleasures. There is in man's nature a secret inclination and motion

Epicurus Greek philosopher (341–270 BC); Bacon's remarks reflect a traditional Christian distortion of his teachings
satis . . . sumus 'we are a large enough theatre to one another' (attributed to Epicurus by Seneca in *Epistles* VII.11)
it hath been well said by the Greek philosopher and biographer Plutarch, in *How a Flatterer may be distinguished from a Friend*
That . . . wise a recollection of one of the *Sententiae* (15) of the Roman dramatist Publilius Syrus, who came to Rome as a slave in the first century BC possibly from Antioch
reciproque reciprocal
the poet's relation Homer's account (in *Iliad* 24)
he Paris, who, bribed by the promise of Helen, judged the beauty of Aphrodite to be superior to that of Juno and Pallas Athena
quitted renounced; Juno had offered riches, Pallas Athena wisdom
keep quarter stay in its proper place
check obstruct

towards love of others, which if it be not spent upon some one or a few, doth naturally spread itself towards many, and maketh men become humane and charitable, as it is seen sometime in friars. Nuptial love maketh mankind; friendly love perfecteth it; but wanton love corrupteth and embaseth† it.

1625

embaseth devalues

Samuel Daniel

1563–1619

Samuel Daniel was born in Somerset, the son of a music teacher. He was educated at Magdelen Hall, Oxford, but did not take a degree. He visited Italy, and then became tutor to William Herbert (son of the Earl of Pembroke), and lived with the Herbert family at Wilton House, near Salisbury. He later became tutor to Lady Anne Clifford, daughter of the Countess of Cumberland, and lived at their home in Skipton (Yorkshire). He served on occasion as a court poet, and eventually retired to a farm in Wiltshire.

Daniel was an immensely versatile writer. His works include a sonnet sequence (*Delia*, 1592), two tragedies, a treatise on poetry (*A Defence of Rhyme*, 1602), several masques for the court of King James, and a verse epic on the Wars of the Roses (*The Civil Wars*, 1595–1609).

From DELIA, Sonnet 12

My spotless love hovers with purest wings
About the temple of the proudest flame;
Where blaze those lights, fairest of earthly things,
Which clear our clouded world with brightest flame.
My ambitious thoughts, confinèd in her face,
Affect no honour, but what she can give;
My hopes do rest in limits of her grace;
I weigh no comfort unless she relieve.
For she that can my heart imparadise,
Holds in her fairest hand what dearest is;
My fortune's wheel, the circle of her eyes,
Whose rolling grace deign once a turn of bliss.
All my life's sweet consists in her alone,
So much I love the most unloving one.

1592

Michael Drayton

1563–1631

Michael Drayton was born in Warwickshire, the son of a tanner. He received his education while serving as a page in the household of Sir Henry Goodere, a local squire who had been a friend of Sir Philip Sidney. He fell in love with Sir Henry's daughter, Anne Goodere, and remained devoted to her after she married; she is the 'Idea' whom Drayton celebrated in his sonnets. Drayton became a prolific poet, favouring long poems on historical subjects. His largest project was *Poly-Olbion*, a vast poem which describes the topography of England. His famous ode 'To the Virginian Voyage' celebrates the voyage of the *Sarah Constant*, the *Godspeed* and the *Discovery* to Virginia in December 1606.

TO THE VIRGINIAN VOYAGE

You brave heroic minds,
Worthy your country's name,
That honour still pursue,
Go, and subdue,
Whilst loitering hinds†
Lurk here at home, with shame.

Britons, you stay too long.
Quickly aboard bestow you,
And with a merry gale
Swell your stretched sail,
With vows as strong,
As the winds that blow you.

hinds a generalised term of abuse

Your course securely steer,
West and by south forth keep,
Rocks, lee-shores, nor shoals,
When Aeolus† scowls,
You need not fear,
So absolute the deep.

And cheerfully at sea,
Success you still entice,
To get the pearl and gold,
And ours to hold,
Virginia,
Earth's only paradise.

Where nature hath in store,
Fowl, venison, and fish,
And the fruitfullest soil,
Without your toil,
Three harvests more,
All greater than you wish.

And the ambitious vine
Crowns with his purple mass,
The cedar reaching high
To kiss the sky,
The cypress, pine
And useful sassafras.†

To whose the golden age
Still nature's laws doth give,
No other cares that tend,
But them to defend
From winter's age,
That long there doth not live.

Aeolus Roman god, ruler of the winds
useful sassafras the bark of the sassafras was used medicinally

When as the luscious smell
Of that delicious land,
   Above the seas that flows,
   The clear wind throws,
Your hearts to swell
Approaching the dear strand.

In kenning* of the shore — seeing
Thanks to God first given,
   O you the happiest men,
   Be frolic* then, — joyous
Let cannons roar,
Frighting the wide heaven.

And in regions far
Such heroes bring ye forth,
   As those from whom we came,
   And plant our name,
Under that star
Not known unto our north.

And as there plenty grows
Of laurel everywhere,
   Apollo's† sacred tree,
   You it may see,
A poet's brows
To crown, that may sing there.

Thy voyages attend.
Industrious Hakluyt,†
   Whose reading shall enflame
   Men to seek fame,
And much commend
To aftertimes thy wit.
1605–6 — 1606

Apollo refers to Apollo as patron of poets; the laurel, which was sacred to Apollo, was used in antiquity for the crowns of poets
Hakluyt Richard Hakluyt (here pronounced as three syllables) was the great Elizabethan chronicler of the discoveries; he described the voyages of explorers such as the Cabots, Drake, Frobisher and Ralegh

Christopher Marlowe

1564–93

Christopher Marlowe was born in Canterbury, the son of a shoemaker. He was educated at the King's School, Canterbury, and then proceeded to Corpus Christi College, Cambridge, where he took his BA in 1584. His supplication for his MA on 31 March 1587 was denied because of his supposed intention to live in Rheims, the seat of the Roman Catholic propaganda campaign which was directed against England. On 29 June the Privy Council intervened and commanded that Marlowe be given his degree 'because it is not Her Majesty's pleasure that anyone employed as he hath been in matters touching the benefit of his country should be defamed by those that are ignorant in the affairs he went about'. The precise nature of these 'affairs' is unknown, but they clearly took the form of some sort of secret government service. In 1589 Marlowe was committed to Newgate on suspicion of murder, but was eventually discharged. By 1591 Marlowe was living in London with the playwright Thomas Kyd, who after Marlowe's death accused him of atheism. On 30 May 1593 Marlowe was killed in a brawl at the Widow Bull tavern in Deptford.

Marlowe wrote seven plays for the Admiral's Men, the chief rivals to the Chamberlain's Men, for whom Shakespeare wrote. His best plays (*Tamburlaine*, *The Jew of Malta* and *Doctor Faustus*) are characterised by a supple and powerful style, and by magnificent protagonists who revel in the quest for power. Marlowe's poems include a verse translation of Ovid's *Amores*, an unfinished erotic Ovidian narrative, *Hero and Leander*, and *The Passionate Shepherd to his Love*, the most famous lyric of the English Renaissance.

From TAMBURLAINE THE GREAT,† Part One, V, i, 135–90

TAMBURLAINE:
Ah, fair Zenocrate,† divine Zenocrate!
Fair is too foul an epithet for thee,
That in thy passion for thy country's love,
And fear to see thy kingly father's harm,
With hair dishevelled wipest thy watery cheeks,
And like to Flora† in her morning's pride,
Shaking her silver tresses in the air,
Rain'st on the earth resolvèd* pearl in showers, melted
And sprinklest sapphires on thy shining face,
Where Beauty, mother to the Muses,† sits,
And comments* volumes with her ivory pen, expounds
Taking instructions from thy flowing eyes;
Eyes, when that Ebena† steps to heaven,
In silence of thy solemn evening's walk,
Making the mantle of the richest night,
The moon, the planets, and the meteors, light;
There angels in their crystal* armours fight transparent
A doubtful battle with my tempted thoughts
For Egypt's freedom and the Soldan's† life,
His life that so consumes Zenocrate,
Whose sorrows lay more siege unto my soul
Than all my army to Damascus walls;
And neither Persians' sovereign nor the Turk
Troubled my senses with conceit of foil†
So much by much as doth Zenocrate.
What is beauty, saith my sufferings, then?
If all the pens that ever poets held
Had fed the feeling of their masters' thoughts,
And every sweetness that inspired their hearts,
Their minds, and muses on admirèd themes;

Tamburlaine the Great Marlowe's *Tamburlaine* is a dramatic presentation of the life of the Tartar conqueror Timur the Lame (1336–1405)
Zenocrate Tamburlaine's wife, whose name Marlowe has coined from Greek, in which it means 'wrath of Zeus'
Flora goddess of flowers
Where Beauty . . . Muses Marlowe has invented the genealogy
Ebena Night, an invented goddess whose name Marlowe has coined from the Greek and Latin word for 'ebony', which was often used figuratively to mean 'darkness'
Soldan Zenocrate is the daughter of the Sultan of Egypt
conceit of foil anticipation of defeat

If all the heavenly quintessence† they still* distil
From their immortal flowers of poesy,
Wherein as in a mirror we perceive
The highest reaches of a human wit;
If these had made one poem's period,†
And all combined in beauty's worthiness,
Yet should there hover in their restless heads
One thought, one grace, one wonder, at the least,
Which into words no virtue can digest.
But how unseemly is it for my sex,
My discipline of arms and chivalry,
My nature, and the terror of my name,
To harbour thoughts effeminate and faint!* feeble
Save only that in beauty's just applause,
With whose instinct the soul of man is touched,
And every warrior that is rapt* with love smitten
Of fame, of valour, and of victory,
Must needs have beauty beat on his conceits:
I thus conceiving and subduing both,
That which hath stopped the tempest of the gods,
Even from the fiery-spangled veil of heaven,
To feel the lovely warmth of shepherd's flames,
And march in cottages of strewèd weeds,* plants
Shall give the world to note, for all my birth,
That virtue solely is the sum of glory,
And fashions men with true nobility.
1587 1590

From EDWARD II,†
I. i. 50–70

GAVESTON.
I must have wanton poets, pleasant wits,
Musicians, that with touching of a string
May draw the pliant king which way I please;
Music and poetry is his delight:
Therefore I'll have Italian masques† by night,

quintessence the 'fifth essence' of which the stars were made
period complete rhetorical structure
Edward II Marlowe's play dramatises the life of King Edward II (1284–1327) from his accession to his abdication and death. The soliloquy printed here is spoken by Piers Gaveston, Edward's favourite
Italian masques Tudor dramatic entertainments for the court, here used anachronistically

Sweet speeches, comedies, and pleasing shows;
And in the day, when he shall walk abroad,
Like sylvan nymphs my pages shall be clad;
My men like satyrs grazing on the lawns
Shall with their goat-feet dance an antic* hay;† grotesque
Sometime a lovely boy in Dian's† shape,
With hair that gilds the water as it glides,
Crownets of pearl about his naked arms,
And in his sportful hands an olive tree
To hide those parts which men delight to see,
Shall bathe him in a spring; and there hard by,
One like Actaeon† peeping through the grove,
Shall by the angry goddess be transformed,
And running in the likeness of an hart,
By yelping hounds pulled down, and seem to die,
Such things as these best please his majesty.

1592 1594

From DOCTOR FAUSTUS†

From Act II, Scene i

Enter Faustus *in his study.*

FAUSTUS. Now, Faustus, must thou needs be damned,
And canst thou not be saved.
What boots* it then to think on God or heaven? avails
Away with such vain fancies, and despair;
Despair in God, and trust in Belzebub.†
Now go not backward; no, Faustus, be resolute.
Why waverest thou? O something soundeth in mine ears,
'Abjure this magic, turn to God again.'
Ay, and Faustus will turn to God again.
To God? He loves thee not.
The God thou servest is thine own appetite,
Wherein is fixed the love of Belzebub.

hay a country dance involving a serpentine movement

Dian Diana, Roman name for the Greek goddess of the hunt

Actaeon a hunter who accidentally saw Diana bathing; Diana transformed him into a stag (*hart*) and he was dismembered by his own hounds

Doctor Faustus Doctor Faustus is a scholar; Mephostophilis is a devil

Belzebub Beelzebub (Hebrew: 'lord of the flies'), a 'prince of the devils' (Matthew 12.24) who later appears in the play

To him I'll build an altar and a church,
And offer lukewarm blood of new-born babes.
Enter the two Angels.
BAD ANGEL. Go forward, Faustus, in that famous art.
GOOD ANGEL. Sweet Faustus, leave that execrable art.
FAUSTUS. Contrition, prayer, repentance, what of these?
GOOD ANGEL. O they are means to bring thee unto heaven.
BAD ANGEL. Rather illusions, fruits of lunacy,
That make them foolish that do use them most.
GOOD ANGEL. Sweet Faustus, think of heaven and heavenly things.
BAD ANGEL. No, Faustus, think of honour and of wealth.
Angels go off
FAUSTUS. Wealth!
Why, the signory of Emden† shall be mine.
When Mephostophilis shall stand by me,
What God can hurt me? Faustus, thou art safe:
Cast* no more doubts. Mephostophilis, come, — consider
And bring glad tidings from great Lucifer.
Is't not midnight? Come, Mephostophilis!
Veni, veni, Mephostophile.†
Enter Mephostophilis.
Now tell me what saith Lucifer thy lord.
MEPHOSTOPHILIS. That I shall wait on Faustus whilst he lives,
So he will buy my service with his soul.
FAUSTUS. Already Faustus hath hazarded that for thee.
MEPHOSTOPHILIS. But now thou must bequeath it solemnly,
And write a deed of gift with thine own blood,
For that security craves Lucifer.
If thou deny it, I must back to hell.
FAUSTUS. Stay, Mephostophilis, and tell me
What good will my soul do thy lord?
MEPHOSTOPHILIS. Enlarge his kingdom.
FAUSTUS. Is that the reason why he tempts us thus?
MEPHOSTOPHILIS. *Solamen miseris socios habuisse doloris.*†
FAUSTUS. Why, have you any pain that torture other?†
MEPHOSTOPHILIS. As great as have the human souls of men.
But tell me, Faustus, shall I have thy soul?
And I will be thy slave and wait on thee,
And give thee more than thou hast wit to ask.

signory of Emden the lordship of Emden, a German seaport
Veni . . . Mephostophile (Latin) 'Come come Mephostophilis'
Solamen . . . doloris (Latin) 'Misery loves company'
torture other tortures others

FAUSTUS. Ay, Mephostophilis, I'll give it him.
MEPHOSTOPHILIS. Then, Faustus, stab thy arm courageously,
And bind thy soul, that at some certain day
Great Lucifer† may claim it as his own,
And then be thou as great as Lucifer.
FAUSTUS. Lo, Mephostophilis, for love of thee
Faustus hath cut his arm, and with his proper* blood — own
Assures† his soul to be great Lucifer's,
Chief lord and regent of perpetual night
View here this blood that trickles from mine arm,
And let it be propitious for my wish.
MEPHOSTOPHILIS. But, Faustus,
Write it in manner of a deed of gift.
FAUSTUS. Ay, so I will. But, Mephostophilis,
My blood congeals and I can write no more.
MEPHOSTOPHILIS. I'll fetch thee fire to dissolve it straight.
Exit.
FAUSTUS. What might the staying of my blood portend?
Is it unwilling I should write this bill?* — contract
Why streams it not that I may write afresh?
'Faustus gives to thee his soul': ah, there it stayed.
Why shouldst thou not? Is not thy soul thine own?
Then write again: 'Faustus gives to thee his soul.'
Enter Mephostophilis *with the chafer*† *of fire.*
MEPHOSTOPHILIS. See, Faustus, here is fire; set it on.
FAUSTUS. So, now the blood begins to clear again;
Now will I make an end immediately.
MEPHOSTOPHILIS. What will not I do to obtain his soul?
FAUSTUS. *Consummatum est*:† this bill is ended,
And Faustus hath bequeathed his soul to Lucifer.
But what is this inscription on mine arm?
Homo fuge:† whither should I fly?
If unto God, he'll throw me down to hell.
My senses are deceived: here's nothing writ!
O yes, I see it plain. Even here is writ
Homo fuge: yet shall not Faustus fly.
MEPHOSTOPHILIS. I'll fetch him somewhat to delight his mind.
Exit
Enter Devils, giving crowns and rich apparel to Faustus; *they dance and then depart. Enter* Mephostophilis.

Lucifer Satan, so called from Isaiah 14.12
assures assigns by a legal agreement
chafer a portable grate
Consummatum est: 'it is finished', the final words of Jesus in the Latin of the Vulgate (John 19. 30)
Homo fuge (Latin) 'fly, man!'

FAUSTUS. What means this show? Speak, Mephostophilis.
MEPHOSTOPHILIS. Nothing, Faustus, but to delight thy mind,
And let thee see what magic can perform.
FAUSTUS. But may I raise such spirits when I please?
MEPHOSTOPHILIS. Ay, Faustus, and do greater things than these.
FAUSTUS. Then, Mephostophilis, receive this scroll,
A deed of gift, of body and of soul:
But yet conditionally that thou perform
All covenants and articles between us both.
MEPHOSTOPHILIS. Faustus, I swear by hell and Lucifer
To effect all promises between us made.
FAUSTUS. Then hear me read it, Mephostophilis.

On these conditions following:

'First, that Faustus may be a spirit in form and substance.

'Secondly, that Mephostophilis shall be his servant, and at his command.

'Thirdly, that Mephostophilis shall do for him and bring him whatsoever.

'Fourthly, that he shall be in his chamber or house invisible.

'Lastly, that he shall appear to the said John Faustus at all times, in what form or shape soever he please.

'I, John Faustus of Wittenberg, doctor, by these presents, do give both body and soul to Lucifer, Prince of the East, and his minister Mephostophilis, and furthermore grant unto them that, four-and-twenty years being expired, the articles above written inviolate,† full power to fetch or carry the said John Faustus, body and soul, flesh, blood or goods, into their habitation wheresoever.

By me John Faustus.'

MEPHOSTOPHILIS. Speak, Faustus, do you deliver this as your deed?
FAUSTUS. Ay, take it, and the devil give thee good of it.
MEPHOSTOPHILIS. So, now, Faustus, ask me what thou wilt.
FAUSTUS. First I will question with thee about hell.
Tell me, where is the place that men call hell?
MEPHOSTOPHILIS. Under the heavens.
FAUSTUS. Ay, so are all things else; but whereabouts?
MEPHOSTOPHILIS. Within the bowels of these elements,
Where we are tortured and remain for ever.
Hell hath no limits, nor is circumscribed

inviolate not having been violated

In one self* place, but where we are is hell, particular
And where hell is, there must we ever be.
And to be short, when all the world dissolves
And every creature shall be purified,
All places shall be hell that is not heaven.
FAUSTUS. I think hell's a fable.
MEPHOSTOPHILIS. Ay, think so still, till experience change thy mind.
FAUSTUS. Why, dost thou think that Faustus shall be damned?
MEPHOSTOPHILIS. Ay, of necessity, for here's the scroll
In which thou hast given thy soul to Lucifer.
FAUSTUS. Ay, and body too, but what of that?
Thinkest thou that Faustus is so fond* to imagine foolish
That after this life there is any pain?
Tush, these are trifles and mere old wives' tales.
MEPHOSTOPHILIS. But I am an instance to prove the contrary,
For I tell thee I am damned, and now in hell.
FAUSTUS. Nay, and this be hell, I'll willingly be damned.
What, sleeping, eating, walking and disputing?

But leaving this, let me have a wife, the fairest maid in Germany, for I am wanton and lascivious, and cannot live without a wife.

MEPHOSTOPHILIS. Well, Faustus, thou shalt have a wife.

He fetches in a woman devil.

FAUSTUS. What sight is this?
MEPHOSTOPHILIS. Now, Faustus, wilt thou have a wife?
FAUSTUS. Here's a hot whore indeed; no. I'll no wife.
MEPHOSTOPHILIS. Marriage is but a ceremonial toy,
And if thou lovest me, think no more of it.
I'll cull thee out the fairest courtesans
And bring them every morning to thy bed:
She whom thine eye shall like, thy heart shall have,
Were she as chaste as was Penelope,†
As wise as Saba,† or as beautiful
As was bright Lucifer before his fall.
Hold, take this book, peruse it thoroughly:
The iterating* of these lines brings gold, repetition
The framing* of this circle on the ground drawing
Brings thunder, whirlwinds, storm and lightning.
Pronounce this thrice devoutly to thyself
And men in harness* shall appear to thee, armour

Penelope wife of Odysseus, famed for her fidelity

Saba the Queen of Sheba (*Saba* is the Vulgate form); see I Kings 10

Ready to execute what thou commandest.
FAUSTUS. Thanks, Mephostophilis, for this sweet book.
This will I keep as chary as my life.

Yet fain would I have a book wherein I might behold all spells and incantations, that I might raise up spirits when I please.

MEPHOSTOPHILIS. Here they are in this book.

There turn to them.

FAUSTUS. Now would I have a book where I might see all characters and planets of the heavens, that I might know their motions and dispositions.†

MEPHOSTOPHILIS. Here they are too. *Turn to them.*

FAUSTUS. Nay, let me have one book more, and then I have done, wherein I might see all plants, herbs and trees that grow upon the earth.

MEPHOSTOPHILIS. Here they be.

FAUSTUS. O thou art deceived.

MEPHOSTOPHILIS. Tut, I warrant* thee. guarantee

Turn to them.
All go off.

From Act V, Scene i, 38–127

OLD MAN. O gentle Faustus, leave this damned art,
This magic, that will charm thy soul to hell,
And quite bereave thee of salvation.
Though thou hast now offended like a man,
Do not persever in it like a devil.
Yet, yet, thou hast an amiable soul,
If sin by custom grow not into nature:
Then, Faustus, will repentance come too late,
Then thou art banished from the sight of heaven;
No mortal can express the pains of hell.
It may be this my exhortation
Seems harsh and all unpleasant; let it not,
For, gentle son, I speak it not in wrath,
Or envy of† thee, but in tender love,
And pity of thy future misery;
And so have hope that this my kind rebuke,
Checking thy body, may amend thy soul.

dispositions the position of a planet for astrological purposes

envy of ill will towards

FAUSTUS. Where are thou, Faustus? Wretch, what hast thou done?
Damned art thou, Faustus, damned: despair and die.
Hell claims his right, and with a roaring voice
Says 'Faustus, come, thine hour is almost come',
Mephostophilis *gives him a dagger.*

And Faustus now will come to do thee right.†
OLD MAN. O stay, good Faustus, stay thy desperate steps.
I see an angel hover o'er thy head,
And with a vial full of precious grace
Offers to pour the same into thy soul
Then call for mercy and avoid despair.
FAUSTUS. O friend, I feel thy words
To comfort my distresséd soul.
Leave me awhile to ponder on my sins.
OLD MAN. Faustus, I leave thee, but with grief of heart,
Fearing the ruin of thy hapless soul.
Exit.
FAUSTUS. Accurséd Faustus, where is mercy now?
I do repent, and yet I do despair.
Hell strives with grace for conquest in my breast;
What shall I do to shun the snares of death?
MEPHOSTOPHILIS. Thou traitor, Faustus, I arrest thy soul
For disobedience to my sovereign lord.
Revolt, or I'll in piecemeal tear thy flesh.
FAUSTUS. I do repent I e'er offended him.
Sweet Mephostophilis, entreat thy lord
To pardon my unjust presumption,
And with my blood again I will confirm
The former vow I made to Lucifer.
MEPHOSTOPHILIS. Do it then, Faustus, with unfeignéd heart,
Lest greater dangers do attend thy drift.* equivocation
FAUSTUS. Torment, sweet friend, that base and crooked age
That durst dissuade me from thy Lucifer,
With greatest torments that our hell affords.
MEPHOSTOPHILIS. His faith is great: I cannot touch his soul;
But what I may afflict his body with
I will attempt, which is but little worth.
FAUSTUS. One thing, good servant, let me crave of thee,
To glut the longing of my heart's desire,

do thee right give you your due

That I may have unto my paramour
That heavenly Helen† which I saw of late,
Whose sweet embracings may extinguish clear
Those thoughts that do dissuade me from my vow,
And keep mine oath I made to Lucifer.

MEPHOSTOPHILIS. This, or what else my Faustus shall desire,
Shall be performed in twinkling of an eye.

Enter Helen *again, passing over between two Cupids.*

FAUSTUS. Was this the face that launched a thousand ships,†
And burnt the topless† towers of Ilium?* Troy
Sweet Helen, make me immortal with a kiss:
Her lips suck forth my soul, see where it flies.
Come, Helen, come, give me my soul again.
Here will I dwell, for heaven is in these lips,
And all is dross that is not Helena.

Enter Old Man.

I will be Paris,† and for love of thee
Instead of Troy shall Wittenberg† be sacked,
And I will combat with weak Menelaus,†
And wear thy colours on my pluméd crest.
Yea, I will wound Achilles† in the heel,
And then return to Helen for a kiss.
O, thou art fairer than the evening's air,
Clad in the beauty of a thousand stars.
Brighter art thou than flaming Jupiter,†
When he appeared to hapless Semele:†
More lovely than the monarch of the sky,
In wanton Arethusa's† azured arms,
And none but thou shalt be my paramour.

[Faustus *and* Helen *go off*].

OLD MAN. Accurséd Faustus, miserable man,
That from thy soul excludest the grace of heaven,
And fliest the throne of his tribunal seat.

Enter the Devils.

Helen Helen of Troy, whose infidelity led to the Trojan War
thousand ships Agamemnon raised a huge fleet to recapture Helen from the Trojans
topless immensely high
Paris the Trojan who abducted Helen
Wittenberg German city, the setting of *Doctor Faustus*
Menelaus Helen's husband, who humiliated Paris in a duel
Achilles warrior killed by Paris after being wounded in the heel
Brighter . . . Semele *Semele* asked her lover *Jupiter* to appear to her in his divine form; he did so, and she was consumed by the heat of his thunderbolts
More lovely . . . arms in classical literature Jupiter never has an affair with the nereid *Arethusa*; perhaps Marlowe is imagining the beauty of the sun's reflection in the blue waters of the spring Arethusa

Satan begins to sift me with his pride,†
As in this furnace God shall try my faith.
My faith, vile hell, shall triumph over thee.
Ambitious fiends, see how the heavens smiles
At your repulse, and laughs your state to scorn.
Hence, hell, for hence I fly unto my God.

All go off.

From Act V, Scene ii, 134–91

The clock strikes eleven.

FAUSTUS. Ah, Faustus,
Now hast thou but one bare hour to live,
And then thou must be damned perpetually.
Stand still, you ever-moving spheres of heaven,
That time may cease and midnight never come.
Fair nature's eye, rise, rise again, and make
Perpetual day; or let this hour be but
A year, a month, a week, a natural day,
That Faustus may repent and save his soul.
O lente, lente, currite noctis equi!†
The stars move still, time runs, the clock will strike.
The devil will come, and Faustus must be damned.
O I'll leap up to my God; who pulls me down?
See, see, where Christ's blood streams in the firmament.
One drop would save my soul, half a drop. Ah, my Christ.
Rend not my heart for naming of my Christ;
Yet will I call on him. O spare me, Lucifer.
Where is it now? 'Tis gone: and see where God
Stretcheth out his arm and bends his ireful brows.
Mountains and hills, come, come, and fall on me,
And hide me from the heavy wrath of God.
No, no!
Then will I headlong run into the earth.
Earth, gape. O no, it will not harbour me.
You stars that reigned at my nativity,
Whose influence hath allotted death and hell,
Now draw up Faustus like a foggy mist
Into the entrails of yon labouring cloud,

sift . . . pride test me with his power
O lente . . . equi! 'O horses of the night, run slowly, slowly', quoted (with an extra 'slowly') from Ovid, *Amores* I,xiii.40

That when you vomit forth into the air
My limbs may issue from your smoky mouths,
So that my soul may but ascend to heaven.
The watch strikes.* clock
Ah, half the hour is past, 'twill all be past anon.
O God,
If thou wilt not have mercy on my soul,
Yet for Christ's sake whose blood hath ransomed me
Impose some end to my incessant pain:
Let Faustus live in hell a thousand years,
A hundred thousand, and at last be saved.
No end is limited to damnéd souls.
Why wert thou not a creature wanting soul?
Or why is this immortal that thou hast?
Ah, Pythagoras' *metempsychosis*,† were that true,
This soul should fly from me, and I be changed
Unto some brutish beast. All beasts are happy,
For when they die
Their souls are soon dissolved in elements,
But mine must live still* to be plagued in hell. always
Cursed be the parents that engendered me!
No, Faustus, curse thyself, curse Lucifer,
That hath deprived thee of the joys of heaven.
The clock strikes twelve.
It strikes, it strikes; now body turn to air,
Or Lucifer will bear thee quick* to hell. alive
Thunder and lightning.
O soul, be changed to little water drops
And fall into the ocean, ne'er be found.
Thunder, and enter the Devils.
My God, my God, look not so fierce on me.
Adders and serpents, let me breathe awhile.
Ugly hell, gape not; come not, Lucifer.
I'll burn my books.† Ah, Mephostophilis! *They go off with him.*
1588–92 1604

Pythagoras' metempsychosis the doctrine of the transmigration of souls was attributed to the pre-Socratic philosopher Pythagoras
books his books of magic

From THE JEW OF MALTA†

Act IV, Scene i, 1–76

Enter Barabas, Ithamore. *Bells within.*

BARABAS. There is no music to† a Christian's knell.
How sweet the bells ring now the nuns are dead
That sound at other times like tinkers' pans!
I was afraid the poison had not wrought,†
Or though it wrought, it would have done no good,
For every year they swell,† and yet they live;
Now all are dead, not one remains alive.

ITHAMORE. That's brave,* master; but think you it will not be known? splendid

BARABAS. How can it, if we two be secret?

ITHAMORE. For my part, fear you not.

BARABAS. I'd cut thy throat, if I did.

ITHAMORE. And reason† too.
But here's a royal* monastery hard by; first-rate
Good master, let me poison all the monks.

BARABAS. Thou shalt not need, for now the nuns are dead
They'll die with grief.

ITHAMORE. Do you not sorrow for your daughter's death?

BARABAS. No, but I grieve because she lived so long;
An Hebrew born, and would become a Christian:
Cazzo† *diavola!** she-devil

ITHAMORE. Look, look, master, here come two religious caterpillars.†

Enter the two Friars.

BARABAS. I smelt 'em ere they came.

ITHAMORE. God-a-mercy, nose;† come, let's be gone.

BARNARDINE. Stay, wicked Jew; repent, I say, and stay.

JACOMO. Thou hast offended, therefore must be damned.

BARABAS. I fear they know we sent the poisoned broth.

ITHAMORE. And so do I, master; therefore speak 'em fair.

BARNARDINE. Barabas, thou hast –

JACOMO. Ay, that thou hast –

BARABAS. True, I have money; what though I have?

BARNARDINE. Thou art a –

The Jew of Malta Barabas is the Jew of Malta; Ithamore is his slave
to comparable to
wrought taken effect
swell swell with pregnancy
reason with good reason
cazzo an Italian obscenity (literally 'penis')
caterpillars primarily 'predators', but also a comparison of the habits of the friars with cocoons
nose the actor playing Barabas wore a false nose

JACOMO. Ay, that thou art, a –
BARABAS. What needs all this? I know I am a Jew.
BARNARDINE. Thy daughter –
JACOMO. Ay, thy daughter –
BARABAS. O, speak not of her, then I die with grief.
BARNARDINE. Remember that –
JACOMO. Ay, remember that –
BARABAS. I must needs say that I have been a great usurer.
BARNARDINE. Thou has committed –
BARABAS. Fornication? But that was in another country, and besides the wench is dead.
BARNARDINE. Ay, but Barabas, remember Mathias and Don Lodowick.†
BARABAS. Why, what of them?
BARNARDINE. I will not say that by a forged challenge they met.
BARABAS. (*aside*). She has confessed, and we are both undone,
My bosom inmates, but I must dissemble.
O holy friars, the burden of my sins
Lie heavy on my soul; then pray you tell me,
Is't not too late now to turn Christian?
I have been zealous in the Jewish faith,
Hard-hearted to the poor, a covetous wretch,
That would for lucre's sake have sold my soul.
A hundred for a hundred† I have taken;
And now for store of wealth may I compare
With all the Jews in Malta: but what is wealth?
I am a Jew, and therefore am I lost.†
Would penance serve for this my sin,
I could afford to whip myself to death.
ITHAMORE. And so could I; but penance will not serve.
BARABAS. To fast, to pray, and wear a shirt of hair,
And on my knees creep to Jerusalem.
Cellars of wine, and sollars† full of wheat,
Warehouses stuffed with spices and with drugs,
Whole chests of gold in bullion and in coin,
Besides I know not how much weight in pearl,
Orient and round, have I within my house;
At Alexandria, merchandise unsold;

Mathias, Don Lodowick refers to characters whom Barabas has tricked into killing each other
hundred for a hundred a Latinism (*centum pro cento*) meaning 100% interest
lost destined to eternal damnation
sollars attic store-rooms

But yesterday two ships went from this town,
Their voyage will be worth ten thousand crowns.
In Florence, Venice, Antwerp, London, Seville,
Frankfort, Lubeck, Moscow, and where not,
Have I debts owing; and in most of these
Great sums of money lying in the banco.†
All this I'll give to some religious house,
So I may be baptized and live therein.
1589–90 1633

From HERO AND LEANDER

Sestiad Two, 227–334

By this, Leander, being near the land,
Cast down his weary feet, and felt the sand.†
Breathless albeit he were, he rested not
Till to the solitary tower he got,
And knocked and called, at which celestial noise
The longing heart of Hero much more joys
Than nymphs and shepherds when the timbrel* rings, tambourine
Or crookèd† dolphin when the sailor sings.
She stayed not for her robes, but straight arose,
And drunk with gladness to the door she goes,
Where seeing a naked man she screeched for fear –
Such sights as this to tender maids are rare –
And ran into the dark herself to hide;
Rich jewels in the dark are soonest spied.
Unto her was he led, or rather drawn,
By those white limbs, which sparkled through the lawn.†
The nearer that he came, the more she fled,
And seeking refuge, slipped into her bed.
Whereon Leander sitting thus began,
Through numbing cold all feeble, faint and wan:
'If not for love, yet, love, for pity sake,
Me in thy bed and maiden bosom take;
At least vouchsafe these arms some little room,

banco Italian: bank
sand of Sestos, to which Leander had just swum across the Hellespont to seek his love Hero
crookèd 'humped', referring to the profile of the dolphin as it breaks the surface of the water
lawn a kind of fine linen

Who, hoping to embrace thee, cheerly swum.
This head was beat with many a churlish billow,
And therefore let it rest upon thy pillow.'
Herewith affrighted Hero shrunk away,
And in her lukewarm place Leander lay,
Whose lively heat, like fire from heaven fet,* fetched
Would animate gross clay, and higher set
The drooping thoughts of base-declining souls
Than dreary* Mars carousing nectar bowls. gloomy
His hands he cast upon her like a snare;
She, overcome with shame and sallow fear,
Like chaste Diana when Actaeon† spied her,
Being suddenly betrayed, dived down to hide her.
And as her silver body downward went,
With both her hands she made the bed a tent,
And in her own mind thought herself secure,
O'ercast with dim and darksome coverture.
And now she lets him whisper in her ear,
Flatter, entreat, promise, protest and swear;
Yet ever as he greedily assayed* attempted
To touch those dainties, she the harpy played,†
And every limb did as a soldier stout
Defend the fort, and keep the foeman out
For though the rising ivory mount he scaled,
Which is with azure circling lines empaled,* enclosed
Much like a globe (a globe may I term this,
By which love sails to regions full of bliss),
Yet there with Sisyphus† he toiled in vain,
Till gentle parley† did the truce obtain.
Wherein Leander on her quivering breast
Breathless spoke something, and sighed out the rest:
Which so prevailed as he with small ado
Enclosed her in his arms and kissed her too.
And every kiss to her was as a charm.
And to Leander as a fresh alarm,
So that the truce was broke, and she alas
(Poor silly maiden) at his mercy was.

Actaeon a hunter who accidentally saw the virgin goddess Diana bathing
the harpy played she withdrew the dainties; harpies were female monsters who tortured men in various ways
Sisyphus was condemned to roll a huge rock up a mountain; each time he approached the summit the rock rolled down again
parley a military term for discussions of terms of ceasefire

Love is not full of pity (as men say)
But deaf and cruel where he means to prey.
Even as a bird, which in our hands we wring,
Forth plungeth, and oft flutters with her wing,
She trembling strove; this strife of hers (like that
Which made the world) another world begat
Of unknown joy. Treason was in her thought,
And cunningly to yield herself she sought.
Seeming not won, yet won she was at length;
In such wars women use but half their strength.
Leander now, like Theban Hercules,†
Entered the orchard of th'Hesperides,†
Whose fruit none rightly can describe but he
That pulls or shakes it from the golden tree.
And now she wished this night were never done,
And sighed to think upon th'approaching sun,
For much it grieved her that the bright daylight
Should know the pleasure of this blessèd night,
And them like Mars† and Erycine† displayed,
Both in each other's arms chained as they laid.
Again she knew not how to frame her look,
Or speak to him who in a moment took
That which so long so charily she kept,
And fain by stealth away she would have crept,
And to some corner secretly have gone,
Leaving Leander in the bed alone.
But as her naked feet were whipping out,
He on the sudden clinged her so about
That mermaid-like unto the floor she slid;
One half appeared, the other half was hid.
Thus near the bed she blushing stood upright,
And from her countenance behold ye might
A kind of twilight break, which through the hair,
As from an orient cloud, glimpsed here and there.
And round about the chamber this false morn
Brought forth the day before the day was born.
So Hero's ruddy cheek Hero betrayed
And her all naked to his sight displayed,

Theban . . . Hesperides one of the twelve labours of *Hercules*, who liberated Thebes, was to steal the golden apples from the garden guarded by the Hesperides ('daughters of the west').

Mars god of war, was married to Venus, who is here called *Erycine* with reference to Mount Eryx, her main sanctuary in Sicily

Whence his admiring eyes more pleasure took
Than Dis† on heaps of gold fixing his look.
By this* Apollo's† golden harp began — this time
To sound forth music to the Ocean,
Which watchful Hesperus† no sooner heard,
But he the day-bright-bearing car* prepared, — chariot
And ran before, as harbinger of light,
And with his flaring beams mocked ugly Night,
Till she, o'ercome with anguish, shame and rage,
Danged* down to hell her loathsome carriage. — hurled

1598

THE PASSIONATE SHEPHERD TO HIS LOVE

Come live with me, and be my love,
And we will all the pleasures prove* — sample
That valleys, groves, hills and fields,
Woods, or steepy mountain yields.

And we will sit upon the rocks,
Seeing the shepherds feed their flocks
By shallow rivers, to whose falls
Melodious birds sing madrigals.

And I will make thee beds of roses,
And a thousand fragrant posies,
A cap of flowers, and a kirtle,* — gown
Embroidered all with leaves of myrtle.

A gown made of the finest wool
Which from our pretty lambs we pull,
Fair-lined slippers for the cold,
With buckles of the purest gold.

Dis Roman god of wealth
Apollo as god of music, was often depicted holding a small harp
Hesperus the evening star

A belt of straw and ivy-buds,
With coral clasps and amber studs,
And if these pleasures may thee move,
Come live with me, and be my love.

The shepherd swains shall dance and sing
For thy delight each May morning.
If these delights thy mind may move,
Then live with me, and be my love.

1600

From OVID'S ELEGIES

Book I, Elegy 5

Corinnae concubitus[†]

In summer's heat, and mid-time of the day,
To rest my limbs upon a bed I lay;
One window shut, the other open stood,
Which gave such light as twinkles in a wood
Like twilight glimpse at setting of the sun,
Or night being past, and yet not day begun.
Such light to shamefast maidens must be shown,
Where they may sport and seem to be unknown.
Then came Corinna in a long loose gown,
Her white neck hid with tresses hanging down,
Resembling fair Semiramis[†] going to bed,
Or Lais[†] of a thousand wooers sped.* experienced
I snatched her gown; being thin, the harm was small,
Yet strived she to be covered therewithal,
And striving thus as one that would be cast,* stripped
Betrayed herself, and yielded at the last.
Stark naked as she stood before mine eye,
Not one wen* in her body could I spy. blemish
What arms and shoulders did I touch and see,
How apt her breasts were to be pressed by me!
How smooth a belly under her waist saw I,
How large a leg, and what a lusty thigh!

Corinnae concubitus (Latin) 'copulation with Corinna', Ovid's mistress

Semiramis Assyrian queen, famed for her voluptuousness

Lais a famous Greek courtesan

To leave the rest, all liked me passing well;
I clinged her naked body, down she fell.
Judge you the rest: being tired she bade me kiss;
Jove send me more such afternoons as this.

1598–9

William Shakespeare

1564–1616

William Shakespeare was born in Stratford, Warwickshire, and was probably educated at the King's New School in Stratford. He married Anne Hathaway in 1582, and their three children were born between 1583 and 1585. His whereabouts and activities for the seven years after 1585 are unknown, but by 1592 he was living alone in London. He earned his living by writing plays (thirty-seven of which survive) and acting for the Lord Chamberlain's Men (later renamed the King's Men). The theatres were closed by the plague from the summer of 1592 to the spring of 1594, during which time Shakespeare composed *Venus and Adonis* and *The Rape of Lucrece*; he wrote his *Sonnets* over a protracted period in the 1590s. In 1597 he bought New Place, a large house in Stratford to which he retired in about 1612. On 23 April 1616 Shakespeare died, possibly as the result of a drinking bout with Ben Jonson and Michael Drayton. In 1623 his former colleagues published the collection of Shakespeare's plays known as the First Folio.

From RICHARD III†

Act I, Scene i, 1–31

RICHARD Now is the winter of our discontent
Made glorious summer by this sun† of York,
And all the clouds that loured upon our house* — York
In the deep bosom of the ocean burièd.

Richard III Richard III was King of England from 1483 until his death at Bosworth Field in 1485. In this opening soliloquy he speaks as Richard Duke of Gloucester, the Yorkist claimant to the throne. At the end of the play he is defeated by a Lancastrian claimant, the Earl of Richmond (later Henry VII). Richard's account of his deformity has no basis in historical fact, but derives ultimately from Sir Thomas More's *History of King Richard the Third*, some of which is printed in the previous volume of this series

sun plays on 'son' of York, Edward IV (Richard's brother), whose heraldic emblem was a sun

Now are our brows bound with victorious wreaths,
Our bruisèd arms hung up for monuments,
Our stern alarums† changed to merry meetings,
Our dreadful marches to delightful measures.* dances
Grim-visaged War hath smoothed his wrinkled front,* forehead
And now, instead of mounting barbèd† steeds
To fright the souls of fearful adversaries,
He capers nimbly in a lady's chamber
To the lascivious pleasing of a lute.
But I, that am not shaped for sportive tricks
Nor made to court an amorous looking-glass;
I, that am rudely stamped,† and want love's majesty
To strut before a wantom ambling nymph;
I, that am curtailed of this fair proportion,
Cheated of feature by dissembling Nature,
Deformed, unfinished, sent before my time
Into this breathing world scarce half made up,
And that so lamely and unfashionable
That dogs bark at me as I halt by them –
Why, I, in this weak piping† time of peace,
Have no delight to pass away the time,
Unless to spy my shadow in the sun
And descant on† mine own deformity.
And therefore, since I cannot prove a lover
To entertain† these fair well-spoken days,
I am determinèd to prove a villain
And hate the idle pleasures of these days.

1592–3 1597

---

alarums calls to arms
barbèd wearing horse-armour
rudely stamped of ill-formed appearance
piping pastoral pipes were associated with peacefulness
descant on talk about
entertain fill in the time of

From ROMEO AND JULIET†

Act I, Scene iv, 53–94

MERCUTIO O then I see Queen Mab† hath been with you.
She is the fairies' midwife, and she comes
In shape no bigger than an agate stone
On the fore-finger of an alderman,
Drawn with a team of little atomies†
Over men's noses as they lie asleep.
Her chariot is an empty hazel-nut,
Made by the joiner squirrel or old grub,†
Time out o' mind the fairies' coachmakers.
Her wagon-spokes made of long spinners'* legs, craneflies
The cover of the wings of grasshoppers,
Her traces of the smallest spider web,
Her collars of the moonshine's watery beams,
Her whip of cricket's bone; the lash, of film;* gossamer
Her wagoner, a small gray-coated gnat,
Not half so big as a round little worm
Pricked from the lazy finger of a maid.
And in this state* she gallops night by night the chariot
Through lovers' brains, and then they dream of love;
O'er courtiers' knees, that dream on curtsies straight;
O'er lawyers' fingers, who straight dream on fees.
O'er ladies' lips, who straight on kisses dream,
Which oft the angry Mab with blisters plagues,
Because their breaths with sweetmeats tainted are.
Sometime she gallops o'er a courtier's nose,
And then dreams he of smelling out a suit;†
And sometime comes she with a tithe-pig's† tail,
Tickling a parson's nose as 'a lies asleep,
Then dreams he of another benefice.
Sometimes she driveth o'er a soldier's neck,
And then dreams he of cutting foreign throats,

Romeo and Juliet In this scene Romeo and his friends (who include Mercutio) are on their way to a feast at the Capulet household, where Romeo will meet Juliet. Mercutio's speech is a response to Romeo's remark that he has had a dream.

Queen Mab an Irish fairy who appears here in English literature for the first time; she subsequently appeared as a fairy queen in works by Shakespeare's friends Ben Jonson and Michael Drayton

atomies little creatures

joiner . . . grub the squirrel chews nuts, the grub bores holes in them

suit a petition which (for a fee) the courtier would present to the monarch

tithe-pig the parson was entitled to one-tenth of every litter of pigs

Of breaches, emboscadas,† Spanish blades,†
Of healths five fathom deep;† and then anon
Drums in his ear, at which he starts and wakes,
And being thus frighted swears a prayer or two,
And sleeps again. This is that very Mab
That plaits the manes of horses in the night,
And bakes the elf-locks† in foul sluttish hairs,
Which once untangled much misfortune bodes.
This is the hag, when maids lie on their backs,
That presses them and learns* them first to bear, teaches
Making them women of good carriage.

1595 1597

From THE TAMING OF THE SHREW†

Act V, Scene ii, 142–79

KATHERINA A woman moved is like a fountain troubled,
Muddy, ill-seeming, thick, bereft of beauty,
And while it is so, none so dry or thirsty
Will deign to sip or touch one drop of it.
Thy husband is thy lord, thy life, thy keeper,
Thy head, thy sovereign; one that cares for thee,
And for thy maintenance commits his body
To painful labour both by sea and land,
To watch the night in storms, the day in cold,
Whilst thou liest warm at home, secure and safe;
And craves no other tribute at thy hands
But love, fair looks, and true obedience –
Too little payment for so great a debt.
Such duty as the subject owes the prince,
Even such a woman oweth to her husband,
And when she is froward, peevish, sullen, sour,
And not obedient to his honest will,

emboscadas Spanish word meaning 'ambushes'
Spanish blades Toledo swords
healths . . . deep drinking heavily to the health of others
elf-locks hair was supposedly matted and tangled by elves

The Taming of the Shrew Katherina is the 'shrew' of the title, and in this speech demonstrates the extent to which she has been 'tamed'

What is she but a foul contending rebel
And graceless* traitor to her loving lord? sinful
I am ashamed that women are so simple
To offer war where they should kneel for peace,
Or seek for rule, supremacy, and sway,
When they are bound to serve, love, and obey.
Why are our bodies soft and weak and smooth,
Unapt* to toil and trouble in the world, unsuited
But that our soft conditions and our hearts
Should well agree with our external parts?
Come, come, you froward and unable† worms,
My mind hath been as big as one of yours,
My heart as great, my reason haply more,
To bandy word for word and frown for frown.
But now I see our lances are but straws,
Our strength as weak, our weakness past compare,
That seeming to be most which we indeed least are.
Then vail your stomachs, for it is no boot,†
And place your hands below your husband's foot.
In token of which duty, if he please,
My hand is ready, may it do him ease.

1590–1 1594

From A MIDSUMMER NIGHT'S DREAM†

Act V, Scene i, 1–22

HIPPOLYTA 'Tis strange, my Theseus, that these lovers speak of.
THESEUS More strange than true. I never may believe
These antique* fables nor these fairy toys.* grotesque tales
Lovers and madmen have such seething brains,
Such shaping fantasies, that apprehend
More than cool reason ever comprehends.
The lunatic, the lover, and the poet
Are of imagination all compact.* composed
One sees more devils than vast hell can hold:

froward and unable refractory and weak
vail . . . boot swallow your pride, for there is no help for it
A Midsummer Night's Dream Hippolyta is Queen of the Amazons. Theseus, the legendary hero of Attica, is in Shakespeare's play presented as Duke of Athens

That is the madman. The lover, all as frantic,
See Helen's beauty in a brow of Egypt.†
The poet's eye, in a fine frenzy rolling,
Doth glance from heaven to earth, from earth to heaven;
And as imagination bodies forth
The forms of things unknown, the poet's pen
Turns them to shapes, and gives to airy nothing
A local habitation and a name.
Such tricks hath strong imagination
That if it would but apprehend some joy
It comprehends some bringer of that joy;
Or in the night, imagining some fear,
How easy is a bush supposed a bear?

1595 1600

From RICHARD II†

Act II, Scene i, 40–68

This royal throne of kings, this sceptred isle,
This earth of majesty, this seat of Mars,†
This other Eden, demi-paradise,
This fortress built by Nature for herself
Against infection and the hand of war,
This happy breed of men, this little world,†
This precious stone set in the silver sea,
Which serves it in the office of a wall –
Or as a moat defensive to a house –
Against the envy of less happier lands;
This blessed plot, this earth, this realm, this England,
This nurse, this teeming womb of royal kings,
Feared* by their breed and famous by their birth, frightening
Renownèd for their deeds as far from home,
For Christian service and true chivalry,
As is the sepulchre in stubborn Jewry†
Of the world's ransom,† blessed Mary's Son;

Helen . . . Egypt the beauty of Helen of Troy in the face of a gypsy

Richard II This prophecy is delivered by John of Gaunt, Duke of Lancaster (1340–99), the father of Henry Bolingbroke, who in the course of the play deposes Richard II and becomes King Henry IV

seat of Mars home of Mars, the god of war

little world world in miniature

Jewry Palestine, which is *stubborn* because of the refusal of the Jews to recognise Jesus as the Messiah

world's ransom Jesus (Mark 10.45)

This land of such dear souls, this dear dear land,
Dear for her reputation through the world,
Is now leased out – I die pronouncing it –
Like to a tenement or pelting* farm. insignificant
England, bound in with the triumphant sea,
Whose rocky shore beats back the envious siege
Of watery Neptune,† is now bound in with shame,
With inky blots and rotten parchment bonds.
That England, that was wont to conquer others,
Hath made a shameful conquest of itself.
Ah, would the scandal vanish with my life,
How happy then were my ensuing death!
1595 1597

From THE MERCHANT OF VENICE†

Act IV, Scene i, 180–204

PORTIA Do you confess the bond?
ANTONIO I do.
PORTIA Then must the Jew be merciful.
SHYLOCK On what compulsion must I? Tell me that.
PORTIA The quality of mercy is not strained;†
It droppeth as the gentle rain from heaven
Upon the place beneath. It is twice blest;
It blesseth him that gives and him that takes.
'Tis mightiest in the mightiest; it becomes
The thronèd monarch better than his crown.
His sceptre shows the force of temporal power,
The attribute to awe and majesty,
Wherein doth sit the dread and fear of kings;
But mercy is above this sceptred sway,
It is enthronèd in the hearts of kings,
It is an attribute to God himself,

Neptune god of the sea
The Merchant of Venice Antonio is the 'merchant of Venice' of the title. Shylock is a moneylender who has lent money to Bassanio, Antonio's friend. Portia, who is betrothed to Bassanio, appears here (disguised as a barrister) in defence of Antonio, who has guaranteed the loan which Bassanio cannot repay
strained forced, constrained

And earthly power doth then show likest God's
When mercy seasons justice. Therefore, Jew,
Though justice be thy plea, consider this –
That in the course of justice none of us
Should see salvation. We do pray for mercy,
And that same prayer† doth teach us all to render
The deeds of mercy. I have spoke thus much
To mitigate the justice of thy plea,
Which if thou follow, this strict court of Venice
Must needs give sentence 'gainst the merchant there.

1596–7

1600

From HENRY IV PART ONE†

Act III, Scene i, 13–63

GLENDOWER At my nativity
The front of heaven was full of fiery shapes
Of burning cressets,† and at my birth
The frame and huge foundation of the earth
Shaked like a coward.

HOTSPUR Why, so it would have done at the same season if your mother's cat had but kittened, though yourself had never been born.

GLENDOWER I say the earth did shake when I was born.

HOTSPUR And I say the earth was not of my mind,
If you suppose as fearing you it shook.

GLENDOWER The heavens were all on fire, the earth did tremble.

HOTSPUR O, then the earth shook to see the heavens on fire,
And not in fear of your nativity.
Diseasèd nature oftentimes breaks forth
In strange eruptions; oft the teeming* earth — pregnant
Is with a kind of colic pinched and vexed

---

prayer the Lord's Prayer

Henry IV Part One This scene is a meeting of the rebel leaders who are plotting against Henry IV. Owen Glendower (*c.* 1354–*c.* 1416) led the Welsh rebellion against Henry. Hotspur is the nickname of Henry Percy, son of the Earl of Northumberland; the historical Hotspur was 39 years old in 1403, when the rebellion took place, but Shakespeare portrays him as a young man. Shakespeare's Edmund Mortimer conflates two historical personages of that name; the Earl of March (1391–1425), who had been recognised as heir presumptive by Richard II, and the Earl's uncle, Sir Edmund Mortimer (1376–*c.* 1409), who had married Glendower's daughter

cressets iron baskets in which fires were lit; they were often suspended from ceilings

By the imprisoning of unruly wind
Within her womb, which, for enlargement striving,
Shakes the old beldam* earth, and topples down — grandmother
Steeples and moss-grown towers. At your birth
Our grandam* earth, having this distemp'rature, — grandmother
In passion* shook. — suffering

GLENDOWER Cousin, of many men
I do not bear these crossings. Give me leave
To tell you once again that at my birth
The front of heaven was full of fiery shapes
The goats ran from the mountains, and the herds
Were strangely clamorous to the frighted fields.
These signs have marked me extraordinary,
And all the courses of my life do show
I am not in the roll of common men.
Where is he living, clipped* in with the sea — bound
That chides the banks of England, Scotland, Wales,
Which calls me pupil or hath read to me?
And bring him out that is but woman's son
Can trace me in the tedious ways of art
And hold me pace in deep experiments.

HOTSPUR I think there's no man speaks better Welsh.
I'll to dinner.

MORTIMER Peace, cousin Percy; you will make him mad.

GLENDOWER I can call spirits from the vasty deep.

HOTSPUR Why, so can I, or so can any man;
But will they come when you do call for them?

GLENDOWER Why, I can teach you, cousin, to command the devil.

HOTSPUR And I can teach thee, coz, to shame the devil
By telling truth; tell truth, and shame the devil.
If thou have power to raise him, bring him hither,
And I'll be sworn I have power to shame him hence.
O, while you live, tell truth and shame the devil!

1596–7

1598

From HENRY IV PART TWO†

Act IV, Scene iii, 83–115

PRINCE JOHN Fare you well, Falstaff. I, in my condition,
Shall better speak of you than you deserve. [*All but* FALSTAFF *go off*]

FALSTAFF I would you had but the wit; 'twere better than your dukedom. Good faith, this same young sober-blooded boy doth not love me, nor a man cannot make him laugh – but that's no marvel, he drinks no wine. There's never none of these demure boys come to any proof, for thin drink doth so overcool their blood, and making many fish meals, that they fall into a kind of male green-sickness,† and then when they marry they get wenches.† They are generally fools and cowards – which some of us should be too, but for inflammation.† A good sherris-sack† hath a twofold operation in it. It ascends me into the brain, dries me there all the foolish and dull and crudy vapours which environ it, makes it apprehensive, quick, forgetive,† full of nimble, fiery, and delectable shapes, which delivered o'er to the voice, the tongue, which is the birth, becomes excellent wit. The second property of your excellent sherris is the warming of the blood, which before – cold and settled – left the liver white and pale, which is the badge of pusillanimity and cowardice; but the sherris warms it, and makes it course from the inwards to the parts' extremes. It illumineth the face, which, as a beacon, gives warning to all the rest of this little kingdom, man, to arm; and then the vital commoners, and inland petty spirits, muster me all to their captain, the heart, who (great and puffed up with this retinue) doth any deed of courage; and this valour comes of sherris. So that skill in the weapon is nothing without sack, for that sets it a-work, and learning a mere hoard of gold kept by a devil, till sack commences it and sets it in act† and use. Hereof comes it that Prince Harry is valiant; for the cold blood he did naturally inherit of his father he hath like lean, sterile, and bare land manured, husbanded, and tilled, with excellent endeavour of drinking good and good store of fertile sherris, that he is become very hot and valiant. If I had a thousand sons, the first human† principle I would teach them should be to forswear thin potations, and to addict themselves to sack.

1597–8 1600

Henry IV Part Two Prince John (1389–1435), whom Shakespeare mistakenly calls Duke of Lancaster, was the third son of King Henry IV. Sir John Falstaff, Shakespeare's greatest comic character, has been the companion of Prince Hal (later Henry V), who at the end of the play repudiates their friendship
green-sickness chlorosis, a form of anaemia peculiar to young women
get wenches beget girls
inflammation passions inflamed by drink
sherris-sack a white wine from Xeres, in southern Spain
forgetive creative
commences . . . act plays on the conferring of degrees: at Cambridge, a 'commencement', and at Oxford, an 'act'
human secular

From MUCH ADO ABOUT NOTHING†

Act II, Scene iii, 49–85

BALTHASAR Because you talk of wooing, I will sing,
Since many a wooer doth commence his suit
To her he thinks not worthy; yet he woos,
Yet will he swear he loves.
DON PEDRO Nay, pray thee come.
Or if thou wilt hold longer argument,
Do it in notes.
BALTHASAR Note this before my notes,
There's not a note of mine that's worth the noting.
DON PEDRO Why, these are very crotchets that he speaks;
Note notes, forsooth, and nothing.

Music

BENEDICK [*Aside*] Now, divine air! Now is his soul ravished! Is it not strange that sheep's guts should hale souls out of men's bodies? Well, a horn† for my money, when all's done.

BALTHASAR *sings*

Sigh no more, ladies, sigh no more,
Men were deceivers ever;
One foot in sea, and one on shore,
To one thing constant never.
Then sigh not so, but let them go
And be you blithe and bonny,
Converting all your sounds of woe
Into hey nonny, nonny,

Sing no more ditties, sing no moe* — more
Of dumps* so dull and heavy, — mournful songs
The fraud of men was ever so
Since Summer first was leavy.
Then sigh not so, but let them go
And be you blithe and bonny,
Converting all your sounds of woe
Into hey nonny, nonny.

Much Ado about Nothing Don Pedro is Prince of Aragon, and Balthasar is his attendant; Benedick is 'a young lord of Padua'

horn a hunting horn, or a bugle summoning to battle

DON PEDRO By my troth, a good song.

BALTHASAR And an ill singer, my lord.

DON PEDRO Ha, no, no; faith, thou sing'st well enough for a shift.†

BENEDICK [*Aside*] An he had been a dog that should have howled thus, they would have hanged him; and I pray God his bad voice bode no mischief. I had as lief have heard the night-raven, come what plague could have come after it.

1598 1600

From HENRY V†

Act IV, Scene iii, 20–67

KING HENRY If we are marked to die, we are enow†
To do our country loss; and if to live,
The fewer men, the greater share of honour.
God's will, I pray thee wish not one man more.
By Jove, I am not covetous for gold,
Nor care I who doth feed upon my cost.
It yearns me not if men my garments wear.
Such outward things dwell not in my desires.
But if it be a sin to covet honour,
I am the most offending soul alive.
No, faith, my coz, wish not a man from England.
God's peace, I would not lose so great an honour
As one man more, methinks, would share from me,
For the best hope I have. O, do not wish one more.
Rather proclaim it, Westmoreland, through my host,
That he which hath no stomach to this fight,
Let him depart. His passport shall be made,
And crowns for convoy put into his purse.
We would not die in that man's company
That fears his fellowship to die with us.
This day* is called the feast of Crispian. 25 October 1415
He that outlives this day and comes safe home
Will stand a tip-toe when this day is named,
And rouse him at the name of Crispian.

shift makeshift

Henry V In this speech Henry V (1387–1422) addresses his troops before the Battle of Agincourt

enow archaic plural of 'enough', i.e. sufficient in number

He that shall see this day, and live old age,
Will yearly on the vigil feast his neighbours
And say, 'Tomorrow is Saint Crispian.'
Then will he strip his sleeve and show his scars
And say, 'These wounds I had on Crispin's day.'
Old men forget; yet all shall be forgot,
But he'll remember with advantages
What feats he did that day. Then shall our names,
Familiar in his mouth as household words,
Harry the King, Bedford and Exeter,
Warwick and Talbot, Salisbury and Gloucester,
Be in their flowing cups freshly remembered.
This story shall the good man teach his son,
And Crispin Crispian† shall ne'er go by
From this day to the ending of the world
But we in it shall be rememberèd –
We few, we happy few, we band of brothers.
For he today that sheds his blood with me
Shall be my brother; be he ne'er so vile,
This day shall gentle his condition.
And gentlemen in England now a-bed
Shall think themselves accursed they were not here,
And hold their manhoods cheap while any speaks
That fought with us upon Saint Crispin's day.

1598–9

1600

From JULIUS CAESAR†

Act III, Scene ii, 77–111

ANTONY Friends, Romans, countrymen, lend me your ears;
I come to bury Caesar, not to praise him.
The evil that men do lives after them,
The good is oft interrèd with their bones;
So let it be with Caesar. The noble Brutus
Hath told you Caesar was ambitious;

Crispin Crispian another name for St Crispin's Day, with reference to the brothers Crispin and Crispinian who were martyred *c.* 285

Julius Caesar this oration is delivered by Mark Antony (*c.* 83–31 BC) to the citizens of Rome after the assassination of Julius Caesar on 15 March 44 BC. Marcus Brutus (85–42 BC) was one of the conspirators who murdered Caesar. Earlier in this scene he had defended the killing of Caesar to the citizens of Rome. Mark Antony's funeral oration is a reply to Brutus

If it were so, it was a grievous fault,
And grievously hath Caesar answered it.
Here, under leave of Brutus and the rest –
For Brutus is an honourable man,
So are they all, all honourable men –
Come I to speak in Caesar's funeral.
He was my friend, faithful and just to me;
But Brutus says he was ambitious,
And Brutus is an honourable man.
He hath brought many captives home to Rome
Whose ransoms did the general coffers fill:
Did this in Caesar seem ambitious?
When that the poor have cried, Caesar hath wept;
Ambition should be made of sterner stuff;
Yet Brutus says he was ambitious,
And Brutus is an honourable man.
You all did see that on the Lupercal†
I thrice presented him a kingly crown,
Which he did thrice refuse. Was this ambition?
Yet Brutus says he was ambitious,
And sure he is an honourable man.
I speak not to disprove what Brutus spoke,
But here I am to speak what I do know.
You all did love him once, not without cause;
What cause withholds you then to mourn for him?
O judgement, thou art fled to brutish beasts,
And men have lost their reason. Bear with me;
My heart is in the coffin there with Caesar,
And I must pause till it come back to me.

1599 1623

From AS YOU LIKE IT†

Act II, Scene vii, 139–66

JAQUES All the world's a stage,
And all the men and women merely players;
They have their exits and their entrances,
And one man in his time plays many parts,

on the Lupercal on the feast of the Lupercalia, 15 February 44 BC

As You Like It Jaques is an attendant lord of the banished Duke Senior

His Acts being seven ages. At first, the infant,
Mewling* and puking in the nurse's arms. crying feebly
Then the whining schoolboy, with his satchel
And shining morning face, creeping like snail
Unwillingly to school. And then the lover,
Sighing like furnace, with a woeful* ballad full of woe
Made to his mistress' eyebrow. Then a soldier,
Full of strange oaths and bearded like the pard,* leopard
Jealous in honour, sudden and quick in quarrel,
Seeking the bubble reputation
Even in the cannon's mouth. And then the justice,
In fair round belly, with good capon lined,
With eyes severe and beard of formal cut,
Full of wise saws and modern instances;
And so he plays his part. The sixth age shifts
Into the lean and slippered pantaloon,†
With spectacles on nose and pouch on side,
His youthful hose, well saved, a world too wide
For his shrunk shank, and his big manly voice,
Turning again toward childish treble, pipes
And whistles in his* sound. Last scene of all, its
That ends this strange eventful history,
Is second childishness and mere oblivion,
Sans† teeth, sans eyes, sans taste, sans everything.

1599–1600 1623

From TWELFTH NIGHT†

Act II, Scene iii, 34–54

FESTE Would you have a love song, or a song of good life?†
SIR TOBY A love song! A love song!
SIR ANDREW Ay, ay, I care not for good life.
FESTE [*Sings*]
O mistress mine! Where are you roaming?
O, stay and hear: your true love's coming,
That can sing both high and low.

---

pantaloon Pantalone, the old man in slippers in the Italian *commedia dell'arte*
sans without (naturalised French)
Twelfth Night Sir Toby Belch lives at the house of his kinswoman Olivia; Sir Andrew Aguecheek is his friend, a foolish suitor to Olivia. Feste is Olivia's household fool
song of good life a drinking song, though Sir Andrew mistakenly takes it to be a song in praise of virtue

Trip no further, pretty sweeting;* sweetheart
Journeys end in lovers meeting,
Every wise man's son† doth know.
SIR ANDREW Excellent good, i'faith.
SIR TOBY Good, good.
FESTE [*Sings*]
What is love? 'Tis not hereafter;
Present mirth hath present laughter,
What's to come is still unsure.
In delay there lies no plenty –
Then come kiss me, sweet and twenty,
Youth's a stuff will not endure.
SIR ANDREW A mellifluous voice, as I am true knight.
SIR TOBY A contagious† breath.
SIR ANDREW Very sweet and contagious, i'faith.
SIR TOBY To hear by the nose, it is dulcet in contagion.

1601 1623

From HAMLET†

Act III, Scene i, 56–88

HAMLET To be, or not to be† – that is the question.
Whether 'tis nobler in the mind to suffer
The slings and arrows of outrageous fortune
Or to take arms against a sea of troubles
And by opposing end them? To die, to sleep;
No more? And by a sleep, to say we end
The heart-ache and the thousand natural shocks
That flesh is heir to. 'Tis a consummation
Devoutly to be wished. To die, to sleep.
To sleep – perchance to dream. Ay, there's the rub.†
For in that sleep of death, what dreams may come
When we have shuffled off this mortal coil* turmoil
Must give us pause. There's the respect
That makes calamity of so long life.

---

a wise man's son was proverbially said to be a fool

contagious means 'pestilential', but Sir Andrew fails to understand the word

Hamlet in this soliloquy Hamlet, Prince of Denmark, meditates on suicide

to be, or not to be to continue to live, or to commit suicide

rub obstacle (in the game of bowls)

For who would bear the whips and scorns of time,
Th'oppressor's wrong, the proud man's contumely,[†]
The pangs of despisèd love, the law's delay,
The insolence of office, and the spurns
That patient merit of th'unworthy takes,
When he himself might his quietus[†] make
With a bare bodkin?* Who would these fardels* bear, dagger burdens
To grunt and sweat under a weary life,
But that the dread of something after death –
The undiscovered country, from whose bourn* realm
No traveller returns – puzzles the will,
And makes us rather bear those ills we have
Than fly to others that we know not of?
Thus conscience* does make cowards of us all. consciousness
And thus the native hue of resolution
Is sicklied o'er with the pale cast of thought,* melancholy
And enterprises of great pitch and moment
With this regard their currents turn awry
And lose the name of action.

1600–1 1603

From OTHELLO[†]

Act IV, Scene iii, 25–57

DESDEMONA My mother had a maid called Barbary:
She was in love; and he she loved proved mad,
And did forsake her. She had a song of 'willow';
An old thing 'twas, but it expressed her fortune,
And she died singing it. That song tonight
Will not go from my mind; I have much to do
But[†] to go hang my head all at one side
And sing it like poor Barbary. Prithee dispatch.
EMILIA Shall I go fetch your night-gown?
DESDEMONA No, unpin me here.
This Ludovico is a proper* man. handsome
EMILIA A very handsome man.

contumely abusive language
quietus the discharging of a debt
Othello Desdemona has been accused of infidelity by her husband Othello; the rift has been caused by Othello's ensign Iago, who is the husband of Emilia
I have much to do/But I must actively resist the urge

DESDEMONA He speaks well.

EMILIA I know a lady in Venice would have walked barefoot to Palestine for a touch of his nether lip.

DESDEMONA [*sings*] *The poor soul sat sighing by a sycamore tree,*
Sing all a green willow;
Her hand on her bosom, her head on her knee.
Sing willow, willow, willow.
The fresh streams ran by her, and murmured her moans;
Sing willow, willow, willow.
Her salt tears fell from her and softened the stones;
Sing willow –
Lay by these –
willow, willow –
Prithee, hie thee; he'll come anon –
Sing all a green willow must be my garland.
Let nobody blame him; his scorn I approve –
Nay, that's not next. Hark! who is't that knocks?

EMILIA It is the wind.

DESDEMONA [*sings*] *I called my love false love, but what said he then?*
Sing willow, willow, willow:
If I court moe women, you'll couch with moe men –* more
So, get thee gone; good night.

1603–4 1622

From KING LEAR†

Act I, Scene i

Enter KENT, GLOUCESTER *and* EDMUND

KENT I thought the king had more affected† the Duke of Albany than Cornwall.

GLOUCESTER It did always seem so to us,† but now in the division of the kingdom it appears not which of the dukes he values most, for

King Lear the play opens with a trial of love in which King Lear, an ancient King of Britain, tests the love of his three daughters with a view to dividing his kingdom amongst them. The play was performed before King James on 26 December 1606. King James, the King of Scotland who had become King of Engand and Ireland in 1603, styled himself (without authority of Parliament) King of Great Britain. The political tensions generated by the fragility of this putative union of Scotland, England and Ireland underlie the occasion of the tragedy of King Lear

had more affected was more fond of

us Edmund and Gloucester

equalities are so weighed that curiosity in neither can make choice of either's moiety.†

KENT Is not this your son, my lord?

GLOUCESTER His breeding,† sir, hath been at my charge.† I have so often blushed to acknowledge him that now I am brazed† to 't.

KENT I cannot conceive† you.

GLOUCESTER Sir, this young fellow's mother could; whereupon she grew round-wombed, and had indeed, sir, a son for her cradle ere she had a husband for her bed. Do you smell a fault?

KENT I cannot wish the fault undone, the issue† of it being so proper.†

GLOUCESTER But I have a son, sir, by order of law,† some year elder than this, who yet is no dearer in my account. Though this knave came something† saucily to the world before he was sent for, yet was his mother fair; there was good sport at his making, and the whoreson must be acknowledged. Do you know this noble gentleman, Edmund?

EDMUND No, my lord.

GLOUCESTER My lord of Kent. Remember him hereafter as my honourable friend.

EDMUND My services to your lordship.

KENT I must love you, and sue† to know you better.

EDMUND Sir, I shall study deserving.†

GLOUCESTER He hath been out† nine years, and away he shall again. The king is coming.

Sennet.† *Enter one bearing a coronet, then* KING LEAR, CORNWALL, ALBANY, GONERIL, REGAN, CORDELIA *and* ATTENDANTS

LEAR Attend† the lords of France and Burgundy, Gloucester.

GLOUCESTER I shall, my liege.† [GLOUCESTER *and* EDMUND *go off*]

LEAR Meantime we shall express our darker purpose.†
Give me the map there. Know that we have divided
In three our kingdom; and 'tis our fast* intent unalterable
To shake all cares and business from our age,
Conferring them on younger strengths while we
Unburdened crawl toward death. Our son of Cornwall,

equalities . . . moiety the portions are so even that neither duke can prefer the portion given to the other; *curiosity* means 'fastidiousness'
breeding upbringing
charge expense
brazed hardened
conceive understand
issue product (refers to Edmund)
proper handsome
by order of law legitimate
something somewhat
sue beg
study deserving strive to deserve your respect
out out of the country
Sennet a ceremonial trumpet fanfare announcing the arrival of the king
attend escort to the king
my liege a feudal term of address to one's superior
darker purpose more secret intention

And you our no less loving son of Albany,
We have this hour a constant will to publish†
Our daughters' several dowers,† that future strife
May be prevented now. The princes, France and Burgundy,
Great* rivals in our youngest daughter's love, noble
Long in our court have made their amorous sojourn,
And here are to be answered. Tell me, my daughters
(Since now we will divest us both of rule,
Interest of* territory, cares of state), title to
Which of you shall we say doth love us most,
That we our largest* bounty may extend most generous
Where nature doth with merit challenge.† Goneril,
Our eldest-born, speak first.

GONERIL Sir, I love you more than word can wield the matter,†
Dearer than eyesight, space and liberty,†
Beyond what can be valued rich or rare,
No less than life, with grace, health, beauty, honour,
As much as child e'er loved, or father found;†
A love that makes breath poor, and speech unable,* inadequate
Beyond all manner of 'so much'† I love you.

CORDELIA [*Aside*] What shall Cordelia speak? Love and be silent.

LEAR Of all these bounds,* even from this line to this boundaries
With shadowy forests and with champains† riched,* enriched
With plenteous rivers and wide-skirted meads,* wide meadows
We make thee lady. To thine and Albany's issues
Be this perpetual. What says our second daughter,
Our dearest Regan, wife of Cornwall?

REGAN I am made of that self mettle* as my sister, same spirit
And prize me† at her worth. In my true heart
I find she names my very deed of love:†
Only she comes too short, that* I profess in that
Myself an enemy to all other joys
Which the most precious square of sense† possesses,
And find I am alone felicitate* made joyful
In your dear highness' love.

---

constant . . . publish fixed intention to make known
several dowers individual dowries
where . . . challenge to the daughter in whom love for her father can be rewarded as if it were objective merit
I love . . . matter the substance of my love is too heavy to be lifted by my words
space and liberty space to move about and freedom to so do
found found himself loved by his child
of 'so much' of comparison
champains flat enclosed countryside
prize me evaluate myself
In . . . love she recites the words of the document of love written on my heart
square of sense properly balanced feelings

CORDELIA [*Aside*] Then poor Cordelia!
And yet not so, since I am sure my love's
More ponderous* than my tongue. [weightier]
LEAR To thee and thine, hereditary ever,
Remain this ample third of our fair kingdom,
No less in space, validity,* and pleasure [value]
Than that conferred on Goneril. Now, our joy.* [Cordelia]
Although our last and least,† to whose young love
The vines of France and milk of Burgundy
Strive to be interessed,† what can you say to draw
A third more opulent than your sisters'? Speak.
CORDELIA Nothing, my lord.
LEAR Nothing?
CORDELIA Nothing.
LEAR Nothing will come of nothing; speak again.
CORDELIA Unhappy that I am, I cannot heave
My heart into my mouth. I love your majesty
According to my bond,† no more nor less.
LEAR How, how, Cordelia? Mend your speech a little,
Lest you may mar your fortunes.
CORDELIA Good my lord,
You have begot me, bred me, loved me. I
Return those duties back as are right fit,* [appropriate]
Obey you, love you, and most honour you.
Why have my sisters husbands, if they say
They love you all? Haply* when I shall wed, [perhaps]
That lord whose hand must take my plight† shall carry
Half my love with him, half my care and duty.
Sure I shall never marry like my sisters,
To love my father all.
LEAR But goes thy heart with this?
CORDELIA Ay, my good lord.
LEAR So young, and so untender?
CORDELIA So young, my lord, and true.
LEAR Let it be so, thy truth then be thy dower.
For by the sacred radiance of the sun,
The mysteries of Hecate† and the night,
By all the operation of the orbs†

---

last and least youngest and therefore last in precedence
be interessed have a right or share
bond status as a daughter
plight vow of marriage
Hecate Greek deity, here invoked as goddess of the moon
operation of the orbs astrological influence of the stars

From whom we do exist and cease to be,
Here I disclaim all my paternal care,
Propinquity† and property of blood,†
And as a stranger to my heart and me
Hold thee from this for ever. The barbarous Scythian,†
Or he that makes his generation messes†
To gorge his appetite, shall to my bosom
Be as well neighboured, pitied, and relieved,
As thou my sometime* daughter. former

KENT Good my liege –

LEAR Peace, Kent!
Come not between the dragon and his wrath.
I loved her most, and thought to set my rest†
On her kind nursery.* Hence, and avoid my sight! care
So be my grave my peace as here I give
Her father's heart from her. Call France! Who stirs?
Call Burgundy! Cornwall and Albany,
With my two daughters' dowers digest the third;
Let pride, which she calls plainness, marry her.†
I do invest you jointly with my power,
Pre-eminence, and all the large effects
That troop with majesty.† Ourself by monthly course,†
With reservation of† an hundred knights
By you to be sustained, shall our abode
Make with you by due turn. Only we shall retain
The name and all th' addition to† a king: the sway,
Revenue,† execution of the rest,†
Belovéd sons, be yours; which to confirm,
This coronet part* between you. share

KENT Royal Lear,
Whom I have ever honoured as my king,
Loved as my father, as my master followed,
As my great patron thought on in my prayers –

LEAR The bow is bent and drawn, make from the shaft.†

propinquity close kinship
property of blood close blood relationship
Scythian the Scythians were an ancient tribe who lived to the east of the Roman empire; they were renowned for their savagery
makes . . . messes kills his children and serves them as food
set my rest stake everything (the term comes from the card game of primero)
marry her enable her to secure a husband
effects/That . . . majesty pomp which accompanies kingship
by monthly course moving once a month from one daughter to the other
reservation of the right to
th'addition to the titles of
revenue accented on the second syllable
execution of the rest discharging the remaining duties
make from the shaft move aside from the path of the arrow

KENT Let it fall rather, though the fork invade
The region of my heart! Be Kent unmannerly
When Lear is mad. What wouldst thou† do, old man?
Think'st thou that duty shall have dread to speak
When power to flattery bows? To plainness honour's bound
When majesty stoops to folly. Reserve thy state,†
And in thy best consideration check
This hideous rashness. Answer my life† my judgement,
Thy youngest daughter does not love thee least,
Nor are those empty-hearted whose low sounds
Reverb no hollowness.†
LEAR Kent, on thy life, no more!
KENT My life I never held but as a pawn
To wage against thine enemies; nor fear to lose it,
Thy safety being motive.* — my motive
LEAR Out of my sight!
KENT See better, Lear, and let me still remain
The true blank† of thine eye.
LEAR Now by Apollo† –
KENT Now by Apollo, king,
Thou swear'st thy gods in vain.
LEAR O vassal! miscreant!* — blasphemer

He reaches for his sword

ALBANY, CORNWALL Dear sir, forbear!
KENT Kill thy physician, and thy fee bestow
Upon the foul disease. Revoke thy gift,
Or whilst I can vent clamour from my throat
I'll tell thee thou dost evil.
LEAR Hear me, recreant,* — traitor
On thine allegiance hear me!
That* thou hast sought to make us break our vow, — because
Which we durst never yet, and with strained pride
To come betwixt our sentence and our power,†
Which nor our nature nor our place can bear,
Our potency made good,† take thy reward.
Five days we do allot thee for provision
To shield thee from disasters of the world,

thou this form of the second-person pronoun is disrespectful, as it is normally reserved for intimates and inferiors
Reserve thy state retain your monarchical power
Answer my life I will stake my life on
Reverb no hollowness are not amplified by the echoing hollowness of their empty hearts
blank centre of the target
Apollo here invoked both as god of the sun and as god of archery
our . . . power my judgement and my execution of that judgement
our . . . good my power being realised

And on the sixth to turn thy hated back
Upon our kingdom. If on the tenth day following
Thy banished trunk* be found in our dominions, — body
The moment is thy death. Away! By Jupiter,
This shall not be revoked.

KENT Fare thee well, king; sith* thus thou wilt appear. — since
Freedom lives hence and banishment is here.
[*To* CORDELIA] The gods to their dear shelter take thee, maid,
That justly think'st and hast most rightly said.
[*To* GONERIL *and* REGAN] And your large speeches may your deeds approve,* — confirm
That good effects* may spring from words of love. — results
Thus Kent, O princes, bids you all adieu;
He'll shape his old course in a country new. [*Exit*

Flourish:† *Enter* GLOUCESTER *with* FRANCE, BURGUNDY *and* ATTENDANTS

GLOUCESTER Here's France and Burgundy, my noble lord.

LEAR My lord of Burgundy,
We first address toward you, who with this king
Hath rivalled for our daughter. What in the least
Will you require in present dower with her,
Or cease your quest of love?

BURGUNDY Most royal majesty,
I crave no more than hath your highness offered,
Nor will you tender less.

LEAR Right noble Burgundy,
When she was dear to us, we did hold her so,
But now her price is fallen. Sir, there she stands.
If aught within that little seeming substance,
Or all of it, with our displeasure pieced,* — supplemented
And nothing more, may fitly like† your grace,
She's there, and she is yours.

BURGUNDY I know no answer.

LEAR Will you, with those infirmities she owes,* — possesses
Unfriended, new adopted to our hate,
Dowered with our curse and strangered with our oath,†
Take her or leave her?

BURGUNDY Pardon me, royal sir,
Election makes not up† in such conditions.

Flourish ceremonial fanfare to mark the formal entrance of royalty
fitly like please by its fitness
strangered . . . oath rendered a stranger by my resolution
Election . . . up one cannot decide

LEAR Then leave her, sir, for by the power that made me
I tell† you all her wealth. [*To* FRANCE] For you, great king,
I would not from your love make such a stray†
To match you where I hate; therefore beseech you
T'avert your liking a more worthier way
Than on a wretch whom Nature is ashamed
Almost t' acknowledge hers.

FRANCE This is most strange,
That she whom even but now was your best object,†
The argument* of your praise, balm of your age, theme
The best, the dearest, should in this trice* of time moment
Commit a thing so monstrous to* dismantle† as to
So many folds of favour. Sure her offence
Must be of such unnatural degree
That monsters it,† or your fore-vouched† affection
Fall into taint; which to believe of her
Must be a faith that reason without miracle
Should never plant in me.

CORDELIA I yet beseech your majesty –
If for I want† that glib and oily art
To speak and purpose not,† since what I well intend,
I'll do 't before I speak – that you make known
It is no vicious blot, murder or foulness,
No unchaste action or dishonoured* step, dishonourable
That hath deprived me of your grace and favour;
But even for want of that for which I am richer,
A still-soliciting† eye, and such a tongue
That I am glad I have not, though not to have it
Hath lost me in your liking.

LEAR Better thou
Hadst not been born than not t' have pleased me better.

FRANCE Is it but this – a tardiness in nature†
Which often leaves the history* unspoke explanation
That* it intends to do? My lord of Burgundy, of what
What say you to the lady? Love's not love
When it is mingled with regards* that stands factors
Aloof from th' entire point.† Will you have her?
She is herself a dowry.

tell disclose to
make . . . stray stray so far
your best object the favourite object of your gaze
dismantle take off (clothes)
monsters it makes it monstrous
fore-vouched previously affirmed
for I want the problem is that I lack
purpose not intend not to do what I say
still-soliciting always soliciting favours
tardiness in nature natural reticence
Aloof . . . point apart from the central issue

BURGUNDY Royal king,
Give but that portion which yourself proposed,
And here I take Cordelia by the hand,
Duchess of Burgundy.

LEAR Nothing. I have sworn; I am firm.

BURGUNDY I am sorry then you have so lost a father
That you must lose a husband.

CORDELIA Peace be with Burgundy!
Since that respects of fortune† are his love,
I shall not be his wife.

FRANCE Fairest Cordelia, that art most rich, being poor,
Most choice, forsaken, and most loved, despised,
Thee and thy virtues here I seize upon;
Be it lawful I take up what's cast away.
Gods, gods! 'Tis strange that from their cold'st neglect
My love should kindle to inflamed respect.
Thy dowerless daughter, king, thrown to my chance,
Is queen of us, of ours, and our fair France.
Not all the dukes of waterish† Burgundy
Can buy this unprized precious maid of me.
Bid them farewell, Cordelia, though unkind;†
Thou losest here,† a better where† to find.

LEAR Thou hast her, France; let her be thine, for we
Have no such daughter, nor shall ever see
That face of hers again. Therefore be gone
Without our grace, our love, our benison.* blessing
Come, noble Burgundy.

[*Flourish.* LEAR, BURGUNDY, CORNWALL, ALBANY *and* ATTENDANTS *all go off*

FRANCE Bid farewell to your sisters.

CORDELIA The jewels of our father, with washèd† eyes
Cordelia leaves you. I know you what you are,
And like a sister am most loath to call
Your faults as they are named. Love well our father.
To your professèd bosoms I commit him,
But yet, alas, stood I within his grace,
I would prefer* him to a better place. promote

respects of fortune considerations of wealth
waterish means both well-watered (referring to the region) and diluted (referring to the duke's lack of resolution)
though unkind though they have not treated you in a manner appropriate to your being a member of their family
here, where both are nouns referring to place
washed means both 'tearful' and 'cleansed of illusion'

So farewell to you both.
REGAN Prescribe not us our duty.
GONERIL Let your study* — endeavour
Be to content your lord, who hath received you
At Fortune's alms.* You have obedience scanted,* — alms-giving — stinted
And well are worth the want that you have wanted.†
CORDELIA Time shall unfold what plighted† cunning hides,
Who covers faults at last with shame derides.†
Well may you prosper.
FRANCE Come, my fair Cordelia.

[FRANCE *and* CORDELIA *go off*

GONERIL Sister, it is not little I have to say of what most nearly appertains to us both. I think our father will hence† tonight.

REGAN That's most certain, and with you; next month with us.

GONERIL You see how full of changes his age is. The observation we have made of it hath not been little. He always loved our sister most, and with what poor judgement he hath now cast her off appears too grossly.

REGAN 'Tis the infirmity of his age; yet he hath ever but slenderly known himself.

GONERIL The best and soundest of his time hath been but rash; then must we look† from his age to receive, not alone the imperfections of long-engraffed† condition, but therewithal the unruly waywardness† that infirm and choleric years bring with them.

REGAN Such unconstant starts† are we like to have from him as this of Kent's banishment.

GONERIL There is further compliment† of leave-taking between France and him. Pray you let us hit together.† If our father carry authority with such disposition as he bears, this last surrender of his will but offend us.

REGAN We shall further think of it.

GONERIL We must do something, and i' th' heat.†

[*All go off*

1605–6 — 1608

want . . . wanted denial of that love which you have lacked
plighted hidden in pleats
with shame derides will be derided with shame
hence depart
look expect
engraffed engrafted
unruly waywardness unpredictable obstinacy
unconstant starts sudden jerks (of a horse)
compliment ceremony
hit together co-ordinate our actions
i' th' heat while the iron is hot (and therefore malleable)

From MACBETH†

Act II, Scene i, 31–64

MACBETH Go bid thy mistress, when my drink is ready,
She strike upon the bell. Get thee to bed.
[*Exit* SERVANT

Is this a dagger which I see before me,
The handle toward my hand? Come, let me clutch thee.
I have thee not, and yet I see thee still.
Art thou not, fatal* vision, sensible† — ominous
To feeling as to sight? Or art thou but
A dagger of the mind, a false creation,
Proceeding from the heat-oppressed brain?
I see thee yet, in form as palpable
As this which now I draw.
Thou marshall'st me the way that I was going,
And such an instrument I was to use.
Mine eyes are made the fools o' th' other senses,
Or else worth all the rest. I see thee still;
And on thy blade and dudgeon* gouts* of blood, — hilt drops
Which was not so before. – There's no such thing:
It is the bloody business which informs†
Thus to mine eyes. Now o'er the one half-world* — hemisphere
Nature seems dead, and wicked dreams abuse
The curtained sleep. Witchcraft celebrates
Pale Hecate's† offerings; and withered Murder,
Alarumed† by his sentinel, the wolf,
Whose howl's his watch, thus with his stealthy pace,
With Tarquin's† ravishing strides, towards his design
Moves like a ghost. Thou sure and firm-set earth,
Hear not my steps, which way they walk, for fear
Thy very stones prate of my whereabout,
And take the present horror from the time,

Macbeth Macbeth (*c.* 1005–57) was King of Scotland from 1040 until his death. Shakespeare compresses the seventeen years of his reign into a short period, with a view to linking Macbeth's murder of King Duncan I (*c.* 1010–40) with Macbeth's eventual murder by Macduff. In this speech the first two lines are addressed to a servant, and the remainder is a soliloquy in which Macbeth hallucinates about the murder which he is about to commit

sensible capable of being perceived

informs assumes a shape

Hecate goddess of the new moon (hence *pale*) and patroness of witchcraft

alarumed roused to action

Tarquin Sextus Tarquinius, who ravished Lucretia, and thus precipitated the fall of the Roman monarchy; Shakespeare wrote a long poem about *The Rape of Lucrece*

Which now suits with it. Whiles I threat, he lives;
Words to the heat of deeds too cold breath gives.

[A bell rings

I go, and it is done; the bell invites me.
Hear it not, Duncan, for it is a knell
That summons thee to heaven, or to hell.

1606 1623

From ANTONY AND CLEOPATRA[†]

Act II, Scene ii, 187–248

ENOBARBUS When she first met Mark Antony, she pursed up[†] his heart upon the river of Cydnus.[†]

AGRIPPA There she appeared indeed! – or my reporter devised well for her.

ENOBARBUS I will tell you.
The barge she sat in, like a burnished throne,
Burned on the water. The poop was beaten gold;
Purple the sails, and so perfumèd that
The winds were lovesick with them. The oars were silver,
Which to the tune of flutes kept stroke, and made
The water which they beat to follow faster,
As* amorous of their strokes. For her own person, as if
It beggared all description. She did lie
In her pavilion – cloth-of-gold, of tissue –
O'erpicturing that Venus where we see
The fancy outwork nature. On each side her
Stood pretty dimpled boys, like smiling Cupids,
With divers-coloured fans, whose wind did seem
To glow the delicate cheeks which they did cool,
And what they undid did.

Antony and Cleopatra in this scene Enobarbus describes the meeting of Antony and Cleopatra in Tarsus in 41 BC. Enobarbus is Shakespeare's recreation of Domitius Ahenobarbus, the Roman statesman who initially took Antony's side in the war against Octavius Caesar, but then defected because of his opposition to Cleopatra's role in the war. Vipsanius Agrippa and Cinius Maecenas were described by the Greek historian Plutarch as the two closest friends of Octavius Caesar

pursed up took possession of

Cydnus a river in a part of Turkey which was then a Roman province

AGRIPPA O, rare for Antony!
ENOBARBUS Her gentlewomen, like the Nereides,†
So many mermaids, tended her i'the eyes,
And made their bends adornings. At the helm
A seeming mermaid steers. The silken tackle
Swell with the touches of those flower-soft hands,
That yarely frame the office.† From the barge
A strange invisible perfume hits the sense
Of the adjacent wharfs.* The city* cast   river-banks   Tarsus
Her people out upon her; and Antony,
Enthroned i' the market-place, did sit alone,
Whistling to the air; which, but for vacancy,†
Had gone to gaze on Cleopatra too
And made a gap in nature.
AGRIPPA Rare Egyptian!
ENOBARBUS Upon her landing, Antony sent to her,
Invited her to supper. She replied
It should be better he became her guest;
Which she entreated. Our courteous Antony,
Whom ne'er the word of 'No' woman heard speak,
Being barbered ten times o'er, goes to the feast,
And, for his ordinary,† pays his heart
For what his eyes eat only.
AGRIPPA Royal wench! –
She made great Caesar lay his sword to bed.
He ploughed her and she cropped.†
ENOBARBUS I saw her once
Hop forty paces through the public street,
And – having lost her breath – she spoke, and panted,
That she did make defect perfection,
And, breathless, power breathe forth.
MAECENAS Now Antony must leave her utterly.
ENOBARBUS Never; he will not.
Age cannot wither her, nor custom stale
Her infinite variety. Other women cloy
The appetites they feed, but she makes hungry
Where most she satisfies. For vilest things

Nereides benign sea-nymphs
yarely . . . office nimbly perform their duties
vacancy because nature was said to abhor a vacuum
ordinary fixed-price meal (here used humorously)
cropped On 23 June 47 BC. Cleopatra had given birth to a son whom she named Ptolemy Caesar, claiming that Julius Caesar was his father

Become themselves† in her, that the holy priests
Bless her when she is riggish.* wanton
MAECENAS If beauty, wisdom, modesty, can settle
The heart of Antony, Octavia is
A blessèd lottery† to him.

1606 1623

From CORIOLANUS†

Act II, Scene iii, 116–36

CITIZENS The gods give you joy, sir, heartily!

[CITIZENS *all go off*

CORIOLANUS Most sweet voices!
Better it is to die, better to starve,
Than crave the hire which first we do deserve.
Why in this wolvish toge* should I stand here toga
To beg of Hob and Dick† that does appear
Their needless vouches?* Custom calls me to't. ratification
What custom wills, in all things should we do't,
The dust on antique time† would lie unswept
And mountainous error be too highly heaped
For truth to o'erpeer. Rather than fool it so,
Let the high office and the honour go
To one that would do thus. I am half through –
The one part suffered, the other will I do.

Enter three CITIZENS *more*

Here come more voices.
Your voices! For your voices I have fought,
Watched for your voices; for your voices, bear
Of wounds two dozen odd. Battles thrice six
I have seen and heard of; for your voices have
Done many things, some less, some more – your voices!
Indeed I would be consul.

1608 1623

become themselves are made becoming
lottery that which has been awarded by lot
Coriolanus Caius Marcius Coriolanus was the eponymous hero of the Volscian city of Corioli, the capture of which earned his cognomen
Hob and Dick derisive allusion to the form of the names Robert and Richard among peasants
antique time antiquated traditions

From THE WINTER'S TALE†

Act IV, Scene iii

Enter AUTOLYCUS, *singing*

AUTOLYCUS

When daffodils begin to peer,* — appear
With heigh, the doxy† over the dale,
Why then comes in the sweet o' the year,
For the red blood reigns in the winter's pale.* — domain

The white sheet bleaching on the hedge,
With heigh, the sweet birds, O how they sing!
Doth set my pugging tooth† on edge,
For a quart of ale is a dish for a king.

The lark, that tirra-lirra chants,
With heigh, with heigh, the thrush and the jay,
Are summer songs for me and my aunts* — women
While we lie tumbling in the hay.

I have served Prince Florizel, and in my time wore three-pile,† but now I am out of service.

But shall I go mourn for that, my dear?
The pale moon shines by night:
And when I wander here and there
I then do most go right.

If tinkers may have leave to live,
And bear the sow-skin budget,* — pouch
Then my account I well may give,
And in the stocks avouch it.

My traffic is sheets; when the kite† builds, look to lesser linen. My father named me Autolycus,† who being, as I am, littered under Mercury,† was likewise a snapper-up of unconsidered trifles. With die

The Winter's Tale Autolycus is aptly described in the list of characters as 'a rogue'
doxy a beggar's mistress
my pugging tooth my urge to steal (the sheet)
three-pile velvet
kite a hawk reputed to steal small pieces of linen as material for its nest
Autolycus in Greek myth, the son of Mercury, and a skilful thief
littered under Mercury born when the dominant planet was Mercury, who (as a god) was the patron of thieves

and drab I purchased this caparison,† and my revenue is the silly cheat. Gallows and knock are too powerful on the highway; beating and hanging are terrors to me. For the life to come, I sleep out the thought of it. A prize! A prize!

1609 1623

From THE TEMPEST†

Act V, Scene i, 33–57

PROSPERO Ye elves of hills, brooks, standing lakes, and groves,
And ye that on the sands with printless foot
Do chase the ebbing Neptune,† and do fly him
When he comes back; you demi-puppets† that
By moonshine do the green sour ringlets† make,
Whereof the ewe not bites; and you whose pastime
Is to make midnight mushrooms,† that rejoice
To hear the solemn curfew, by whose aid
(Weak masters though ye be) I have bedimmed
The noontide sun, called forth the mutinous winds,
And 'twixt the green sea and the azured vault
Set roaring war; to the dread rattling thunder
Have I given fire, and rifted Jove's stout oak†
With his own bolt; the strong-based promontory
Have I made shake, and by the spurs* plucked up side-shoots
The pine and cedar; graves at my command
Have waked their sleepers, oped, and let 'em forth
By my so potent art. But this rough† magic
I here abjure: and when I have required
Some heavenly music – which even now I do –
To work mine end upon their senses, that
This airy charm is for, I'll break my staff,
Bury it certain fathoms in the earth,
And deeper than did ever plummet sound
I'll drown my book.

1611 1623

with die . . . caparison with gambling and whores I came to be dressed in these rags
The Tempest Prospero is the Duke of Milan, living in exile on an island
Neptune the sea; Neptune was the Roman god of the sea
demi-puppets fairies half the size of puppets
green sour ringlets fairy-rings, i.e. circles of grass discoloured by the effect of certain fungi, a phenomenon popularly attributed to fairies
midnight mushrooms mushrooms which appear overnight
Jove's stout oak the oak was sacred to Jove
rough dealing merely with the material world

From SONNETS

18

Shall I compare thee to a summer's day?
Thou art more lovely and more temperate.
Rough winds do shake the darling buds of May,
And summer's lease hath all too short a date:
Sometime too hot the eye of heaven shines,
And often is his gold complexion dimmed;
And every fair from fair some time declines,
By chance, or nature's changing course, untrimmed;†
But thy eternal summer shall not fade
Nor lose possession of that fair thou ow'st;* ownest
Nor shall Death brag thou wanderest in his shade,
When in eternal lines to time thou growest.†
  So long as men can breathe or eyes can see,
  So long lives this, and this gives life to thee.

30

When to the sessions of sweet silent thought
I summon up remembrance of things past,
I sigh the lack of many a thing I sought,
And with old woes new wail my dear time's waste.
Then can I drown an eye, unused to flow,
For precious friends hid in death's dateless* night, endless
And weep afresh love's long since cancelled woe,
And moan th' expense* of many a vanished sight. loss
Then can I grieve at grievances foregone,
And heavily from woe to woe tell* o'er count
The sad account of fore-bemoanèd moan,
Which I new pay as if not paid before.
  But if the while I think on thee, dear friend
  All losses are restored, and sorrows end.

untrimmed stripped of ornament *growest* become incorporated in

73

That time of year thou mayst in me behold
When yellow leaves, or none, or few, do hang
Upon those boughs which shake against the cold,
Bare ruined choirs where late the sweet birds sang.
In me thou seest the twilight of such day
As after sunset fadeth in the west,
Which by and by black night doth take away,
Death's second self, that seals up all in rest.
In me thou seest the glowing of such fire
That on the ashes of his* youth doth lie. its
As the death-bed whereon it must expire,
Consumed with that which it was nourished by.
  This thou perceivest which makes thy love more strong,
  To love that well which thou must leave ere long.

116

Let me not to the marriage of true minds
Admit impediments. Love is not love
Which alters when it alteration finds,
Or bends with the remover to remove.
O, no! It is an ever-fixèd mark,†
That looks on tempests and is never shaken;
It is the star to every wandering bark,
Whose worth's unknown, although his* height be taken. its
Love's not Time's fool, though rosy lips and cheeks
Within his bending sickle's compass come;
Love alters not with his brief hours and weeks,
But bears it out even to the edge of doom.
  If this be error, and upon me proved,
  I never writ, nor no man ever loved.

mark a device for marking a spot at sea

129

The expense of spirit in a waste of shame
Is lust† in action; and till action, lust
Is perjured, murderous, bloody, full of blame,
Savage, extreme, rude,* cruel, not to trust; brutal
Enjoyed no sooner but despisèd straight;
Past reason hunted, and, no sooner had,
Past reason hated, as a swallowed bait,
On purpose laid to make the taker mad –
Mad in pursuit, and in possession so;
Had, having, and in quest to have, extreme;
A bliss in proof, and proved, a very woe;
Before, a joy proposed; behind, a dream.
All this the world well knows; yet none knows well
To shun the heaven that leads men to this hell.

130

My mistress' eyes are nothing like the sun;
Coral is far more red than her lips' red;
If snow be white, why then her breasts are dun;
If hairs be wires, black wires grow on her head.
I have seen roses damasked,* red and white, variegated
But no such roses see I in her cheeks;
And in some perfumes is there more delight
Than in the breath that from my mistress reeks.* emanates
I love to hear her speak, yet well I know
That music hath a far more pleasing sound;
I grant I never saw a goddess go* – walk
My mistress when she walks treads on the ground.
And yet, by heaven, I think my love as rare†
As any she belied with false compare.

1609

lust is the grammatical subject of the sentence
my love as rare the object of my love as splendid

King James
1566–1625

James was born in Edinburgh Castle, the son of Henry Stewart (Lord Darnley) and Mary Queen of Scots; he received a formidable education from his tutor George Buchanan. When his mother was forced to abdicate on 24 July 1567 he became King James VI of Scotland; when Queen Elizabeth died on 24 March 1603 he was proclaimed James I of England.

James had a scholarly temperament, and produced a considerable body of poetry (in English, Scots and Latin) and prose; he also translated Du Bartas, Lucan and a selection of psalms. His best known works are a treatise on the art of government (*Basilikon Doron*, 1599), a tract opposing the new fashion of smoking (*A Counterblast to Tobacco*, 1604) and an attack on Buchanan's argument (in *De Jure Regni*) that the king is responsible to his people (*True Law of Free Monarchies*, 1598, of which James's authorship is not certain).

From A COUNTERBLAST TO TOBACCO†

[*The History of Tobacco*]

That the manifold abuses of this vile custom of tobacco-taking may the better be espied, it is fit that first you enter into consideration both of the first original thereof, and likewise of the reasons of the first entry thereof into this country. For certainly as such customs, that have their first institution either from a godly, necessary or honourable ground, and are first brought in, by the means of some worthy, virtuous and great personage, are ever, and most justly, holden in great and reverent estimation and account by all wise, virtuous and temperate spirits; so should it by the contrary, justly bring a great disgrace into that sort of customs, which having their original from base corruption and barbarity, do in like sort make their first entry into a country by an inconsiderate and childish affectation of novelty, as is the true case of the first

† *A Counterblast to Tobacco* tobacco was first brought to England from Virginia in 1586, and the habit of smoking it quickly became established among Elizabethan courtiers

invention of tobacco-taking, and of the first entry thereof among us. For tobacco being a common herb, which (though under divers names) grows almost everywhere, was first found out by some of the barbarous Indians, to be a preservative or antidote against the pox, a filthy disease whereunto these barbarous people are (as all men know) very much subject, what through the uncleanly and adust† constitution of their bodies, and what through the intemperate heat of their climate; so that from them was first brought into Christendom that most detestable disease, so from them likewise was brought this use of tobacco, as a stinking and unsavoury antidote, for so corrupted and execrable a malady, the stinking suffumigation† whereof they yet use against that disease, making so one canker or venom to eat out another.

And now good countrymen, let us (I pray you) consider what honour or policy can move us to imitate the barbarous and beastly manners of the wild, godless and slavish Indians, especially in so vile and stinking a custom? Shall we that disdain to imitate the manners of our neighbour France (having the style of the first Christian Kingdom) and that cannot endure the spirit of the Spaniards (their king being now comparable in largeness of dominions to the great emperor of Turkey), shall we, I say, that have been so long civil and wealthy in peace, famous and invincible in war, fortunate in both, we that have been ever able to aid any of our neighbours (but never deafed any of their ears with any of our supplications for assistance), shall we, I say, without blushing, abase ourselves so far as to imitate those beastly Indians, slaves to the Spaniards, refuse to the world, as yet aliens from the holy covenant of God? Why do we not as well imitate them in walking naked as they do? In preferring glasses, feathers and such toys to gold and precious jewels, as they do? Yea why do we not deny God and adore the devil, as they do?

[*The Filthy Habit*]

And for the vanities committed in this filthy custom, is it not both great vanity and uncleanness that at the table, a place of respect, of cleanliness, of modesty, men should not be ashamed to sit tossing of tobacco pipes, and puffing of the smoke of tobacco one to another, making the filthy smoke and stink thereof, to exhale athwart the dishes and infect the air when very often men that abhor it are at their repast? Surely smoke becomes a kitchen better than a dining chamber, and yet it makes a kitchen also oftentimes in the inward parts of men, soiling

adust dry
suffumigation medicinal fumes produced by burning plants

and infecting them with an unctuous and oily kind of soot, as hath been found in some great tobacco-takers that after their death were opened. And not only meat time, but no other time nor action is exempted from the public use of this uncivil trick: so as if the wives of Dieppe list† to contest with this nation for good manners, their worst manners would in all reason be found at least not as dishonest† as ours are on this point. The public use whereof at all times and in all places hath now so far prevailed, as divers men very sound both in judgement and complexion have been forced to take it also without desire, partly because they were ashamed to seem singular (like the two philosophers who were forced to duck themselves in that rainwater, and so become fools as well as the rest of the people) and partly to be as one that was content to eat garlic (which he did not love) that he might not be troubled with the smell of it in the breath of his fellows. And is it not a great vanity that a man cannot heartily welcome his friend now but straight they must be in hand with tobacco? No, it is become in place of a cure, a point of good fellowship, and he that will refuse to take a pipe of tobacco among his fellows (though by his own election he would rather feel the savour of a sink) is accounted peevish and no good company, even as they do with tippling in the cold eastern countries. Yea the mistress cannot in a more mannerly kind entertain her servant than by giving him out of her fair hand a pipe of tobacco. But herein is not only a great vanity, but a great contempt of God's good gifts, that the sweetness of man's breath, being a good gift of God, should be wilfully corrupted by this stinking smoke, wherein I must confess it hath too strong a virtue; and so that which is an ornament of nature, and can neither by any artifice be at the first acquired, nor once lost be recovered again, shall be filthily corrupted with an incurable stink, which vile quality is as directly contrary to that wrong opinion which is holden of the wholesomeness thereof, as the venom of putrefaction is contrary to the virtue preservative.

Moreover, which is a great iniquity and against all humanity, the husband shall not be ashamed to reduce thereby his delicate, wholesome and clean-complexioned wife to that extremity, that either she must also corrupt her sweet breath therewith, or else resolve to live in a perpetual stinking torment.

Have you not reason then to be ashamed, and to forbear this filthy novelty so basely grounded, so foolishly received and so grossly mistaken in the right use thereof? In your abuse thereof sinning against God, harming yourselves both in persons and goods, and taking also thereby

list wished *dishonest* shameful

the marks and notes of vanity upon you; by the custom thereof making yourselves to be wondered at by all foreign civil nations, and by all strangers that come among you to be scorned and condemned. A custom loathsome to the eye, hateful to the nose, harmful to the brain, dangerous to the lungs, and in the black stinking fume thereof nearest resembling the horrible Stygian† smoke of the pit that is bottomless.

1604

Stygian hellish; 'Styx' was the river in the classical underworld, but also a poetical name for the underworld itself

Thomas Nashe

(1567–1601)

Thomas Nashe was born in Lowestoft, the son of a curate. He was educated at St John's College, Cambridge, travelled in France and Italy, and in 1588 settled in London as a writer. His first publication, a preface to Robert Greene's *Menaphon*, was an attack on the writings of his contemporaries. He probably wrote one or more of the anti-Puritan attacks on the Marprelate tracts. He became involved in prolonged literary battles, the best product of which is *Pierce Penniless his supplication to the devil*. His prose ranges from the pious *Christ's Tears over Jerusalem* to his violent picaresque masterpiece, *The Unfortunate Traveller*; his Ovidian romance, *The Choice of Valentines*, is a witty and obscene poem. He collaborated in a controversial play, *The Isle of Dogs*, which was suppressed and is now lost.

From SUMMER'S LAST WILL AND TESTAMENT

[Spring]

THE SONG

Spring, the sweet spring, is the year's pleasant king,
Then blooms each thing, then maids dance in a ring;
Cold doth not sting, the pretty birds do sing,
Cuckoo, jug jug, pu we, to witta woo.

The palm and may† make country houses gay,
Lambs frisk and play, the shepherds pipe all day,
And we hear aye birds tune this merry lay,
Cuckoo, jug, jug, pu we, to witta woo.

palm and may celebrations of Palm Sunday and Mayday

The fields breathe sweet, the daisies kiss our feet,
Young lovers meet, old wives a-sunning sit;
In every street these tunes our ears do greet,
Cuckoo, jug, jug, pu we, to witta woo.
  Spring, the sweet spring.

[Autumn[†]]

THE SONG

Autumn hath all the Summer's fruitful treasure;
Gone is our sport, fled is poor Croydon's pleasure.
Short days, sharp days, long nights come on apace;
Ah, but who shall hide us from the winter's face?
Cold doth increase, the sickness will not cease,
And here we lie, God knows, with little ease:
    From winter, plague and pestilence, good Lord, deliver us.
London doth mourn, Lambeth is quite forlorn,
Trades cry 'Woe worth'[†] that ever they were born,
The want of term[†] is town and city's harm;
Close chambers we do want, to keep us warm;
Long banished must we live from our friends;
This low-built[†] house will bring us to our ends.
    From winter, plague and pestilence, good Lord, deliver us.

Adieu, farewell earth's bliss

Adieu, farewell earth's bliss,
This world uncertain is,
Fond are life's lustful joys,
Death proves them all but toys,* trifles
None from his darts can fly;
I am sick, I must die:
  Lord, have mercy on us.

Autumn in Nashe's time Croydon and Lambeth were villages to the south of London
Woe worth a curse upon (our birth)
term confined areas (to prevent the spread of plague)
low-built built on low ground, and therefore believed to be unhealthy

Rich men, trust not in wealth,
Gold cannot buy you health;
Physic† himself must fade,
All things to end are made,
The plague full swift goes by;
I am sick, I must die:
Lord, have mercy on us.

Beauty is but a flower,
Which wrinkles will devour,
Brightness falls from the air,†
Queens have died young and fair,
Dust hath closed Helen's† eye.
I am sick, I must die:
Lord, have mercy on us.

Strength stoops unto the grave,
Worms feed on Hector† brave,
Swords may not fight with fate,
Earth still holds ope* her gate. open
Come, come, the bells† do cry.
I am sick, I must die:
Lord, have mercy on us.

Wit with his wantonness,
Tasteth death's bitterness;
Hell's executioner
Hath no ears for to hear
What vain art can reply.
I am sick, I must die:
Lord, have mercy on us.

Haste therefore each degree,
To welcome destiny:
Heaven is our heritage,
Earth but a player's stage,
Mount we unto the sky.
I am sick, I must die:
Lord, have mercy on us.

1592 1600

physic the art of medicine
air possibly a misprint for 'hair'
Helen Helen of Troy, who was famed for her beauty
Hector the most valiant of the Trojan warriors in Homer's *Iliad*
bells passing bells, which were tolled to announce a death

From THE UNFORTUNATE TRAVELLER†

[*The Battle of Marignano*]

It was my good luck or my ill, I know not which, to come just to the fighting of the battle, where I saw a wonderful spectacle of bloodshed on both sides. Here unwieldly Switzers wallowing in their gore like an ox in his dung; there the sprightly French sprawling and turning on the stained grass like a roach new taken out of the stream. All the ground was strewed as thick with battle-axes as the carpenter's yard with chips: the plain appeared like a quagmire, overspread as it was with trampled dead bodies. In one place might you behold a heap of dead murthered men overwhelmed with a falling steed instead of a tombstone; in another place a bundle of bodies fettered together in their own bowels. And as the tyrant Roman Emperor used to tie condemned living caitiffs face to face to dead corpses, so were the half-living here mixed with squeezed carcases long putrefied. Any man might give arms that was an actor in that battle, for there were more arms and legs scattered in the field that day than will be gathered up till Doomsday. The French King himself in this conflict was much distressed; the brains of his own men sprinkled in his face; thrice was his courser slain under him, and thrice was he struck on the breast with a spear. But in the end, by the help of the Venetians, the Helvetians or Switzers were subdued, and he crowned a victor, a peace concluded, and the city of Millaine† surrendered unto him as a pledge of reconciliation.

1593 1594

From CHRIST'S TEARS OVER JERUSALEM

Ladies of the Court

Just to dinner they will arise, and after dinner go to bed again, and lie until supper. Yea, sometimes, by no sickness occasioned, they will lie in bed three days together, provided every morning before four o'clock they have their broths and their cullises† with pearl and gold sodden in

The Unfortunate Traveller the narrator, Jack Wilton, encounters on his travels the Battle of Marignano (13–14 September 1515), one of the decisive battles of the Italian Wars; the French, under Francis I, defeated an army of 25,000 Swiss infantrymen near Milan.

Millaine Milan

cullises strong meat broths

them. If haply† they break their hours and rise more early to go a-banqueting, they stand practising half a day with their looking-glasses, how to pierce and to glance and to look alluringly amiable. Their feet are not so well framed to the measures† as are their eyes to move and bewitch. Even as angels are painted in church-windows with glorious golden fronts beset with sunbeams, so beset they their foreheads on either side with glorious borrowed gleamy bushes; which, rightly interpreted, should signify beauty to sell, since a bush† is not else hanged forth but to invite men to buy. And in Italy, where they set any beast to sale, they crown his head with garlands, and bedeck it with gaudy blossoms, as full as ever it may stick.

Their heads, with their top and top-gallant† lawn† baby-caps and snow-resembled silver curlings, they make a plain puppet stage of. Their breasts they embusk up on high, and their round roseate buds immodestly lay forth, to show at their hands there is fruit to be hoped. In their curious† antic† woven garments, they imitate and mock the worms and adders that must eat them. They show the swellings of their mind in the swellings and plumpings out of their apparel. Gorgeous ladies of the Court, never was I admitted so near any of you as to see how you torture poor old Time with sponging, pinning and pouncing,† but they say, his sickle you have burst in twain to make your periwigs† more elevated arches of.

I dare not meddle with ye, since the philosopher† that too intentively gazed on the stars stumbled and fell into a ditch; and many gazing too immoderately on our earthly stars fall in the end into the ditch of all uncleanness. Only this humble caveat let me give you by the way, that you look the devil come not to you in the likeness of a tailor or painter; that however you disguise your bodies, you lay not on your colours so thick that they sink into your souls. That your skins being too white without, your souls be not all black within.

It is not your pinches,† your purls,† your flowery jaggings,† superfluous interlacings, and puffings up, that can any way offend God, but the puffings up of your souls which therein you express. For as the biting of a bullet is not that which poisons the bullet, but the lying of the gunpowder in the dint† of the biting, so it is not the wearing of costly

haply by chance
measures stately dances
bush the sign-board of a tavern
top and top-gallant names of sails
lawn linen
curious artfully made
antic grotesque
pouncing cutting the edges of a garment into points and scallops
periwigs wigs
philosopher Thales of Miletus, the earliest (sixth century BC) Greek physicist; Nashe's story derives from Plato's *Theaetetus*
pinches pleats
purls frills
jaggings fringes
dint indentation

burnished apparel that shall be objected unto you for sin, but the pride of your hearts which, like the moth, lies closely shrouded amongst the threads of that apparel. Nothing else is garish apparel but Pride's ulcer broken forth. How will you attire yourselves, what gown, what head-tire† will you put on, when you shall live in hell amongst hags and devils?

As many jags, blisters and scars shall toads, cankers and serpents make on your pure sins in the grave, as now you have cuts, jags or raisings upon your garments. In the marrow of your bones snakes shall breed. Your mornlike crystal countenances shall be netted over and, masker-like, caul-vizarded† with crawling venomous worms. Your orient† teeth toads shall steal into their heads for pearl; of the jelly of your decayed eyes shall they engender them young. In their hollow caves (their transplendent† juice so pollutionately† employed) shelly snails shall keep house.

1593 1593

head-tire head-dress
caul-vizarded having the face concealed under a netted veil
orient having the lustre of a pearl
transplendent brilliantly translucent
pollutionately foully

Thomas Campion

1567–1620

Thomas Campion was born in London, the son of a legal official. He was educated at Peterhouse, Cambridge, but did not proceed to a degree. After leaving Cambridge he entered Gray's Inn to study law, but was not called to the bar. He eventually turned to the study of medicine, and received an MD from the University of Caen in 1605.

Campion's early poetry was written in Latin, and his fondness for classical versification can be felt in his later English verse. He was a skilled composer, and many of his finest poems are set to music in his four *Books of Airs*. He wrote a treatise on English poetry (1602) which contains several of his own poems as illustrations. He also composed four masques for the court of King James.

FOLLOW YOUR SAINT

Follow your saint, follow with accents sweet;
Haste you, sad notes, fall at her flying feet.
Here, wrapped in cloud of sorrow, pity move,
And tell the ravisher of my soul I perish for her love.
But if she scorns my never-ceasing pain,
Then burst with sighing in her sight and ne'er return again.

All that I sang still to her praise did tend,
Still she was first, still she my songs did end.
Yet she my love and music both doth fly,
The music that her echo is, and beauty's sympathy.
Then let my notes pursue her scornful flight;
It shall suffice that they were breathed and died for her delight.

1601

ROSE-CHEEKED LAURA

Rose-cheeked Laura, come,
Sing thou smoothly with thy beauty's
Silent music, either other
Sweetly gracing.

Lovely forms do flow
From concent* divinely framèd; harmony
Heaven is music, and thy beauty's
Birth is heavenly.

These dull notes we sing
Discords need for helps to grace them;
Only beauty purely loving
Knows no discord.

But still moves delight,
Like clear springs renewed by flowing,
Ever perfect, ever in them-
Selves eternal.

1602

NOW WINTER NIGHTS

Now winter nights enlarge
The number of their hours,
And clouds their storms discharge
Upon the airy towers.
Let now the chimneys blaze,
And cups o'erflow with wine,
Let well-tuned words amaze
With harmony divine.
Now yellow waxen lights
Shall wait on honey love,
While youthful revels, masques and courtly sights
Sleep's leaden spells remove.

This time doth well dispense
With lovers' long discourse;
Much speech hath some defence,
Though beauty no remorse.
All do not all things well;
Some measures comely tread,
Some knotted riddles tell,
Some poems smoothly read.
The summer hath his joys
And winter his delights;
Though love and all his pleasures are but toys,* trifles
They shorten tedious nights.

1617

Ben Jonson
1572–1637

Benjamin Jonson was born in London and educated for a short time at Westminster School. On leaving school he followed his stepfather into the bricklaying trade, which he carried on (with a brief interval for military service in the Netherlands) until 1597, when he was employed by Philip Henslowe as an actor-writer. The following year he killed the actor Gabriel Spencer, and was sentenced to hang, but escaped execution by benefit of clergy, although he was dispossessed and branded; while in prison he was converted to Roman Catholicism. He began to write plays for children's companies, and for the Lord Chamberlain's Men, and thus became a colleague of Shakespeare; after the accession of King James, he wrote masques for the court for almost thirty years, often collaborating with Inigo Jones. In about 1610 he reverted to Anglicanism. In 1618 he walked to Scotland, where he stayed for a year and a half; there he met William Drummond, who recorded their conversations. In 1619 he was awarded an honorary MA by the University of Oxford, and began to teach rhetoric at Gresham College in London. In 1628 he was paralysed by a stroke, and was probably bedridden for the last nine years of his life.

Plays such as *Volpone* (1606), *The Alchemist* (1610) and *Bartholomew Fair* (1614) establish Jonson as the finest writer of satirical comedy of the English Renaissance, and he was also the greatest exponent of the masque. His poems, which are written in a deceptively plain style, are often imitations of the Latin and Greek poems of classical antiquity.

ON MY FIRST SON

Farewell, thou child of my right hand,† and joy;
My sin was too much hope of thee, loved boy.†
Seven years thou wert lent to me, and I thee pay,
Exacted by thy fate, on the just day.
O, could I lose all father, now. For why
Will man lament the state he should envy?
To have so soon 'scaped world's, and flesh's rage,
And, if no other misery, yet age!
Rest in soft peace, and, asked, say here doth lie
Ben Jonson his best piece of poetry.
For whose sake, henceforth, all his vows be such,
As what he loves may never like too much.

1603 1616

INVITING A FRIEND TO SUPPER

Tonight, grave sir, both my poor house, and I
Do equally desire your company:
Not that we think us worthy such a guest,
But that your worth will dignify our feast,
With those that come; whose grace may make that seem
Something, which, else, could hope for no esteem.
It is the fair acceptance, sir, creates
The entertainment perfect: not the cates.* delicacies
Yet shall you have, to rectify* your palate, cleanse
An olive, capers, or some better salad
Ush'ring the mutton; with a short-legged hen,
If we can get her, full of eggs, and then,
Lemons, and wine for sauce: to these, a cony
Is not to be despaired of, for our money;
And, though fowl, now, be scarce, yet there are clerks,
The sky not falling, think we may have larks.
I'll tell you of more, and lie, so you will come:
Of partridge, pheasant, woodcock, of which some

---

child of my right hand the boy's name was Benjamin, which means 'child of the right hand' in Hebrew

My sin . . . loved boy an imitation of a line by the Roman poet Martial (*c.* AD 40–104) which may be translated 'whatever you love, pray that it does not please you too much' (VI,xxix,8)

May yet be there; and godwit,† if we can:
Knat, rail,† and ruff too. Howsoe'er, my man†
Shall read a piece of Virgil, Tacitus,†
Livy, or of some better book to us,
Of which we'll speak our minds, amidst our meat;
And I'll profess no verses to repeat:
To this, if aught appear, which I not know of,
That will the pastry, not my paper, show of.
Digestive cheese, and fruit there sure will be;
But that, which most doth take my muse, and me,
Is a pure cup of rich canary† wine,
Which is the Mermaid's† now, but shall be mine:
Of which had Horace,† or Anacreon† tasted,
Their lives, as do their lines, till now had lasted.
Tobacco, nectar, or the Thespian spring,†
Are all but Luther's† beer, to this I sing.
Of this we will sup free, but moderately,
And we will have no Pooly,† or Parrot by;
Nor shall our cups make any guilty men:
But, at our parting, we will be, as when
We innocently met. No simple word,
That shall be uttered at our mirthful board,
Shall make us sad next morning: or affright
The liberty, that we'll enjoy tonight.

1616

godwit a kind of sandpiper, extolled as England's finest delicacy
knat, rail, ruff knot (*knat*) and ruff are species of sandpiper; as the other three birds are all waterside birds, *rail* must be the water-rail
man Jonson had trained his servant Richard Broom to read in Latin
Tacitus, Livy Roman historians
canary i.e. from the Canary Islands
Mermaid tavern on Bread Street frequented by Jonson, Ralegh, Donne and Shakespeare
Horace Roman poet
Anacreon Greek poet
Thespian spring Aganippe (near Thespiae), at the foot of Mount Helicon; its water inspired poets
Luther's perhaps 'inferior' because of its association with the Reformer
Pooly, Parrot Robert Pooly was a government spy; presumably the unidentified Parrot was another

TO PENSHURST†

Thou art not, Penshurst, built to envious show,
Of touch,† or marble; nor canst boast a row
Of polished pillars, or a roof of gold:
Thou hast no lantern,† whereof tales are told;
Or stair, or courts; but stand'st an ancient pile,
And these grudged at, art reverenced the while.
Thou joy'st in better marks, of soil, of air,
Of wood, of water: therein thou art fair.
Thou hast thy walks for health, as well as sport:
Thy mount, to which the dryads† do resort,
Where Pan,† and Bacchus† their high feasts have made,
Beneath the broad beech, and the chestnut shade;
That taller tree, which of a nut was set,
At his great birth,† where all the muses met.
There, in the writhèd bark, are cut the names
Of many a sylvan,† taken with his flames.†
And thence, the ruddy satyrs† oft provoke
The lighter fauns,† to reach thy lady's oak.†
Thy copse, too, named of Gamage,† thou hast there,
That never fails to serve thee seasoned deer,
When thou would'st feast, or exercise thy friends.
The lower land, that to the river bends,
Thy sheep, thy bullocks, kine, and calves do feed:
The middle grounds thy mares, and horses breed.
Each bank doth yield thee conies,* and the tops   rabbits
Fertile of wood, Ashore,† and Sidney's copse,†
To crown thy open table, doth provide
The purpled pheasant, with the speckled side:

Penshurst the country house of the Sidney family, in Kent. The head of the family was Robert Sidney (Viscount Lisle, later the Earl of Leicester; 1563–1626), the younger brother of Sir Philip Sidney
touch touchstone, here referring to black marble or basalt
lantern a small windowed tower surmounting a dome
dryads tree nymphs
Pan is here invoked as god of the countryside, and *Bacchus* as god of cultivation
at his great birth Sir Philip Sidney's birth at Penshurst in 1554 had been marked by the planting of an oak tree
sylvan a rural lover
flames flames of love
satyrs, fauns woodland attendants of Bacchus were known to the Greeks as satyrs and to the Romans as fauns
lady's oak 'My Lady's Oak' is the name of a tree at Penshurst, apparently so termed because a lady of the house went into labour under it
Gamage Viscount Lisle's wife was Lady Barbara Gamage, after whom a copse called 'Lady Gamage's Bower' is named
Ashore, Sidney's copse names of copses in the park

The painted partridge lies in every field,
And, for thy mess, is willing to be killed.
And if the high-swoll'n Medway[†] fail thy dish,
Thou hast thy ponds, that pay thee tribute fish,
Fat, agéd carps, that run into thy net.
And pikes, now weary their own kind to eat,
As loth, the second draught, or cast to stay,
Officiously,* at first, themselves betray. dutifully
Bright eels, that emulate them, and leap on land,
Before the fisher, or into his hand.
Then hath thy orchard fruit, thy garden flowers,
Fresh as the air, and new as are the hours.
The early cherry, with the later plum,
Fig, grape, and quince, each in his time doth come:
The blushing apricot, and woolly peach
Hang on thy walls, that every child may reach.
And though thy walls be of the country stone,
They are reared with no man's ruin, no man's groan,
There's none, that dwell about them, wish them down;
But all come in, the farmer, and the clown:* peasant
And no one empty-handed, to salute
Thy lord, and lady, though they have no suit.
Some bring a capon, some a rural cake,
Some nuts, some apples; some that think they make
The better cheeses, bring them; or else send
By their ripe daughters, whom they would commend
This way to husbands; and whose baskets bear
An emblem of themselves, in plum, or pear.
But what can this (more than express their love)
Add to thy free provisions, far above
The need of such? Whose liberal board doth flow,
With all, that hospitality doth know!
Where comes[†] no guest, but is allowed to eat,
Without his fear, and of thy lord's own meat:
Where the same beer, and bread, and self-same wine,
That is his lordship's, shall be also mine.
And I not fain to sit (as some, this day,
At great men's tables) and yet dine away.[†]

Medway a river close to Penshurst
Where comes . . . dine away Sir Robert Sidney does not subscribe to the custom of serving fine food to those at the family end of the long table and coarse food to those 'below the salt', but rather shares the fine food with all his guests

Here no man tells* my cups; nor, standing by, counts
A waiter, doth my gluttony envy;
But gives me what I call, and lets me eat,
He knows, below, he shall find plenty of meat,
Thy tables hoard not up for the next day,
Nor, when I take my lodging, need I pray
For fire, or lights, or livery:* all is there; food
As if thou, then, wert mine, or I reigned here:
There's nothing I can wish, for which I stay.* wait
That found King James, when hunting late, this way,
With his brave* son, the prince,† they saw thy fires splendid
Shine bright on every hearth as the desires
Of thy Penates† had been set on flame,
To entertain them; or the country came,
With all their zeal, to warm their welcome here.
What (great, I will not say, but) sudden cheer
Didst thou, then, make them! And what praise was heaped
On thy good lady, then! Who, therein, reaped
The just reward of her high huswifery;
To have her linen, plate, and all things nigh,
When she was far: and not a room, but dressed,
As if it had expected such a guest!
These, Penshurst, are thy praise, and yet not all.
Thy lady's noble, fruitful, chaste withal.
His children thy great lord may call his own:
A fortune, in this age, but rarely known.
They are, and have been taught religion: thence
Their gentler spirits have sucked innocence.
Each morn, and even, they are taught to pray,
With the whole household, and may, every day,
Read, in their virtuous parents' noble parts,
The mysteries of manners, arms, and arts.
Now, Penshurst, they that will proportion thee
With other edifices, when they see
Those proud, ambitious heaps, and nothing else,
May say, their lords have built, but thy lord dwells.

1611–12 1616

prince Henry (1594–1612), who had been created Prince of Wales in 1610

Penates Roman household gods (pronounced as three syllables)

EPITAPH ON S.P., A CHILD OF Q[UEEN] EL[IZABETH'S] CHAPEL†

Weep with me all you that read
  This little story:
And know, for whom a tear you shed,
  Death's self is sorry.
'Twas a child, that so did thrive
  In grace, and feature,
As Heaven and Nature seemed to strive
  Which owned the creature.
Years he numbered scarce thirteen
  When Fates turned cruel,
Yet three filled zodiacs† had he been
  The stage's jewel;
And did act (what now we moan)
  Old men so duly,* skilfully
As, sooth, the Parcae† thought him one,
  He played so truly.
So, by error, to his fate
  They all consented;
But viewing him since (alas, too late)
  They have repented.
And have sought (to give new birth)
  In baths to steep him;
But, being so much too good for earth,
  Heaven vows to keep him.

1602 1616

Epitaph on S.P. 'S.P.' is Salathiel Pavy, a member of the Children of the Chapel, a company of boy actors; he played the part of Anaides in Jonson's *Cynthia's Revels*

three filled zodiacs for three years

Parcae the 'Fates' of line 10, goddesses who determined the lifespan of mortals

EPITAPH ON ELIZABETH, L.H.†

Wouldst thou hear, what man can say
In a little? Reader, stay.
Underneath this stone doth lie
As much beauty, as could die:
Which in life did harbour give
To more virtue, than doth live.
If, at all, she had a fault,
Leave it buried in this vault.
One name was Elizabeth,
The other let it sleep with death:
Fitter, where it died, to tell,
Than that it lived at all. Farewell.

1616

SONG. TO CELIA†

Drink to me, only, with thine eyes,
  And I will pledge with mine;
Or leave a kiss but in the cup,
  And I'll not look for wine.
The thirst, that from the soul doth rise,
  Doth ask a drink divine:
But might I of Jove's nectar sup,
  I would not change for thine.
I sent thee, late, a rosy wreath,
  Not so much honouring thee,
As giving it a hope, that there
  It could not withered be.
But thou thereon didst only breathe,
  And send'st it back to me:
Since when it grows, and smells, I swear,
  Not of itself, but thee.

1616

Epitaph on Elizabeth, L.H. the identity of 'L.H.' is not known

Song. To Celia the song is loosely based on the erotic *Epistles* of Philostratus, a Greek writer of the second century AD

TO THE MEMORY OF MY BELOVÈD, THE AUTHOR MR WILLIAM SHAKESPEARE: AND WHAT HE HATH LEFT US

To draw no envy (Shakespeare) on thy name,
Am I thus ample to thy book, and fame:
While I confess thy writings to be such,
As neither man, nor muse, can praise too much.
'Tis true, and all men's suffrage. But these ways
Were not the paths I meant unto thy praise:
For seeliest* ignorance on these may light, blindest
Which, when it sounds at best, but echoes right;
Or blind affection, which doth ne'er advance
The truth, but gropes, and urgeth all by chance;
Or crafty malice, might pretend this praise,
And think to ruin, where it seemed to raise.
These are, as some infamous bawd, or whore,
Should praise a matron. What could hurt her more?
But thou art proof against them, and indeed
Above the ill fortune of them, or the need.
I therefore will begin. Soul of the age!
The applause, delight, the wonder of our stage!
My Shakespeare, rise; I will not lodge thee by
Chaucer,† or Spenser,† or bid Beaumont† lie
A little further, to make thee a room:
Thou art a monument, without a tomb,
And art alive still, while thy book doth live,
And we have wits to read, and praise to give.
That I not mix thee so, my brain excuses;
I mean with great, but disproportioned muses:
For, if I thought my judgement were of years,
I should commit thee surely with thy peers,
And tell, how far thou didst our Lyly† outshine,
Or sporting Kyd,† or Marlowe's mighty line.
And though thou hadst small Latin, and less Greek,
From thence to honour thee, I would not seek

Chaucer, Spenser, Beaumont all three are buried in Westminster Abbey; Francis Beaumont had died only six weeks before Shakespeare

Lyly the poet and dramatist John Lyly

Kyd 'sporting' refers not to his plays (such as *The Spanish Tragedy*) but to his name (i.e. 'small goat')

For names; but call forth thundering Aeschylus,
Euripides, and Sophocles to us,
Pacuvius, Accius,† him of Cordova† dead,
To life again, to hear thy buskin† tread,
And shake a stage: or, when thy socks† were on,
Leave thee alone, for the comparison
Of all that insolent Greece, or haughty Rome
Sent forth, or since did from their ashes come.
Triumph, my Britain, thou hast one to show,
To whom all scenes of Europe homage owe.
He was not of an age, but for all time!
And all the muses still were in their prime,
When like Apollo† he came forth to warm
Our ears, or like a Mercury† to charm!
Nature herself was proud of his designs,
And joyed to wear the dressing of his lines!
Which were so richly spun, and woven so fit,
As, since, she will vouchsafe no other wit.
The merry Greek, tart Aristophanes,†
Neat Terence, witty Plautus,† now not please;
But antiquated, and deserted lie
As they were not of nature's family.
Yet must I not give nature all: thy art,
My gentle Shakespeare, must enjoy a part.
For though the poet's matter, nature be,
His art doth give the fashion. And, that he,
Who casts to write a living line, must sweat,
(Such as thine are) and strike the second heat
Upon the muses' anvil: turn the same,
(And himself with it) that he thinks to frame;
Or for the laurel he may gain a scorn,
For a good poet's made, as well as born.
And such wert thou. Look how the father's face
Lives in his issue, even so, the race
Of Shakespeare's mind, and manners brightly shines
In his well-turnéd, and true-filéd lines:

Pacuvius and *Accius* Roman tragedians whose plays survive only in fragments; the Roman philosopher and tragedian Seneca was born in *Cordova*
buskin the high thick-soled boot worn in Athenian tragedy
socks the low-heeled shoe (Latin *soccus*) worn in Athenian comedy
Apollo god of music, and god of the sun
Mercury the Roman god Mercury was associated with enchantment
Aristophanes Greek comic dramatist
Terence, *Plautus* Roman comic dramatists

In each of which, he seems to shake a lance,[†]
As brandished at the eyes of ignorance.
Sweet swan of Avon,[†] what a sight it were
To see thee in our waters yet appear,
And make those flights upon the banks of Thames,
That so did take Eliza,[†] and our James![†]
But stay, I see thee in the hemisphere
Advanced, and made a constellation there!
Shine forth, thou star of poets, and with rage,[†]
Or influence,[†] chide, or cheer the drooping stage;
Which, since thy flight from hence, hath mourned like night.
And despairs day, but for thy volume's light.

1623

From TIMBER: OR DISCOVERIES

[*On Shakespeare*]

I remember, the players have often mentioned it as an honour to Shakespeare, that in his writing (whatsoever he penned) he never blotted out line. My answer hath been, would he had blotted a thousand. Which they thought a malevolent speech. I had not told posterity this, but for their ignorance, who choose that circumstance to commend their friend by, wherein he most faulted. And to justify mine own candour (for I loved the man, and do honour his memory – on this side idolatry – as much as any). He was (indeed) honest, and of an open, and free nature: had an excellent fancy; brave notions, and gentle expressions: wherein he flowed with that facility, that sometime it was necessary he should be stopped: *sufflaminandus erat*;[†] as Augustus said of Haterius.[†] His wit was in his own power; would the rule of it had

shake a lance a pun on Shakespeare's name
Avon the river which runs through Stratford, Shakespeare's birthplace
Eliza, James Queen Elizabeth and her successor King James
Shine . . . rage in the ancient world heroes were deemed to rise to a place in the stars after death
influence i.e. the astrological influence of the star
sufflaminandus erat Latin 'what he needs is a brake'
Haterius Roman orator and declaimer

been so too. Many times he fell into those things, could not escape laughter: as when he said in the person of Caesar, one speaking to him; 'Caesar, thou dost me wrong'. He replied: 'Caesar did never wrong, but with just cause': and such like; which were ridiculous. But he redeemed his vices, with his virtues. There was ever more in him to be praised, than to be pardoned.

1640

From VOLPONE†

Act III, Scene vii, 185–279

VOLPONE: Why droops my Celia?
Thou hast in place of a base husband found
A worthy lover; use thy fortune well,
With secrecy and pleasure. See, behold,
What thou art queen of; not in expectation,
As I feed others, but possessed and crowned.
See, here, a rope of pearl, and each more orient†
Than that the brave† Egyptian queen caroused;
Dissolve and drink 'em.† See, a carbuncle†
May put out both the eyes of our St Mark;†
A diamond would have bought Lollia Paulina†
When she came in like star-light, hid with jewels
That were the spoils of provinces; take these,
And wear, and lose 'em; yet remains an ear-ring
To purchase them again, and this whole state.
A gem but worth a private patrimony
Is nothing: we will eat such at a meal.

Volpone in this scene Volpone, whose name (meaning 'fox' in Italian) is indicative of his cunning, attempts to seduce the virtuous Celia, but is prevented from doing so by Bonario, a young gentleman

orient pearls from the east were particularly valuable

brave splendidly costumed

dissolve and drink 'em like Cleopatra, who once met Antony's challenge to spend ten million sesterces on a meal by drinking a priceless pearl dissolved in vinegar

carbuncle precious red stone

St Mark the precise reference is unclear, but it may refer to the relics of St Mark in the Venetian cathedral named after him

Lollia Paulina an immensely wealthy first-century Roman woman

The heads of parrots, tongues of nightingales,
The brains of peacocks, and of ostriches
Shall be our food, and, could we get the phœnix,†
Though nature lost her kind, she were our dish.

CELIA: Good sir, these things might move a mind affected
With such delights; but I, whose innocence
Is all I can think wealthy, or worth th' enjoying,
And which, once lost, I have nought to lose beyond it,
Cannot be taken with these sensual baits.
If you have conscience –

VOLPONE: 'Tis the beggar's virtue.
If thou hast wisdom, hear me, Celia.
Thy baths shall be the juice of July-flowers,†
Spirit of roses, and of violets,
The milk of unicorns, and panthers' breath
Gathered in bags and mixed with Cretan wines.
Our drink shall be preparèd gold and amber,
Which we will take until my roof whirl round
With the vertigo; and my dwarf shall dance,
My eunuch sing, my fool make up the antic.†
Whilst we, in changèd shapes, act Ovid's tales,†
Thou like Europa† now, and I like Jove,
Then I like Mars,† and thou like Erycine;†
So of the rest, till we have quite run through,
And wearied all the fables of the gods.
Then will I have thee in more modern forms,
Attirèd like some sprightly dame of France,
Brave Tuscan lady, or proud Spanish beauty;
Sometimes unto the Persian Sophy's† wife,
Or the Grand Signior's† mistress; and, for change,
To one of our most artful courtesans,
Or some quick* Negro, or cold Russian; vigorous
And I will meet thee in as many shapes;
Where we may so transfuse our wand'ring souls
Out at our lips and score up sums of pleasures,

phoenix a mythical bird which came to Egypt every 500 or 1641 years, was consumed by fire in its nest, and rose again from its ashes
July-flowers gillyflowers, which are clove-scented
antic grotesque dance
Ovid's tales the *Metamorphoses* of the Roman poet Ovid contains many such tales
Europa a mortal abducted by *Jove*, who disguised himself as a bull, enticed her onto his back, and carried her off to Crete
Erycine Venus, here named after her temple at Eryx (in Sicily), was the wife of *Mars*, god of war
Sophy shah, the supreme ruler of Persia
Grand Signior the Sultan of Turkey

[*Sings*] That the curious shall not know
How to tell them as they flow;
And the envious, when thy find
What their number is, be pined.

CELIA: If you have ears that will be pierced, or eyes
That can be opened, a heart may be touched,
Or any part that yet sounds man about you;
If you have touch of holy saints, or heaven,
Do me the grace to let me 'scape. If not,
Be bountiful and kill me. You do know
I am a creature hither ill betrayed
By one whose shame I would forget it were.
If you will deign me neither of these graces,
Yet feed your wrath, sir, rather than your lust,
(It is a vice comes nearer manliness)
And punish that unhappy crime of nature,
Which you miscall my beauty: flay my face,
Or poison it with ointments for seducing
Your blood to this rebellion. Rub these hands
With what may cause an eating leprosy,
E'en to my bones and marrow; anything
That may disfavour* me, save in my honour, disfigure
And I will kneel to you, pray for you, pay down
A thousand hourly vows, sir, for your health;
Report, and think you virtuous –

VOLPONE: Think me cold,
Frozen, and impotent, and so report me?
That I had Nestor's† hernia thou wouldst think.
I do degenerate and abuse my nation
To play with opportunity thus long;
I should have done the act, and then have parleyed.
Yield, or I'll force thee.
[*He seizes her.*]

CELIA: O! just God!

VOLPONE: In vain –

BONARIO: Forbear, foul ravisher! libidinous swine!
He leaps out from where MOSCA *had placed him.*
Free the forcèd lady, or thou diest, impostor.
But that I am loath to snatch thy punishment
Out of the hand of justice, thou shouldst yet
Be made the timely sacrifice of vengeance,
Before this altar, and this dross, thy idol.

Nestor the ancient warrior of the Trojan War

Lady, let's quit the place, it is the den
Of villainy; fear nought, you have a guard;
And he ere long shall meet his just reward.
[BONARIO *and* CELIA *go off.*]
VOLPONE: Fall on me, roof, and bury me in ruin!
Become my grave, that wert my shelter! O!
I am unmasked, unspirited, undone,
Betrayed to beggary, to infamy –

1606 1607

From THE ALCHEMIST†

Act IV, Scene vii, 1–72

[*Re-enter* FACE *with* KASTRIL.]
[FACE:] Why, now's the time, if ever you will quarrel
Well, as they say, and be a true-born child.
The Doctor and your sister both are abused.
KASTRIL: Where is he? Which is he? He is a slave.
Whate'er he is, and the son of a whore. – Are you
The man, sir, I would know?
SURLY: I should be loath, sir,
To confess so much.
KASTRIL: Then you lie i' your throat.
SURLY: How!
FACE: [*to* KASTRIL]: A very arrant rogue, sir, and a cheater,
Employed here by another conjurer
That does not love the Doctor, and would cross him,
If he knew how.
SURLY: Sir, you are abused.
KASTRIL: You lie:
And 'tis no matter.
FACE: Well said, sir! He is
The impudent'st rascal –
SURLY: You are indeed. Will you hear me, sir?
FACE: By no means. Bid him be gone.
KASTRIL: Begone, sir, quickly.

† *The Alchemist* Subtle, the alchemist of the title, and Face, a servant who has been left in charge of the house of his master Lovewit, attempt to dupe the other characters, including Kastril (a country bumpkin), Drugger (a tobacconist), Surly (a gambler) and Ananias (a Puritan)

SURLY: This's strange! – Lady, do you inform your brother.
FACE: There is not such a foist† in all the town.
The Doctor had him presently; and finds yet
The Spanish Count will come here. – [*Aside*] Bear up, Subtle.
SUBTLE: Yes, sir, he must appear within this hour.
FACE: And yet this rogue would come in a disguise,
By the temptation of another spirit,
To trouble our art, though he could not hurt it.
KASTRIL: Ay,
I know – [*To his sister*] Away, you talk like a foolish mauther.* girl
SURLY: Sir, all is truth she says.
FACE: Do not believe him, sir.
He is the lying'st swabber!† Come your ways, sir.
SURLY: You are valiant out of company!
KASTRIL: Yes, how then, sir?
[*Enter* DRUGGER *with a piece of damask*.]
FACE: Nay, here's an honest fellow, too, that knows him,
And all his tricks. – [*Aside to* DRUGGER] Make good what I say,
Abel;
This cheater would ha' cozened thee o' the window. –
He owes this honest Drugger here seven pound,
He has had on him in twopenny'orths of tobacco.
DRUGGER: Yes, sir. And he's damned himself three terms to pay me.
FACE: And what does he owe for lotion?
DRUGGER: Thirty shillings, sir;
And for six syringes.
SURLY: Hydra† of villainy!
FACE: Nay, sir, you must quarrel him out o' the house.
KASTRIL: I will.
– Sir, if you get not out o' doors, you lie;
And you are a pimp.
SURLY: Why, this is madness, sir,
Not valour in you. I must laugh at this.
KASTRIL: It is my humour; you are a pimp and a trig* dandy
And an Amadis de Gaul,† or a Don Quixote
DRUGGER: Or a knight o' the curious coxcomb, do you see?
[*Enter* ANANIAS.]
ANANIAS: Peace to the household!
KASTRIL: I'll keep peace for no man.

foist a cheat or rogue
swabber a term of contempt (naval term for someone who cleans the decks)
hydra mythical giant water serpent with several heads
Amadis de Gaul eponymous hero of the Spanish romance *Amadis de Gaula*

ANANIAS: Casting of dollars is concluded lawful.
KASTRIL: Is he the Constable?
SUBTLE: Peace, Ananias.
FACE: No, sir.
KASTRIL: Then you are an otter,† and a shad,† a whit,†
A very tim.†
SURLY: You'll hear me, sir?
KASTRIL: I will not.
ANANIAS: What is the motive?
SUBTLE: Zeal in the young gentleman,
Against his Spanish slops.
ANANIAS: They are profane,
Lewd, superstitious, and idolatrous breeches.
SURLY: New rascals!
KASTRIL: Will you be gone, sir?
ANANIAS: Avoid, Satan!
Thou art not of the light! That ruff of pride
About thy neck betrays thee, and is the same
With that which the unclean birds,† in seventy-seven,†
Were seen to prank it with on divers coasts:
Thou look'st like Antichrist,* in that lewd hat. i.e. the Pope
SURLY: I must give way.
KASTRIL: Be gone, sir.
SURLY: But I'll take
A course with you –
ANANIAS: Depart, proud Spanish fiend!
SURLY: Captain and Doctor –
ANANIAS: Child of perdition!
KASTRIL: Hence, sir! –
[*Exit* SURLY.]
Did I not quarrel bravely?
FACE: Yes, indeed, sir.
KASTRIL: Nay, an' I give my mind to't, I shall do't.
FACE: O, you must follow, sir, and threaten him tame.
He'll turn again else.
KASTRIL: I'll re-turn him then.
[*Exit.*]
FACE: Drugger, this rogue prevented us, for thee.
We had determined that thou should'st ha' come
In a Spanish suit, and ha' carried her so; and he,
A brokerly slave, goes, puts it on himself.

otter, shad, whit, tim the precise sense of these abusive terms is unknown

unclean birds see Revelation 18.2

seventy-seven 1577 (allusion unknown)

Hast brought the damask?
DRUGGER: Yes, sir.
FACE: Thou must borrow
A Spanish suit. Hast thou no credit with the players?
DRUGGER: Yes, sir; did you never see me play the Fool?
FACE: I know not, Nab. – [*Aside*] Thou shalt, if I can help it. –
Hieronimo's† old cloak, ruff, and hat will serve;
I'll tell thee more when thou bring'st 'em.
[*Exit* DRUGGER.]

1610 1612

From BARTHOLOMEW FAIR

The Induction† on the Stage

[*Enter* STAGE-KEEPER.]

STAGE-KEEPER:] Gentlemen, have a little patience, they are e'en upon coming, instantly. He that should begin the play, Master Littlewit,† the Proctor,† has a stitch new fall'n in his black silk stocking; twill be drawn up ere you can tell twenty. He plays one o' the Arches,† that dwells about the Hospital,† and he has a very pretty part. But for the whole play, will you ha' the truth on't? (I am looking, lest the poet hear me, or his man, Master Brome,† behind the arras) it is like to be a very conceited† scurvy one, in plain English. When't comes to the Fair once, you were e'en as good go to Virginia, for anything there is of Smithfield. He has not hit the humours,† he does not know 'em; he has not conversed with the Barthol'mew-birds, as they say; he has ne'er a sword-and-buckler man in his Fair, nor a little Davy† to take toll o' the bawds there, as in my time, nor a Kindheart,† if anybody's teeth should chance to ache in his play. Nor a juggler with a well-educated ape to come over the chain for the King of England and back again for the Prince, and sit still on his arse for the Pope and the King of Spain! None o' these fine sights! Nor has he the canvas-cut i' the night for a hobby-horse-man to creep in to his she-neighbour and take his leap there! Nothing! No, an' some writer (that I know) had had but the penning o' this matter, he

Hieronimo hero of Thomas Kyd's *The Spanish Tragedy*, a part which Jonson had acted
Induction an 'induction' is an introduction or prologue; Jonson introduced many of his plays in this manner
Littlewit a legal official (*proctor*) serving in the ecclesiastical Court of *Arches*; the *Hospital* is St Bartholomew's, in Smithfield, where the annual fair took place on 24 August, St Bartholomew's Day
Brome Richard Brome, playwright and secretary to Jonson
conceited fanciful
humours idiosyncrasies
little Davy a notorious bully
Kindheart an itinerant dentist

would ha' made you such a jig-a-jog i' the booths, you should ha' thought an earthquake had been i' the Fair! But these master-poets, they will ha' their own absurd courses; they will be informed of nothing! He has, sir reverence,† kicked me three or four times about the tiring-house,† I thank him, for but offering to put in, with my experience. I'll be judged by you, gentlemen, now, but for one conceit of mine! Would not a fine pump upon the stage ha' done well for a property now? And a punk† set under upon her head, with her stern upward, and ha' been soused by my witty young masters o' the Inns o' Court?† What think you o' this for a show, now? He will not hear o' this! I am an ass, I? And yet I kept the stage in Master Tarlton's† time, I thank my stars. Ho! an'† that man had lived to have played in *Barthol'mew Fair*, you should ha' seen him ha' come in, and ha' been cozened i' the cloth-quarter,† so finely! And Adams,† the rogue, ha' leaped and capered upon him, and ha' dealt his vermin about as though they had cost him nothing. And then a substantial watch to ha' stol'n in upon 'em, and taken 'em away with mistaking words, as the fashion is in the stage-practice.

[*Enter*] BOOK-HOLDER† [*and*] SCRIVENER† *to him.*

BOOK-HOLDER: How now? What rare discourse you are fall'n upon, ha! Ha' you found any familiars here, that you are so free? What's the business?

STAGE-KEEPER: Nothing, but the understanding† gentlemen o' the ground here asked my judgement.

BOOK-HOLDER: Your judgement, rascal? For what? Sweeping the stage? Or gathering up the broken apples for the bears within?† Away rogue, it's come to a fine degree in these spectacles when such a youth as you pretend to a judgement.

[*Exit* STAGE-KEEPER.]

And yet he may, i' the most o' this matter i' faith; for the author hath writ it just to his meridian, and the scale of the grounded judgements here, his play-fellows in wit. – Gentlemen, not for want of a prologue, but by way of a new one, I am sent out to you here with a scrivener, and certain articles drawn out in haste between our author and you; which if you please to hear, and as they appear reasonable, to approve of, the play will follow presently.

1614 1631

sir-reverence with apologies
tiring-house backstage area which contained the dressing rooms
punk prostitute
Inns of Court houses for law students
Tarlton Richard Tarlton, a comic actor who had died in 1588
'an if
cloth-quarter the market-stalls on the north wall of St Bartholomew's Church; one of *Tarlton's Jests* (1613) relates how his clothes were stolen there
Adams John Adams, who acted with Tarlton
Book-holder prompter
Scrivener notary
understanding a punning reference to spectators standing in the pit
bears within the play was performed at the Hope Theatre, which doubled as a bear-baiting arena

John Donne

1572–1631

John Donne was born into a Roman Catholic family in London. He was educated at home by Catholic tutors. At the age of twelve he entered Hart Hall, Oxford, which had no chapel and was therefore suitable for Catholics. He did not take a degree, as he could not subscribe to the Thirty-nine Articles or the Oath of Supremacy, both of which were obligatory. After three years at Oxford Donne migrated to Cambridge, where he was not attached to a college (the oaths in Cambridge were administered by colleges, not by the university as in Oxford) and did not take a degree. From 1589 to 1591 he probably travelled in Spain and Italy, and on his return studied law at Lincoln's Inn for four years, during which time he renounced Roman Catholicism. He served as a soldier on expeditions to Cadiz (1596) and the Azores (1597). In 1597 he became secretary to Sir Thomas Egerton, Lord Keeper of the Great Seal, and later entered Parliament. In 1601 he secretly married Ann More, Lady Egerton's niece. Ann More's father strongly disapproved of the marriage, and marriage without the consent of the bride's father was an offence against both canon law and social decorum. Donne was dismissed from his post as Egerton's secretary, imprisoned for a short period, and for the next fourteen years suffered irregular employment. In 1615 he entered the church in compliance with the wish of the king, who forced the University of Cambridge to award a DD to Donne. In 1621 Donne successfully cultivated (and possibly bribed) the Duke of Buckingham, who used his influence to have Donne appointed as Dean of St Paul's Cathedral, where he became the most celebrated preacher of his generation.

The poems in *Songs and Sonnets*, most of which cannot be dated, were published posthumously, as were his sermons. His *Satires* and *Elegies* date from the 1590s, and the *Anniversaries* were written in 1601. Most of the Divine Poems were written between 1606 and 1611. His prose works include a treatise on suicide (*Biathanatos*, *c.* 1608), two anti-Roman Catholic tracts (*Pseudo-Martyr*, 1610, and *Ignatius His Conclave*, 1611) and his *Devotions upon Emergent Occasions* (1624).

From SONGS AND SONNETS

Air and Angels

Twice or thrice had I loved thee,
Before I knew thy face or name;
So in a voice, so in a shapeless flame,
Angels affect† us oft, and worshipped be;
  Still* when, to where thou wert, I came, always
Some lovely glorious nothing I did see,
  But since my soul, whose child love is,
Takes limbs of flesh, and else could nothing do,
  More subtle* than the parent is rarefied
Love must not be, but take a body too,
  And therefore what thou wert, and who
    I bid love ask, and now
That it assume thy body, I allow,
And fix itself in thy lip, eye, and brow.

Whilst thus to ballast love, I thought,
And so more steadily to have gone,
With wares which would sink admiration,
I saw, I had love's pinnace† overfraught,
  Every thy hair for love to work upon
Is much too much, some fitter must be sought;
  For, nor in nothing, nor in things
Extreme, and scattering bright, can love inhere;
  Then as an angel, face and wings
Of air, not pure as it, yet pure doth wear,
  So thy love may be my love's sphere;
    Just such disparity
As is 'twixt air and angels' purity,
'Twixt women's love, and men's will ever be.

1633

The Bait†

Come live with me, and be my love,
And we will some new pleasures prove
Of golden sands, and crystal brooks,
With silken lines, and silver hooks.

---

affect means both 'influence' and 'love'
pinnace a small sailing boat

The Bait this poem is a response to Marlowe's 'The Passionate Shepherd to his Love'

There will the river whispering run
Warmed by thy eyes, more than the sun.
And there th'enamoured fish will stay,
Begging themselves they may betray.

When thou wilt swim in that live bath,
Each fish, which every channel hath,
Will amorously to thee swim,
Gladder to catch thee, than thou him.

If thou, to be so seen, be'st loth,
By sun, or moon, thou darkenest both,
And if myself have leave to see,
I need not their light, having thee.

Let others freeze with angling reeds,†
And cut their legs, with shells and weeds,
Or treacherously poor fish beset,
With strangling snare, or windowy net:

Let coarse bold hands, from slimy nest
The bedded fish in banks out-wrest,
Or curious† traitors, sleavesilk flies†
Bewitch poor fishes' wandering eyes.

For thee, thou need'st no such deceit,
For thou thyself art thine own bait,
That fish, that is not catched thereby,
Alas, is wiser far than I.

1612

reeds fishing rods made from reeds
curious artfully constructed
sleavesilk flies lures made out of sleaved (i.e. unravelled) silk

The Canonization

For God's sake hold your tongue, and let me love,
Or chide my palsy, or my gout,
My five grey hairs, or ruined fortune flout,
With wealth your state, your mind with arts improve
Take you a course,† get you a place,†
Observe his Honour, or his Grace,†
Or the King's real, or his stampèd face†
Contemplate; what you will, approve,* try out
So you will let me love.

Alas, alas, who's injured by my love?
What merchant's ships have my sighs drowned?
Who says my tears have overflowed his ground?
When did my colds a forward spring remove?
When did the heats which my veins fill
Add one more to the plaguy bill?†
Soldiers find wars, and lawyers find out still
Litigious men, which quarrels move,
Though she and I do love.

Call us what you will, we are made such by love;
Call her one, me another fly,†
We are tapers* too, and at our own cost die,† candles
And we in us find the eagle† and the dove,†
The phoenix riddle† hath more wit
By us; we two being one, are it.
So to one neutral thing both sexes fit
We die and rise the same, and prove
Mysterious by this love.

course a method for advancing yourself
place place at court
Observe . . . Grace i.e. court a nobleman or a bishop
stampèd face i.e. on coins
plaguy bill the weekly list of those who have died of the plague
fly here refers to a moth which is attracted to the flame of a candle
at our own cost die the candle consumes itself as it burns the moth. There is a secondary reference to the belief that sexual relations (a common sense of *die*) shorten one's lifespan
eagle represents masculine strength
dove represents feminine gentleness
phoenix a mythical Arabian bird; its *riddle* is that when it died it was resurrected from its own ashes

We can die by it, if not live by love,
And if unfit for tombs and hearse†
Our legend† be, it will be fit for verse;
And if no piece of chronicle† we prove,
We'll build in sonnets† pretty rooms;†
As well a well wrought urn becomes†
The greatest ashes, as half-acre tombs,
And by these hymns, all shall approve* confirm
Us canonized for love:

And thus invoke us; 'You whom reverend love
Made one another's hermitage;
You, to whom love was peace, that now is rage;
Who did the whole world's soul contract, and drove
Into the glasses of your eyes
(So made such mirrors, and such spies,
That they did all to you epitomize,)
Countries, towns, courts: beg from above
A pattern of your love!'

1633

The Flea†

Mark but this flea, and mark in this,
How little that which thou denyest me is;
Me it sucked first, and now sucks thee,
And in this flea, our two bloods mingled be;†
Confess it, this cannot be said
A sin, or shame, or loss of maidenhead,
Yet this enjoys before it woo,
And pampered swells with one blood made of two,
And this, alas, is more than we would do.

hearse a canopy over a tomb
legend an account of the life of a saint
piece of chronicle masterpiece of history
sonnets love poems
rooms in Italian the word for room is *stanza*
becomes is appropriate for
The Flea a late medieval pseudo-Ovidian erotic poem about a flea occasioned a large number of Renaissance poems in several languages in which poets envy the freedom of the flea to explore the lady's body and celebrate the joy of the flea in dying at the hand of the lady. A French collection of more than fifty such poems played on the pun between *puce* ('flea') and *pucelage* ('virginity')
two bloods mingled be according to an Aristotelian tradition sexual intercourse was thought to involve the mingling of bloods

Oh stay, three lives in one flea spare,
Where we almost, nay more than married are.
This flea is you and I, and this
Our marriage bed, and marriage temple is;
Though parents grudge, and you, we are met,
And cloistered in these living walls of jet.
Though use* make you apt to kill me, habit
Let not to this, self-murder added be,
And sacrilege, three sins in killing three.

Cruel and sudden, hast thou since
Purpled thy nail, in blood of innocence?
In what could this flea guilty be,
Except in that drop which it sucked from thee?
Yet thou triumphest, and sayest that thou
Findest not thyself, nor me the weaker now;
'Tis true, then learn how false, fears be;
Just so much honour, when thou yield'st to me,
Will waste, as this flea's death took life from thee.

1633

The Good Morrow†

I wonder by my troth, what thou, and I
Did, till we loved? were we not weaned till then,
But sucked on country pleasures, childishly?
Or snorted* we in the seven sleepers' den?† slept
'Twas so; but* this, all pleasures fancies be. except for
If ever any beauty I did see,
Which I desired, and got, 'twas but a dream of thee.

And now good morrow to our waking souls,
Which watch not one another out of fear;
For love, all love of other sights controls,
And makes one little room, an every where.
Let sea-discoverers to new worlds have gone,
Let maps† to others,* worlds on worlds have shown, other people
Let us possess one world, each hath one, and is one.

the Good Morrow this poem is an *aubade*, a form of song to be sung at dawn

seven sleepers' den the cave near Ephesus in which seven young Christians, buried alive in the persecution of the Roman emperor Decius (AD 249), slept for 187 years

maps probably refers to heart-shaped maps which depicted the two hemispheres of the earth

My face in thine eye, thine in mine appears,
And true plain hearts do in the faces rest,
Where can we find two better hemispheres
Without sharp* north, without declining west? cold
Whatever dies, was not mixed equally;
If our two loves be one, or, thou and I
Love so alike, that none do slacken, none can die.

1633

A Lecture upon the Shadow

Stand still, and I will read to thee
A lecture, love, in love's philosophy.
These three hours that we have spent,
Walking here, two shadows went
Along with us, which we ourselves produced;
But, now the sun is just above our head,
We do those shadows tread;
And to brave* clearness all things are reduced. splendid
So whilst our infant loves did grow,
Disguises did, and shadows, flow,
From us, and our cares; but, now 'tis not so.

That love hath not attained the high'st degree,
Which is still diligent lest others see.

Except our loves at this noon stay,
We shall new shadows make the other way.
As the first were made to blind
Others; these which come behind
Will work upon ourselves, and blind our eyes.
If our loves faint, and westwardly decline;
To me thou, falsely, thine,
And I do thee mine actions shall disguise.
The morning shadows wear away,
But these grow longer all the day
But oh, love's day is short, if love decay.

Love is a growing, or full constant light;
And his first minute, after noon, is night.

1633

The Relic

When my grave is broke up again
Some second guest to entertain,†
(For graves have learned that woman-head†
To be to more than one a bed)
And he that digs it, spies
A bracelet of bright hair about the bone,
Will he not let us alone,
And think that there a loving couple lies,
Who thought that this device might be some way
To make their souls, at the last busy day,†
Meet at this grave, and make a little stay?

If this fall in a time, or land,
Where mis-devotion* doth command, idolatry
Then, he that digs us up, will bring
Us, to the Bishop, and the King,
To make us relics; then
Thou shalt be a Mary Magdalen,† and I
A something else† thereby;
All women shall adore us, and some men;
And since at such time, miracles are sought,
I would have that age by this paper* taught poem
What miracles we harmless lovers wrought.

First, we loved well and faithfully,
Yet knew not what we loved, nor why,
Difference of sex no more we knew,
Than our guardian angels do;
Coming and going, we
Perchance might kiss, but not between those meals;†
Our hands ne'er touched the seals,†
Which nature, injured by late law, sets free:
These miracles we did; but now alas,
All measure, and all language, I should pass,* surpass
Should I tell what a miracle she was.

1633

When . . . entertain old graves were regularly reopened to create space for additional occupants
woman-head 'womanhood', with an implied contrast to 'maidenhead'
last busy day the day of judgement
Mary Magdalen the devoted follower of Jesus
a something else probably one of Mary's former lovers, but possibly 'a Jesus Christ'
meals refers to the riotous love-feasts (*agapai*) celebrated by early Christians (e.g. II Peter 2.13)
seals refers primarily to restrictions on love, but glances at the slang sense of 'genitals'

Song

Go, and catch a falling star,
Get with child a mandrake† root,
Tell me, where all past years are,
Or who cleft the Devil's foot,
Teach me to hear mermaids† singing,
Or to keep off envy's stinging,
And find
What wind
Serves to advance an honest mind.

If thou be'est born to strange sights,
Things invisible to see,
Ride ten thousand days and nights,
Till age snow white hairs on thee,
Thou, when thou return'st, wilt tell me
All strange wonders that befell thee,
And swear
No where
Lives a woman true, and fair.

If thou find'st one, let me know,
Such a pilgrimage were sweet,
Yet do not, I would not go,
Though at next door we might meet,
Though she were true, when you met her,
And last, till you write your letter,
Yet she
Will be
False, ere I come, to two, or three.

1633

mandrake kind of potato with a forked root, said to resemble the human form
mermaids the Sirens who in Greek mythology lured sailors to their deaths with their enchanting songs

The Sun Rising

Busy* old fool, unruly sun, meddlesome
Why dost thou thus,
Through windows, and through curtains call on us?
Must to thy motions lovers' seasons run?
Saucy pedantic wretch, go chide
Late school-boys, and sour prentices,* apprentices
Go tell court-huntsmen,† that the King will ride,
Call country ants to harvest offices;†
Love, all alike,† no season knows, nor clime,
Nor hours, days, months, which are the rags of time.

Thy beams, so reverend, and strong
Why shouldst thou think?
I could eclipse and cloud them with a wink,
But that I would not lose her sight so long:
If her eyes have not blinded thine,
Look, and tomorrow late, tell me,
Whether both the Indias of spice and mine†
Be where thou left'st them, or lie here with me.
Ask for those kings whom thou saw'st yesterday,
And thou shalt hear, All here in one bed lay.

She is all states, and all princes,† I,
Nothing else is.
Princes do but play us; compared to this,
All honour's mimic; all wealth alchemy.†
Thou sun art half as happy as we,
In that the world's contracted thus;
Thine age asks* ease, and since thy duties be requires
To warm the world, that's done in warming us.
Shine here to us, and thou art everywhere;
This bed thy centre is, these walls, thy sphere.†

1633

court-huntsmen courtiers who hunted stags with King James I
Call . . . offices i.e. call industrious farmers to their harvesting duties
all alike always the same
both . . . mine spices came from the Spice Islands in the East Indies, and gold was mined in the West Indies, a name which included the mainland of South America
princes the term could apply to female rulers
alchemy Donne regarded alchemy as a fraudulent science
This bed . . . sphere in the Ptolemaic cosmology the earth was the centre of the sphere of the sun's orbit

A Valediction: forbidding Mourning

As virtuous men pass mildly away,
And whisper to their souls, to go,
Whilst some of their sad friends do say,
The breath goes now, and some say, no:

So let us melt and make no noise,
No tear-floods, nor sigh-tempests move,* provoke
'Twere profanation of our joys
To tell the laity our love.

Moving of th' earth* brings harms and fears, earthquakes
Men reckon what it did and meant,
But trepidation of the spheres,†
Though greater far, is innocent.

Dull sublunary† lovers' love
(Whose soul is sense†) cannot admit
Absence,† because it doth remove
Those things† which elemented it.

But we by a love, so much refined,
That our selves know not what it is,
Inter-assurèd of the mind,†
Care less, eyes, lips, and hands to miss.

Our two souls therefore, which are one,
Though I must go, endure not yet
A breach, but an expansion,
Like gold† to airy thinness beat.

---

trepidation of the spheres in the Ptolemaic cosmology the eighth sphere (to which the fixed stars were attached) and the ninth sphere were subject to trepidation (i.e. oscillation), which was held to be responsible for the precession of the equinoxes

sublunary below the moon, and therefore earthly and subject to change

sense means both sensual, and subject to the senses

absence plays on the Latin meaning of *ab* ('from') and the English meaning of 'sense'

things the proximity of the lovers gave substance to (*elemented*) their love

Inter-assured . . . mind mutually assured of each other's fidelity

gold the chemical symbol for gold, a circle with a dot at the centre, anticipates the compass image below

If they be two, they are two so
As stiff twin compasses† are two,
Thy soul the fixed foot, makes no show
To move, but doth, if th'other do.

And though it in the centre sit,
Yet when the other far doth roam,
It leans, and hearkens after it,
And grows erect, as that comes home.

Such wilt thou be to me, who must
Like th' other foot, obliquely† run;
Thy firmness makes my circle just,* perfect
And makes me end, where I begun.

1611 1633

Woman's Constancy

Now thou hast loved me one whole day,
Tomorrow when thou leav'st, what wilt thou say?
Wilt thou then antedate some new made vow?
Or say that now
We are not just those persons, which we were?
Or, that oaths made in reverential fear
Of Love, and his wrath, any may forswear?
Or, as true deaths, true marriages untie,
So lovers' contracts, images of those,
Bind but till sleep, death's image, them unloose?
Or, your own end to justify,
For having purposed change, and falsehood, you
Can have no way but falsehood to be true?
Vain lunatic,† against these scapes† I could
Dispute, and conquer, if I would,
Which I abstain to do,
For by tomorrow, I may think so too.

1633

twin compasses the two legs of a compass; the compass was a traditional image of the constancy of lovers
obliquely diverging from a straight line
lunatic under the influence of the moon, and therefore inconstant
scapes escapes (from an agreement)

From HOLY SONNETS

10 Death be not proud

Death be not proud, though some have called thee
Mighty and dreadful, for, thou art not so,
For, those, whom thou think'st, thou dost overthrow,
Die not, poor death, nor yet canst thou kill me;
From rest and sleep, which but thy pictures be,
Much pleasure, then from thee, much more must flow,
And soonest our best men with thee do go,
Rest of their bones, and soul's delivery.†
Thou art slave to fate, chance, kings, and desperate men,
And dost with poison, war, and sickness dwell,
And poppy,† or charms† can make us sleep as well,
And better than thy stroke; why swell'st† thou then?
One short sleep past, we wake eternally,
And death shall be no more, Death thou shalt die.

1633

14 Batter my heart

Batter my heart, three-personed† God; for, you
As yet but knock, breathe, shine, and seek to mend;
That I may rise, and stand, o'erthrow me, and bend
Your force, to break, blow, burn, and make me new.
I, like an usurped town, to another due,
Labour to admit you, but oh, to no end,
Reason your viceroy in me, me should defend,
But is captived, and proves weak or untrue,
Yet dearly'I love you, and would be loved fain,* eagerly
But am betrothed unto your enemy,
Divorce me, untie, or break that knot again,
Take me to you, imprison me, for I
Except you enthral† me, never shall be free,
Nor ever chaste, except you ravish me.

1633

Rest . . . delivery death is a rest for the body and a liberation (delivery) for the soul
poppy opium was used as a sedative
charms magic spells
swell'st puff up with pride
three-personed Father, Son, and Holy Spirit
except you enthral unless you enslave

19 Oh, to vex me

Oh, to vex me, contraries meet in one:
Inconstancy unnaturally hath begot
A constant habit; that when I would not
I change in vows, and in devotion.†
As humorous† is my contrition†
As my profane love, and as soon forgot:
As riddlingly distempered,† cold and hot,
As praying, as mute; as infinite, as none.
I durst not view heaven yesterday; and today
In prayers, and flattering speeches I court God:
Tomorrow I quake with true fear of his rod.
So my devout fits come and go away
Like a fantastic ague:† save that here
Those are my best days, when I shake with fear.

1633

From ELEGIES

Elegy 10 The Dream

Image of her whom I love, more than she,†
  Whose fair impression in my faithful heart,
Makes me her medal,† and makes her love me,
  As kings do coins, to which their stamps impart
The value: go, and take my heart from hence,
  Which now is grown too great and good for me:
Honours oppress weak spirits, and our sense
  Strong objects dull; the more,† the less we see.

devotion pronounced as four syllables
humorous changeable (with reference to the 'humours' which were deemed to determine disposition)
contrition pronounced as four syllables
riddlingly distempered enigmatically unbalanced
fantastic ague a hallucinatory fever with paroxysms of trembling
more than she the poet's mental image is more real than is the lady herself
medal a commemorative medal
the more the stronger the impact on our senses

When you are gone, and reason gone with you,
Then fantasy is queen and soul, and all;
She can present joys meaner† than you do;
Convenient, and more proportional.
So, if I dream I have you, I have you,
For, all our joys are but fantastical.†
And so I 'scape* the pain, for pain is true,* escape actual
And sleep which locks up sense, doth lock out all.

After a such fruition I shall wake,
And, but the waking, nothing shall repent;
And shall to love more thankful sonnets† make,
Than if more honour, tears, and pains were spent.
But dearest heart, and dearer image stay;
Alas, true joys at best are dream enough;
Though you stay here you pass too fast away:
For even at first life's taper is a snuff.†

Filled with her love, may I be rather grown
Mad with much heart, than idiot† with none.

1633

From SATIRES

Satire 1 Away thou fondling

Away thou fondling* motley† humourist,† foolish
Leave me, and in this standing wooden chest,†
Consorted with these few books, let me lie
In prison, and here be coffined, when I die;
Here are God's conduits,† grave divines; and here
Nature's secretary, the Philosopher;†

meaner nearer the mean, therefore more moderate
fantastical produced by fantasy (line 10)
sonnets love poems, not necessarily of 14 lines
taper is a snuff candle is a burnt wick
idiot a person lacking reason and sense
motley the parti-coloured dress of the court fool
humourist a person subject to 'humours' or fantasies
standing wooden chest a desk (with bookshelves) in a school or college, partitioned off to form a small study
conduits the channels through which God speaks
the Philosopher Aristotle, who studied the secrets of nature (hence 'secretary') in his scientific works

And jolly[†] statesmen, which teach how to tie
The sinews of a city's mystic body;[†]
Here gathering chroniclers,[†] and by them stand
Giddy fantastic[†] poets of each land.
Shall I leave all this constant company,
And follow headlong, wild uncertain thee?
First swear by thy best love in earnest[†]
(If thou which lov'st all, canst love any best)
Thou wilt not leave me in the middle street,
Though some more spruce companion thou dost meet,
Not though a captain do come in thy way
Bright parcel gilt,[†] with forty dead men's pay,[†]
Nor though a brisk perfumed pert courtier
Deign with a nod, thy courtesy to answer.
Nor come a velvet Justice with a long
Great train of blue coats,[†] twelve, or fourteen strong,
Wilt thou grin or fawn on him, or prepare
A speech to court his beauteous son and heir.
For better or worse take me, or leave me:
To take, and leave me is adultery.
Oh monstrous, superstitious puritan,* — purist
Of refined manners, yet ceremonial man,
That when thou meet'st one, with inquiring eyes
Dost search, and like a needy broker* prize* — merchant — appraise
The silk, and gold he wears, and to that rate
So high or low, dost raise thy formal hat:
That wilt consort none, until thou have known
What lands he hath in hope, or of his own,
As though all thy companions should make thee
Jointures,[†] and marry thy dear company.
Why shouldst thou (that dost not only approve,
But in rank itchy lust, desire, and love
The nakedness and barrenness to enjoy,
Of thy plump muddy[†] whore, or prostitute boy)
Hate virtue, though she be naked, and bare?
At birth, and death, our bodies naked are;

jolly splendid (possibly used ironically)
mystic body the 'body politic', the city in its corporate character as opposed to its physical existence
gathering chroniclers historians who gather information
giddy fantastic capricious fanciful
earnest pronounced as three syllables
parcel gilt partly gilded, with a play on 'guilt'
dead men's pay corrupt officers would draw the pay of their dead soldiers
blue coats refers to the uniforms of beadles, who were minor legal officials
jointures property owned jointly by husband and wife
muddy morally impure

And till our souls be unapparelled
Of bodies, they from bliss are banished.
Man's first blessed state was naked, when by sin
He lost that, yet he was clothed but in beast's skin,†
And in this coarse attire, which I now wear,
With God, and with the Muses I confer.
But since thou like a contrite penitent,
Charitably warned of thy sins, dost repent
These vanities and giddinesses, lo
I shut my chamber door, and come, let's go.
But sooner may a cheap whore, that hath been
Worn by as many several men in sin,
As are black feathers, or musk-colour hose,†
Name her child's right true father, 'mongst all those:
Sooner may one guess, who shall bear away
The Infanta* of London, heir to an India;† princess
And sooner may a gulling weather-spy†
By drawing forth heaven's scheme* tell certainly a horoscope
What fashioned hats, or ruffs, or suits next year
Our subtle-witted antic* youths will wear; fantastic
Than thou, when thou depart'st from me, canst show
Whither, why, when, or with whom thou wouldst go.
But how shall I be pardoned my offence
That thus have sinned against my conscience?
Now we are in the street; he first of all
Improvidently proud, creeps to the wall,†
And so imprisoned, and hemmed in by me
Sells for a little state* his liberty; status
Yet though he cannot skip forth now to greet
Every fine silken painted fool we meet,
He them to him with amorous smiles allures,
And grins, smacks, shrugs, and such an itch endures,
As 'prentices, or school-boys which do know
Of some gay sport abroad, yet dare not go.
And as fiddlers stop lowest, at highest sound,†
So to the most brave, stoops he nigh'st the ground.

---

he lost . . . skin refers to Adam (Genesis 3.21)
As are . . . hose refers to contemporary fashions
an India enormous wealth
gulling weather-spy deceitful astrologer
wall the inside position on the side of the street was reserved for those of high social standing
And as . . . sound instruments of the viol family were held upright, so the highest notes are played when the player stops the vibration at the lowest point

But to a grave man, he doth move no more
Than the wise politic† horse would heretofore,
Or thou o elephant or ape wilt do,
When any names the King of Spain to you.
Now leaps he upright, jogs me, and cries, 'Do you see
Yonder well-favoured youth?' 'Which?' 'Oh, 'tis he
That dances so divinely'; 'Oh,' said I,
'Stand still, must you dance here for company?'
He drooped, we went, till one (which did excel
Th' Indians, in drinking his tobacco† well)
Met us; they talked; I whispered, 'Let us go,
'T may be you smell him not, truly I do.'
He hears not me, but on the other side
A many-coloured peacock having spied,
Leaves him and me; I for my lost sheep stay;
He follows, overtakes, goes on the way
Saying, 'Him whom I last left, all repute
For his device,* in handsoming* a suit, invention embellishing
To judge of lace, pink,† panes,† print,† cut,* and pleat shape
Of all the Court, to have the best conceit.'* conception
'Our dull comedians† want him, let him go;
But oh, God strengthen thee, why stoop'st thou so?'
'Why? he hath travelled.' 'Long?' 'No, but to me
(Which understand none), he doth seem to be
Perfect French, and Italian'; I replied,
'So is the pox',† he answered not, but spied
More men of sort, of parts, and qualities;
At last his love he in a window spies,
And like light dew exhaled, he flings from me
Violently ravished to his lechery.
Many were there, he could command† no more;
He quarrelled, fought, bled; and turned out of door
Directly came to me hanging the head,
And constantly a while must keep his bed.

1633

politic cunning; the horse belonged to a showman called Banks, who taught it to respond to requests from the audience
drinking his tobacco before the smoking of tobacco became fashionable, it was used (like tea leaves) for making a hot drink
pink decorative eyelet
panes decorative strips of cloth
print the crimping of pleats
dull comedians comic actors who dressed as clowns
pox syphilis, which was associated with France and Italy
command have at his disposal

From PARADOXES

A Defence of Women's Inconstancy

That women are inconstant, I with any man confess. But that inconstancy is a bad quality I against any man will maintain; for every thing, as it is one better than another, so is it fuller of change. The heavens themselves continually turn, the stars move, the moon changeth, fire whirleth, air flieth, water ebbs and flows, the face of the earth altereth her looks, time stays not, the colour that hath most light will take most dyes; so in men, they that have the most reason are the most alterable in their designs, and the darkest and most ignorant do seldomest change. Therefore women changing more than men have also more reason, they cannot be immutable like stocks,† like stones, like the earth's dull centre. Gold that lieth still rusteth, water corrupteth, and air that moveth not poisoneth. Then why should that which is the perfection of other things be imputed to women as greatest imperfection? Because thereby they deceive men? Are not your wits pleased with those jests which cozen† your expectation? You can call it pleasure to be beguiled in trifles, and in the most excellent toy in the world you call it treachery. I would you had your mistresses so constant that they would never change, no not so much as their smocks, then should you see what a sluttish virtue constancy were. Inconstancy is a most commendable and cleanly quality; and women in this quality are far more absolute than the heavens, than the stars, than moon, or anything beneath it, for long observation hath picked certainty out of this mutability. The learned are so well acquainted with the stars signs and planets that they make them but characters to read the meaning of the heaven in his own forehead. Every simple fellow can bespeak the change of the moon a great while before hand. But I would fain have the learnedest man so skilful as to tell when the simplest woman meaneth to vary. Learning affords no rules to know, much less knowledge to rule the mind of a woman. For as philosophy teacheth us, that light things do always tend upwards, and heavy things decline downwards, experience teacheth us otherwise, that the disposition of a light woman is to fall down; the nature of women being contrary to all art and nature. Women are like flies which feed amongst us at our table, or fleas sucking our very blood, who leave not our most retired places free from their familiarity. Yet for all their fellowship will they never be tamed, nor commanded by us. Women are like the sun which is violently carried one way, yet hath a proper course contrary. So though they (by the mastery of some overruling churlish husbands) are forced to his bias, yet have they a motion of

stocks tree stumps

cozen cheat

their own, which their husbands never know of. It is the nature of nice and fastidious minds to know things only to be weary of them. Women by their sly-changeableness, and pleasing doubleness, prevent even the mislike of those, for they can never be so well known, but that there is still more unknown. Every women is a science, for he that plods upon a woman all his life long shall at length find himself short of the knowledge of her. They are born to take down the pride of wit and ambition of wisdom, making fools wise in the adventuring to win them, wise men fools with conceit of losing their labour, witty men stark mad being confounded with their uncertainties. Philosophers write against them for spite, not desert, that having attained to some knowledge in all other things in them only they know nothing but are merely ignorant. Active and experienced men rail against them because they love in their lifeless and decrepit age, when all goodness leaves them. These envious libellers ballad against them because having nothing in themselves able to deserve their love, they maliciously discommend all they cannot obtain; thinking to make men believe they know much because they are able to dispraise much, and rage against inconstancy when they were never admitted into so much favour as to be forsaken. In mine opinion such men are happy that women are inconstant, for so they may chance to be beloved of some excellent woman (when it comes to their turn) out of their inconstancy, and mutability, though not out of their own desert. And what reason is there to clog any woman with one man be he never so singular? Women had rather (and it is far better, and more judicial) to enjoy all the virtues in several men, than but some of them in one, for otherwise they lose their taste like divers sorts of meat minced together in one dish. And to have all excellencies in one man (if it were possible) is confusion, not diversity. Now who can deny, but such as are obstinately bent to undervalue their worth, are those that have not soul enough to comprehend their excellency, women being the most excellent creatures, in that man is able to subject all things else, and to grow wise in every thing, but still persists a fool in woman. The greatest scholar, if he once take a wife, is found so unlearned that he must begin his hornbook,† and all is by inconstancy. To conclude, therefore, this name of inconstancy which hath been so much poisoned with slanders ought to be changed into variety, for the which the world is so delightful, and a woman for that the most delightful thing in the world.

1633

hornbook a piece of paper containing the alphabet and the ten digits, protected against its young users by a thin plate of translucent horn; the term also puns on the horns of a cuckold

From DEVOTIONS

Meditation

Perchance he for whom this bell tolls, may be so ill, as that he knows not it tolls for him; and perchance I may think myself so much better than I am, as that they who are about me, and see my state, may have caused it to toll for me, and I know not that. The church is catholic, universal, so are all her actions; all that she does, belongs to all. When she baptizes a child, that action concerns me; for that child is thereby connected to that head which is my head too, and engraffed into that body, whereof I am a member. And when she buries a man, that action concerns me. All mankind is of one author, and is one volume; when one man dies, one chapter is not torn out of the book, but translated into a better language; and every chapter must be so translated; God employs several translators; some pieces are translated by age, some by sickness, some by war, some by justice; but God's hand is in every translation; and his hand shall bind up all our scattered leaves again, for that library where every book shall lie open to one another. As therefore the bell that rings to a sermon, calls not upon the preacher only, but upon the congregation to come: so this bell calls us all: but how much more me, who am brought so near the door by this sickness. There was a contention as far as a suit† (in which both piety and dignity, religion and estimation, were mingled) which of the religious orders should ring to prayers first in the morning; and it was determined, that they should ring first that rose earliest. If we understand aright the dignity of this bell, that tolls for our evening prayer, we would be glad to make it ours, by rising early, in that application, that it might be ours, as well as his, whose indeed it is. The bell doth toll for him that thinks it doth; and though it intermit again, yet from that minute, that that occasion wrought upon him, he is united to God. Who casts not up his eye to the sun when it rises? But who takes off his eye from a comet when that breaks out? Who bends not his ear to any bell, which upon any occasion rings? But who can remove it from that bell, which is passing a piece of himself out of this world? No man is an island, entire of itself; every man is a piece of the continent, a part of the main;† if a clod be washed away by the sea, Europe is the less, as well as if a promontory were, as well as if a manor of thy friends, or of thine own were; any man's death diminishes me, because I am involved in mankind; and therefore never send to know for whom the bell tolls; it tolls for thee.

1624

suit a dispute in canon law

main mainland

From A SERMON PREACHED AT WHITEHALL, 8 MARCH 1622

[Death] comes equally to us all, and makes us all equal when it comes. The ashes of an oak in the chimney, are no epitaph of that oak, to tell me how high or how large that was; it tells me not what flocks it sheltered while it stood, nor what men it hurt when it fell. The dust of great persons' graves is speechless too, it says nothing, it distinguishes nothing. As soon the dust of a wretch whom thou wouldest not, as of a prince whom thou couldest not look upon, will trouble thine eyes, if the wind blow it thither; and when a whirlwind hath blown the dust of the churchyard into the church, and the man sweeps out the dust of the church into the churchyard, who will undertake to sift those dusts again, and to pronounce, 'This is the patrician, this is the noble flour, and this the yeomanly, this the plebeian bran'?

1622 1640

Richard Barnfield

1574–1627

Richard Barnfield was born in Shropshire, and was educated at Brasenose College, Oxford, where he took his BA in 1592. He lived as a gentleman in London, where his friends were poets and playwrights, until about 1600, and then retired for the rest of his life to his manor in Staffordshire.

In 1594 Barnfield published *The Affectionate Shepherd*, a collection of poems modelled on Virgil's second *Eclogue*, and the following year he published a collection of sonnets in *Cynthia*; both collections of love poems are addressed to a boy, but it is not clear to what extent this was a literary affectation; the Commonplace Book attributed to Barnfield portrays him as robustly heterosexual.

From THE AFFECTIONATE SHEPHERD

The Tears of an Affectionate Shepherd Sick for Love
or
The Complaint of Daphnis for the Love of Ganymede

If it be sin to love a sweet-faced boy
(Whose amber locks trussed up in golden trammels
Dangle adown his lovely cheeks with joy,
When pearl and flowers his fair hair enamels)
If it be sin to love a lovely lad
Oh then sin I, for whom my soul is sad.

His ivory-white and alabaster skin
Is stained throughout with rare vermilion red,
Whose twinkling starry lights do never blin* cease
To shine on lovely Venus (beauty's bed);
But as the lily and the blushing rose
So white and red on him in order grows.

1594

From CYNTHIA

Sonnet 3

The Stoics think (and they come near the truth)
That virtue is the chiefest good of all;
The Academics* on Idea call, Platonists
The Epicures in pleasure spend their youth.
The Peripatetics* judge felicity Aristotelians
To be the chiefest good above all other.
One man thinks this, and that conceives another,
So that in one thing very few agree.
Let Stoics have their virtue if they will,
And all the rest their chief-supposèd good;
Let cruel martialists* delight in blood, soldiers
And misers joy their bags with gold to fill;
My chiefest good, my chief felicity,
Is to be gazing on my love's fair eye.

Sonnet 8

Sometimes I wish that I his pillow were,
So I might steal a kiss, and yet not seen,
So might I gaze upon his sleeping eyne,* eyes
Although I did it with a panting fear.
But when I well consider how vain my wish is,
Ah foolish bees (think I) that do not suck
His lips for honey; but poor flowers do pluck
Which have no sweet in them, when his sole kisses
Are able to revive a dying soul.
Kiss him, but sting him not, for if you do,
His angry voice your flying will pursue.
But when they hear his tongue, what can control
Their back-return? For then they plain may see
How honey-combs from his lips dropping be.

Sonnet 17

Cherry-lipped Adonis† in his snowy shape,
Might not compare with his pure ivory white,
On whose fair front* a poet's pen may write, forehead
Whose roseate red excels the crimson grape.
His love-enticing delicate soft limbs,
Are rarely framed t'entrap poor gazing eyes;
His cheeks, the lily and carnation dyes
With lovely tincture which Apollo's dims.
His lips ripe strawberries in nectar wet,
His mouth a hive, his tongue a honey-comb
Where muses (like bees) make their mansion,
His teeth pure pearl in blushing coral set.
Oh how can such a body sin-procuring
Be slow to love, and quick to hate, enduring.

1595

Adonis a beautiful youth loved by Venus

Cyril Tourneur

1575?–1626

Cyril Tourneur was probably born in the 1570s, but nothing is known of his parentage or early life. He seems to have spent much of his adult life in military service abroad. He published a satirical poem in 1600, and in 1611 his play *The Atheist's Tragedy* was published. His authorship of *The Revenger's Tragedy* (1607) is not certain.

From THE REVENGER'S TRAGEDY†

Act III, Scene v, 141–98

DUKE
How sweet can a duke breathe? Age has no fault.
Pleasure should meet in a perfumed mist.
Lady, sweetly encountered: I came from Court,
I must be bold with you – oh! What's this? Oh!
[*He kisses the skull*]

VINDICE
Royal villain, white devil†

DUKE
Oh!

VINDICE
Brother – place the torch here that his affrighted eyeballs
May start into those hollows. Duke, dost know
Yon dreadful vizard?* View it well; 'tis the skull face
Of Gloriana, whom thou poisonedst last.

DUKE
Oh 't'as poisoned me!

VINDICE
Didst not know that till now?

DUKE
What are you two?

The Revenger's Tragedy in this scene Vindice (whose name means 'revenger') murders the duke by encouraging him to kiss the poisoned skull of his mistress

white devil a devil who pretends to be virtuous

VINDICE
Villains all three! The very ragged bone
Has been sufficiently revenged.

DUKE
Oh Hippolito – call treason! [*Falls*]

HIPPOLITO
Yes my good lord. Treason, treason, treason!
Stamping on him

DUKE
Then I'm betrayed.

VINDICE
Alas poor lecher: in the hands of knaves
A slavish duke is baser than his slaves.

DUKE
My teeth are eaten out.

VINDICE
Hadst any left?

HIPPOLITO
I think but few.

VINDICE
Then those that did eat are eaten.

DUKE
Oh my tongue!

VINDICE
Your tongue? 'Twill teach you to kiss closer,
Not like a slobbering Dutchman. You have eyes still:
Look, monster, what a lady hast thou made me
My once betrothed wife.

DUKE
Is it thou villain? Nay then –

VINDICE
'Tis I, 'tis Vindice, 'tis I!

HIPPOLITO
And let this comfort thee. Our lord and father
Fell sick upon the infection of thy frowns
And died in sadness. Be that thy hope of life.

DUKE
Oh!

VINDICE
He had his tongue, yet grief made him die speechless.
Puh, 'tis but early yet; now I'll begin
To stick thy soul with ulcers; I will make
Thy spirit grievous sore, it shall not rest
But like some pestilent man, toss in thy breast.
Mark me, duke,
Thou'rt a renowned, high, and mighty cuckold!

DUKE
Oh!

VINDICE
Thy bastard, thy bastard rides a-hunting in thy brow.

DUKE
Millions of deaths!
VINDICE
Nay to afflict thee more,
Here in this lodge they meet for damned clips:* embraces
Those eyes shall see the incest of their lips.
DUKE
Is there a hell besides this, villains?
VINDICE
Villain?
Nay heaven is just, scorns are the hires of scorns,
I ne'er knew yet adulterer without horns.
HIPPOLITO
Once ere they die 'tis quitted. [*Noises within*]
VINDICE
Hark the music,
Their banquet is prepared, they're coming –
DUKE
Oh kill me not with that sight.
VINDICE
Thou shalt not lose that sight for all thy dukedom.
DUKE
Traitors, murderers!
VINDICE
What, is not thy tongue eaten out yet?
Then we'll invent a silence. Brother, stifle the torch.
DUKE
Treason! Murder!
VINDICE
Nay faith, we'll have you hushed now with thy dagger.
Nail down his tongue, and mine shall keep possession
About his heart; if he but gasp he dies,
We dread not death to quittance* injuries. Brother, recompense
If he but wink, not brooking* the foul object tolerating
Let our two other hands tear up his lids
And make his eyes, like comets, shine through blood.
When the bad bleeds, then is the tragedy good.

1607

John Fletcher and Francis Beaumont

1579–1625 1584–1616

John Fletcher was born at Rye, in Sussex, the son of a minister who was later to become Bishop of London. He was probably educated at Corpus Christi College, Cambridge. By 1605 he had established himself as a playwright in London; he died of the plague in 1625. Francis Beaumont was born in Leicestershire, the son of an eminent judge. He attended Broadgates Hall (later Pembroke College), Oxford, but left in his second year to study law at the Inner Temple. He became a poet and playwright, and soon began to collaborate with Fletcher, with whom he lived for many years in a house close to the Globe Theatre. Beaumont married in about 1613, and retired to Kent. From 1606 to 1613 Beaumont and Fletcher collaborated in about fifteen plays, the most famous of which is *The Maid's Tragedy*, which was written in 1610.

From THE MAID'S TRAGEDY†

Act II, Scene i, 34–75

EVADNE

I thank thee, Dula. Would thou couldst instil
Some of thy mirth into Aspatia.
Nothing but sad thoughts in her breast do dwell;
Methinks a mean betwixt you would do well.

DULA

She is in love; hang me if I were so,
But I could run my country. I love too
To do those things that people in love do.

The Maid's Tragedy in this passage Aspatia laments the loss of her fiancé Amintor to Evadne, the king's mistress

ASPATIA
It were a timeless* smile should prove my cheek: untimely
It were a fitter hour for me to laugh
When at the altar the religious priest
Were pacifying the offended powers
With sacrifice, than now. This should have been
My rite, and all your hands have been employed
In giving me a spotless offering
To young Amintor's bed, as we are now
For you. Pardon, Evadne, would my worth
Were great as yours, or that the king, or he,
Or both thought so. Perhaps he found me worthless,
But till he did so, in these ears of mine,
These credulous ears, he poured the sweetest words
Thou art or love could frame. If he were false,
Pardon it, Heaven; and if I did want
Virtue, you safely may forgive that too,
For I have lost none that I had from you.

EVADNE
Nay, leave this sad talk, madam.

ASPATIA Would I could,
Then I should leave the cause.

EVADNE
See, if you have not spoiled all Dula's mirth!

ASPATIA
Thou think'st thy heart hard, but if thou be'st caught,
Remember me; thou shalt perceive a fire
Shot suddenly into thee.

DULA That's not so good;
Let 'em shoot anything but fire, and I
Fear 'em not.

ASPATIA Well, wench, thou may'st be taken.

EVADNE
Ladies, good night, I'll do the rest myself.

DULA
Nay, let your lord do some.

ASPATIA [*singing*].
Lay a garland on my hearse of the dismal yew –

EVADNE
That's one of your sad songs, madam.

ASPATIA
Believe me, 'tis a very pretty one.

EVADNE
How is it, madam?

ASPATIA

SONG

Lay a garland on my hearse of the dismal yew;
Maidens, willow branches bear; say I died true.
My love was false, but I was firm, from my hour of birth;
Upon my buried body lay lightly, gentle earth!

1610–11 1619

Thomas Middleton

1580–1627

Thomas Middleton was born in London, the son of a prosperous bricklayer. He was educated at Queen's College, Oxford, but left without a degree. By 1600 he had moved to London and was associated with the theatres. During the next twenty years he wrote a large number of plays (often in collaboration with others), pageants and masques. His best-known plays are *The Roaring Girl* (written with Thomas Dekker), *A Fair Quarrel*, and *A Chaste Maid in Cheapside* (written with William Rowley). 'Midnight's bell' is a song in his play *Blurt, Master Constable.*

From BLURT, MASTER CONSTABLE

Midnight's bell

Midnight's bell goes ting, ting, ting, ting, ting,
Then dogs do howl, and not a bird does sing
But the nightingale, and she cries twit, twit, twit.
Owls then on every bough do sit,
Ravens croak on chimney's tops,
The cricket in the chamber hops,
And the cats cry mew, mew, mew.
The nibbling mouse is not asleep,
But he goes peep, peep, peep, peep, peep,
  And the cats cry mew, mew, mew,
  And still the cats cry mew, mew, mew.

1602

John Webster

1580?–1634?

John Webster was born in London, the son of a coachmaker; little is known of his private life. He became a freeman of the Merchant Taylors' Company, and assumed a double career of coachmaker and playwright. Most of his plays were written in collaboration with others; of the three surviving plays which he wrote himself, the most powerful are the tragedies *The White Devil* (*c.* 1609) and *The Duchess of Malfi* (*c.* 1612). Both plays are based on Italian *novelle*, and are characterised by the artistic use of horror, and by powerful and markedly literary language. He also wrote a tragi-comedy, *The Devil's Law Case* (*c.* 1619).

From THE WHITE DEVIL[†]

The Arraignment of Vittoria

Enter FRANCISCO, MONTICELSO, *the six lieger*[†] AMBASSADORS, BRACHIANO, VITTORIA, [ZANCHE, FLAMINEO, MARCELLO,] LAWYER, *and a guard.*

MONTICELSO: Forbear my lord, here is no place assigned you.
The business by his holiness is left
To our examination.
BRACHIANO: May it thrive with you!
Lays a rich gown under him.
FRANCISCO: A chair there for his lordship.
BRACHIANO: Forbear your kindness; an unbidden guest
Should travel as Dutch women go to church:
Bear their stools with them.
MONTICELSO: At your pleasure sir.
Stand to the table gentlewomen. Now signior
Fall to your plea.

The White Devil in this scene, which is sufficiently important to warrant a title, Vittoria Corombona is tried for murder and adultery. Monticelso, the uncle of Vittoria's murdered husband, is a Cardinal. Francisco de Medici is Duke of Florence; Brachiano is Vittoria's lover (afterwards husband). The plot, though not the trial scene, is based on events which took place in Italy in the 1580s

lieger resident

LAWYER: *Domine Judex converte oculos in hanc pestem*
mulierum corruptissimam.†
VITTORIA: What's he?
FRANCISCO: A lawyer, that pleads against you.
VITTORIA: Pray my lord, let him speak his usual tongue.
I'll make no answer else.
FRANCISCO: Why you understand Latin.
VITTORIA: I do sir, but amongst this auditory
Which come to hear my cause, the half or more
May be ignorant in't.
MONTICELSO: Go on sir.
VITTORIA: By your favour,
I will not have my accusation clouded
In a strange tongue: all this assembly
Shall hear what you can charge me with.
FRANCISCO: Signior,
You need not stand on't much; pray change your language.
MONTICELSO: O for God sake; gentlewoman, your credit
Shall be more famous by it.
LAWYER: Well then have at you.
VITTORIA: I am at the mark sir, I'll give aim to† you,
And tell you how near you shoot.
LAWYER: Most literated judges, please your lordships,
So to connive your judgements to the view
Of this debauched and diversivolent† woman
Who such a black concatenation
Of mischief hath effected, that to extirp
The memory of't, must be the consummation
Of her and her projections –
VITTORIA: What's all this?
LAWYER: Hold your peace.
Exorbitant sins must have exulceration.
VITTORIA: Surely my lords this lawyer here hath swallowed
Some pothecary's bills,† or proclamations.
And now the hard and undigestible words
Come up like stones we use give hawks for physic.
Why this is Welsh† to Latin.

Domine . . . corruptissimam (Latin) 'My Lord Judge, turn your eyes to this plague, the most corrupt of women'
give aim to you act as the marker at the archery butts
diversivolent desiring strife
pothecary's bills prescriptions, which were written in Latin
Welsh here used in the sense of 'incomprehensible gibberish'

LAWYER: My lords, the woman
Knows not her tropes nor figures, nor is perfect
In the academic derivation
Of grammatical elocution.
FRANCISCO: Sir your pains
Shall be well spared, and your deep eloquence
Be worthily applauded amongst those
Which understand you.
LAWYER My good lord.
FRANCISCO *speaks this as in scorn*: Sir,
Put up your papers in your fustian bag –
Cry mercy sir, 'tis buckram† – and accept
My notion of your learned verbosity.
LAWYER: I most graduatically thank your lordship.
I shall have use for them elsewhere.
[*Exit.*]
MONTICELSO: I shall be plainer with you, and paint out
Your follies in more natural red and white
Than that upon your cheek.
VITTORIA: O you mistake.
You raise a blood as noble in this cheek
As ever was your mother's.
MONTICELSO: I must spare you till proof cry whore to that;
Observe this creature here my honoured lords,
A woman of a most prodigious spirit
In her effected.
VITTORIA: Honourable my lord,
It doth not suit a reverend cardinal
To play the lawyer thus.
MONTICELSO: O your trade instructs your language!
You see my lords what goodly fruit she seems,
Yet like those apples travellers report
To grow where Sodom and Gomorrah stood†
I will but touch her and you straight shall see
She'll fall to soot and ashes.
VITTORIA: Your envenomed
Pothecary should do't.

Put up . . . buckram Francisco plays on two senses of the term *fustian*, which refers both to a coarse cloth and to inflated language, and then mockingly begs the pardon of the lawyer ('cry mercy sir') and corrects himself by observing that the bag is made of buckram, the traditional fabric of lawyers' bags

Like those apples . . . stood the legend of the apples of Sodom and Gomorrah derives from Josephus, and is ultimately based on Deuteronomy 32.32

MONTICELSO: I am resolved
Were there a second paradise to lose
This devil would betray it.
VITTORIA: O poor charity!
Thou art seldom found in scarlet.†
MONTICELSO: Who knows not how, when several night by night
Her gates were choked with coaches, and her rooms
Outbraved the stars with several kind of lights
When she did counterfeit a prince's court?
In music, banquets and most riotous surfeits
This whore, forsooth, was holy.
VITTORIA: Ha? whore? what's that?
MONTICELSO: Shall I expound whore to you? Sure I shall;
I'll give their perfect character.† They are first
Sweetmeats which rot the eater: in man's nostril
Poisoned perfumes. They are cozening alchemy,
Shipwrecks in calmest weather! What are whores?
Cold Russian winters, that appear so barren,
As if that nature had forgot the spring.
They are the true material fire of hell,
Worse than those tributes i'th' Low Countries paid,
Exactions upon meat, drink, garments, sleep;
Ay even on man's perdition, his sin.
They are those brittle evidences of law
Which forfeit all a wretched man's estate
For leaving out one syllable. What are whores?
They are those flattering bells have all one tune,
At weddings, and at funerals: your rich whores
Are only treasuries by extortion filled
And emptied by cursed riot. They are worse,
Worse than dead bodies, which are begged at gallows
And wrought upon by surgeons, to teach man†
Wherein he is imperfect. What's a whore?
She's like the guilty counterfeited coin
Which whosoe'er first stamps it brings in trouble
All that receive it.

1610–12 1612

---

scarlet the colour of Cardinal Monticelso's gown
character character sketch in the tradition of the Greek writer Theophrastus
to teach man i.e. for anatomy lessons

From THE DUCHESS OF MALFI[†]

Act IV, Scene ii, 117–234

BOSOLA: I am come to make thy tomb.

DUCHESS: Ha! my tomb?
Thou speakest as if I lay upon my death-bed,
Gasping for breath: dost thou perceive me sick?

BOSOLA: Yes, and the more dangerously, since thy sickness is insensible.[†]

DUCHESS: Thou art not mad, sure; dost know me?

BOSOLA: Yes.

DUCHESS: Who am I?

BOSOLA: Thou art a box of worm seed,[†] at best, but a salvatory of green mummy:[†] what's this flesh? a little crudded[†] milk, fantastical puff-paste: our bodies are weaker than those paper prisons boys use to keep flies in: more contemptible; since ours is to preserve earth-worms: didst thou ever see a lark in a cage? such is the soul in the body: this world is like her little turf of grass, and the heaven o'er our heads, like her looking-glass, only gives us a miserable knowledge of the small compass of our prison.

DUCHESS: Am not I thy Duchess?

BOSOLA: Thou art some great woman, sure; for riot begins to sit on thy forehead (clad in grey hairs) twenty years sooner than on a merry milkmaid's. Thou sleep'st worse, than if a mouse should be forced to take up her lodging in a cat's ear: a little infant, that breeds its teeth, should it lie with thee, would cry out, as if thou wert the more unquiet bedfellow.

DUCHESS: I am Duchess of Malfi still.

BOSOLA: That makes thy sleeps so broken:
Glories, like glow-worms, afar off shine bright,
But looked to near, have neither heat nor light.

DUCHESS: Thou art very plain.

BOSOLA: My trade is to flatter the dead, not the living; I am a tomb-maker.

DUCHESS: And thou comest to make my tomb?

BOSOLA: Yes.

DUCHESS: Let me be a little merry;
Of what stuff wilt thou make it?

The Duchess of Malfi in this scene the Duchess of Malfi and her servant ('waiting-woman') Cariola are murdered by Bosola, a former galley-slave who has been employed by the Duchess's brothers

insensible not perceivable through the senses

worm seed the dried heads of this plant were used as an anthelmintic

salvatory of green mummy a medicine box containing green mummified human flesh, which was esteemed as a medicine

crudded curdled

BOSOLA: Nay, resolve† me first, of what fashion?
DUCHESS: Why, do we grow fantastical in our death-bed?
Do we affect fashion in the grave?
BOSOLA: Most ambitiously. Princes' images on their tombs
Do not lie as they were wont, seeming to pray
Up to Heaven: but with their hands under their cheeks,
As if they died of the tooth-ache; they are not carved
With their eyes fixed upon the stars; but as
Their minds were wholly bent upon the world,
The self-same way they seem to turn their faces.
DUCHESS: Let me know fully therefore the effect
Of this thy dismal preparation,
This talk, fit for a charnel.* — cemetery
BOSOLA: Now I shall;
[*Enter* EXECUTIONERS *with*] *a coffin, cords, and a bell.*
Here is a present from your princely brothers,
And may it arrive welcome, for it brings
Last benefit, last sorrow.
DUCHESS: Let me see it.
I have so much obedience, in my blood,
I wish it in their veins, to do them good.
BOSOLA: This is your last presence chamber.
CARIOLA: O my sweet lady!
DUCHESS: Peace; it affrights not me.
BOSOLA: I am the common bellman,†
That usually is sent to condemned persons,
The night before they suffer.
DUCHESS: Even now thou said'st
Thou wast a tomb-maker?
BOSOLA: 'Twas to bring you
By degrees to mortification. Listen:
[*He rings the bell.*]
Hark, now every thing is still,
The screech-owl and the whistler shrill
Call upon our Dame, aloud,
And bid her quickly don her shroud.
Much you had of land and rent,
*Your length in clay's now competent.** — sufficient
A long war disturbed your mind,
Here your perfect peace is signed.

resolve explain to
common bellman an official sent by a charity to recite an uplifting speech (accompanied by a tolling handbell) outside the cell of a prisoner due to be executed

Of what is't fools make such vain keeping?
Sin their conception, their birth, weeping:
Their life, a general mist of error,
Their death, a hideous storm of terror.
Strew your hair with powders sweet:
Don clean linen, bathe your feet,
And, the foul fiend more to check,
A crucifix let bless your neck.
'Tis now full tide 'tween night and day,
End your groan, and come away.
[EXECUTIONERS *approach.*]
CARIOLA: Hence villains, tyrants, murderers. Alas!
What will you do with my lady? Call for help.
DUCHESS: To whom, to our next neighbours? They are mad-folks.
BOSOLA: Remove that noise.
[EXECUTIONERS *seize* CARIOLA, *who struggles.*]
DUCHESS: Farewell Cariola,
In my last will I have not much to give;
A many hungry guests have fed upon me,
Thine will be a poor reversion.* bequest
CARIOLA: I will die with her.
DUCHESS: I pray thee look thou givest my little boy
Some syrup for his cold, and let the girl
Say her prayers, ere she sleep.
[CARIOLA *is forced off.*]
Now what you please,
What death?
BOSOLA: Strangling: here are your executioners.
DUCHESS: I forgive them:
The apoplexy, catarrh, or cough o'th' lungs
Would do as much as they do.
BOSOLA: Doth not death fright you?
DUCHESS: Who would be afraid on't?
Knowing to meet such excellent company
In th'other world.
BOSOLA: Yet, methinks,
The manner of your death should much afflict you,
The cord should terrify you?
DUCHESS: Not a whit:
What would it pleasure me, to have my throat cut
With diamonds? or to be smothered
With cassia? or to be shot to death, with pearls?
I know death hath ten thousand several doors
For men to take their exits; and 'tis found

They go on such strange geometrical hinges,
You may open them both ways: any way, for Heaven sake,
So I were out of your whispering. Tell my brothers
That I perceive death, now I am well awake,
Best gift is, they can give, or I can take.
I would fain put off my last woman's fault,
I'ld not be tedious to you.

EXECUTIONERS: We are ready.

DUCHESS: Dispose my breath how please you, but my body
Bestow upon my women, will you?

EXECUTIONERS: Yes.

DUCHESS: Pull, and pull strongly, for your able strength
Must pull down heaven upon me:
Yet stay, heaven gates are not so highly arched
As princes' palaces: they that enter there
Must go upon their knees. Come violent death,
Serve for mandragora† to make me sleep;
Go tell my brothers, when I am laid out,
They then may feed in quiet.

They strangle her.

BOSOLA: Where's the waiting woman?
Fetch her. Some other strangle the children.

1612–14 1623

From THE DEVIL'S LAW-CASE†

Act V, Scene iv, 106–35

CAPUCHIN: O, I tremble for you:
For I do know you have a storm within you,
More terrible than a sea fight, and your soul
Being heretofore drowned in security,
You know not how to live, nor how to die:
But I have an object that shall startle you,
And make you know whither you are going.

ROMELIO: I am armed for't.

---

mandragora mandrake, which has narcotic properties

The Devil's Law Case in this scene a Capuchin Friar presents a dumbshow to the merchant Romelio

Enter LEONORA *with two coffins borne by her servants, and two winding sheets† stuck with flowers; presents one to her son,† and the other to* JULIO.

'Tis very welcome, this is a decent garment
Will never be out of fashion. I will kiss it.
All the flowers of the spring
Meet to perfume our burying:
These have but their growing prime,
And man does flourish but his time.
Survey our progress from our birth,
We are set, we grow, we turn to earth.
Soft music [*is played*].
Courts adieu, and all delights,
All bewitching appetites;
Sweetest breath, and clearest eye,
Like perfumes go out and die;
And consequently* this is done, inevitably
As shadows wait upon the sun.
Vain the ambition of kings,
Who seek by trophies and dead things,
To leave a living name behind,
And weave but nets to catch the wind.
O you have wrought a miracle, and melted
A heart of adamant: you have comprised
In this dumb pageant, a right excellent form
Of penitence.

CAPUCHIN: I am glad you so receive it.

1620 1623

winding sheets linen in which bodies were wrapped

her son Romelio

William Drummond of Hawthornden

1585–1649

William Drummond was born in Hawthornden near Edinburgh, the son of a courtier. He was educated at Edinburgh High School, Edinburgh University and the University of Bourges (where he studied law). He travelled in England and Europe until 1610, when his father's death made him Laird of Hawthornden, whereupon he abandoned his plans for a legal career and retired to Hawthornden for the rest of his life. Drummond brought to Hawthornden a large collection (now in the Edinburgh University Library) of literary works in English, French, Spanish and Italian. He read widely, and eventually began to write poetry himself. He wrote most of his poetry between 1612 and 1623, and then turned to a history of Scotland, which was published posthumously; in his old age he wrote pamphlets for the royalist cause.

Drummond's early poems are sonnets and madrigals in the Petrarchan tradition. In 1623 he published a collection of religious poems (*Flowers of Sion*) together with a prose meditation on death, *A Cypress Grove*.

SLEEP, SILENCE CHILD

Sleep, silence child, sweet father of soft rest,
Prince whose approach peace to all mortals brings,
Indifferent host to shepherds and to kings,
Sole comforter of minds with grief oppressed.
Lo, by thy charming rod all breathing things

Lie slumbering, with forgetfulness possessed,
And yet o're me to spread thy drowsy wings
Thou spares (alas) who cannot be thy guest.
Since I am thine, o come, but with that face
To inward light which thou art wont to show,
With fainéd solace ease a true felt woe,
Or if deaf God thou do deny that grace,
  Come as thou wilt, and what thou wilt bequeath,
  I long to kiss the image of my death.

1614

ALEXIS, HERE SHE STAYED

Alexis,† here she stayed among these pines
(Sweet hermitress) she did alone repair,
Here did she spread the treasure of her hair,
More rich than that brought from the Colchian† mines.
She set her by these musket eglantines,†
The happy place the print seems yet to bear,
Her voice did sweeten here thy sugared lines,
To which winds, trees, beasts, birds did lend their ear.
Me here she first perceived, and here a morn
Of bright carnations did o'respread her face,
Here did she sigh, here first my hopes were born,
And I first got a pledge of promised grace:
  But (ah) what served it to be happy so?
  Sith* passéd pleasures double but new woe. since

1614

FOR THE BAPTIST†

The last and greatest herald of heaven's king,
Girt with rough skins, hies to the deserts wild,
Among that savage brood the woods forth bring,
Which he than man more harmless found and mild:
His food was blossoms, and what young doth spring,

Alexis a common pastoral name, here representing Drummond's friend Sir William Alexander
Colchian Jason brought the golden fleece back from Colchis (now Soviet Georgia)
musket eglantines perfumed sweet-briars
Baptist John the Baptist, precursor and second cousin of Jesus

With honey that from virgin hives distilled;
Parched body, hollow eyes, some uncouth thing
Made him appear, long since from earth exiled.
There burst he forth; all ye, whose hopes rely
On God, with me amidst these deserts mourn,
Repent, repent, and from old errors turn.
Who listened to his voice, obeyed his cry?
  Only the Echoes which he made relent,
  Rung from their marble caves, repent, repent.

1623

MADRIGAL

On this cold world of ours,
Flower of the seasons, season of the flowers,
Son of the sun sweet spring,
Such hot and burning days why dost thou bring?
Is this for that those high eternal powers
Flash down that fire this all environing?
Or that now Phœbus† keeps his sister's sphere?
Or doth some Phaëton†
Enflame the sea and air?
Or rather is it (usher of the year)
For that last day amongst thy flowers alone
Unmasked thou sawest my fair?
  And whilst thou on her gazed she did thee burn,
  And in thy brother summer doth thee turn.

1614

Phœbus epithet of Apollo as god of the sun; his twin sister was Phœbe, goddess of the moon

Phaëton the son of Phœbus; his inability to control the horses of the chariot of the sun nearly caused the earth to be burnt

From A CYPRESS GROVE

[*On Death*]

If there be any evil in death, it would appear to be that pain and torment, which we apprehend to arise from the breaking of those straight bands which keep the soul and body together; which, sith not without great struggling and motion, seemeth to prove it self vehement and most extreme. The senses are the only cause of pain, but before the last trances of death they are so brought under, that they have no (or very little) strength, and their strength lessening the strength of pain too must be lessened. How should we doubt but the weakness of sense lesseneth pain, sith we know, that weakened and maimed parts which receive not nourishment, are a great deal less sensible than the other parts of the body; and see, that old strengthless, decrepit persons leave this world almost without pain, as in a sleep? If bodies of the most sound and wholesome constitution be these which most vehemently feel pain, it must then follow that they of a distempered and crazy† constitution, have least feeling of pain; and by this reason, all weak and sick bodies should not much feel pain; for if they were not distempered and evil complexioned, they would not be sick. That the sight, hearing, taste, smelling, leave us without pain, and unawares, we are undoubtedly assured: And why should we not think the same of the feeling? That, by which we are capable of feeling, is the vital spirits animated by the brain, which in a man in perfect health, by veins and arteries are spread and extended through the whole body, and hence it is that the whole body is capable of pain: but, in dying bodies we see, that by pauses and degrees those parts which are furthest removed from the heart, become cold, and being deprived of natural heat, all the pain which they feel, is that they do feel no pain. Now, even as ere the sick be aware, the vital spirits have withdrawn themselves from the whole extension of the body, to succour the heart (like distressed citizens which finding their walls battered down, fly to the defence of their citadel) so they abandon the heart without any sensible touch. As the flame, the oil failing, leaveth the wick, or as the light the air which it doth invest. As to those shrinking motions, and convulsions of sinews and members, which appear to witness great pain, let one represent to himself the strings of an high-tuned lute, which breaking, retire to their natural windings, or a piece of ice, that without any outward violence, cracketh at a thaw; no otherwise do the sinews of the body, finding themselves slack and unbended from the brain, and their wonted

crazy diseased

labours and motions cease, struggle, and seem to stir themselves, but without either pain or sense. Sowning† is a true portrait of death, or rather it is the same, being a cessation from all action, motion, and function of sense and life: But in sowning there is no pain, but a silent rest, and so deep and sound a sleep, that the natural is nothing in comparison of it; what great pain then can there be in death, which is but a continued sowning, a sweet ignorance of cares, and a never again returning to the works and dolorous felicity of life? The wise and all provident Creator hath made death by many signs of pain appear terrible, to the effect, that if man, for relief of miseries and present evils, should have unto it recourse, it being (apparently) a worser, he should rather constantly endure what he knoweth, than have refuge unto that which he feareth and knoweth not, the terrors of death seem the guardians of life.

Now although death were an extreme pain, sith it comes in an instant, what can it be? Why should we fear it? For, while we are, it cometh not, and it being come, we are no more. Nay, though it were most painful, long continuing, and terrible-ugly, why should we fear it? Sith fear is a foolish passion but where it may preserve; but it can not preserve us from death, yea, rather fear maketh us to meet with that which we would shun, and banishing the comforts of present contentments bringeth death more near unto us. That is ever terrible which is unknown; so do little children fear to go in the dark, and their fear is increased with tales.

1623

sowning swooning

Thomas Hobbes

1588–1679

Thomas Hobbes was born in Malmesbury, Wiltshire, the son of a vicar. His early education, which was partly private, and partly at Malmesbury School, turned him into a precocious classicist: he was learning Greek and Latin at the age of six, and at thirteen translated Euripides' *Medea* from Greek into Latin iambics. He studied at Magdalen Hall, Oxford, and for the next twenty years served at Chatsworth and on the continent as tutor (and later secretary) to William Cavendish (who became the second Earl of Devonshire); after the second Earl's death in 1628, Hobbes became tutor to his son William Cavendish, the third Earl. In 1640 Hobbes completed a controversial political treatise, and fled to France to escape the wrath of Parliament. He lived in France until 1651, when he fled back to England to escape the wrath of the churchmen occasioned by the publication of *Leviathan*. He submitted to the Commonwealth government, and after the Restoration was granted a royal pension. At the age of eighty-four he wrote his autobiography in Latin verse, and two years later he completed his translation of Homer's epics.

Hobbes was a philosopher of science and of politics. His greatest work is *The Leviathan, or the Matter, Form and Power of a Commonwealth*, which he published in English in 1651 and in Latin in 1668. The metaphor of the leviathan refers to the state as an organism. Hobbes believed that mankind was by nature selfish and anti-social, and therefore needed to be ruled by a sovereign power, which could either be a single man or a parliament, but not both. Only such a sovereign power could ensure a peaceful existence for mankind.

From LEVIATHAN

Of the Natural Condition of Mankind, as concerning their Felicity, and Misery

Nature hath made men so equal, in the faculties of body, and mind; as that though there be found one man sometimes manifestly stronger in body, or of quicker mind than another; yet when all is reckoned together, the difference between man and man, is not so considerable, as that one man can thereupon claim to himself any benefit, to which another may not pretend, as well as he. For as to the strength of body, the weakest has strength enough to kill the strongest, either by secret machination, or by confederacy with others, that are in the same danger with himself.

And as to the faculties of the mind, (setting aside the arts grounded upon words, and especially that skill of proceeding upon general, and infallible rules, called science; which very few have, and but in few things; as being not a native faculty, born with us; nor attained, as prudence, while we look after somewhat else,) I find yet a greater equality amongst men, than that of strength. For prudence is but experience; which equal time, equally bestows on all men, in those things they equally apply themselves unto. That which may perhaps make such equality incredible, is but a vain conceit of one's own wisdom, which almost all men think they have in a greater degree, than the vulgar; that is, than all men but themselves, and a few others, whom by fame, or for concurring with themselves, they approve. For such is the nature of men, that howsoever they may acknowledge many others to be more witty, or more eloquent, or more learned; yet they will hardly believe there be many so wise as themselves: for they see their own wit at hand, and other men's at a distance. But this proveth rather that men are in that point equal, than unequal. For there is not ordinarily a greater sign of the equal distribution of any thing, than that every man is contented with his share.

From this equality of ability, ariseth equality of hope in the attaining of our ends. And therefore if any two men desire the same thing, which nevertheless they cannot both enjoy, they become enemies; and in the way to their end (which is principally their own conservation, and sometimes their delectation only) endeavour to destroy, or subdue one another. And from hence it comes to pass, that where an invader hath no more to fear, than an other man's single power; if one plant, sow, build, or possess a convenient seat† others may probably be expected

seat home

to come prepared with forces united, to dispossess and deprive him, not only of the fruit of his labour, but also of his life, or liberty. And the invader again is in the like danger of another.

And from this diffidence of one another, there is no way for any man to secure himself, so reasonable, as anticipation; that is, by force, or wiles, to master the persons of all men he can, so long, till he see no other power great enough to endanger him: and this is no more than his own conservation requireth, and is generally allowed. And because there be some, that taking pleasure in contemplating their own power in the acts of conquest, which they pursue farther than their security requires; if others, that otherwise would be glad to be at ease within modest bounds, should not by invasion increase their power, they would not be able, long time, by standing only on their defence, to subsist. And by consequence, such augmentation of dominion over men, being necessary to a man's conservation, it ought to be allowed him.

Again, men have no pleasure (but on the contrary a great deal of grief) in keeping company, where there is no power able to overawe them all. For every man looketh that his companion should value him, at the same rate he sets upon himself: and upon all signs of contempt, or undervaluing, naturally endeavours, as far as he dares (which amongst them that have no common power to keep them in quiet, is far enough to make them destroy each other) to extort a greater value from his contemners,† by dommage;† and from others, by the example.

So that in the nature of man, we find three principal causes of quarrel: first, competition: secondly, diffidence: thirdly, glory.

The first, maketh men invade for gain; the second, for safety; and the third, for reputation. The first use violence, to make themselves masters of other men's persons, wives, children, and cattle; the second, to defend them; the third, for trifles, as a word, a smile, a different opinion, and any other sign of undervalue, either direct in their persons, or by reflection in their kindred, their friends, their nation, their profession, or their name.

Hereby it is manifest, that during the time men live without a common power to keep them all in awe, they are in that condition which is called war; and such a war, as is of every man, against every man. For war consisteth not in battle only, or the act of fighting; but in a tract of time, wherein the will to contend by battle is sufficiently known: and therefore the notion of time, is to be considered in the nature of war, as it is in the nature of weather. For as the nature of foul weather, lieth not in a shower or two of rain, but in an inclination thereto of many days together; so the nature of war, consisteth not in actual

contemners those who despise him

dommage damage

fighting, but in the known disposition thereto, during all the time there is no assurance to the contrary. All other time is peace.

Whatsoever therefore is consequent to a time of war, where every man is enemy to every man; the same is consequent to the time, wherein men live without other security, than what their own strength, and their own invention shall furnish them withall. In such condition, there is no place for industry; because the fruit thereof is uncertain: and consequently no culture[†] of the earth, no navigation, nor use of the commodities that may be imported by sea; no commodious building; no instruments of moving, and removing such things as require much force; no knowledge of the face of the earth; no account of time; no arts, no letters; no society; and which is worst of all, continual fear, and danger of violent death; and the life of man, solitary, poor, nasty, brutish, and short.

1651

culture cultivation

Robert Herrick

1591–1674

Robert Herrick was born in London, the son of a Leicestershire goldsmith. When Robert was sixteen months old his father committed suicide, and the seven Herrick children became wards of their uncle Sir William Hericke. Herrick may have attended Westminster School, and in 1607 he was apprenticed to his guardian as a goldsmith. He was released from his apprenticeship in 1613 to enter St John's College, Cambridge; in 1616 he migrated to Trinity Hall, where he took his degrees. He was ordained in 1623, and for several years lived in literary circles in London. In 1627 he served as an army chaplain in France, and for this service was awarded the living of Dean Prior, in rural Devonshire. He was ejected in 1647 for Royalist sympathies, and during his years of ecclesiastical exile he lived in London, supported by wealthy friends and relatives. He was restored to his living in 1662, and returned to Dean Prior for the rest of his life.

In 1648 Herrick collected his secular poems (*Hesperides*) and his religious poems (*Noble Numbers*) and published them in one volume; thereafter he seems not to have written any more poetry. The 1200 poems collected in this volume establish Herrick as one of the greatest lyric poets to have written in English; his poems are graceful and highly polished, witty and epigrammatic.

CORINNA'S† GOING A-MAYING

Get up, get up for shame, the blooming morn
Upon her wings presents the god unshorn.†
See how Aurora† throws her fair
Fresh-quilted colours through the air:
Get up, sweet slug-a-bed, and see
The dew bespangling herb and tree.
Each flower has wept and bowed toward the east
Above an hour since: yet you not dressed;
Nay! not so much as out of bed?
When all the birds have matins said
And sung their thankful hymns, 'tis sin,
Nay, profanation to keep in,
Whereas a thousand virgins on this day
Spring, sooner than the lark, to fetch in May.

Rise and put on your foliage, and be seen
To come forth, like the spring-time, fresh and green,
And sweet as Flora.† Take no care
For jewels for your gown or hair:
Fear not; the leaves will strew
Gems in abundance upon you:
Besides, the childhood of the day has kept,
Against you come, some orient pearls unwept;
Come and receive them while the light
Hangs on the dew-locks of the night:
And Titan† on the eastern hill
Retires himself, or else stands still
Till you come forth. Wash, dress, be brief in praying:
Few beads* are best when once we go a-Maying. prayers

Corinna's Going a-Maying *Corinna*: the name recalls that of Ovid's mistress
god unshorn Phoebus Apollo, the sun-god, whose hair (the rays of the sun) is never cut
Aurora goddess of the dawn
Flora goddess of flowers
Titan the sun-god, who in Greek mythology was one of the Titans

Come, my Corinna, come; and, coming, mark
How each field turns a street, each street a park
Made green and trimmed with trees: see how
Devotion gives each house a bough
Or branch: each porch, each door ere this
An ark, a tabernacle is,
Made up of white-thorn neatly interwove;
As if here were those cooler shades of love.
Can such delights be in the street
And open fields and we not see it?
Come, we'll abroad; and let's obey
The proclamation made for May:
And sin no more, as we have done, by staying;
But, my Corinna, come, let's go a-Maying.

There's not a budding boy or girl this day
But is got up, and gone to bring in May.
A deal of youth, ere this, is come
Back, and with white-thorn laden home.
Some have despatched their cakes and cream
Before that we have left* to dream: ceased
And some have wept, and wooed, and plighted troth,
And chose their priest, ere we can cast off sloth:
Many a green-gown† has been given;
Many a kiss, both odd and even:†
Many a glance too has been sent
From out the eye, love's firmament;
Many a jest told of the keys betraying
This night, and locks picked, yet we're not a-Maying.

green-gown a gown greened by tumbling in the grass

odd and even a reference to kissing games

Come, let us go while we are in our prime;
And take the harmless folly of the time.
We shall grow old apace, and die
Before we know our liberty.
Our life is short, and our days run
As fast away as does the sun;
And, as a vapour or a drop of rain,
Once lost, can ne'er be found again,
So when or you or I are made
A fable, song, or fleeting shade,
All love, all liking, all delight
Lies drowned with us in endless night.
Then while time serves, and we are but decaying,
Come, my Corinna, come, let's go a-Maying.

1648

HIS PRAYER TO BEN JONSON†

When I a verse shall make,
Know I have prayed thee,
For old religion's† sake,
Saint Ben, to aid me.

Make the way smooth for me,
When I, thy Herrick,
Honouring thee, on my knee
Offer my lyric.

Candles I'll give to thee,
And a new altar,
And thou, Saint Ben, shalt be
Writ in my Psalter.

1648

His Prayer to Ben Jonson Herrick considered himself to be a disciple of Jonson; he was, as Jonson phrased it (borrowing from Revelation 7.8), 'sealed of the tribe of Ben'

old religion Roman Catholicism

TO THE VIRGINS, TO MAKE MUCH OF TIME

Gather ye rosebuds while ye may,
Old time is still a-flying:
And this same flower that smiles to-day
To-morrow will be dying.

The glorious lamp of heaven, the sun,
The higher he's a-getting,
The sooner will his race be run,
And nearer he's to setting.

That age is best which is the first,
When youth and blood are warmer;
But being spent, the worse, and worst
Times still succeed the former.

Then be not coy, but use your time,
And while ye may go marry:
For having lost but once your prime
You may for ever tarry.

1648

POEMS TO JULIA†

Her Bed

See'st thou that cloud as silver clear,
Plump, soft, and swelling everywhere?
'Tis Julia's bed, and she sleeps there.

Her Legs

Fain would I kiss my Julia's dainty leg,
Which is as white and hairless as an egg.

Poems to Julia Julia was one of Herrick's imaginary mistresses

Upon Julia's Clothes

When as in silks my Julia goes,
Then, then, methinks, how sweetly flows
The liquefaction of her clothes.

Next, when I cast mine eyes and see
That brave vibration each way free;
O how that glittering taketh me!

Upon Julia's Breasts

Display thy breasts, my Julia – there let me
Behold that circummortal purity,
Between whose glories there my lips I'll lay,
Ravish'd in that fair *via lactea*.†

Upon Julia's Voice

So smooth, so sweet, so silvery is thy voice,
As, could they hear, the damned would make no noise,
But listen to thee, walking in thy chamber,
Melting melodious words to lutes of amber.

1648

UPON MISTRESS SUSANNA SOUTHWELL, HER FEET†

Her pretty feet
Like snails did creep
A little out, and then,
As if they played at Bo-Peep,
Did soon draw in again.

1648

via lactea the Latin term for the Milky Way
Upon Mistress Susanna Southwell, Her Feet the precise identity of Susanna Southwell is not known, but she was presumably related to Herrick's friend Sir Thomas Southwell

TO ANTHEA, WHO MAY COMMAND HIM ANYTHING†

Bid me to live, and I will live
  Thy Protestant to be,
Or bid me love, and I will give
  A loving heart to thee.

A heart as soft, a heart as kind,
  A heart as sound and free
As in the whole world thou canst find,
  That heart I'll give to thee.

Bid that heart stay, and it will stay
  To honour thy decree:
Or bid it languish quite away,
  And't shall do so for thee.

Bid me to weep, and I will weep
  While I have eyes to see:
And, having none, yet I will keep
  A heart to weep for thee.

Bid me despair, and I'll despair
  Under that cypress-tree:
Or bid me die, and I will dare
  E'en death to die for thee.

Thou art my life, my love, my heart,
  The very eyes of me:
And hast command of every part
  To live and die for thee.

1648

To Anthea, Who May Command Him Anything Anthea was another of Herrick's imaginary mistresses

HIS LITANY TO THE HOLY SPIRIT

In the hour of my distress,
When temptations me oppress,
And when I my sins confess,
Sweet Spirit, comfort me!

When I lie within my bed,
Sick in heart and sick in head,
And with doubts discomforted,
Sweet Spirit, comfort me!

When the house doth sigh and weep,
And the world is drowned in sleep,
Yet mine eyes the watch do keep,
Sweet Spirit, comfort me!

When the artless doctor sees
No one hope, but of his fees,
And his skill runs on the lees,[†]
Sweet Spirit, comfort me!

When his potion and his pill
Has, or none, or little skill,
Meet for nothing, but to kill;
Sweet Spirit, comfort me!

When the passing bell[†] doth toll,
And the Furies[†] in a shoal
Come to fright a parting soul,
Sweet Spirit, comfort me!

When the tapers now burn blue,
And the comforters are few,
And that number more than true,
Sweet Spirit, comfort me!

lees dregs (of medicine, and of life)
passing-bell a bell tolled to announce the death of a parishioner
Furies Roman avenging goddesses

When the priest his last hath prayed,
And I nod to what is said,
'Cause my speech is now decayed,
Sweet Spirit, comfort me!

When, God knows, I'm tossed about,
Either with despair, or doubt;
Yet before the glass be out,
Sweet Spirit, comfort me!

When the tempter me pursueth
With the sins of all my youth,
And half damns me with untruth,
Sweet Spirit, comfort me!

When the flames and hellish cries
Fright mine ears, and fright mine eyes,
And all terrors me surprise,
Sweet Spirit, comfort me!

When the judgment is revealed,
And that open'd which was sealed,
When to Thee I have appealed,
Sweet Spirit, comfort me!

1648

THIS CROSSTREE HERE

This crosstree here
Doth Jesus bear,
Who sweetened first
The death accursed.
Here all things ready are, make haste, make haste away;
For long this work will be, and very short this day.
Why then, go on to act: here's wonders to be done
Before the last least sand of Thy ninth hour be run;
Or ere dark clouds do dull or dead the mid-day's sun.
Act when Thou wilt,
Blood will be spilt:
Pure balm, that shall
Bring health to all.
Why then, begin
To pour first in
Some drops of wine,
Instead of brine,
To search the wound
So long unsound:
And, when that's done,
Let oil next run
To cure the sore
Sin made before.
And O! dear Christ,
E'en as Thou di'st,
Look down, and see
Us weep for Thee.
And tho', love knows,
Thy dreadful woes
We cannot ease,
Yet do Thou please,
Who mercy art,
T' accept each heart
That gladly would
Help if it could.
Meanwhile let me,
Beneath this tree,
This honour have,
To make my grave.

1648

Henry King

1592–1669

Henry King was born in Buckinghamshire, the son of an eminent clergyman. He was educated at Westminster School (where George Herbert was his exact contemporary) and Christ Church, Oxford. He became a prebend of St Paul's in 1616, and eventually became Bishop of Chichester, but he was ejected from this post in 1643. He lived with various friends during the Interregnum, was restored to his bishopric in 1660.

King wrote poetry all his life, and many of his best poems are elegies. He is remembered chiefly for *An Exequy*, which commemorates his wife Anne, who died in January 1624.

From AN EXEQUY TO HIS MATCHLESS NEVER-TO-BE-FORGOTTEN FRIEND

Accept, thou shrine of my dead saint
Instead of dirges, this complaint;†
And for sweet flowers to crown thy hearse,
Receive a strew* of weeping verse — scattering
From thy grieved friend, whom thou might'st see
Quite melted into tears for thee.

complaint lyric which expresses grief

Dear loss, since thy untimely fate,
My task hath been to meditate
On thee, on thee; thou art the book
The library whereon I look,
Though almost blind. For thee (loved clay)
I languish out, not live, the day,
Using no other exercise
But what I practise with mine eyes.
By which wet glasses I find out
How lazily Time creeps about
To one that mourns; this, only this
My exercise and business is,
So I compute the weary hours
With sighs dissolvèd into showers.

. . .

But hark! My pulse, like a soft drum
Beats my approach, tells thee I come;
And, slow howe're my marches be,
I shall at last sit down by thee.

The thought of this bids me go on,
And wait my dissolution†
With hope and comfort. Dear (forgive
The crime), I am content to live
Divided, with but half a heart,
Till we shall meet and never part.
1624 1657

dissolution pronounced as five syllables

Francis Quarles

1592–1644

Francis Quarles was born in Essex, the son of a courtier, and was educated at a local county school. He studied at Christ's College, Cambridge, and Lincoln's Inn. In 1613 he went to Germany as an attendant of Princess Elizabeth. In about 1620 he returned to London, where he published a series of Biblical paraphrases. He moved to Dublin in about 1628 as private secretary to Archbishop Ussher. Four years later he retired to Essex, where he composed his *Emblems* (1635) and *Hieroglyphics of the Life of Man* (1638). In 1639 he was appointed chronologer to the city of London; he seems to have written nothing in his official capacity, but he did compose a series of Royalist pamphlets.

Quarles's reputation rests on his *Emblems*, a collection of short devotional poems, each of which is based on a verse from the Bible, and illustrated by an engraving.

From EMBLEMS

Proverbs xxiii.5

Wilt thou set thine eyes upon that which is not? for riches make themselves wings; they fly away as an eagle.

False world, thou liest: thou canst not lend
        The least delight;
Thy favours cannot gain a friend,
        They are so slight;
Thy morning pleasures make an end
        To please at night;
Poor are the wants that thou suppliest;
And yet thou vauntest, and yet thou viest
With heaven! fond earth, thou boastest; false world, thou liest.

Thy babbling tongue tells golden tales
        Of endless treasure;
Thy bounty offers easy sales
        Of lasting pleasure;
Thou askest the Conscience what she ails,
        And swearest to ease her:
There's none can want where thou suppliest;
There's none can give where thou deniest:
Alas! fond world, thou boastest; false world, thou liest.

What well-adviséd ear regards
        What Earth can say?
Thy words are gold, but thy rewards
        Are painted clay;
Thy cunning can but pack the cards,
        Thou canst not play;
Thy game at weakest, still thou viest;†
If seen, and then revied,† deniest:
Thou art not what thou seemest false world, thou liest.

Thy tinsel bosom seems a mint
        Of new-coined treasure;
A paradise, that has no stint,
        No change, no measure;
A painted cask, but nothing in it,
        Nor wealth, nor pleasure:
Vain earth, that falsely thus compliest
With man; vain man, that thus reliest
On earth: vain man, thou dotest; vain Earth, thou liest.

What mean dull souls, in this high measure
        To haberdash†
In earth's base wares, whose greatest treasure
        Is dross and trash;
The height of whose enchanting pleasure
        Is but a flash?
Are these the goods that thou suppliest
Us mortals with? Are these the highest?
Can these bring cordial† peace? False world, thou liest.

1635

thou viest you bid on the strength of the cards which you hold
revied your opponent raises the stakes
haberdash to sell small items of dress, etc.
cordial comforting to the heart

George Herbert

1593–1633

George Herbert, the unofficial patron saint of Anglicanism, was born into a prominent family in Montgomery and educated at Westminster School and Trinity College, Cambridge, where he had a brilliant career. He had entered Trinity as a King's Scholar in 1609, and was elected to a Minor Fellowship in 1614 and a Major Fellowship in 1616. In 1618 he was appointed Reader in Rhetoric, and two years later became Public Orator, a post which brought him into contact with the court of King James. In 1624 and 1625 he sat as a Member of Parliament for Montgomery. In 1626 he was ordained as a deacon, and appointed prebend of a ruined church at Leighton Bromswold, Huntingdonshire, which was very close to Little Gidding, where Herbert's Cambridge friend Nicholas Ferrar had established a religious community. Herbert offered to transfer the prebend to Little Gidding, but Ferrar suggested that he restore the ruined church, which Herbert did. Ferrar's influence during this period doubtless contributed to the development of a religious sensibility in Herbert. In 1630 Herbert was ordained as a priest and appointed rector of Bemerton (near Salisbury), where he lived for the last three years of his life.

During his lifetime Herbert's only published poems were written in Latin. On his deathbed he sent his English poems to Ferrar, who published them as *The Temple* a few weeks after Herbert died of consumption. Various translations and prose works appeared in the course of the next thirty years; his finest prose work is a description of a model country parson entitled *A Priest to the Temple* (1652). The poems in *The Temple* use traditional forms, types and images to illustrate a wide variety of devotional themes and moods.

From THE TEMPLE

The Altar

A broken altar, Lord, thy servant rears,
Made of a heart, and cemented with tears:
Whose parts are as thy hand did frame;
No workman's tool hath touched the same.
A heart alone
Is such a stone,
As nothing but
Thy power doth cut.
Wherefore each part
Of my hard heart
Meets in this frame,
To praise thy name:
That, if I chance to hold my peace,
These stones to praise thee may not cease.
O let thy blessed sacrifice be mine,
And sanctify this altar to be thine.

1633

Easter Wings

Lord, who createdst man in wealth and store,
Though foolishly he lost the same,
Decaying more and more,
Till he became
Most poor:
With thee
Oh let me rise
As larks, harmoniously,
And sing this day thy victories:
Then shall the fall further the flight in me.

My tender age in sorrow did begin:
And still with sicknesses and shame
Thou did'st so punish sin,
That I became
Most thin.
With thee
Let me combine,
And feel this day thy victory,
For, if I imp† my wing on thine,
Affliction shall advance the flight in me.

1633

Sin

Lord, with what care hast thou begirt us round!
Parents first season us: then schoolmasters
Deliver us to laws; they send us bound
To rules of reason, holy messengers,

Pulpits and Sundays, sorrow dogging sin,
Afflictions sorted,* anguish of all sizes. assorted
Fine nets and stratagems to catch us in,
Bibles laid open, millions of surprises,

Blessings beforehand, ties of gratefulness,
The sound of glory ringing in our ears;
Without, our shame; within, our consciences;
Angels and grace, eternal hopes and fears.

Yet all these fences and their whole array
One cunning bosom-sin blows quite away.

1633

imp engraft (a metaphor from falconry)

Prayer

Prayer, the church's banquet, angels' age,†
God's breath in man returning to his birth,
The soul in paraphrase, heart in pilgrimage,
The Christian plummet sounding† heaven and earth;
Engine† against the Almighty, sinner's tower,
Reversed thunder, Christ-side-piercing spear,†
The six days' world-transposing† in an hour,
A kind of tune, which all things hear and fear;
Softness and peace and joy and love and bliss,
Exalted manna,† gladness of the best,
Heaven in ordinary,† men well dressed,
The milky way, the bird of paradise,
Church bells beyond the stars heard, the soul's blood,
The land of spices, something understood.

1633

Jordan† (I)

Who says that fictions only and false hair
Become a verse? Is there in truth no beauty?
Is all good structure in a winding stair?
May no lines pass, except they do their duty
Not to a true, but painted chair?

Is it not verse, except enchanted groves
And sudden arbours shadow coarse-spun lines?
Must purling* streams refresh a lover's loves? murmuring
Must all be veiled, while he that reads, divines,
Catching the sense at two removes?

angels' age angels are eternal, so prayer puts us in contact with eternity
sounding measuring the depth of
engine here refers to a siege machine
spear the spear which pierced the side of Jesus was said to have touched his heart, and prayer can do likewise
transposing changing to another musical key
manna here used typologically of the bread of the communion service
ordinary draws on the Latin sense of the word, and refers to the form of prayer in the church service
Jordan refers literally to the river which miraculously divided when the Hebrews entered the Promised Land (Joshua 3.16), and in which Jesus was baptised, and metaphorically to the achievement of purity

Shepherds are honest people; let them sing:
Riddle who list, for me, and pull for prime,†
I envy no man's nightingale or spring;
Nor let them punish me with loss of rhyme,
Who plainly say, 'My God, my King'.

1633

Unkindness

Lord, make me coy and tender† to offend:
In friendship, first I think, if that agree,
Which I intend,
Unto my friend's intent and end.
I would not use a friend, as I use Thee.

If any touch my friend, or his good name,
It is my honour and my love to free
His blasted fame
From the least spot or thought of blame.
I could not use a friend, as I use Thee.

My friend may spit upon my curious† floor:
Would he have gold? I lend it instantly;
But let the poor,
And thou within them, starve at door.
I cannot use a friend, as I use Thee.

When that my friend pretendeth to a place,†
I quit my interest, and leave it free:
But when thy grace
Sues for my heart, I thee displace;
Nor would I use a friend, as I use Thee.

Yet can a friend what Thou has done fulfil?
O write in brass, 'My God upon a tree
His blood did spill,
Only to purchase my good-will:
Yet use I not my foes, as I use Thee.'

1633

pull for prime draw winning cards (in the game of primero)
coy and tender quiet and reluctant
curious beautiful and ornate
pretendeth to a place aspires to a position

Jordan† (II)

When first my lines of heavenly joys made mention,
Such was their lustre, they did so excel,
That I sought out quaint words, and trim invention;
My thoughts began to burnish, sprout, and swell,
Curling with metaphors a plain intention,
Decking the sense, as if it were to sell.

Thousands of notions in my brain did run,
Offering their service, if I were not sped:* successful
I often blotted what I had begun;
This was not quick* enough, and that was dead. lively
Nothing could seem too rich to clothe the sun,†
Much less those joys which trample on his head.

As flames do work and wind, when they ascend;
So did I weave myself into the sense.
But while I bustled, I might hear a friend
Whisper, 'How wide is all this long pretence!
There is in love a sweetness ready penned:
Copy out only that, and save expense.'

1633

The Collar†

I struck the board,* and cried, 'No more; table
I will abroad.
What? shall I ever sigh and pine?
My lines and life are free; free as the road,
Loose as the wind, as large as store.
Shall I be still in suit?†
Have I no harvest but a thorn
To let me blood, and not restore
What I have lost with cordial fruit?
Sure there was wine,
Before my sighs did dry it: there was corn,
Before my tears did drown it.
Is the year only lost to me?

Jordan (II) this poem is a sacred imitation of the first sonnet in Sidney's *Astrophil and Stella*
sun plays on 'Son' (of God)
The Collar refers not to the clerical collar (which was not a distinctive feature of clerical dress) but to the yoke, and plays on 'choler' and 'caller'
in suit acting as a petitioner

Have I no bays to crown it?
No flowers, no garlands gay? all blasted?
All wasted?
Not so, my heart: but there is fruit,
And thou hast hands.
Recover all thy sigh-blown age
On double pleasures: leave thy cold dispute
Of what is fit, and not: forsake thy cage,
Thy rope of sands,
Which petty thoughts have made, and made to thee
Good cable, to enforce and draw,
And be thy law,
While thou didst wink and wouldst not see.
Away; take heed:
I will abroad.
Call in thy death's-head† there: tie up thy fears.
He that forbears
To suit and serve his need,
Deserves his load.'
But as I raved and grew more fierce and wild
At every word,
Methought I heard one calling, 'Child':
And I replied, 'My Lord.'

1633

The Pulley†

When God at first made man,
Having a glass of blessings standing by;
'Let us', said he, 'pour on him all we can:
Let the world's riches, which dispersed lie,
Contract into a span'.

So strength first made a way;
Then beauty flowed, then wisdom, honour, pleasure:
When almost all was out, God made a stay,
Perceiving that alone, of all his treasure,
Rest in the bottom lay.

---

death's-head a human skull which acted as an emblem of mortality

The Pulley the poem is a sacred adaptation of the legend of Pandora's box, according to which Pandora brought to her husband a box of plagues and disasters which were let loose when she opened it; she tried to shut the box quickly, but all that remained inside was Hope

'For if I should', said he,
'Bestow this jewel also on my creature,
He would adore my gifts instead of me,
And rest in Nature, not the God of Nature:
So both should losers be.

Yet let him keep the rest,†
But keep them with repining restlessness:
Let him be rich and weary, that at least,
If goodness lead him not, yet weariness
May toss him to my breast'.

1633

The Flower

How fresh, O Lord, how sweet and clean
Are thy returns! even as the flowers in spring;
To which, besides their own demean,†
The late-past frosts tributes of pleasure bring.
Grief melts away
Like snow in May,
As if there were no such cold thing.

Who would have thought my shrivelled heart
Could have recovered greenness? It was gone
Quite under ground; as flowers depart
To see their Mother-root, when they have blown;* bloomed
Where they together
All the hard weather,
Dead to the world, keep house unknown.

These are thy wonders, Lord of power,
Killing and quickening, bringing down to hell
And up to heaven in an hour;
Making a chiming of a passing-bell.†
We say amiss,
This or that is:
Thy Word is all, if we could spell.

---

rest means both 'remainder' and 'repose'
demean demesne (i.e. estate), with a play on 'demeanour'
passing-bell a bell tolled to signal a death

O that I once past changing were,
Fast in thy Paradise, where no flower can wither!
Many a spring I shoot up fair,
Offering* at heaven, growing and groaning thither: aiming
Nor doth my flower
Want a spring-shower,
My sins and I joining together.

But while I grow in a straight line,
Still upwards bent, as if heaven were mine own,
Thy anger comes, and I decline:
What frost to that? what pole is not the zone
Where all things burn,
When thou dost turn,
And the least frown of thine is shown?

And now in age I bud again,
After so many deaths I live and write;
I once more smell the dew and rain,
And relish versing: O my only light,
It cannot be
That I am he,
On whom thy tempests fell at night.

These are thy wonders, Lord of love,
To make us see we are but flowers that glide:
Which when we once can find and prove,
Thou hast a garden for us, where to bide.
Who would be more,
Swelling through store,
Forfeit their Paradise by their pride.

1633

The Twenty-third Psalm

The God of love my shepherd is,
And he that doth me feed:
While he is mine, and I am his,
What can I want or need?

He leads me to the tender grass,
Where I both feed and rest;
Then to the streams that gently pass:
In both I have the best.

Or if I stray, he doth convert,
  And bring my mind in frame:
And all this not for my desert,
  But for his holy name.

Yea, in death's shady, black abode
  Well may I walk, not fear:
For thou art with me, and thy rod
  To guide, thy staff to bear.

Nay, thou dost make me sit and dine,
  Even in my enemies' sight;
My head with oil, my cup with wine
  Runs over day and night.

Surely thy sweet and wondrous love
  Shall measure all my days;
And as it never shall remove,
  So neither shall my praise.

1633

Discipline

Throw away thy rod,
Throw away thy wrath:
    O my God,
Take the gentle path.

For my heart's desire
Unto thine is bent:
    I aspire
To a full consent.

Not a word or look
I affect to own,
    But by book,
And thy book alone.

Though I fail, I weep:
Though I halt in pace,
    Yet I creep
To the throne of grace.

Then let wrath remove;
Love will do the deed:
For with love
Stony hearts will bleed.

Love is swift of foot;
Love's a man of war,†
And can shoot,
And can hit from far.

Who can 'scape his bow?
That which wrought on thee,
Brought thee low,
Needs must work on me.

Throw away thy rod;
Though man frailties hath,
Thou art God:
Throw away thy wrath.

1633

Love

Love bade me welcome; yet my soul drew back,
Guilty of dust and sin.
But quick-eyed Love, observing me grow slack
From my first entrance in,
Drew nearer to me, sweetly questioning,
If I lacked any thing.

A guest, I answered, worthy to be here:
Love said, You shall be he.
I the unkind, ungrateful? Ah, my dear,
I cannot look on thee.
Love took my hand, and smiling did reply,
Who made the eyes but I?

man of war refers both to God (Exodus 15.3) and to Cupid

Truth, Lord, but I have marred them: let my shame
Go where it doth deserve.
And know you not, says Love, who bore the blame?
My dear, then I will serve.
You must sit down, says Love, and taste my meat:†
So I did sit and eat.

1633

From A PRIEST TO THE TEMPLE
Chapter 2
The Parson's Life

The country parson is exceeding exact in his life, being holy, just, prudent, temperate, bold, grave in all his ways. And because the two highest points of life, wherein a Christian is most seen, are patience, and mortification; patience in regard of afflictions, mortification in regard of lusts and affections, and the stupefying and deading of all the clamorous powers of the soul, therefore he hath thoroughly studied these, that he may be an absolute master and commander of himself, for all the purposes which God hath ordained him. Yet in these points he labours most in those things which are most apt to scandalize his parish. And first, because country people live hardly, and therefore as feeling their own sweat, and consequently knowing the price of money, are offended much with any, who by hard usage increase their travail, the country parson is very circumspect in avoiding all covetousness, neither being greedy to get, nor niggardly to keep, nor troubled to lose any worldly wealth; but in all his words and actions slighting, and disesteeming it, even to a wondering, that the world should so much value wealth, which in the day of wrath hath not one dram of comfort for us. Secondly, because luxury is a very visible sin, the parson is very careful to avoid all the kinds thereof, but especially that of drinking, because it is the most popular vice; into which if he come, he prostitutes himself both to shame, and sin, and by having fellowship, with the unfruitful works of darkness, he disableth himself of authority to reprove them. For sins make all equal, whom they find together; and then they are worst, who ought to be best. Neither is it for the servant of Christ to haunt inns, or taverns, or ale-houses, to the dishonour of his person and office. The parson doth not so, but orders his life in

You must . . . meat see Luke 12.37

such a fashion, that when death takes him, as the Jews and Judas did Christ, he may say as He did, 'I sat daily with you teaching in the Temple'. Thirdly, because country people (as indeed all honest men) do much esteem their word, it being the life of buying, and selling, and dealing in the world; therefore the parson is very strict in keeping his word, though it be to his own hindrance, as knowing, that if he be not so, he will quickly be discovered, and disregarded: neither will they believe him in the pulpit, whom they cannot trust in his conversation. As for oaths, and apparel, the disorders thereof are also very manifest. The parson's yea is yea, and nay nay; and his apparel plain, but reverend, and clean, without spots, or dust, or smell; the purity of his mind breaking out, and dilating it self even to his body, clothes, and habitation.

1652

LETTER

For my dear sick Sister†

Most dear Sister,

Think not my silence forgetfulness; or, that my love is as dumb as my papers; though businesses may stop my hand, yet my heart, a much better member, is always with you: and which is more, with our good and gracious God, incessantly begging some ease of your pains, with that earnestness, that becomes your griefs, and my love. God who knows and sees this writing, knows also that my soliciting him has been much, and my tears many for you; judge me then by those waters, and not by my ink, and then you shall justly value

Your most truly,
most heartily,
affectionate Brother,
and Servant,
George Herbert.

Decem. 6. 1620.
Trin: Coll.
1620

1670

† *For my dear sick Sister* Herbert's sister, Lady Elizabeth Johnes, was ill for fourteen years, but outlived her brother George by more than a year

Izaak Walton

1593–1683

Izaak Walton was born in Stafford, the son of a yeoman. He was apprenticed in London to a relative who was an ironmonger. By 1614 he had opened a shop in Fleet Street, where his vicar was John Donne, whose life Walton later wrote. He lived in London until 1644; for the next eighteen years his movements cannot be traced in any detail, but at times he lived in London or Stafford. In 1662 he retired to a flat in the Bishop's Palace at Winchester, and occasionally travelled to his friend Charles Cotton's fishing house on the River Dove.

Walton wrote biographies of several of his contemporaries, including John Donne (1640), Richard Hooker (1665) and George Herbert (1670). His most famous work is *The Complete Angler* (1653, and heavily revised in 1655), a fishing manual filled with practical information and recipes, but also with literary and philosophical reflections on the life of retirement. Such retirement had been forced on many Royalist priests, and Walton's book can be seen as a consolation for the 'complete Anglican' in exile.

From THE COMPLETE ANGLER Preface to the fifth edition

The Epistle to the Reader

To all Readers of this discourse, but especially to the honest Angler

I think fit to tell thee these following truths; that I did neither undertake, nor write, nor publish, and much less own, this discourse to please myself: and, having been too easily drawn to do all to please others, as I propose not the gaining of credit by this undertaking, so I would not willingly lose any part of that to which I had a just title before I began it; and do therefore desire and hope, if I deserve not commendations, yet I may obtain pardon.

And though this discourse may be liable to some exceptions, yet I cannot doubt but that most readers may receive so much pleasure or profit by it, as may make it worthy the time of their perusal, if they be not too grave or too busy men. And this is all the confidence that I can put on, concerning the merit of what is here offered to their consideration and censure; and if the last prove too severe, as I have a liberty, so I am resolved to use it, and neglect all sour censures.

And I wish the reader also to take notice, that in writing of it I have made myself a recreation of a recreation; and that it might prove so to him, and not read dull and tediously, I have in several places mixed, not any scurrility, but some innocent, harmless mirth, of which, if thou be a severe, sour-complexioned man, then I here disallow thee to be a competent judge; for divines say, there are offences given, and offences not given but taken.

And I am the willinger to justify the pleasant part of it, because though it is known I can be serious at seasonable times, yet the whole discourse is, or rather was, a picture of my own disposition, especially in such days and times as I have laid aside business, and gone a-fishing with honest Nat. and R. Roe; but they are gone, and with them most of my pleasant hours, even as a shadow that passeth away and returns not.

And next let me add this, that he that likes not the book, should like the excellent picture of the trout and some of the other fish, which I may take a liberty to commend, because they concern not myself.

Next, let me tell the reader, that in that which is the more useful part of this discourse, that is to say, the observations of the nature and breeding, and seasons, and catching of fish, I am not so simple as not to know, that a captious reader may find exceptions against something said of some of these; and therefore I must entreat him to consider, that experience teaches us to know that several countries alter the time, and I think, almost the manner, of fishes' breeding, but doubtless of their being in season; as may appear by three rivers in Monmouthshire, namely, Severn, Wye, and Usk, where Camden observes, that in the river Wye, salmon are in season from September to April; and we are certain, that in Thames and Trent, and in most other rivers, they be in season the six hotter months.

Now for the art of catching fish, that is to say, how to make a man that was none to be an angler by a book, he that undertakes it shall undertake a harder task than Mr Hales, a most valiant and excellent fencer, who in a printed book called *A Private School of Defence* undertook to teach that art or science, and was laughed at for his labour. Not but that many useful things might be learned by that book, but he was laughed at because that art was not to be taught by words, but practice: and so must angling. And note also, that in this discourse I do not undertake to say all that is known, or may be said of it, but I undertake to acquaint the reader with many things that are not usually known to every angler; and I shall leave gleanings and observations enough to be made out of the experience of all that love and practise this recreation, to which I shall encourage them. For angling may be said to be so like the mathematics, that it can never be fully learnt; at least not so fully, but that there will be more new experiments left for the trial of other men that succeed us.

But I think all that love this game may here learn something that may be worth their money, if they be not poor and needy men: and in case they be, I then wish them to forbear to buy it; for I write not to get money, but for pleasure, and this discourse boasts of no more, for I hate to promise much, and deceive the reader.

And however it proves to him, yet I am sure I have found a high content in the search and conference of what is here offered to the reader's view and censure. I wish him as much in the perusal of it, and so I might here take my leave; but will stay a little and tell him, that whereas it is said by many, that in fly-fishing for a trout, the angler must observe his twelve several flies for the twelve months of the year, I say, he that follows that rule, shall be as sure to catch fish, and be as wise, as he that makes hay by the fair days in an almanac, and no surer; for those very flies that used to appear about, and on, the water in one month of the year, may the following year come almost a month sooner or later, as the same year proves colder or hotter: and yet, in the following discourse, I have set down the twelve flies that are in reputation with many anglers; and they may serve to give him some observations concerning them. And he may note, that there are in Wales, and other countries, peculiar flies, proper to the particular place or country; and doubtless, unless a man makes a fly to counterfeit that very fly in that place, he is like to lose his labour, or much of it; but for the generality, three or four flies neat and rightly made, and not too big, serve for a trout in most rivers, all the summer: and for winter fly-fishing it is as useful as an almanac out of date. And of these, because as no man is born an artist, so no man is born an angler, I thought fit to give thee this notice.

When I have told the reader, that in this fifth impression there are many enlargements, gathered both by my own observation, and the communication with friends, I shall stay him no longer than to wish him a rainy evening to read this following discourse; and that if he be an honest angler, the east wind may never blow when he goes a-fishing.

1676

From THE LIFE OF MR GEORGE HERBERT

[*The Death of Herbert*]

Thus he continued meditating, and praying, and rejoicing, till the day of his death; and on that day said to Mr Woodnot, 'My dear friend, I am sorry I have nothing to present to my merciful God but sin and misery; but the first is pardoned, and a few hours will now put a period to the latter; for I shall suddenly go hence, and be no more seen.' Upon which expression Mr Woodnot took occasion to remember him of the re-edifying Layton Church, and his many acts of mercy. To which he made answer, saying, 'They be good works, if they be sprinkled with the blood of Christ and not otherwise.' After this discourse he became more restless, and his soul seemed to be weary of her earthly tabernacle; and this uneasiness became so visible, that his wife, his three nieces, and Mr Woodnot stood constantly about his bed, beholding him with sorrow, and an unwillingness to lose the sight of him, whom they could not hope to see much longer. As they stood thus beholding him, his wife observed him to breathe faintly, and with much trouble, and observed him to fall into a sudden agony; which so surprised her, that she fell into a sudden passion, and required of him to know how he did. To which his answer was, 'that he had passed a conflict with his last enemy, and had overcome him by the merits of his master Jesus.' After which answer he looked up, and saw his wife and nieces weeping to an extremity, and charged them, if they loved him, to withdraw into the next room, and there pray every one alone for him; for nothing but their lamentations could make his death uncomfortable. To which request their sighs and tears would not suffer them to make any reply; but they yielded him a sad obedience, leaving only with him Mr Woodnot and Mr Bostock. Immediately after they had left him, he said to Mr Bostock, 'Pray, sir, open that door, then look into that cabinet, in which you may easily find my last will, and give it into my hand': which being done, Mr Herbert delivered it into the hand of Mr Woodnot, and said, 'My old friend, I here deliver you my last will, in which you will find that I have made you my sole executor for the good of my wife and nieces; and I desire you to show kindness to them, as they shall need it: I do not desire you to be just; for I know you will be so for your own sake; but I charge you by the religion of our friendship, to be careful of them.' And having obtained Mr Woodnot's promise to be so, he said, 'I am now ready to die.' After which words he said, 'Lord, forsake me not now my strength faileth me: but grant me mercy for the merits of my Jesus. And now, Lord – Lord, now receive my soul.' And with those words he breathed forth his divine soul, without any apparent disturbance, Mr Woodnot and Mr Bostock attending his last breath, and closing his eyes.

Thus he lived, and thus he died, like a saint, unspotted of the world, full of alms-deeds, full of humility, and all the examples of a virtuous life; which I cannot conclude better, than with this borrowed observation:

– All must to their cold graves:
But the religious actions of the just
Smell sweet in death, and blossom in the dust.

Mr George Herbert's have done so to this, and will doubtless do so to succeeding generations.

1670

From THE LIFE OF DR JOHN DONNE

[*The Youth of Donne*]

Master John Donne was born in London, in the year 1573, of good and virtuous parents; and, though his own learning and other multiplied merits may justly appear sufficient to dignify both himself and his posterity, yet the reader may be pleased to know that his father was masculinely and lineally descended from a very ancient family in Wales, where many of his name now live, that deserve, and have great reputation in that country.

By his mother he was descended of the family of the famous and learned Sir Thomas More, sometime Lord Chancellor of England: as also, from that worthy and laborious judge Rastall,† who left posterity the vast statutes of the law of this nation most exactly abridged.

He had his first breeding in his father's house, where a private tutor had the care of him, until the tenth year of his age; and, in his eleventh year, was sent to the University of Oxford; having at that time a good command both of the French and Latin tongue. This, and some other of his remarkable abilities, made one then give this censure of him: That this age had brought forth another Picus Mirandola;† of whom story says that he was rather born than made wise by study.

There he remained for some years in Hart Hall, having, for the advancement of his studies, tutors of several sciences to attend and

Rastell William Rastell, editor of a large collection of statutes and of the works of Sir Thomas More

Picus Mirandola Giovanni Pico della Mirandola, fifteenth-century Italian humanist and philosopher

instruct him, till time made him capable, and his learning expressed in public exercises declared him worthy, to receive his first degree in the schools, which he forbore by advice from his friends, who, being for their religion of the Romish persuasion, were conscionably averse to some parts of the oath that is always tendered at those times, and not to be refused by those that expect the titulary honour of their studies.

About the fourteenth year of his age he was transplanted from Oxford to Cambridge, where, that he might receive nourishment from both soils, he stayed till his seventeenth year; all which time he was a most laborious student, often changing his studies, but endeavouring to take no degree, for the reasons formerly mentioned.

About the seventeenth year of his age he was removed to London, and then admitted into Lincoln's Inn, with an intent to study the law; where he gave great testimonies of his wit, his learning, and of his improvement in that profession; which never served him for other use than an ornament and self-satisfaction.

His father died before his admission into this society, and, being a merchant, left him his portion in money. (It was £3,000.) His mother, and those to whose care he was committed, were watchful to improve his knowledge, and to that end appointed him tutors, both in the mathematics and in all other liberal sciences, to attend him. But with these arts they were advised to instil into him particular principles of the Romish Church, of which those tutors professed, though secretly, themselves to be members.

They had almost obliged him to their faith; having for their advantage, besides many opportunities, the example of his dear and pious parents, which was a most powerful persuasion, and did work much upon him, as he professeth in his Preface to his *Pseudo-Martyr*, a book of which the reader shall have some account in what follows.

He was now entered into the eighteenth year of his age, and at that time had betrothed himself to no religion that might give him any other denomination than a Christian. And reason and piety had both persuaded him that there could be no such sin as schism, if an adherence to some visible church were not necessary.

About the nineteenth year of his age, he, being then unresolved what religion to adhere to, and considering how much it concerned his soul to choose the most orthodox, did therefore, – though his youth and health promised him a long life, – to rectify all scruples that might concern that, presently laid aside all study of the law, and of all other sciences that might give him a denomination; and began seriously to survey and consider the body of divinity, as it was then controverted betwixt the reformed and the Roman Church. And as God's blessed Spirit did then awaken him to the search, and in that industry did never forsake him, – they be his own words, – so he calls the same Holy Spirit to witness this protestation; that in that disquisition and search he proceeded with humility and diffidence in himself, and by that which he took to be the safest way, namely, frequent prayers, and an indifferent affection to both parties; and indeed, truth had too much light about her to be hid from so sharp an enquirer; and he had too much ingenuity not to acknowledge he had found her.

1640

Thomas Carew

1595?–1640

Thomas Carew (pronounced 'Carey') was born in London, the son of a prominent court official. He was educated at Merton College, Oxford, and studied law at the Middle Temple. From 1613 to 1616 he served as private secretary to Sir Dudley Carleton in Venice, Turin and The Hague. He lived for some time at the French court, and in 1629 became a courtier at the court of King Charles.

Carew wrote a court masque, *Coelum Britannicum*, and a famous elegy on the death of John Donne. Many of his finest poems are elegant and witty songs.

A SONG

Ask me no more where Jove† bestows,
When June is past, the fading rose;
For in your beauty's orient deep,
These flowers, as in their causes,† sleep.

Ask me no more whither do stray
The golden atoms† of the day;
For in pure love heaven did prepare
These powders to enrich your hair.

Ask me no more whither do haste
The nightingale when May is past;
For in your sweet dividing* throat — harmonious
She winters, and keeps warm her note.

Jove here invoked as god of the bright sky
in their causes in the philosophical tradition descending from Aristotle things were deemed to lie dormant in their progenitors. In Carew's compliment the flowers of the next summer are said to lie latent in the lady's beauty
atoms particles of sunlight

Ask me no more where those stars light,
That downwards fall in dead of night;
For in your eyes they sit, and there
Fixèd become, as in their sphere.

Ask me no more if east or west
The phoenix† builds her spicy nest;
For unto you at last she flies,
And in your fragrant bosom dies.

1640

phoenix a mythical bird said to rise from its own ashes; it is an eastern bird, hence its nest is said to be built from spicy shrubs

Sir Thomas Browne

1605–82

Thomas Browne was born in London, the son of a mercer. He was educated at Winchester College, and in 1623 entered Broadgates Hall, Oxford (which became Pembroke Hall in 1624). He travelled in Ireland before studying medicine at Montpellier, Padua and Leiden. He settled in Norwich, and practised medicine there for the rest of his life. He was knighted by Charles II in 1671.

Browne wrote *Religio Medici* in the mid 1630s, and it was published without his permission in 1642. His most ambitious work, *Pseudodoxia Epidemica* (known popularly as *Vulgar Errors* from its running title) was published in 1646. This enormous work is an encyclopaedic analysis of errors in many fields of knowledge; its extraordinary range and prodigious learning were remarkable even by the standards of the period. Of his shorter works, the best-known are *Hydriotaphia*, or *Urn Burial*, an archaeological treatise on funerary practices, and its companion piece, *The Garden of Cyrus*, a study of the occurrence of the number five in art (especially gardens), nature and philosophy.

From RELIGIO MEDICI[†]

The First Part

1. For my religion, though there be several circumstances that might persuade the world I have none at all, as the general scandal of my profession,[†] the natural[†] course of my studies, the indifferency of my behaviour, and discourse in matters of religion, neither violently defending one, nor with that common ardour and contention opposing another; yet in despite hereof I dare, without usurpation, assume the honourable style of a Christian: not that I merely owe this title to the

Religio Medici (Latin) The Religion of a Physician

scandal of my profession cf. the proverb *ubi tres medici, duo athei* (two out of three physicians are atheists)

natural scientific

font, my education, or clime wherein I was born, as being bred up either to confirm those principles my parents instilled into my unwary understanding; or by a general consent proceed in the religion of my country. But having, in my riper years, and confirmed judgement, seen and examined all, I find myself obliged by the principles of grace, and the law of mine own reason, to embrace no other name but this; neither doth herein my zeal so far make me forget the general charity I owe unto humanity, as rather to hate than pity Turks, infidels, and (what is worse) Jews, rather contenting myself to enjoy that happy style, than maligning those who refuse so glorious a title.

2. But because the name of a Christian is become too general to express our faith, there being a geography of religions as well as lands, and every clime distinguished not only by their laws and limits, but circumscribed by their doctrines and rules of faith; to be particular, I am of that reformed new-cast Religion, wherein I dislike nothing but the name,† of the same belief our Saviour taught, the apostles disseminated, the fathers authorised, and the martyrs confirmed; but by the sinister ends of princes, the ambition and avarice of prelates, and the fatal corruption of times, so decayed, impaired, and fallen from its native beauty, that it required the careful and charitable hand of these times to restore it to its primitive integrity. Now the accidental occasion whereon, the slender means whereby, the low and abject condition of the person† by whom so good a work was set on foot, which in our adversaries beget contempt and scorn, fills me with wonder, and is the very same objection the insolent pagans† first cast at Christ and his disciples.

3. Yet have I not so shaken hands with those desperate Resolutions,† who had rather venture at large their decayed bottom, than bring her in to be new trimmed in the dock;† who had rather promiscuously retain all, than abridge any, and obstinately be what they are, than what they have been, as to stand in diameter and swords, point with them: we have reformed from them, not against them. For omitting those improperations† and terms of scurrility betwixt us, which only difference our affections, and not our cause, there is between us one common name and appellation, one faith, and necessary body of principles common to us both; and therefore I am not scrupulous to converse and live with them, to enter their churches in defect of ours, and either pray with them, or for them: I could never perceive any rational consequence from those many texts which prohibit the children

the name Protestantism
person Luther, who was the son of a miner
pagans members of the synagogue who denounced Jesus as a carpenter's son (Mark 6.3)
Resolutions refers to Roman Catholics
venture . . . dock i.e. sail a rotten ship rather than bring it into dock for refitting
improperations taunts

of Israel to pollute themselves with the temples of the heathens; we being all Christians, and not divided by such detested impieties as might profane our prayers, or the place wherein we make them; or that a resolved conscience may not adore her Creator any where, especially in places devoted to his service; where if their devotions offend him, mine may please him, if theirs profane it, mine may hallow it; holy water and crucifix (dangerous to the common people) deceive not my judgement, nor abuse my devotion at all. I am, I confess, naturally inclined to that which misguided zeal terms superstition; my common conversation I do acknowledge austere, my behaviour full of rigour, sometimes not without morosity; yet at my devotion I love to use the civility of my knee, my hat, and hand, with all those outward and sensible motions, which may express, or promote my invisible devotion. I should violate my own arm rather than a church, nor willingly deface the memory† of saint or martyr. At the sight of a cross or crucifix I can dispense with my hat, but scarce with the thought or memory of my Saviour; I cannot laugh at but rather pity the fruitless journeys of pilgrims, or condemn the miserable condition of friars; for though misplaced in circumstance, there is something in it of devotion. I could never hear the Ave Maria bell† without an elevation, or think it a sufficient warrant, because they erred in one circumstance, for me to err in all, that is in silence and dumb contempt; whilst therefore they directed their devotions to her, I offered mine to God, and rectified the errors of their prayers by rightly ordering mine own; at a solemn procession I have wept abundantly, while my consorts, blind with opposition and prejudice, have fallen into an access of scorn and laughter. There are questionless both in Greek, Roman, and African† Churches, solemnities, and ceremonies, whereof the wiser zeals do make a Christian use, and stand condemned by us; not as evil in themselves, but as allurements and baits of superstition to those vulgar heads that look asquint on the face of truth, and those unstable judgements that cannot consist in the narrow point and centre of virtue without a reel or stagger to the circumference.

4. As there were many reformers, so likewise many reformations; every country proceeding in a particular way and method, according as their national interest together with their constitution and clime inclined them, some angrily and with extremity, others calmly, and with mediocrity, not rending, but easily dividing the community, and leaving an honest possibility of a reconciliation, which though peaceable spirits do desire, and may conceive that revolution of time, and the

memory memorial shrine
Ave Maria bell a bell rung at certain hours to tell the faithful to say a 'Hail Mary'
African the Coptic church

mercies of God may effect; yet that judgement that shall consider the present antipathies between the two extremes, their contrarieties in condition, affection and opinion, may with the same hopes expect an union in the poles of Heaven.

The Second Part

9. I was never yet once, and commend their resolutions who never marry twice, not that I disallow of second marriage; as neither in all cases of polygamy, which considering some times and the unequal number of both sexes may be also necessary. The whole world was made for man, but the twelfth part of man for woman: man is the whole world and the breath of God, woman the rib and crooked piece of man. I could be content that we might procreate like trees, without conjunction, or that there were any way to perpetuate the world without this trivial and vulgar way of coition; it is the foolishest act a wise man commits in all his life, nor is there any thing that will more deject his cold imagination, when he shall consider what an odd and unworthy piece of folly he hath committed; I speak not in prejudice, nor am averse from that sweet sex, but naturally amorous of all that is beautiful; I can look a whole day with delight upon a handsome picture, though it be but of an horse. It is my temper, and I like it the better, to affect all harmony, and sure there is music even in the beauty, and the silent note which Cupid strikes, far sweeter than the sound of an instrument. For there is a music wherever there is a harmony, order or proportion; and thus far we may maintain the music of the spheres; for those well ordered motions, and regular paces, though they give no sound unto the ear, yet to the understanding they strike a note most full of harmony. Whatsoever is harmonically composed, delights in harmony; which makes me much distrust the symmetry† of those heads which declaim against all church music. For myself, not only from my obedience but my particular genius, I do embrace it; for even that vulgar and tavern music, which makes one man merry, another mad, strikes in me a deep fit of devotion, and a profound contemplation of the first Composer, there is something in it of Divinity more than the ear discovers. It is an hieroglyphical† and shadowed lesson of the whole world, and creatures of God, such a melody to the ear, as the whole world well understood, would afford the understanding. In brief, it is a sensible fit of that harmony, which intellectually sounds in the ears of God. I will not say with Plato, the Soul is an harmony, but harmonical, and hath its nearest sympathy unto music; thus some, whose temper of body agrees, and

symmetry balance

hieroglyphical having a hidden meaning

humours the constitution of their souls, are born poets, though indeed all are naturally inclined unto rhythm. This made Tacitus in the very first line of his story, fall upon a verse; and Cicero, the worst of poets, but declaiming for a poet, falls in the very first sentence upon a perfect hexameter. I feel not in me those sordid, and unchristian desires of my profession, I do not secretly implore and wish for plagues, rejoice at famines, revolve ephemerides† and almanacs, in expectation of malignant aspects, fatal conjunctions, and eclipses: I rejoice not at unwholesome springs, nor unseasonable winters; my prayer goes with the husbandman's; I desire everything in its proper season, that neither men nor the times be out of temper. Let me be sick myself, if sometimes the malady of my patient be not a disease unto me, I desire rather to cure his infirmities than my own necessities, where I do him no good methinks it is scarce honest gain, though I confess 'tis but the worthy salary of our well-intended endeavours: I am not only ashamed, but heartily sorry, that besides death, there are diseases incurable, yet not for my own sake, or that they be beyond my art, but for the general cause and sake of humanity whose common cause I apprehend as mine own. And to speak more generally, those three noble professions which all civil commonwealths do honour, are raised upon the fall of Adam, and are not any exempt from their infirmities; there are not only diseases incurable in physic,† but cases indissoluble in laws, vices incorrigible in divinity: if General Councils may err, I do not see why particular courts should be infallible, their perfectest rules are raised upon the erroneous reasons of man, and the laws of one, do but condemn the rules of another; as Aristotle oft-times the opinions of his predecessors, because, though agreeable to reason, yet were not consonant to his own rules, and the logic of his proper principles. Again, to speak nothing of the sin against the Holy Ghost, whose cure not only, but whose nature is unknown; I can cure the gout or stone in some, sooner than divinity, pride, or avarice in others. I can cure vices by physic, when they remain incurable by divinity, and shall obey my pills, when they condemn their precepts. I boast nothing, but plainly say, we all labour against our own cure, for death is the cure of all diseases. There is no catholicon† or universal remedy I know but this, which though nauseous to queasy stomachs, yet to prepared appetites is nectar and a pleasant potion of immortality.

1635–6 1642

resolve ephemerides study astronomical almanacs

physic medicine

catholicon another word for universal remedy

Edmund Waller

1606–87

Edmund Waller was born at the manor house in Coleshill (which was then in Hertfordshire) and grew up in Beaconsfield. He was educated at Eton College, King's College, Cambridge (which he left without a degree), and Lincoln's Inn, where he studied law. At the age of sixteen he entered Parliament, at first as an unofficial Member for Amersham (a seat which was then in abeyance). In 1631 he married, but his wife died three years later. He soon became enamoured of Lady Dorothy Sidney, the 'Sacharissa' of Waller's poems. His affection seems not to have been reciprocated, and in due course they married others. Waller remained in Parliament for much of his life, though on occasion his allegiance changed between king and Parliament.

Waller's earliest surviving poem, written when he was nineteen, a celebration of the king's escape from shipwreck, was one of the first to use heroic couplets. He collected his poems in 1645, and in 1685 published his *Divine Poems*. His poems are characterised by a rare elegance and simplicity.

OF ENGLISH VERSE

Poets may boast, as safely vain,
Their works shall with the world remain:
Both, bound together, live or die,
The verses and the prophecy.

But who can hope his line should long
Last in a daily changing tongue?
While they are new, envy prevails;
And as that dies, our language fails.

When architects have done their part,
The matter may betray their art;
Time, if we use ill-chosen stone,
Soon brings a well-built palace down.

Poets that lasting marble seek,
Must carve in Latin, or in Greek;
We write in sand, our language grows,
And like the tide, our work o'erflows.

Chaucer his sense can only boast;
The glory of his numbers* lost! poems
Years have defaced his matchless strain;
And yet he did not sing in vain.

The beauties which adorned that age,
The shining subjects of his rage,
Hoping they should immortal prove,
Rewarded with success his love.

This was the generous poet's scope;
And all an English pen can hope,
To make the fair approve his flame,
That can so far extend their fame.

Verse, thus designed, has no ill fate,
If it arrive but at the date
Of fading beauty; if it prove
But as long-lived as present love.

1668

GO, LOVELY ROSE

Go, lovely Rose,
Tell her that wastes her time and me,
That now she knows,
When I resemble* her to thee, compare
How sweet and fair she seems to be.

Tell her that's young,
And shuns to have her graces spied,
That hadst thou sprung
In deserts, where no men abide,
Thou must have uncommended died.

Small is the worth
    Of beauty from the light retired;
Bid her come forth,
    Suffer herself to be desired,
    And not blush so to be admired.

Then die, that she
    The common fate of all things rare
May read in thee
    How small a part of time they share
    That are so wondrous sweet and fair!

1645

John Milton

1608–74

John Milton was born in London, the son of a scrivener. He was educated at St Paul's School and Christ's College, Cambridge. On leaving Cambridge Milton returned to his father's house in Hammersmith, and in about 1635 the family moved to Horton, in Buckinghamshire; during these years Milton undertook a vigorous programme of private study. In 1638 and 1639 he travelled in Italy, and when he returned to England became a schoolteacher in his own home. In 1649 Milton was appointed Secretary for Foreign Tongues to the Council of State. He was already blind in one eye, and in 1652 he lost the sight of his other eye. After the restoration of Charles II in 1660 Milton retired to private life.

Most of Milton's early poems were written in Latin. His first great English poem, an ode 'On the Morning of Christ's Nativity', was written in 1629, just after his twenty-first birthday. In 1634 he received a commission to write a masque for the Earl of Bridgewater; the masque, which is now known as *Comus*, is Milton's first important work to deal with the theme of temptation, which was to be the central theme of his epics. In 1637 Milton composed 'Lycidas', a pastoral elegy which commemorates a fellow student at Cambridge. During the Commonwealth and Protectorate Milton wrote a large number of prose works, and also composed his sonnets. Blindness and enforced retirement gave him the leisure to write *Paradise Lost*, *Paradise Regained* and (if it is a late work), *Samson Agonistes*.

SONNET 1

O nightingale, that on yon bloomy spray
  Warblest at eve, when all the woods are still,
  Thou with fresh hope the lover's heart dost fill,
  While the jolly Hours† lead on propitious May,
Thy liquid notes that close the eye of day,
  First heard before the shallow cuckoo's bill
  Portend success in love; O if Jove's will
  Have linked that amorous power to thy soft lay,
Now timely sing, ere the rude bird of hate†
  Foretell my hopeless doom in some grove nigh:
  As thou from year to year hast sung too late
For my relief; yet hadst no reason why,
  Whether the Muse, or Love call thee his mate,
  Both them I serve, and of their train am I.

1645

From ON THE MORNING OF CHRIST'S NATIVITY

I

This is the month, and this the happy morn
Wherein the Son of heaven's eternal King,
Of wedded maid, and virgin mother born,
Our great redemption from above did bring;
For so the holy sages† once did sing,
  That he our deadly forfeit should release,
And with his Father work us a perpetual peace.

II

That glorious form, that light unsufferable,
And that far-beaming blaze of majesty,
Wherewith he wont at heaven's high council-table,
To sit the midst of trinal unity,
He laid aside; and here with us to be,
  Forsook the courts of everlasting day,
And chose with us a darksome house of mortal clay.

Hours goddesses of the seasons
bird of hate the cuckoo
holy sages Hebrew prophets

III

Say heavenly Muse,† shall not thy sacred vein
Afford a present to the infant God?
Hast thou no verse, no hymn, or solemn strain,
To welcome him to this his new abode,
Now while the heaven by the sun's team untrod,
Hath took no print of the approaching light,
And all the spangled host keep watch in squadrons bright?

IV

See how from far upon the eastern road
The star-led wizards haste with odours sweet,
O run, prevent* them with thy humble ode, anticipate
And lay it lowly at his blessed feet;
Have thou the honour first, thy Lord to greet,
And join thy voice unto the angel quire,
From out his secret altar touched with hallowed fire.

1629 1645

ON SHAKESPEARE†

What needs my Shakespeare for his honoured bones,
The labour of an age in piled stones,
Or that his hallowed relics should be hid
Under a star-ypointing† pyramid?
Dear son of memory, great heir of fame,
What need'st thou such weak witness of thy name?
Thou in our wonder and astonishment
Hast built thyself a live-long monument.
For whilst to the shame of slow-endeavouring art,
Thy easy numbers flow, and that each heart
Hath from the leaves of thy unvalued* book, invaluable
Those Delphic lines† with deep impression took,
Then thou our fancy of itself bereaving,
Dost make us marble with too much conceiving;
And so sepulchred in such pomp dost lie,
That kings for such a tomb would wish to die.

1630 1632

heavenly Muse Urania, in antiquity the muse of astronomy, and in the Renaissance the muse of Christian poetry

On Shakespeare the poem was first published in the Second Folio of Shakespeare (1632)

star-ypointing an archaic present participle

Delphic lines Apollo, the patron of poetry, had his oracle at Delphi

ON THE UNIVERSITY CARRIER†

Here lies old Hobson, Death hath broke his girt,* saddle girth
And here alas, hath laid him in the dirt,
Or else the ways being foul, twenty to one,
He's here stuck in a slough, and overthrown.
'Twas such a shifter,* that if truth were known, trickster
Death was half glad when he had got him down;
For he had any time this ten years full,
Dodged with him, betwixt Cambridge and the Bull.†
And surely, Death could never have prevailed,
Had not his weekly course of carriage failed;
But lately finding him so long at home,
And thinking now his journey's end was come,
And that he had ta'en up his latest inn,
In the kind office of a chamberlain†
Showed him his room where he must lodge that night,
Pulled off his boots, and took away the light:
If any ask for him, it shall be said,
Hobson has supped, and 's newly gone to bed.
1631 1645

SONNET 7

How soon hath time the subtle thief of youth,
Stol'n on his wing my three and twentieth year!
My hasting days fly on with full career,
But my late spring no bud or blossom showeth.
Perhaps my semblance* might deceive the truth, appearance
That I to manhood am arrived so near,
And inward ripeness doth much less appear,
That some more timely* happy spirits endueth.† seasonable
Yet be it less or more, or soon or slow,
It shall be still* in strictest measure even, forever
To* that same lot, however mean or high, equal to
Toward which time leads me, and the will of heaven;
All is, if I have grace to use it so,
As ever in my great task-master's eye.
1631 1645

On the University Carrier Thomas Hobson, who drove a weekly coach from Cambridge to London, had been a well-known figure in Cambridge for over 60 years

Bull the Bull Inn, Bishopsgate, London

chamberlain an attendant in charge of the bed-chambers at an inn

endueth is inherent in

SONG FROM ARCADES†

O'er the smooth enamelled† green
Where no print of step hath been,
Follow me as I sing,
And touch the warbled string.
Under the shady roof
Of branching elm star-proof.
Follow me,
I will bring you where she sits
Clad in splendour as befits
Her deity.
Such a rural queen
All Arcadia hath not seen.

1645

ON TIME

Fly envious Time, till thou run out thy race,
Call on the lazy leaden-stepping hours,
Whose speed is but the heavy plummet's† pace;
And glut thyself with what thy womb devours,
Which is no more than what is false and vain,
And merely mortal dross,
So little is our loss,
So little is thy gain.
For when as each thing bad thou hast entombed,
And last of all thy greedy self consumed,
Then long eternity shall greet our bliss
With an individual* kiss; inseparable
And joy shall overtake us as a flood,
When every thing that is sincerely* good purely
And perfectly divine,
With truth, and peace, and love shall ever shine

Arcades a brief pastoral entertainment which Milton wrote for Alice, Dowager Countess of Derby; it was performed at Harefield, her estate near Uxbridge. The title refers to the inhabitants of ancient Arcadia, a mountainous area in Greece which was often used as the setting of Renaissance pastoral fictions

enamelled beautified with various colours

plummet the weight (not the pendulum) of a clock

About the supreme throne
Of him, to whose happy-making sight[†] alone,
When once our heavenly-guided soul shall climb,
Then all this earthy grossness quit,
Attired with stars, we shall for ever sit,
  Triumphing over Death, and Chance, and thee
  O Time.

1645

From COMUS: A MASQUE PRESENTED AT LUDLOW CASTLE[†]

Comus. O foolishness of men! that lend their ears
To those budge doctors[†] of the Stoic[†] fur,
And fetch their precepts from the Cynic tub,[†]
Praising the lean and sallow Abstinence.
Wherefore did Nature pour her bounties forth,
With such a full and unwithdrawing hand,
Covering the earth with odours, fruits, and flocks,
Thronging the seas with spawn innumerable,
But all to please, and sate the curious taste?
And set to work millions of spinning worms,
That in their green shops weave the smooth-haired silk
To deck her sons, and that no corner might
Be vacant of her plenty, in her own loins
She hutched the all-worshipped ore, and precious gems
To store her children with; if all the world
Should in a pet of temperance feed on pulse,
Drink the clear stream, and nothing wear but frieze,[†]
The all-giver would be unthanked, would be unpraised,
Not half his riches known, and yet despised,
And we should serve him as a grudging master,
As a penurious niggard of his wealth,
And live like Nature's bastards, not her sons,

happy-making sight an Anglicised form of the scholastic term 'beatific vision', i.e. the sight of God promised in Matthew 5.8

A Masque Presented at Ludlow Castle Milton's masque has been popularly known as *Comus* since the late seventeenth century

budge doctors . . . Cynic tub Stoics and Cynics were ancient groups of philosophers who abjured all luxury; budge (i.e. solemn) doctors of the Stoic school include Zeno, Seneca and Marcus Aurelius. Diogenes, one of the leaders of the Cynic school, lived in a tub

frieze coarse woollen cloth

Who would be quite surcharged with her own weight,
And strangled with her waste fertility;
The earth cumbered, and the winged air darked with plumes,
The herds would over-multitude their lords,
The sea o'erfraught would swell, and the unsought diamonds
Would so emblaze the forehead[†] of the deep,[†]
And so bestud with stars, that they below[†]
Would grow inured to light, and come at last
To gaze upon the sun with shameless brows.
List Lady be not coy, and be not cozened
With that same vaunted name virginity,
Beauty is Nature's coin, must not be hoarded,
But must be current, and the good thereof
Consists in mutual and partaken bliss,
Unsavoury in the enjoyment of itself.
If you let slip time, like a neglected rose
It withers on the stalk with languished head.
Beauty is Nature's brag, and must be shown
In courts, at feasts, and high solemnities
Where most may wonder at the workmanship;
It is for homely features to keep home,
They had their name thence; coarse complexions
And cheeks of sorry grain* will serve to ply — hue
The sampler, and to tease the housewife's wool.
What need a vermeil-tinctured lip for that
Love-darting eyes, or tresses like the morn?
There was another meaning in these gifts,
Think what, and be advised, you are but young yet.
Lady. I had not thought to have unlocked my lips
In this unhallowed air, but that this juggler* — sorcerer
Would think to charm my judgement, as mine eyes
Obtruding false rules pranked[†] in reason's garb.
I hate when vice can bolt[†] her arguments,
And virtue has no tongue to check her pride:
Imposter do not charge most innocent Nature,
As if she would her children should be riotous.
With her abundance she good cateress
Means her provision only to the good
That live according to her sober laws,
And holy dictate of spare temperance:

deep the centre of the earth, the *forehead* of which is the roof of the inside of the earth
they below the spirits of the underworld
pranked showily dressed
bolt may mean refine or utter hastily

If every just man that now pines with want
Had but a moderate and beseeming share
Of that which lewdly-pampered Luxury
Now heaps upon some few with vast excess,
Nature's full blessings would be well-dispensed
In unsuperfluous even proportion,
And she no whit encumbered with her store,
And then the giver would be better thanked,
His praise due paid, for swinish gluttony
Ne'er looks to heaven amidst his gorgeous feast,
But with besotted† base ingratitude
Crams, and blasphemes his feeder. Shall I go on?
Or have I said enough? To him that dares
Arm his profane tongue with contemptuous words
Against the sun-clad power of chastity;
Fain would I something say, yet to what end?
Thou hast nor ear, nor soul to apprehend
The sublime notion, and high mystery
That must be uttered to unfold the sage
And serious doctrine of virginity,
And thou art worthy that thou shouldst not know
More happiness than this thy present lot.
Enjoy your dear wit, and gay rhetoric
That hath so well been taught her dazzling fence,* — fencing
Thou art not fit to hear thyself convinced;
Yet should I try, the uncontrollèd* worth — indisputable
Of this pure cause would kindle my rapt spirits
To such a flame of sacred vehemence,
That dumb things would be moved to sympathize,
And the brute Earth would lend her nerves,* and shake, — sinews
Till all thy magic structures reared so high,
Were shattered into heaps o'er thy false head.
Comus. She fables not, I feel that I do fear
Her words set off by some superior power;
And though not mortal, yet a cold shuddering dew
Dips me all o'er, as when the wrath of Jove†
Speaks thunder, and the chains of Erebus†
To some of Saturn's crew.† I must dissemble,
And try her yet more strongly. Come, no more,
This is mere moral babble, and direct
Against the canon laws of our foundation;

besotted morally stupefied
Wrath of Jove . . . Saturn's crew Jove used thunderbolts to depose his father Saturn, and then chained Saturn and his supporters (crew) the Titans in *Erebus*, the underworld

I must not suffer this, yet 'tis but the lees*   sediment
And settlings of a melancholy blood;
But this will cure all straight, one sip of this
Will bathe the drooping spirits in delight
Beyond the bliss of dreams. Be wise, and taste. . . .
1634   1637

LYCIDAS†

Yet once more, O ye laurels, and once more
Ye myrtles brown, with ivy never sere,*   dry
I come to pluck your berries harsh and crude,†
And with forced fingers rude,†
Shatter your leaves before the mellowing year.
Bitter constraint, and sad occasion dear,
Compels me to disturb your season due:
For Lycidas is dead, dead ere his prime,†
Young Lycidas, and hath not left his peer:
Who would not sing for Lycidas? he knew
Himself to sing, and build the lofty rhyme.
He must not float upon his watery bier
Unwept, and welter* to the parching wind,   writhe
Without the meed* of some melodious tear,†   reward
  Begin then, sisters† of the sacred well,†
That from beneath the seat of Jove† doth spring,
Begin, and somewhat loudly sweep the string.
Hence with denial vain, and coy excuse,
So may some gentle muse
With lucky words favour my destined urn,
And as he passes turn,
And bid fair peace be to my sable* shroud.   black
For we were nursed upon the self-same hill,
Fed the same flock; by fountain, shade, and rill.

Lycidas 'Lycidas' is a common name in pastoral verse; here it represents Edward King, a Fellow of Christ's College Cambridge, who had drowned on his way to Ireland on 10 August 1637

crude used in the Latin sense of 'unripe'

rude used in the Latin sense of 'unskilled'

ere his prime King was 25

tear has a secondary meaning of 'elegy'

sisters . . . Jove the sisters are the muses, the *sacred well* is Aganippe, on Mount Helicon, which is *the seat of Jove*

Together both, ere the high lawns appeared
Under the opening eye-lids of the morn,
We drove a-field, and both together heard
What time the grey-fly winds her sultry horn,
Battening our flocks with the fresh dews of night,
Oft till the star that rose, at evening, bright,
Toward heaven's descent had sloped his westering wheel.
Meanwhile the rural ditties were not mute,
Tempered to the oaten flute,
Rough satyrs danced, and fauns with cloven heel,
From the glad sound would not be absent long,
And old Damaetas† loved to hear our song.
But O the heavy change, now thou art gone,
Now thou art gone, and never must return!
Thee shepherd, thee the woods, and desert caves,
With wild thyme and the gadding vine o'ergrown,
And all their echoes mourn.
The willows, and the hazel copses green,
Shall now no more be seen,
Fanning their joyous leaves to thy soft lays.
As killing as the canker to the rose,
Or taint-worm to the weanling herds that graze,
Or frost to flowers, that their gay wardrobe wear,
When first the white-thorn blows;
Such, Lycidas, thy loss to shepherd's ear.
Where were ye nymphs when the remorseless deep
Closed o'er the head of your loved Lycidas?
For neither were ye playing on the steep,†
Where your old bards, the famous Druids, lie.
Nor on the shaggy top of Mona* high, Anglesey
Nor yet where Deva† spreads her wizard stream:
Ay me, I fondly dream!
Had ye been there . . . for what could that have done?
What could the muse† herself that Orpheus† bore,
The muse herself for her enchanting son
Whom universal nature did lament,
When by the rout that made the hideous roar,
His gory visage down the stream was sent,
Down the swift Hebrus† to the Lesbian† shore.

Damaetas a pastoral name, here probably used in allusion to a tutor at Christ's College
steep the island of Bardsey, off the coast of Wales
Deva The river Dee, in Cheshire
the muse . . . Lesbian shore the muse is Calliope, whose son Orpheus was dismembered by Thracian women, who threw his head into the *Hebrus* River, whence it floated to the island of Lesbos

Alas! What boots* it with uncessant care — avails
To tend the homely slighted shepherd's trade,
And strictly meditate the thankless muse,
Were it not better done as others use,
To sport with Amaryllis† in the shade,
Or with the tangles of Neaera's† hair?
Fame is the spur that the clear spirit doth raise
(That last infirmity of noble mind)
To scorn delights, and live laborious days;
But the fair guerdon when we hope to find,
And think to burst out into sudden blaze,
Comes the blind Fury† with th' abhorred shears,
And slits the thin-spun life. But not the praise,
Phoebus† replied, and touched my trembling ears;
Fame is no plant that grows on mortal soil,
Nor in the glistering foil†
Set off to the world, nor in broad rumour lies,
But lives and spreads aloft by those pure eyes,
And perfect witness of all-judging Jove;
As he pronounces lastly on each deed,
Of so much fame in heaven expect thy meed.
O fountain Arethuse,† and thou honoured flood,
Smooth-sliding Mincius,† crowned with vocal reeds,
That strain I heard was of a higher mood:* — musical mode
But now my oat proceeds,
And listens to the herald† of the sea
That came in Neptune's plea,
He asked the waves, and asked the felon* winds, — savage
What hard mishap had doomed this gentle swain?
And questioned every gust of rugged wings
That blows from off each beaked promontory;
They knew not of his story,
And sage Hippotades† their answer brings,
That not a blast was from his dungeon† strayed,
The air was calm, and on the level brine,
Sleek Panope† with all her sisters played.

Amaryllis, Neaera common pastoral names
Fury Atropos is one of the three Fates, but Milton endows her with the repulsive character of a Fury
Phoebus sun-god, patron of poetry
foil the setting of a jewel
Arethuse represents the Greek pastoral poetry of Sicily
Mincius represents Roman pastoral poetry, especially that of Virgil, who was born in Mantua, which is built on two islands in the Mincio river
herald Triton, son of Neptune; he blew on his conch-shell to calm the seas, hence 'herald'
Hippotades Aeolus, god of the winds
dungeon the cave of Aeolus, in which Jove imprisoned the winds
Panope one of the 50 sea-nymphs ('nereids')

It was that fatal and perfidious bark
Built in the eclipse, and rigged with curses dark,
That sunk so low that sacred head of thine.
  Next Camus,† reverend sire, went footing slow,
His mantle hairy, and his bonnet sedge,
Inwrought with figures dim, and on the edge
Like to that sanguine flower† inscribed with woe.
Ah; who hath reft (quoth he) my dearest pledge?* child
Last came, and last did go,
The pilot† of the Galilean lake,
Two massy keys he bore of metals twain,
(The golden opes, the iron shuts amain)†
He shook his mitred† locks, and stern bespake,
How well could I have spared for thee, young swain,
Enow† of such as for their bellies' sake,
Creep and intrude, and climb into the fold?
Of other care they little reckoning make,
Than how to scramble at the shearers' feast,
And shove away the worthy bidden guest;
Blind mouths! that scarce themselves know how to hold
A sheep-hook, or have learned aught else the least
That to the faithful herdman's art belongs!†
What recks it them? What need they? They are sped,* satisfied
And when they list,* their lean and flashy* songs choose trifling
Grate on their scrannel* pipes of wretched straw, thin
The hungry sheep look up, and are not fed,
But swoll'n with wind, and the rank mist they draw,
Rot inwardly, and foul contagion spread:
Besides what the grim wolf with privy paw
Daily devours apace, and nothing said,
But that two-handed engine at the door,
Stands ready to smite once, and smite no more.
  Return Alpheus,† the dread voice is past,
That shrunk thy streams; return Sicilian muse,

Camus the river Cam represents the University of Cambridge
flower the hyacinth. Hyacinthus was accidentally killed by his lover Apollo, who turned him into a flower
pilot the apostle Peter, who was a Galilean fisherman when Jesus called him
amain with full force
mitred Peter was the first bishop of the church, and so wears a mitre
lines 113–21 see the parable in John 10.1–28
enow plural of 'enough'
Alpheus a river in Arcadia. The youth Alpheus loved Arethusa (line 85), who fled to Sicily and became a fountain; he was changed into a river and flowed to her in a hidden channel under the sea

And call the vales, and bid them hither cast
Their bells, and flowrets of a thousand hues.
Ye valleys low where the mild whispers use,* go habitually
Of shades and wanton winds, and gushing brooks,
On whose fresh lap the swart star† sparely looks,
Throw hither all your quaint enamelled eyes,
That on the green turf suck the honied showers,
And purple all the ground with vernal flowers.
Bring the rathe* primrose that forsaken dies, early
The tufted crow-toe, and pale jessamine,
The white pink, and the pansy freaked with jet,
The glowing violet
The musk-rose, and the well-attired woodbine,
With cowslips wan that hang the pensive head,
And every flower that sad embroidery wears:
Bid amaranthus† all his beauty shed,
And daffadillies fill their cups with tears,
To strew the laureate hearse where Lycid lies.
For so to interpose a little ease,
Let our frail thoughts dally with false surmise.
Ay me! Whilst thee the shores, and sounding seas
Wash far away, where'er thy bones are hurled,
Whether beyond the stormy Hebrides
Where thou perhaps under the whelming tide
Visit'st the bottom of the monstrous world;†
Or whether thou to our moist vows denied,
Sleep'st by the fable of Bellerus† old,
Where the great vision of the guarded mount†
Looks toward Namancos† and Bayona's† hold;
Look homeward angel now, and melt with ruth.* pity
And, O ye dolphins, waft the hapless youth.†
Weep no more, woeful shepherds weep no more,
For Lycidas your sorrow is not dead,
Sunk though he be beneath the watery floor,
So sinks the day-star* in the ocean bed, the sun
And yet anon repairs his drooping head,

swart star Sirius, the heliacal rising of which occurs in midsummer; *swart* (blackened by heat) has been transferred from effect to cause
amaranthus a flower that was an ancient symbol of immortality; its name means 'unfading' in Greek
monstrous world the world of sea-monsters
Bellerus Milton's invention, by analogy to Bellerium, the Latin name for Land's End
Where . . . mount according to a Cornish legend in the year 495 St Michael appeared to some fishermen who saw him standing on the mount which now bears his name
Namancos, Bayona represent Spain, the Catholicism of which St Michael guards against
waft the hapless youth bring his body ashore for burial

And tricks* his beams, and with new spangled ore, adorns
Flames in the forehead of the morning sky:
So Lycidas sunk low, but mounted high,
Through the dear might of him† that walked the waves;
Where other groves, and other streams along,
With nectar pure his oozy locks he laves,
And hears the unexpressive* nuptial song, inexpressible
In the blest kingdoms meek of joy and love.
There entertain him all the saints above,
In solemn troops, and sweet societies
That sing, and singing in their glory move,
And wipe the tears for ever from his eyes.
Now Lycidas the shepherds weep no more;
Henceforth thou art the genius† of the shore,
In thy large recompense, and shalt be good
To all that wander in that perilous flood.
  Thus sang the uncouth† swain to the oaks and rills,
While the still morn went out with sandals grey,
He touched the tender stops of various quills,
With eager thought warbling his Doric lay:†
And now the sun had stretched out all the hills,
And now was dropped into the western bay;
At last he rose, and twitched his mantle blue:
Tomorrow to fresh woods, and pastures new.
1637 1638

From THE REASON OF CHURCH GOVERNMENT URGED AGAINST PRELATY† Book II, Preface

[*Milton's Vocation as a Poet*]

I would be heard only, if it might be, by the elegant and learned reader, to whom principally for a while I shall beg leave I may address myself. To him it will be no new thing, though I tell him that if I hunted after praise, by the ostentation of wit and learning, I should not write thus

him Jesus; see Matthew 14.25–31
genius local protective deity
uncouth may mean 'unknown' or 'rustic'
Doric lay pastoral song; the Greek pastoral poets of Sicily wrote in the Doric dialect

The Reason of Church Government Urged Against Prelaty this passage is part of a personal digression in a tract which is otherwise concerned with the administration of the church; it was published early in 1642 out of mine own season when I have neither yet completed to my mind the full circle of my private studies, although I complain not of any insufficiency to the matter in hand; or were I ready to my wishes, it were a folly to commit anything elaborately composed to the careless and interrupted listening of these tumultuous times. Next, if I were wise only to my own ends, I would certainly take such a subject as of itself might catch applause, whereas this hath all the disadvantages on the contrary; and such a subject as the publishing whereof might be delayed at pleasure, and time enough to pencil it over with all the curious touches of art, even to the perfection of a faultless picture; whenas in this argument the not deferring is of great moment to the good speeding, that, if solidity have leisure to do her office, art cannot have much. Lastly, I should not choose this manner of writing, wherein knowing myself inferior to myself, led by the genial power of nature to another task, I have the use, as I may account, but of my left hand.

And though I shall be foolish in saying more to this purpose, yet, since it will be such a folly wisest men go about to commit, having only confessed and so committed, I may trust with more reason, because with more folly, to have courteous pardon. For although a poet, soaring in the high region of his fancies, with his garland and singing robes about him, might, without apology, speak more of himself than I mean to do; yet for me sitting here below in the cool element of prose, a mortal thing among many readers of no empyreal conceit,† to venture and divulge unusual things of myself, I shall petition to the gentler sort, it may not be envy† to me.

I must say, therefore, that after I had for my first years, by the ceaseless diligence and care of my father (whom God recompense!), been exercised to the tongues and some sciences, as my age would suffer, by sundry masters and teachers, both at home and at the schools, it was found that whether aught was imposed me by them that had the overlooking, or betaken to of mine own choice in English, or other tongue, prosing or versing, but chiefly by this latter, the style, by certain vital signs it had, was likely to live. But much latelier in the private academies of Italy, whither I was favoured to resort, perceiving that some trifles which I had in memory, composed at under twenty or thereabout (for the manner is, that everyone must give some proof of his wit and reading there), met with acceptance above what was looked for; and other things, which I had shifted in scarcity of books and conveniences to patch up amongst them, were received with written encomiums, which the Italian is not forward to bestow on men of this side the Alps; I began thus far to assent both to them and divers of my friends here at home, and not less to an inward prompting which now

empyreal conceit elevated concepts *envy* cause for disrespect

grew daily upon me, that by labour and intense study (which I take to be my portion in this life), joined with the strong propensity of nature, I might perhaps leave something so written to aftertimes, as they should not willingly let it die.

These thoughts at once possessed me, and these other; that if I were certain to write as men buy leases, for three lives† and downward, there ought no regard be sooner had than to God's glory, by the honour and instruction of my country. For which cause, and not only for that I knew it would be hard to arrive at the second rank among the Latins, I applied myself to that resolution, which Ariosto† followed against the persuasions of Bembo,† to fix all the industry and art I could unite to the adorning of my native tongue; not to make verbal curiosities the end (that were a toilsome vanity), but to be an interpreter and relater of the best and sagest things among mine own citizens throughout this island in the mother dialect. That, what the greatest and choicest wits of Athens, Rome, or modern Italy, and those Hebrews of old did for their country, I, in my proportion, with this over and above, of being a Christian, might do for mine; not caring to be once named abroad, though perhaps I could attain to that, but content with these British islands as my world; whose fortune hath hitherto been that, if the Athenians, as some say, made their small deeds great and renowned by their eloquent writers, England hath had her noble achievements made small by the unskilful handling of monks and mechanics.†

Time serves not now, and perhaps I might seem too profuse, to give any certain account of what the mind at home, in the spacious circuits of her musing, hath liberty to propose to herself, though of highest hope and hardest attempting; whether that epic form whereof the two poems of Homer, and those other two of Virgil and Tasso,† are a diffuse, and the book of Job a brief model: or whether the rules of Aristotle herein are strictly to be kept, or nature to be followed, which in them that know art, and use judgement, is no transgression, but an enriching of art; and lastly, what king or knight, before the conquest, might be chosen in whom to lay the pattern of a Christian hero. And as Tasso gave to a prince of Italy† his choice whether he would command him to write of Godfrey's expedition against the Infidels,† or Belisarius†

leases, for three lives leases which remain in force during the life of the most long-lived of three specified persons

Ariosto sixteenth-century Italian author of *Orlando Furioso*

Bembo Pietro Bembo, the sixteenth-century Italian humanist

mechanics an abusive term suggesting lack of education

Tasso sixteenth-century Italian author of *Gerusalemme Liberata*

prince of Italy Alfonso II d'Este, Duke of Ferrara

Godfrey . . . Infidels the First Crusade, in which Godfrey of Bouillon beseiged the Muslims in Jerusalem; this was the subject of Tasso's poem

Belisarius Justinian's general, who twice led expeditions to rid Italy of the Goths, a Germanic people who had earlier migrated to Italy

against the Goths, or Charlemagne† against the Lombards; if to the instinct of nature and the emboldening of art aught may be trusted, and that there be nothing adverse in our climate, or the fate of this age, it haply would be no rashness, from an equal diligence and inclination, to present the like offer in our own ancient stories; or whether those dramatic constitutions, wherein Sophocles and Euripides reign, shall be found more doctrinal and exemplary to a nation.

The scripture also affords us a divine pastoral drama in the Song of Solomon, consisting of two persons, and a double chorus, as Origen† rightly judges. And the Apocalypse of St John is the majestic image of a high and stately tragedy, shutting up and intermingling her solemn scenes and acts with a sevenfold chorus of hallelujahs and harping symphonies: and this my opinion the grave authority of Paraeus,† commenting that book, is sufficient to confirm. Or if occasions shall lead, to imitate those magnific odes and hymns, wherein Pindarus† and Callimachus† are in most things worthy, some others in their frame judicious, in their matter most and end faulty. But those frequent songs throughout the law and prophets beyond all these, not in their divine argument alone, but in the very critical art of composition, may be easily made appear over all the kinds of lyric poesy to be incomparable.

These abilities, wheresoever they be found, are the inspired gift of God, rarely bestowed, but yet to some (though most abuse) in every nation; and are of power, beside the office of a pulpit, to imbreed and cherish in a great people the seeds of virtue and public civility, to allay the perturbations of the mind, and set the affections in right tune; to celebrate in glorious and lofty hymns the throne and equipage of God's almightiness, and what he works, and what he suffers to be wrought with high providence in his church; to sing victorious agonies of martyrs and saints, the deeds and triumphs of just and pious nations, doing valiantly through faith against the enemies of Christ; to deplore the general relapses of kingdoms and states from justice and God's true worship.

Lastly, whatsoever in religion is holy and sublime, in virtue amiable or grave, whatsoever hath passion or admiration in all the changes of that which is called fortune from without, or the wily subtleties and refluxes of man's thoughts from within; all these things with a solid and treatable smoothness to paint out and describe. Teaching over the whole book of sanctity and virtue, through all the instances of example, with such delight to those especially of soft and delicious temper, who

Charlemagne king of the Franks, who mounted an attack on the Lombards, a Germanic people who had settled in northern Italy

Origen third-century Alexandrian theologian

Paraeus David Paraeus, German Reformation theologian

Pindarus Pindar, the ancient Greek lyric poet

Callimachus ancient Greek writer of poetry and prose

will not so much as look upon truth herself, unless they see her elegantly dressed; that whereas the paths of honesty and good life appear now rugged and difficult, though they be indeed easy and pleasant, they will then appear to all men both easy and pleasant, though they were rugged and difficult indeed. And what a benefit this would be to our youth and gentry, may be soon guessed by what we know of the corruption and bane which they suck in daily from the writings and interludes of libidinous and ignorant poetasters; who, having scarce ever heard of that which is the main consistence of a true poem, the choice of such persons as they ought to introduce, and what is moral and decent to each one, do for the most part lay up vicious principles in sweet pills to be swallowed down, and make the taste of virtuous documents harsh and sour.

But because the spirit of man cannot demean itself lively in this body, without some recreating intermission of labour and serious things, it were happy for the commonwealth, if our magistrates, as in those famous governments of old, would take into their care, not only the deciding of our contentious law-cases and brawls, but the managing of our public sports and festival pastimes; that they might be, not such as were authorized a while since, the provocations of drunkenness and lust, but such as may inure and harden our bodies by martial exercises to all warlike skill and performance; and may civilize, adorn, and make discreet our minds by the learned and affable meeting of frequent academies, and the procurement of wise and artful recitations, sweetened with eloquent and graceful enticements to the love and practice of justice, temperance, and fortitude, instructing and bettering the nation at all opportunities, that the call of wisdom and virtue may be heard everywhere, as Solomon† saith: 'She crieth without, she uttereth her voice in the streets, in the top of high places, in the chief concourse, and in the openings of the gates.' Whether this may not be, not only in pulpits, but after another persuasive method, at set and solemn panegyries,† in theatres,† porches,† or what other place or way may win most upon the people to receive at once both recreation and instruction, let them in authority consult.

The thing which I had to say, and those intentions which have lived within me ever since I could conceive myself anything worth to my country, I return to crave excuse that urgent reason hath plucked from me, by an abortive and foredated discovery. And the accomplishment of them lies not but in a power above man's to promise; but that none hath by more studious ways endeavoured, and with more unwearied

Solomon King of Israel to whom the Book of Proverbs was attributed; see Proverbs 1.20–1
panegyries religious festivals
theatres lecture theatres
porches church-porches, which in the mid seventeenth century were used for religious ceremonies

spirit that none shall, that I dare almost aver of myself, as far as life and free leisure will extend; and that the land had once enfranchised herself from this impertinent yoke of prelaty, under whose inquisitorious and tyrannical duncery no free and splendid wit can flourish.

Neither do I think it shame to covenant with any knowing reader, that for some few years yet I may go on trust with him toward the payment of what I am now indebted, as being a work not to be raised from the heat of youth, or the vapours of wine; like that which flows at waste from the pen of some vulgar amorist, or the trencher fury† of a rhyming parasite; not to be obtained by the invocation of Dame Memory† and her siren daughters; but by devout prayer to that eternal Spirit, who can enrich with all utterance and knowledge, and sends out his seraphim, with the hallowed fire of his altar,† to touch and purify the lips of whom he pleases: to this must be added industrious and select reading, steady observation, insight into all seemly and generous arts and affairs; till which in some measure be compassed, at mine own peril and cost, I refuse not to sustain this expectation from as many as are not loth to hazard so much credulity upon the best pledges that I can give them.

Although it nothing content me to have disclosed thus much beforehand, but that I trust hereby to make it manifest with what small willingness I endure to interrupt the pursuit of no less hopes than these, and leave a calm and pleasing solitariness, fed with cheerful and confident thoughts, to embark in a troubled sea of noises and hoarse disputes, put from beholding the bright countenance of truth in the quiet and still air of delightful studies, to come into the dim reflection of hollow antiquities sold by the seeming bulk, and there be fain to club quotations with men whose learning and belief lies in marginal stuffings; who, when they have, like good sumpters,† laid ye down their horse-loads of citations and fathers at your door with a rhapsody of who and who were bishops here or there, ye may take off their pack-saddles, their day's work is done, and episcopacy, as they think, stoutly vindicated. Let any gentle apprehension, that can distinguish learned pains from unlearned drudgery, imagine what pleasure or profoundness can be in this, or what honour to deal against such adversaries.

But were it the meanest under-service, if God by his secretary† conscience enjoin it, it were sad for me if I should draw back; for me especially, now when all men offer their aid to help, ease, and lighten the difficult labours of the church, to whose service, by the intentions

trencher fury poetic creativity inspired by the prospect of material reward
Dame Memory Mnemosyne, mother of the muses, who are here called sirens with reference to their singing
altar Isaiah 6.6
sumpters pack-horse drivers
secretary entrusted with the commands of God

of my parents and friends, I was destined of a child, and in mine own resolutions: till coming to some maturity of years, and perceiving what tyranny had invaded the church, that he who would take orders must subscribe slave, and take an oath withal, which unless he took with a conscience that would retch, he must either straight perjure, or split his faith; I thought it better to prefer a blameless silence before the sacred office of speaking, bought and begun with servitude and forswearing. Howsoever, thus church-outed by the prelates, hence may appear the right I have to meddle in these matters, as before the necessity and constraint appeared.

1641–2 — 1642

From AREOPAGITICA[†]

[*On Liberty*]

Lords and Commons of England, consider what nation it is whereof ye are, and whereof ye are the governors: a nation not slow and dull, but of a quick, ingenious and piercing spirit, acute to invent, subtle and sinewy to discourse, not beneath the reach of any point, the highest that human capacity can soar to. Therefore the studies of learning in her deepest sciences have been so ancient and so eminent among us, that writers of good antiquity and ablest judgement have been persuaded that even the school of Pythagoras[†] and the Persian wisdom[†] took beginning from the old philosophy of this island. And that wise and civil Roman, Julius Agricola,[†] who governed once here for Caesar,[†] preferred the natural wits of Britain before the laboured studies of the French. Nor is it for nothing that the grave and frugal Transylvanian[†] sends out yearly from as far as the mountainous borders of Russia, and beyond the Hercynian wilderness,[†] not their youth, but their staid men, to learn our language and our theologic arts.

Yet that which is above all this, the favour and the love of Heaven, we have great argument to think in a peculiar manner propitious and

Areopagitica is a tract addressed to Parliament in defence of the freedom to publish books without prior censorship. It was published in November 1644

school of Pythagoras an ancient society of ascetics, founded by Pythagoras for the study of mathematics and astronomy

Persian wisdom Zoroastrianism, which in Milton's time was associated with the wisdom of the Magi

Julius Agricola Roman legate of Britain, whose governorship is described by Tacitus

Caesar a title of the Roman emperor, in this case Vespasian

Transylvania in Milton's time, a semi-autonomous Protestant state

Hercynian wilderness the wooded mountains of Germany

propending towards us. Why else was this nation chosen before any other, that out of her, as out of Sion, should be proclaimed and sounded forth the first tidings and trumpet of Reformation to all Europe? And had it not been the obstinate perverseness of our prelates against the divine and admirable spirit of Wycliffe to suppress him as a schismatic and innovator, perhaps neither the Bohemian Huss and Jerome,† no nor the name of Luther or of Calvin, had been ever known: the glory of reforming all our neighbours had been completely ours. But now, as our obdurate clergy have with violence demeaned the matter, we are become hitherto the latest and backwardest scholars, of whom God offered to have made us the teachers. Now once again by all concurrence of signs, and by the general instinct of holy and devout men, as they daily and solemnly express their thoughts, God is decreeing to begin some new and great period in His Church, even to the reforming of Reformation itself: what does He then but reveal Himself to His servants, and as His manner is, first to His Englishmen? I say, as His manner is, first to us, though we mark not the method of His counsels, and are unworthy.

Behold now this vast city: a city of refuge, the mansion house of liberty, encompassed and surrounded with His protection; the shop of war hath not there more anvils and hammers waking, to fashion out the plates and instruments of armed justice in defence of beleaguered truth, than there be pens and heads there, sitting by their studious lamps, musing, searching, revolving new notions and ideas wherewith to present, as with their homage and their fealty, the approaching Reformation: others as fast reading, trying all things, assenting to the force of reason and convincement. What could a man require more from a nation so pliant and so prone to seek after knowledge? What wants there to such a towardly† and pregnant soil, but wise and faithful labourers, to make a knowing people, a nation of prophets, of sages, and of worthies? We reckon more than five months yet to harvest; there need not be five weeks; had we but eyes to lift up, the fields are white already.

Where there is much desire to learn, there of necessity will be much arguing, much writing, many opinions; for opinion in good men is but knowledge in the making. Under these fantastic terrors of sect and schism, we wrong the earnest and zealous thirst after knowledge and understanding which God hath stirred up in this city. What some lament of, we rather should rejoice at, should rather praise this pious forwardness among men, to reassume the ill-reputed care of their

Bohemian Huss and Jerome John Huss, the Bohemian reformer, and his friend Jerome of Prague, were both disciples of the English reformer John Wycliffe

towardly promising

religion into their own hands again. A little generous prudence, a little forbearance of one another, and some grain of charity might win all these diligences to join, and unite in one general and brotherly search after truth; could we but forgo this prelatical tradition of crowding free consciences and Christian liberties into canons and precepts of men. I doubt not, if some great and worthy stranger should come among us, wise to discern the mould and temper of a people, and how to govern it, observing the high hopes and aims, the diligent alacrity of our extended thoughts and reasonings in the pursuance of truth and freedom, but that he would cry out as Pyrrhus† did, admiring the Roman docility and courage. If such were my Epirots, I would not despair the greatest design that could be attempted, to make a church or kingdom happy.

Yet these are the men cried out against for schismatics and sectaries; as if, while the temple of the Lord was building, some cutting, some squaring the marble, others hewing the cedars, there should be a sort of irrational men who could not consider there must be many schisms and many dissections made in the quarry and in the timber, ere the house of God can be built. And when every stone is laid artfully together, it cannot be united into a continuity, it can but be contiguous in this world; neither can every piece of the building be of one form; nay rather the perfection consists in this, that, out of many moderate varieties and brotherly dissimilitudes that are not vastly disproportional, arises the goodly and the graceful symmetry that commends the whole pile and structure.

Let us therefore be more considerate builders, more wise in spiritual architecture, when great reformation is expected. For now the time seems come, wherein Moses the great prophet may sit in heaven rejoicing to see that memorable and glorious wish of his fulfilled, when not only our seventy Elders, but all the Lord's people, are become prophets. No marvel then though some men, and some good men too perhaps, but young in goodness, as Joshua then was, envy them. They fret, and out of their own weakness are in agony, lest these divisions and subdivisions will undo us. The adversary again applauds, and waits the hour. 'When they have branched themselves out', saith he, 'small enough into parties and partitions, then will be our time.' Fool! he sees not the firm root, out of which we all grow, though into branches: nor will be ware until he see our small divided maniples† cutting through at every angle of his ill-united and unwieldy brigade. And that we are to hope better of all these supposed sects and schisms, and that we shall not need that solicitude, honest perhaps though over-timorous of them that vex in

Pyrrhus king of Epirus who on several occasions defeated the Romans

maniples small bands of soldiers

this behalf, but shall laugh in the end at those malicious applauders of our differences, I have these reasons to persuade me.

First, when a city shall be as it were besieged and blocked about, her navigable river infested, inroads and incursions round, defiance and battle oft rumoured to be marching up even to her walls and suburb trenches, that then the people, or the greater part, more than at other times, wholly taken up with the study of highest and most important matters to be reformed, should be disputing, reasoning, reading, inventing, discoursing, even to a rarity and admiration, things not before discoursed or written of, argues first a singular goodwill, contentedness and confidence in your prudent foresight and safe government, Lords and Commons; and from thence derives itself to a gallant bravery and well-grounded contempt of their enemies, as if there were no small number of as great spirits among us, as his was, who when Rome was nigh besieged by Hannibal, being in the city, bought that piece of ground at no cheap rate, whereon Hannibal himself encamped his own regiment.

Next, it is a lively and cheerful presage of our happy success and victory. For as in a body, when the blood is fresh, the spirits pure and vigorous, not only to vital but to rational faculties, and those in the acutest and the pertest operations of wit and subtlety, it argues in what good plight and constitution the body is so when the cheerfulness of the people is so sprightly up, as that it has not only wherewith to guard well its own freedom and safety, but to spare, and to bestow upon the solidest and sublimest points of controversy and new invention, it betokens us not degenerated, nor drooping to a fatal decay, but casting off the old and wrinkled skin of corruption to outlive these pangs and wax young again, entering the glorious ways of truth and prosperous virtue, destined to become great and honourable in these latter ages. Methinks I see in my mind a noble and puissant nation rousing herself like a strong man after sleep, and shaking her invincible locks. Methinks I see her as an eagle mewing her mighty youth, and kindling her undazzled eyes at the full midday beam; purging and unscaling her long-abused sight at the fountain itself of heavenly radiance; while the whole noise of timorous and flocking birds, with those also that love the twilight, flutter about, amazed at what she means, and in their envious gabble would prognosticate a year of sects and schisms.

What would ye do then? should ye suppress all this flowery crop of knowledge and new light sprung up and yet springing daily in this city? should ye set an oligarchy of twenty engrossers† over it, to bring a famine upon our minds again, when we shall know nothing but what is measured to us by their bushel? Believe it, Lords and Commons, they

engrossers monopolists

who counsel ye to such a suppressing do as good as bid ye suppress yourselves; and I will soon show how. If it be desired to know the immediate cause of all this free writing and free speaking, there cannot be assigned a truer than your own mild and free and humane government. It is the liberty, Lords and Commons, which your own valorous and happy counsels have purchased us, liberty which is the nurse of all great wits; this is that which hath rarefied and enlightened our spirits like the influence of heaven; this is that which hath enfranchised, enlarged and lifted up our apprehensions degrees above themselves.

Ye cannot make us now less capable, less knowing, less eagerly pursuing of the truth, unless ye first make yourselves, that made us so, less the lovers, less the founders of our true liberty. We can grow ignorant again, brutish, formal and slavish, as ye found us; but you then must first become that which ye cannot be, oppressive, arbitrary and tyrannous, as they were from whom ye have freed us. That our hearts are now more capacious, our thoughts more erected to the search and expectation of greatest and exactest things, is the issue of your own virtue propagated in us; ye cannot suppress that, unless ye reinforce an abrogated and merciless law, that fathers may dispatch at will their own children. And who shall then stick closest to ye, and excite others? not he who takes up arms for coat and conduct, and his four nobles of Danegelt.[†] Although I dispraise not the defence of just immunities, yet love my peace better, if that were all. Give me the liberty to know, to utter, and to argue freely according to conscience, above all liberties.

1644

1644

four nobles of Danegelt i.e. a few pounds of land-tax

SONNET 16

When I consider how my light is spent,
Ere half my days, in this dark world and wide,
And that one talent† which is death to hide,
Lodged with me useless, though my soul more bent
To serve therewith my maker, and present
My true account, lest he returning chide,†
Doth God exact day-labour, light denied,
I fondly ask; but Patience to prevent
That murmur, soon replies, God doth not need
Either man's work or his own gifts, who best
Bear his mild yoke, they serve him best, his state
Is kingly. Thousands at his bidding speed
And post o'er land and ocean without rest:
They also serve who only stand and wait.

1652 1673

SONNET 19

Methought I saw my late espousèd saint
Brought to me like Alcestis† from the grave,
Whom Jove's great son† to her glad husband gave,†
Rescued from death by force though pale and faint.
Mine as whom washed from spot of childbed taint,
Purification in the old Law did save,
And such, as yet once more I trust to have
Full sight of her in heaven without restraint,
Came vested all in white, pure as her mind:
Her face was veiled, yet to my fancied sight,
Love, sweetness, goodness in her person shined
So clear, as in no face with more delight.
But O as to embrace me she inclined
I waked, she fled, and day brought back my night.

1673

one talent . . . chide see the parable of the talents, Matthew 25.14–30

like Alcestis . . . husband gave in *Alcestis*, a play by the Greek tragedian Euripides (*c.*485–*c.*406 BC). Hercules (*Jove's great son*) rescues Alcestis from Death and returns her, veiled, to her husband

From PARADISE LOST Book I†

Of man's first disobedience, and the fruit
Of that forbidden tree, whose mortal taste
Brought death into the world, and all our woe,
With loss of Eden, till one greater man* Jesus
Restore us, and regain the blissful seat,
Sing heavenly Muse,† that on the secret top
Of Oreb,† or of Sinai, didst inspire
That shepherd, who first taught the chosen seed,†
In the beginning how the heavens and earth
Rose out of chaos: or if Sion hill†
Delight thee more, and Siloa's† brook that flowed
Fast by the oracle of God; I thence
Invoke thy aid to my adventurous song,
That with no middle flight intends to soar
Above the Aonian mount,† while it pursues
Things unattempted yet in prose or rhyme.
And chiefly thou O Spirit, that dost prefer
Before all temples the upright heart and pure,
Instruct me, for thou know'st; thou from the first
Wast present, and with mighty wings outspread
Dove-like sat'st brooding on the vast abyss
And madest it pregnant: what in me is dark
Illumine, what is low raise and support;
That to the highth of this great argument
I may assert eternal providence,
And justify the ways of God to men.

1667

Paradise Lost I this is the opening invocation of *Paradise Lost.* An invocation is an appeal for divine assistance in the writing of a poem. In antiquity such requests were addressed to the muses, but Milton invokes the Christian god

heavenly Muse Urania, muse of astronomy and of Christian poetry

Of Oreb . . . chosen seed Moses (the *shepherd*) saw the burning bush on Mount Horeb, which is sometimes called Sinai; the chosen seed is Israel

Sion hill the site of the temple in Jerusalem

Siloa a pool near the temple in Jerusalem; see John 9.7,11

Aonian mount Helicon, home of the muses

From PARADISE LOST, Book IV†

When Adam thus to Eve: 'Fair consort, the hour
Of night, and all things now retired to rest
Mind us of like repose, since God hath set
Labour and rest, as day and night to men
Successive, and the timely dew of sleep
Now falling with soft slumbrous weight inclines
Our eyelids; other creatures all day long
Rove idle unemployed, and less need rest;
Man hath his daily work of body or mind
Appointed, which declares his dignity,
And the regard of heaven on all his ways;
While other animals unactive range,
And of their doings God takes no account.
To morrow ere fresh morning streak the east
With first approach of light, we must be risen,
And at our pleasant labour, to reform
Yon flowery arbours, yonder alleys green,
Our walk at noon, with branches overgrown,
That mock our scant manuring,* and require — cultivating
More hands than ours to lop their wanton growth:
Those blossoms also, and those dropping gums,
That lie bestrewn unsightly and unsmooth,
Ask riddance, if we mean to tread with ease;
Mean while, as nature wills, night bids us rest.'
To whom thus Eve with perfect beauty adorned.
'My author and disposer, what thou bid'st
Unargued I obey; so God ordains,
God is thy law, thou mine: to know no more
Is woman's happiest knowledge and her praise.
With thee conversing I forget all time,
All seasons* and their change, all please alike. — times of day
Sweet is the breath of morn, her rising sweet,
With charm* of earliest birds; pleasant the sun — song
When first on this delightful land he spreads
His orient beams, on herb, tree, fruit, and flower,
Glistering with dew; fragrant the fertile earth
After soft showers; and sweet the coming on
Of grateful evening mild, then silent night

Paradise Lost IV this conversation between Adam and Eve takes place while they are still innocent residents of the garden of Eden

With this her solemn bird and this fair moon,
And these the gems of heaven, her starry train:
But neither breath of morn when she ascends
With charm of earliest birds, nor rising sun
On this delightful land, nor herb, fruit, flower,
Glistering with dew, nor fragrance after showers,
Nor grateful evening mild, nor silent night
With this her solemn bird, nor walk by moon,
Or glittering starlight without thee is sweet.'

1667

From PARADISE LOST, Book XII†

So spake our mother Eve, and Adam heard
Well pleased, but answered not; for now too nigh
The archangel stood, and from the other hill
To their fixed station, all in bright array
The cherubim descended; on the ground
Gliding meteorous, as evening mist
Risen from a river o'er the marish* glides, marsh
And gathers ground fast at the labourer's heel
Homeward returning. High in front advanced,
The brandished sword of God before them blazed
Fierce as a comet; which with torrid heat,†
And vapour as the Lybian† air adust,†
Began to parch that temperate clime; whereat
In either hand the hastening angel caught
Our lingering parents, and to the eastern gate
Led them direct, and down the cliff as fast
To the subjected plain; then disappeared.
They looking back, all the eastern side beheld
Of Paradise, so late their happy seat,
Waved over by that flaming brand, the gate
With dreadful faces thronged and fiery arms:
Some natural tears they dropped, but wiped them soon;
The world was all before them, where to choose
Their place of rest, and providence their guide:
They hand in hand with wandering steps and slow,
Through Eden took their solitary way.

1667

Paradise Lost XII in these closing lines of *Paradise Lost* Adam and Eve are expelled from Eden by the archangel Michael
Fierce . . . heat according to an ancient tradition the 'flaming sword' (Genesis 3,24) was the heat of the tropics (hence *Lybian*); *adust* means scorched

From PARADISE REGAINED, Book III[†]

To whom our Saviour calmly thus replied.
'Thou neither dost persuade me to seek wealth
For empire's sake, nor empire to affect
For glory's sake by all thy argument.
For what is glory but the blaze of fame,
The people's praise, if always praise unmixed?
And what the people but a herd confused,
A miscellaneous rabble, who extol
Things vulgar, and well weighed, scarce worth the praise,
They praise and they admire they know not what;
And know not whom, but as one leads the other;
And what delight to be by such extolled,
To live upon their tongues and be their talk,
Of whom to be dispraised were no small praise?
His lot who dares be singularly good.
The intelligent among them and the wise
Are few, and glory scarce of few is raised.
This is true glory and renown, when God,
Looking on the earth, with approbation marks
The just man, and divulges[†] him through heaven
To all his angels, who with true applause
Recount his praises; thus he did to Job,
When to extend his fame through heaven and earth,
As thou to thy reproach may'st well remember,
He asked thee, Hast thou seen my servant Job?
Famous he was in heaven, on earth less known;
Where glory is false glory, attributed
To things not glorious, men not worthy of fame.
They err who count it glorious to subdue
By conquest far and wide, to overrun
Large countries, and in field great battles win,
Great cities by assault: what do these worthies,
But rob and spoil, burn, slaughter, and enslave
Peaceable nations, neighbouring, or remote,
Made captive, yet deserving freedom more
Than those their conquerors, who leave behind
Nothing but ruin wheresoe'er they rove,

Paradise Regained III *Paradise Regained* presents the temptation of Jesus in the desert. In this speech Jesus replies to Satan's offer of earthly glory

divulges publicly proclaims

And all the flourishing works of peace destroy,
Then swell with pride, and must be titled gods,†
Great benefactors† of mankind, deliverers,†
Worshipped with temple, priest, and sacrifice;
One is the son of Jove,† of Mars† the other,
Till conqueror Death discover them scarce men,
Rolling in brutish vices, and deformed,
Violent or shameful death their due reward.
But if there be in glory aught of good,
It may by means far different be attained
Without ambition, war, or violence;
By deeds of peace, by wisdom eminent,
By patience, temperance; I mention still
Him whom thy wrongs with saintly patience borne,
Made famous in a land and times obscure;
Who names not now with honour patient Job?
Poor Socrates (who next more memorable?)
By what he taught and suffered for so doing,
For truth's sake suffering death unjust, lives now
Equal in fame to proudest conquerors.
Yet if for fame and glory aught be done,
Aught suffered; if young African† for fame
His wasted country freed from Punic† rage,
The deed becomes unpraised, the man at least,
And loses, though but verbal, his reward.
Shall I seek glory then, as vain men seek
Oft not deserved? I seek not mine, but his
Who sent me, and thereby witness whence I am.'

1667–70 1671

titled gods dead Roman emperors were usually accorded the title 'divine' by the Senate

benefactors a title conferred by the Greeks on various eminent persons

deliverers the title of deliverer, or saviour, was used by the Greeks of kings to imply deification; in the New Testament it is often applied to Jesus

The son of Jove is Alexander the Great; the son *of Mars* is Romulus, first king of Rome and (after his translation to heaven) the god Quirinus

young African Scipio, who at the age of 32 drove Hannibal out of Italy, and thus freed his country from *Punic* (i.e. Carthaginian) *rage*; he went on to conquer 'Africa' (the Carthaginian Empire), and so was named Africanus

From SAMSON AGONISTES†

The Scene before the Prison in Gaza

Samson A little onward lend thy guiding hand
To these dark steps, a little further on;
For yonder bank hath choice of sun or shade,
There I am wont to sit, when any chance
Relieves me from my task of servile toil,
Daily in the common prison else enjoined me,
Where I a prisoner chained, scarce freely draw
The air imprisoned also, close and damp,
Unwholesome draught: but here I feel amends,
The breath of heaven fresh blowing, pure and sweet,
With day-spring* born; here leave me to respire. dawn
This day a solemn feast the people hold
To Dagon† their sea-idol, and forbid
Laborious works, unwillingly this rest
Their superstition yields me; hence with leave
Retiring from the popular noise, I seek
This unfrequented place to find some ease,
Ease to the body some, none to the mind
From restless thoughts, that like a deadly swarm
Of hornets armed, no sooner found alone,
But rush upon me thronging, and present
Times past, what once I was, and what am now.
O wherefore was my birth from heaven foretold
Twice by an angel, who at last in sight
Of both my parents all in flames ascended
From off the altar, where an offering burned,
As in a fiery column charioting
His godlike presence, and from some great act
Or benefit revealed to Abraham's race?
Why was my breeding ordered and prescribed
As of a person separate to God,†
Designed for great exploits; if I must die
Betrayed, captived, and both my eyes put out,
Made of my enemies the scorn and gaze;
To grind in brazen fetters under task

Samson Agonistes in this opening speech the blinded Samson reflects on his captivity by the Philistines

Dagon the national god of the Philistines, commonly represented as half-man and half-fish (hence *sea-idol*)

person separate to God an English translation of the Hebrew word Nazarite, used of Hebrews (including Samson) who had been consecrated to abstinence

With this heaven-gifted strength? O glorious strength
Put to the labour of a beast, debased
Lower than bond-slave! Promise was that I
Should Israel from Philistian yoke deliver;
Ask for this great deliverer now, and find him
Eyeless in Gaza at the mill with slaves,
Himself in bonds under Philistian yoke;
Yet stay, let me not rashly call in doubt
Divine prediction; what if all foretold
Had been fulfilled but through mine own default,
Whom have I to complain of but myself?
Who this high gift of strength committed to me,
In what part lodged, how easily bereft me,
Under the seal of silence could not keep,
But weakly to a woman must reveal it,
O'ercome with importunity and tears.
O impotence of mind, in body strong!
But what is strength without a double share
Of wisdom, vast, unwieldly, burdensome,
Proudly secure, yet liable to fall
By weakest subtleties, not made to rule,
But to subserve where wisdom bears command.
God, when he gave me strength, to show withal
How slight the gift was, hung it in my hair.
But peace, I must not quarrel with the will
Of highest dispensation, which herein
Haply had ends above my reach to know:
Suffices that to me strength is my bane,
And proves the source of all my miseries;
So many, and so huge, that each apart
Would ask a life to wail, but chief of all,
O loss of sight, of thee I most complain!
Blind among enemies, O worse than chains,
Dungeon, or beggary, or decrepit age!
Light the prime work of God to me is extinct,
And all her various objects of delight
Annulled, which might in part my grief have eased,
Inferior to the vilest now become
Of man or worm; the vilest here excel me,
They creep, yet see, I dark in light exposed
To daily fraud, contempt, abuse and wrong,
Within doors, or without, still* as a fool, invariably
In power of others, never in my own;
Scarce half I seem to live, dead more than half.

O dark, dark, dark, amid the blaze of noon,
Irrecoverably dark, total eclipse
Without all hope of day!
O first-created beam, and thou great word,
Let there be light, and light was over all;
Why am I thus bereaved thy prime decree?
The sun to me is dark
And silent* as the moon, — not shining
When she deserts the night
Hid in her vacant* interlunar cave. — at leisure
Since light so necessary is to life,
And almost life itself, if it be true
That light is in the soul,
She all in every part; why was the sight
To such a tender ball as the eye confined?
So obvious* and and so easy to be quenched, — exposed
And not as feeling through all parts diffused,
That she might look at will through every pore?
Then had I not been thus exiled from light;
As in the land of darkness yet in light,
To live a life half dead, a living death,
And buried; but O yet more miserable!
Myself, my sepulchre, a moving grave,
Buried, yet not exempt
By privilege of death and burial
From worst of other evils, pains and wrongs,
But made hereby obnoxious* more — exposed to harm
To all the miseries of life,
Life in captivity
Among inhuman foes.

1671

Sir John Suckling

1609–42

John Suckling was born in Middlesex into a wealthy Norfolk family; he was educated at Trinity College, Cambridge, and Gray's Inn. On the death of his father in 1628 he inherited large estates and assumed the life of a courtier; he was knighted in 1630. He served as a Royalist soldier from 1639 to 1641, and then fled to the Continent, where he died in mysterious circumstances, possibly by suicide. His literary works were collected posthumously. They include poems, songs, three plays, letters to various eminent figures, and an unorthodox religious tract.

SONG†

Why so pale and wan, fond lover?
Prithee,† why so pale?
Will, when looking well can't move her,
Looking ill prevail?
Prithee, why so pale?

Why so dull and mute, young sinner?
Prithee, why so mute?
Will, when speaking well can't win her,
Saying nothing do't?
Prithee, why so mute?

Quit, quit, for shame, this will not move;
This cannot take her.
If of herself she will not love,
Nothing can make her.
The devil take her!

1638

Song this song appears in Suckling's play, *Aglaura*

prithee colloquialism for 'I pray thee'

Richard Crashaw

1613?–49

Richard Crashaw was born in London, the son of a prominent puritan divine. He was educated at Charterhouse and Pembroke Hall, Cambridge. In 1636 he migrated to Peterhouse, where he was elected to a Fellowship. He was ejected from his Fellowship by the parliamentary commissioners in 1643. In 1646 he travelled to Paris, and had by this time been converted to Roman Catholicism. In about 1648 he travelled to Italy. He was appointed to a post at the shrine of Loreto, where he died shortly thereafter.

In 1634 Crashaw published a book of sacred epigrams (in Latin). He collected his English poems in 1646; his religious poems appeared as *Steps to the Temple*, and his secular poems as *The Delights of the Muses*; in 1652 his poems were collected as *Carmen Deo Nostro* ('A Song to our Lord'). Crashaw's poetry has traditionally been read in the light of the Roman Catholicism which he embraced in his last years, but it is more profitably understood as the verse of the greatest poet of the Laudian wing of the Anglican church. His devotional poetry is characterised by baroque conceits, sensuality and the celebration of ecstasy.

A HYMN OF THE NATIVITY, SUNG AS BY THE SHEPHERDS

Chorus

Come we shepherds whose blessed sight
  Hath met love's noon in nature's night,
Come lift we up our loftier song,
  And wake the sun that lies too long.

To all our world of well-stolen joy
He slept, and dreamt of no such thing,
While we found out heaven's fairer eye
And kissed the cradle of our king.
Tell him he rises now too late
To show us aught worth looking at.

Tell him we now can show him more
Than he e'er showed to mortal sight,
Than he himself e'er saw before,
Which to be seen needs not his light;
Tell him, Tityrus, where th' hast been;
Tell him, Thyrsis, what th' hast seen.

Tityrus

Gloomy night embraced the place
Where the noble infant lay.
The babe looked up and showed his face;
In spite of darkness it was day.
It was thy day, sweet! and did rise
Not from the east but from thine eyes.

Chorus

It was thy day, sweet! *etc.*

Thyrsis

Winter chid aloud, and sent
The angry north to wage his wars.
The north forgot his fierce intent,
And left perfumes instead of scars;
By those sweet eyes' persuasive powers,
Where he meant frost, he scattered flowers.

Chorus

By those sweet eyes' *etc.*

Both

We saw thee in thy balmy nest,
Bright dawn of our eternal day!
We saw thine eyes break from their east,
And chase the trembling shades away.
We saw thee, and we blessed the sight,
We saw thee by thine own sweet light.

Tityrus

Poor world (said I), what wilt thou do
To entertain this starry stranger?
Is this the best thou canst bestow,
A cold, and not too cleanly, manger?
Contend ye powers of heaven and earth
To fit a bed for this huge birth.

Chorus

Contend ye powers *etc.*

Thyrsis

Proud world (said I), cease your contest,
And let the mighty babe alone.
The phoenix builds the phoenix' nest.
Love's architecture is his own.
The babe whose birth embraves* this morn, glorifies
Made his own bed ere he was born.

Chorus

The babe whose birth *etc.*

Tityrus

I saw the curled drops, soft and slow,
Come hovering o'er the place's head,
Off'ring their whitest sheets of snow
To furnish the fair infant's bed.
Forbear (said I), be not too bold:
Your fleece is white, but 'tis too cold.

Chorus

Forbear (said I) *etc.*

Thyrsis

I saw the obsequious* seraphins† dutiful
Their rosy fleece of fire bestow,
For well they now can spare their wings
Since heaven itself lies here below.
Well done (said I), but are you sure
Your down so warm will pass for pure?

seraphins the highest order of angels; they were associated with purifying fire

Chorus

Well done (said I) *etc.*

Tityrus

No, no, your king's not yet to seek
Where to repose his royal head.
See, see, how soon his new-bloomed cheek
Twixt's mother's breasts is gone to bed.
Sweet choice, (said I), no way but so
Not to lie cold, yet sleep in snow.

Chorus

Sweet choice (said I) *etc.*

Both

We saw thee in thy balmy nest,
Bright dawn of our eternal day!
We saw thine eyes break from their east,
And chase the trembling shades away.
We saw thee, and we blessed the sight,
We saw thee by thine own sweet light.

Chorus

We saw thee *etc.*

Full Chorus

Welcome, all wonders in one sight!
Eternity shut in a span,
Summer in winter, day in night,
Heaven in earth, and God in man.
Great little one! whose all-embracing birth
Lifts earth to heav'n, stoops heav'n to earth.

Welcome, though not to gold nor silk,
To more than Caesar's birthright is:
Two sister-seas of virgin milk,
With many a rarely tempered kiss
That breathes at once both maid and mother,
Warms in the one, cools in the other.

She sings thy tears asleep, and dips
   Her kisses in thy weeping eye;
She spreads the red leaves of thy lips
   That in their buds yet blushing lie.
She 'gainst those mother-diamonds tries
The points of her young eagle's eyes.

Welcome, though not to those gay flies†
   Gilded i' th' beams of earthly kings,
Slippery souls in smiling eyes,
   But to poor shepherds, homespun things,
Whose wealth's their flock, whose wit to be
Well read in their simplicity.

Yet when young April's husband showers
   Shall bless the fruitful Maia's† bed,
We'll bring the first-born of her flowers
   To kiss thy feet and crown thy head,
To thee, dread lamb! whose love must keep
The shepherds more than they their sheep.

To thee, meek majesty! soft king
   Of simple graces and sweet loves,
Each of us his lamb will bring,
   Each his pair of silver doves,
Till, burnt at last in fire of thy fair eyes,
Ourselves become our own best sacrifice.

1646

THE TEAR

What bright soft thing is this,
   Sweet Mary, thy fair eyes' expense?
A moist spark it is,
   A watery diamond, from whence
The very term, I think, was found,
The water of a diamond.

gay flies showily-dressed courtiers
Maia Roman goddess of fertility after whom the month of May was named

O, 'tis not a tear,
'Tis a star about to drop
From thine eye, its sphere.
The sun will stoop and take it up.
Proud will his sister be to wear
This thine eye's jewel in her ear.

O, 'tis a tear,
Too true a tear, for no sad eyne,†
How sad soe'er,
Rain so true a tear as thine:
Each drop, leaving a place so dear,
Weeps for itself, is its own tear.

Such a pearl as this is
(Slipped from Aurora's† dewy breast)
The rose-bud's sweet lip kisses,
And such the rose itself, that's vexed
With ungentle flames, does shed,
Sweating in a too warm bed.

Such the maiden gem,
By the purpling vine put on,
Peeps from her parent stem
And blushes on the bridegroom sun:
The watery blossom of thy eyne,
Ripe, will make the richer wine.

Fair drop, why quakest thou so?
'Cause thou straight must lay thy head
In the dust? O no,
The dust shall never be thy bed:
A pillow for thee will I bring,
Stuffed with down of angel's wing.

Thus carried up on high
(For to heaven thou must go),
Sweetly shalt thou lie
And in soft slumbers bathe thy woe
Till the singing orbs awake thee
And one of their bright chorus make thee.

eyne archaic plural of eye

Aurora goddess of the dawn

There thyself shalt be
An eye, but not a weeping one;
Yet I doubt of thee
Whether th' hadst rather there have shone
An eye of heaven, or still shine here
In the heaven of Mary's eye, a tear.

1646

ON THE WOUNDS OF OUR CRUCIFIED LORD

O these wakeful wounds of thine!
Are they mouths? Or are they eyes?
Be they mouths or be they eyne,
Each bleeding part some one supplies.

Lo, a mouth, whose full-bloomed lips
At too dear a rate are roses.
Lo, a bloodshot eye that weeps
And many a cruel tear discloses.

O thou, that on this foot hast laid
Many a kiss and many a tear,
Now thou shalt have all repaid
Whatso'er thy charges were.

This foot hath got a mouth and lips
To pay the sweet sum of thy kisses;
To pay thy tears, an eye that weeps
Instead of tears such gems as this is.

The difference only this appears
(Nor can the change offend),
The debt is paid in ruby tears
Which thou in pearls did'st lend.

1646

ON MARRIAGE

I would be married, but I'd have no wife,
I would be married to a single life.

1646

Richard Lovelace

1618–58

Richard Lovelace was born in Woolwich, the son of a wealthy courtier. He was educated at the Charterhouse School and Gloucester Hall, Oxford (now part of Worcester College). He was created MA after only two years in Oxford, on the occasion of a visit by the king and queen in 1636. He became a courtier, and served as a soldier in Scotland. He presented a royalist petition to Parliament in 1642, and while imprisoned for this offence wrote 'To Althea', the last stanza of which is justly famous. On his release he joined the king's forces, and in 1648 was again sent to prison, where he wrote 'To Lucasta, Going to the Wars'. He died in extreme poverty.

TO ALTHEA, FROM PRISON

When Love with unconfinèd wings
Hovers within my gates,
And my divine Althea brings
To whisper at the grates;
When I lie tangled in her hair,
And fettered to her eye,
The birds that wanton in the air
Know no such liberty.

When flowing cups run swiftly round
With no allaying Thames,†
Our careless heads with roses bound,
Our hearts with loyal flames;
When thirsty grief in wine we steep,
When healths and draughts go free,
Fishes that tipple in the deep,
Know no such liberty.

no allaying Thames no water diluting the wine

When, like committed* linnets, I
With shriller voice shall sing
The sweetness, mercy, majesty,
And glories of my king;
When I shall voice aloud, how good
He is, how great should be;
Enlargèd winds that curl the flood,
Know no such liberty.

caged

Stone walls do not a prison make,
Nor iron bars a cage;
Minds innocent and quiet take
That for an hermitage.
If I have freedom in my love,
And in my soul am free,
Angels alone that soar above,
Enjoy such liberty.

1649

TO LUCASTA,† GOING TO THE WARS

Tell me not, sweet, I am unkind,
That from the nunnery
Of thy chaste breast, and quiet mind,
To war and arms I fly.

True, a new mistress now I chase,
The first foe in the field,
And with a stronger faith embrace
A sword, a horse, a shield.

Yet this inconstancy is such,
As you too shall adore;
I could not love thee, dear, so much,
Loved I not honour more.

1649

Lucasta the name means 'chaste light'

Abraham Cowley

1618–67

Abraham Cowley was born in London, the posthumous son of a stationer. He was educated at Westminster School and Trinity College, Cambridge. He collected his poems as *Poetical Blossoms* when he was fifteen; one of the poems in the collection, 'Pyramus and Thisbe', was written when he was ten. He was elected to a Minor Fellowship at Trinity in 1640, and stayed at Cambridge until he was ejected in 1643. At Cambridge he continued to write poetry, composed plays in Latin and English, and started writing an epic (which he never finished) on King David. After his ejection he moved to Oxford, where he wrote pamphlets and poems in the Royalist cause, and in 1644 moved to the court of Henrietta Maria in Paris. In 1654 he returned to England and made his peace with Cromwell's government. He took up medicine, and was granted an MD by Oxford in 1657. After the Restoration he retired to Kent.

ANACREONTIC† ON DRINKING

The thirsty earth soaks up the rain,
And drinks, and gapes for drink again.
The plants suck in the earth, and are
With constant drinking fresh and fair.
The sea itself, which one would think
Should have but little need of drink,
Drinks ten thousand rivers up,
So filled that they o'erflow the cup.
The busy sun (and one would guess
By's drunken fiery face no less)
Drinks up the sea, and when h'as done,
The moon and stars drink up the sun.
They drink and dance by their own light,
They drink and revel all the night.

Anacreontic verses in praise of wine, women and pleasure in imitation of Anacreon, the ancient Greek poet

Nothing in nature's sober found,
But an eternal health goes round.
Fill up the bowl then, fill it high,
Fill all the glasses there, for why
Should every creature drink but I,
Why, man of morals, tell me why?

1656

Lucy Hutchinson

1620–?80

Lucy Apsley was born in the Tower of London, of which her father Sir Allen Apsley was Lieutenant. She records that her parents 'spared no cost' in her education, which was conducted by a large number of tutors and included the study of Greek, Hebrew, Latin and French. In 1638 she married John Hutchinson, a soldier and parliamentarian who later became one of the signatories to the death warrant of the king. After the Restoration she pleaded for her husband's life to be spared; he was spared, but was subsequently arrested again, and died in captivity in 1664.

Lucy Hutchinson decided to commemorate her husband with a memoir, which was eventually published in 1806 as the *Life of Colonel Hutchinson*. Her biography is a vivid portrayal of life in seventeenth-century England, told from a Baptist point of view. The passage printed here occurs is an autobiographical fragment which prefaces the biography.

From LIFE OF COLONEL HUTCHINSON

[*On England*]

Whoever considers England, will find it no small favour of God to have been made one of its natives, both upon spiritual and outward accounts. The happiness of the soil and air contribute all things that are necessary to the use or delight of man's life. The celebrated glory of this isle's inhabitants, ever since they received a mention in history, confers some honour upon every one of her children, and with it an obligation to continue in that magnanimity and virtue, which hath famed this island, and raised her head in glory higher than the great kingdoms of the neighbouring continent. Britain hath been as a garden enclosed, wherein all things that man can wish, to make a pleasant life, are planted and grow in her own soil, and whatsoever foreign countries yield, to increase admiration and delight, are brought in by her fleets. The people, by the plenty of their country, not being forced to toil for bread, have ever addicted themselves to more generous employments, and been reckoned, almost in all ages, as valiant warriors as any part of the world sent forth: insomuch, that the greatest Roman captains thought it not unworthy of their expeditions, and took great glory in triumphs for imperfect conquests. Lucan[†] upbraids Julius Cæsar for returning hence with a repulse, and it was two hundred years before the land could be reduced into a Roman province, which at length was done, and such of the nation, then called Picts, as scorned servitude, were driven into the barren country of Scotland, where they have ever since remained a perpetual trouble to the successive inhabitants of this place. The Britons, that thought it better to work for their conquerors in a good land, than to have the freedom to starve in a cold or barren quarter, were by degrees fetched away, and wasted in the civil broils of these Roman lords, till the land, almost depopulated, lay open to the incursions of every borderer, and were forced to call a stout warlike people, the Saxons, out of Germany, to their assistance. These willingly came at their call, but were not so easily sent out again, nor persuaded to let their hosts inhabit with them, for they drove the Britons into the mountains of Wales, and seated themselves in those pleasant countries which from the new masters received a new name, and ever since retained it, being called England; and on which the warlike Dane made many attempts, with various success, but after about two or three hundred years' vain contest, they were for ever driven out, with shame and loss, and the Saxon Heptarchy[†] melted into a monarchy, which continued till the superstitious prince,[†] who was sainted for his ungodly chastity, left an empty throne to him that could seize it. He[†] who first set up his standard in it, could not hold it, but with his life left it again for the Norman usurper,[†] who partly by violence, partly by falsehood, laid here the foundation of his monarchy, in the people's blood, in which it hath swam about five hundred years, till the flood that bore it was ploughed into such deep furrows, as had almost sunk the proud vessel. Of those Saxons that remained subjects to the Norman conqueror,

Lucan Roman poet (AD 39–65) who recorded the exploits of Caesar in the poem known as *Pharsalia*. After Caesar's second raid in 54 BC, the Romans did not return to England until 43 AD; the northern frontier was eventually stabilised with the construction of Hadrian's Wall in 122 – hence Lucy Hutchinson's 'two hundred years'

Heptarchy the seven English kingdoms (Northumbria, East Anglia, Essex, Mercia, Wessex, Sussex and Kent) which existed in a confederation from the sixth to ninth centuries. The Heptarchy 'melted into a monarchy' with the accession of Athelstan as king of England in 926

prince Edward the Confessor, king of England from 1042 to 1066. His marriage was supposedly unconsummated. In common with many seventeenth-century Protestants, Lucy Hutchinson believed that celibacy was ungodly, partly because it was associated with Roman Catholicism, and partly because it was deemed to be a repudiation of God's injunction to produce children. In the case of Edward, his chastity 'left an empty throne' because he failed to produce an heir. He was canonised (sainted) in 1161

He Harold II, who was king of England from January–October 1066.

Norman usurper William ('the Conqueror'), Duke of Normandy, defeated King Harold at Hastings in 1066, and ruled as king of England from 1066 to 1087

my father's family descended; of those Normans that came in with him, my mother's was derived; both of them, as all the rest in England, contracting such affinity, by mutual marriages, that the distinction remained but a short space; Normans and Saxons becoming one people, who by their valour grew terrible to all the neighbouring princes, and have not only bravely acquitted themselves in their own defence, but have showed abroad how easily they could subdue the world, if they did not prefer the quiet enjoyment of their own part above the conquest of the whole.

Better laws and a happier constitution of government no nation ever enjoyed, it being a mixture of monarchy, aristocracy, and democracy, with sufficient fences against the pest of every one of those forms – tyranny, faction, and confusion; yet is it not possible for man to devise such just and excellent bounds, as will keep in wild ambition, when prince's flatterers encourage that beast to break his fence, which it hath often done, with miserable consequences both to the prince and people; but could never in any age so tread down popular liberty, but that it arose again with renewed vigour, till at length it trod on those that trampled it before. And in the just bounds, wherein our kings were so well hedged in, the surrounding princes have with terror seen the reproof of their usurpations over their free brethren, whom they rule rather as slaves than subjects, and are only served for fear, but not for love; whereas this people have ever been as affectionate to good, as unpliable to bad sovereigns.

Nor is it only valour and generosity that renown this nation; in arts we have advanced equal to our neighbours, and in those that are most excellent, exceeded them. The world hath not yielded more men famous in navigation, nor ships better built or furnished. Agriculture is as ingeniously practised; the English archers were the terror of Christendom, and their clothes the ornament; but these low things bounded not their great spirits, in all ages it hath yielded men as famous in all kinds of learning, as Greece or Italy can boast of.

And to complete the crown of all their glory, reflected from the lustre of their ingenuity, valour, wit, learning, justice, wealth, and bounty, their piety and devotion to God, and his worship, hath made them one of the most truly noble nations in the Christian world. God having as it were enclosed a people here, out of the waste common of the world, to serve him with a pure and undefiled worship. Lucius† the British king was one of the first monarchs of the earth that received the faith

Lucius legendary second-century king of Britain, popularly believed to be the first Christian king of Britain

of Christ into his heart and kingdom; Henry the Eighth,† the first prince that broke the antichristian yoke off from his own and his subjects' necks. Here it was that the first Christian emperor† received his crown; here began the early dawn of Gospel light, by Wycliffe† and other faithful witnesses, whom God raised up after the black and horrid midnight of antichristianism; and a more plentiful harvest of devout confessors, constant martyrs, and holy worshippers of God, hath not grown in any field of the church, throughout all ages, than those whom God hath here glorified his name and gospel by. Yet hath not this wheat been without its tares; God in comparison with other countries hath made this as a paradise, so, to complete the parallel, the serpent hath in all times been busy to seduce, and not unsuccessful; ever stirring up opposers to the infant truths† of Christ.

1664–71 1806

Henry the Eighth Henry VIII, king of England from 1509 to 1547, was responsible for the spate of legislation (1532–6) which separated the Church of England from the Roman Catholic Church ('the antichristian yoke', in the view of seventeenth-century Protestants)

first Christian emperor Constantine, who was not yet a Christian when he was proclaimed emperor in York in 306

Wycliffe John Wycliffe (*c.* 1330–84), the church reformer, was thought by seventeenth-century English Protestants to have led the Reformation; Luther was thus reduced to the status of one of Wycliffe's continental successors

infant truths the earliest truths of the church, i.e. the teaching of Jesus

Andrew Marvell

1621–78

Andrew Marvell was born in Yorkshire, the son of a vicar. He was educated at Hull Grammar School and Trinity College, Cambridge. For the ten years after he left Cambridge his movements are largely unknown, except that at some point he travelled in Holland, France, Italy and Spain. In about 1651 he moved to the Yorkshire home of General Fairfax as tutor to his daughter Mary, and in 1653 took a similar post at Eton. In 1657 he was appointed Latin Secretary to the Council of State, and worked in the same office as Milton. He was elected Member of Parliament for Hull in 1659, and held the seat for the rest of his life. From 1662 to 1665 he visited Russia, Sweden and Denmark on government service. He died from incompetent medical treatment, and three years later his *Miscellaneous Poems* were published by his housekeeper, who claimed to be his widow.

Marvell was a highly accomplished writer of satire (in both poetry and prose) and of lyric verse. He was a pioneer of poems in the 'country house' genre. Poems such as 'An Horatian Ode upon Cromwell's Return from Ireland' establish him as the most distinguished writer of political poems in English.

THE DEFINITION OF LOVE

My love is of a birth as rare
As 'tis for object strange and high:
It was begotten by Despair
Upon Impossibility.

Magnanimous Despair alone
Could show me so divine a thing,
Where feeble Hope could ne'er have flown
But vainly flapped its tinsel wing.

And yet I quickly might arrive
Where my extended soul is fixed,
But Fate does iron wedges drive,
And always crowds itself betwixt.

For Fate with jealous eye does see
Two perfect loves, nor lets them close:†
Their union would her ruin be,
And her tyrannic power depose.

And therefore her decrees of steel
Us as the distant Poles have placed,
(Though Love's whole world on us doth wheel)
Not by themselves to be embraced,

Unless the giddy heaven fall,
And earth some new convulsion tear;
And, us to join, the world should all
Be cramped into a planisphere.†

As lines (so loves) oblique may well
Themselves in every angle greet:
But ours so truly parallel,
Though infinite, can never meet.

Therefore the love which us doth bind,
But Fate so enviously debars,
Is the conjunction† of the mind,
And opposition† of the stars.

1681

close come together
planisphere a map on which a sphere is projected onto a plane
conjunction an astrological term for the appearance of two planets in the same longitude
opposition an astrological term for the appearance of two planets 180° apart (hence 'star-crossed')

TO HIS COY MISTRESS

Had we but world enough, and time,
This coyness, Lady, were no crime.
We would sit down, and think which way
To walk, and pass our long love's day.
Thou by the Indian Ganges' side
Shouldst rubies find: I by the tide
Of Humber† would complain. I would
Love you ten years before the flood:
And you should, if you please, refuse
Till the conversion of the Jews.†
My vegetable† love should grow
Vaster than empires, and more slow.
An hundred years should go to praise
Thine eyes, and on thy forehead gaze.
Two hundred to adore each breast:
But thirty thousand to the rest.
An age at least to every part,
And the last age should show your heart:
For, Lady, you deserve this state;
Nor would I love at lower rate.
But at my back I always hear
Time's wingèd chariot hurrying near:
And yonder all before us lie
Deserts of vast eternity.
Thy beauty shall no more be found;
Nor, in thy marble vault, shall sound
My echoing song: then worms shall try
That long-preserved virginity:
And your quaint honour† turn to dust;
And into ashes all my lust.
The grave's a fine and private place,
But none, I think, do there embrace.
Now, therefore, while the youthful glue
Sits on thy skin like morning dew,
And while thy willing soul transpires
At every pore with instant fires,

Humber Hull, where Marvell lived, is on the River Humber, which is a tidal estuary
Till . . . Jews in Protestant theology one of the signs of the Last Judgement will be the conversion of the Jews
vegetable growing like a plant
quaint honour fastidious chastity

Now let us sport us while we may;
And now, like amorous birds of prey,
Rather at once our time devour,
Than languish in his slow-chapped† power.
Let us roll all our strength, and all
Our sweetness, up into one ball:
And tear our pleasures with rough strife,
Thorough* the iron grates of life. through
Thus, though we cannot make our sun
Stand still, yet we will make him run.†

1681

AN HORATIAN ODE† UPON CROMWELL'S† RETURN FROM IRELAND

The forward youth that would appear
Must now forsake his muses dear,
  Nor in the shadows sing
  His numbers languishing†
'Tis time to leave the books in dust,
And oil th' unusèd armour's rust:
  Removing from the wall
  The corslet of the hall.
So restless Cromwell could not cease
In the inglorious arts of peace,
  But through adventurous war
  Urgèd his active star.
And, like the three-forked lightning, first
Breaking the clouds where it was nursed,
  Did thorough his own side
  His fiery way divide.
(For 'tis all one to courage high
The emulous or enemy:

slow-chapped slowly devouring
Thus . . . him run see Joshua 10.12
An Horatian Ode upon Cromwell's Return from Ireland an Horatian ode is a poem on the model of the Roman poet Horace, in which the first stanza establishes a metrical pattern which is duplicated in subsequent stanzas. Keats's 'Ode to a Nightingale' is another example of the genre
Cromwell Oliver Cromwell returned from his Irish campaign in May 1650
numbers languishing love poems

And with such to enclose
Is more than to oppose.)
Then burning through the air he went,
And palaces and temples rent:
And Caesar's head at last
Did through his laurels blast.†
'Tis madness to resist or blame
The force of angry heaven's flame:
And, if we would speak true,
Much to the man is due,
Who, from his private gardens, where
He lived reservèd and austere,
As if his highest plot
To plant the bergamot,†
Could by industrious valour climb
To ruin the great work of time,
And cast the kingdoms old
Into another mould.
Though justice against fate complain,
And plead the ancient rights in vain:
But those do hold or break
As men are strong or weak.
Nature, that hateth emptiness,
Allows of penetration less:
And therefore must make room
Where greater spirits come.
What field of all the Civil Wars,
Where his were not the deepest scars?
And Hampton† shows what part
He had of wiser art,
Where, twining subtle fears with hope,
He wove a net of such a scope,
That Charles himself might chase
To Carisbrooke's† narrow case:* cage
That thence the royal actor born
The tragic scaffold might adorn:
While round the armèd bands
Did clap their bloody hands

And Caesar's . . . blast every Roman emperor (Caesar) wore a laurel wreath; according to an ancient tradition, lightning did not strike the laurel tree
bergamot a kind of pear
Hampton refers to the flight of Charles I from Hampton Court Palace on 11 November 1647
Carisbrooke the castle on the Isle of Wight where King Charles was imprisoned

He nothing common did or mean
Upon that memorable scene:
But with his keener eye
The axe's edge did try:†
Nor called the gods with vulgar spite
To vindicate his helpless right,
But bowed his comely head,
Down, as upon a bed.
This was that memorable hour
Which first assured the forcèd* power. achieved
So when they did design
The Capitol's† first line,
A bleeding head where they begun,
Did fright the architects to run;†
And yet in that the State
Foresaw its happy fate.
And now the Irish are ashamed
To see themselves in one year tamed:†
So much one man can do,
That does both act and know.
They can affirm his praises best,
And have, though overcome, confessed
How good he is, how just,
And fit for highest trust:
Nor yet grown stiffer with command,
But still* in the Republic's hand: always
How fit he is to sway
That can so well obey.
He to the Commons' feet presents
A kingdom, for his first year's rents:
And, what he may, forbears
His fame, to make it theirs:
And has his sword and spoils ungirt,
To lay them at the public's skirt.
So when the falcon high
Falls heavy from the sky,
She, having killed, no more does search
But on the next green bough to perch,

try put to the test
The Capitol's . . . to run ancient authors record that when the foundations of the Temple of Jupiter on the Capitol (the hill on which the temple was built) were being dug, a severed head was discovered; the priests interpreted the discovery as a portent of the supremacy of Rome
in one year tamed Cromwell ruthlessly tamed the Irish between August 1649 and May 1650

Where, when he first does lure,
The falconer has her sure.
What may not then our isle presume
While Victory his crest does plume?
What may not others fear
If thus he crowns each year?
A Caesar,[†] he, ere long to Gaul,
To Italy an Hannibal,[†]
And to all states not free
Shall climactèric[†] be.
The Pict[†] no shelter now shall find
Within his parti[†]-coloured mind,
But from this valour sad* — constant
Shrink underneath the plaid:
Happy, if in the tufted brake
The English hunter him mistake,
Nor lay his hounds in near
The Caledonian* deer. — Scottish
But thou, the Wars' and Fortune's son,
March indefatigably on,
And for the last effect
Still keep thy sword erect;
Besides the force it has to fright
The spirits of the shady night,
The same arts that did gain
A power, must it maintain.

1650 — 1681

A Caesar . . . Hannibal Julius Caesar invaded Gaul in 58 BC, and the Carthaginian general Hannibal invaded Italy in 218 BC. In line 23 Caesar was Charles; here he stands for Cromwell

climactèric of critical importance

Pict Scot (Cromwell had returned from Ireland in order to invade Scotland)

parti- *picti*, the Latin word for the Scots, means the 'painted people'; there is also a *parti-/party* pun

THE GARDEN

How vainly men themselves amaze
To win the palm,† the oak,† or bays,†
And their uncessant labours see
Crowned from some single herb or tree,
Whose short and narrow vergèd shade
Does prudently their toils upbraid,
While all flowers and all trees do close* — unite
To weave the garlands of repose.

Fair Quiet, have I found thee here,
And Innocence, thy sister dear!
Mistaken long, I sought you then
In busy companies of men.
Your sacred plants, if here below,
Only among the plants will grow.
Society is all but rude,
To this delicious solitude.

No white nor red was ever seen
So amorous as this lovely green.
Fond lovers, cruel as their flame,
Cut in these trees their mistress' name.
Little, alas, they know, or heed,
How far these beauties hers exceed!
Fair trees! wheres'e'er your barks I wound,
No name shall but your own be found.

When we have run our passion's heat,
Love hither makes his best retreat.
The gods, that mortal beauty chase,
Still* in a tree did end their race. — always
Apollo† hunted Daphne† so,
Only that she might laurel† grow.
And Pan† did after Syrinx† speed,
Not as a nymph, but for a reed.†

---

palm, oak, bays in antiquity the palm was awarded for athletic or military prowess, the oak for civic merit or valour, and the bay for poetic excellence or military victory

Apollo . . . Daphne so the god Apollo pursued the nymph Daphne, who was transformed into a *laurel* (the *bays* of line 2)

Pan . . . reed the god Pan pursued the nymph *Syrinx*, who was transformed into a reed, out of which he made his flute

What wondrous life is this I lead!
Ripe apples drop about my head;
The luscious clusters of the vine
Upon my mouth do crush their wine;
The nectarene, and curious* peach, — lovely
Into my hands themselves do reach;
Stumbling on melons, as I pass,
Ensnared with flowers, I fall on grass.

Meanwhile the mind, from pleasures less,* — lesser pleasures
Withdraws into its happiness:
The mind, that ocean where each kind
Does straight* its own resemblance find,† — immediately
Yet it creates, transcending these,
Far other worlds, and other seas,
Annihilating* all that's made — reducing
To a green thought in a green shade.

Here at the fountain's sliding foot,
Or at some fruit-tree's mossy root,
Casting the body's vest* aside, — vestment
My soul into the boughs does glide:
There like a bird it sits, and sings,
Then whets,* and combs its silver wings; — preens
And, till prepared for longer flight,
Waves in its plumes the various light.

Such was that happy garden-state,
While man there walked without a mate:
After a place so pure, and sweet,
What other help could yet be meet!
But 'twas beyond a mortal's share* — lot
To wander solitary there:
Two paradises 'twere in one
To live in paradise alone.

---

its . . . find alludes to the ancient belief that the flora and fauna of the land have equivalents in the sea

How well the skilful gardener drew
Of flowers and herbs this dial† new,
Where from above the milder sun
Does through a fragrant zodiac run;
And, as it works, the industrious bee
Computes its time as well as we.
How could such sweet and wholesome hours
Be reckoned but with herbs and flowers!
1650–2 1681

ON A DROP OF DEW

See how the orient† dew,
Shed from the bosom of the morn
Into the blowing* roses, — blossoming
Yet careless of its mansion new,
For* the clear region where 'twas born — because of
Round in itself encloses:
And in its little globe's extent,
Frames as it can its native element.* — heaven
How it the purple flower does slight,
Scarce touching where it lies,
But gazing back upon the skies,
Shines with a mournful light,
Like its own tear,
Because so long divided from the sphere.
Restless it rolls and unsecure,
Trembling lest it grow impure,
Till the warm sun pity its pain,
And to the skies exhale it back again.
So the soul, that drop, that ray
Of the clear fountain of eternal day,
Could it within the human flower be seen,
Remembering still its former height,
Shuns the sweet leaves and blossoms green,
And recollecting† its own light,

dial a garden planted as a floral sundial which shows both time of day and season
orient gleaming like a pearl
recollecting means both 'collecting again' and 'remembering'

Does, in its pure and circling thoughts, express
The greater heaven in an heaven less.
    In how coy* a figure wound, modest
    Every way it turns away:
    So the world excluding round,
    Yet receiving in the day,
    Dark beneath, but bright above,
    Here disdaining, there in love.
  How loose and easy hence to go,
  How girt and ready to ascend,
  Moving but on a point below,
  It all about does upwards bend.
Such did the manna's sacred dew distil,†
White and entire, though congealed and chill,
Congealed on earth: but does, dissolving, run
Into the glories of th' almighty sun.
1650–2 1681

THE MOWER† TO THE GLOWWORMS

Ye living lamps, by whose dear light
The nightingale does sit so late,
And studying all the summer night,
Her matchless songs does meditate;

Ye country comets, that portend
No war, nor prince's funeral,
Shining unto no higher end
Than to presage the grass's fall;

Ye glowworms, whose officious* flame obliging
To wandering mowers shows the way,
That in the night have lost their aim,
And after foolish fires† do stray;

Such did . . . distil Exodus 16.21
mower Marvell substitutes a mower (one who cuts crops with a scythe) for the conventional shepherd of pastoral poetry
foolish fires refers primarily to the will-o'-the-wisps which lead men astray, but also to the flames of love

Your courteous lights in vain you waste,
Since Juliana† here is come,
For she my mind hath so displaced
That I shall never find my home.

1681

BERMUDAS

Where the remote Bermudas ride
In the ocean's bosom unespied,
From a small boat, that rowed along,
The listening winds received this song.
'What should we do but sing his praise
That led us through the watery maze,
Unto an isle so long unknown,†
And yet far kinder than our own?
Where he the huge sea-monsters wracks,
That lift the deep upon their backs,
He lands us on a grassy stage,
Safe from the storms, and prelate's rage.
He gave us this eternal spring,
Which here enamels everything,
And sends the fowl to us in care,
On daily visits through the air.
He hangs in shades the orange bright,
Like golden lamps in a green night,
And does in the pom'granates close
Jewels more rich than Ormus† shows.
He makes the figs our mouths to meet,
And throws the melons at our feet,
But apples* plants of such a price, pineapples
No tree could ever bear them twice.
With cedars, chosen by his hand,
From Lebanon, he stores the land,
And makes the hollow seas, that roar,
Proclaim the ambergris† on shore.

Juliana the country woman loved by the mower

so long unknown the Bermudas may have been discovered by Juan Bermudez early in the sixteenth century, but were not colonised until 1612

Ormus a trading city at the mouth of the Persian Gulf (now Hormuz, Iran)

ambergris a secretion from the sperm whale which was found floating in tropical seas and used to make perfume

He cast (of which we rather boast)
The gospel's pearl upon our coast,
And in these rocks for us did frame
A temple, where to sound his name.
Oh let our voice his praise exalt,
Till it arrive at heaven's vault:
Which thence (perhaps) rebounding, may
Echo beyond the Mexique Bay.'
  Thus sung they, in the English boat,[†]
An holy and a cheerful note,
And all the way, to guide their chime,
With falling oars they kept the time.

1653–4 1681

AN EPITAPH UPON —[†]

Enough: and leave the rest to fame.
'Tis to commend her but to name.
Courtship, which living she declined,
When dead to offer were unkind.
Where never any could speak ill,
Who would officious praises spill?
Nor can the truest wit or friend,
Without detracting, her commend.
To say she lived a virgin chaste,
In this age loose and all unlaced;
Nor was, when vice is so allowed,
Of virtue or ashamed, or proud;
That her soul was on heaven so bent
No minute but it came and went;
That ready her last debt to pay
She summed her life up every day;
Modest as morn; as midday bright;
Gentle as evening; cool as night;
'Tis true: but all so weakly said,
'Twere more significant, *she's dead.*

1672 1681

Thus . . . boat the fact that the boat is English may suggest that the passengers are Puritan refugees escaping religious persecution

An Epitaph Upon — the poem commemorates Frances Jones (daughter of Lord Ranelagh), who died on 28 March 1672

Henry Vaughan

1622–95

Henry Vaughan was born in Breconshire, the son of a Welsh gentleman. He was educated privately by a tutor in Llangattock. Details of his adult life are exceedingly obscure; he may have studied at Oxford and at one of the Inns of Court. In 1645 he served as a soldier (on the Royalist side) in the Welsh campaign. Vaughan eventually turned to medicine, which he practised in Wales for the rest of his life.

As a poet Vaughan was a self-confessed disciple of George Herbert. The religious poems for which he is remembered appeared in his second collection, *Silex Scintillans* ('The Sparking Flint'), which appeared in 1650 and (in an enlarged version) 1655. He published three other collections of poetry and several translations of devotional works. His poetry is uneven in quality, but at its best it examines the spiritual qualities in nature at a level of poetical sophistication unmatched until Wordsworth.

THE RETREAT

Happy those early days! when I
Shined in my Angel-infancy.
Before I understood this place
Appointed for my second race,
Or taught my soul to fancy aught* — anything
But a white, celestial thought,
When yet I had not walked above
A mile, or two, from my first love,
And looking back (at that short space,)
Could see a glimpse of his bright face;
When on some gilded cloud or flower
My gazing soul would dwell an hour,
And in those weaker glories spy
Some shadows of eternity;
Before I taught my tongue to wound
My conscience with a sinful sound,

Or had the black art to dispense
A several* sin to every sense, separate
But felt through all this fleshly dress
Bright shoots of everlastingness.
  O how I long to travel back
And tread again that ancient track!
That I might once more reach that plain,
Where first I left my glorious train,
From whence th'enlightened spirit sees
That shady city of palm trees;
But (ah!) my soul with too much stay
Is drunk, and staggers in the way.
Some men a forward motion love,
But I by backward steps would move,
And when this dust falls to the turn
In that state I came return.

1650

PEACE

My soul, there is a country
    Far beyond the stars,
Where stands a wingèd sentry
    All skilful in the wars,
There above noise, and danger
    Sweet peace sits crowned with smiles,
And one born in a manger
    Commands the beauteous files,†
He is thy gracious friend,
    And (O my soul awake!)
Did in pure love descend
    To die here for thy sake,
If thou canst get but thither,
    There grows the flower of peace,
The rose that cannot wither,
    Thy fortress, and thy ease;
Leave then thy foolish ranges;†
    For none can thee secure,
But one, who never changes,
    Thy God, thy life, thy cure.

1650

files military formations

ranges lines of soldiers

MAN

1

Weighing the steadfastness and state* stability
Of some mean things which here below reside,
Where birds like watchful clocks the noiseless date
And intercourse of times divide,
Where bees at night get home and hive, and flowers
Early, as well as late,
Rise with the sun, and set in the same bowers;

2

I would (said I) my God would give
The staidness of these things to man! for these
To his divine appointments ever cleave,
And no new business breaks their peace;
The birds nor sow, nor reap, yet sup and dine,
The flowers† without clothes live,
Yet Solomon was never dressed so fine.†

3

Man hath still* either toys,* or care, always frivolities
He hath no root, nor to one place is tied,
But ever restless and irregular
About this earth doth run and ride,
He knows he hath a home, but scarce knows where,
He says it is so far
That he hath quite forgot how to go there.

4

He knocks at all doors, strays and roams,
Nay hath not so much wit as some stones* have lodestones
Which in the darkest nights point to their homes,
By some hid sense their Maker gave;
Man is the shuttle, to whose winding quest
And passage through these looms
God ordered motion, but ordained no rest.

1650

The flowers . . . fine paraphrase of the words of Jesus in Matthew 6.28–9

'THEY ARE ALL GONE INTO THE WORLD OF LIGHT!'

They are all gone into the world of light!
And I alone sit lingering here;
Their very memory is fair and bright,
And my sad thoughts doth clear.

It glows and glitters in my cloudy breast
Like stars upon some gloomy grove,
Or those faint beams in which this hill is dressed,
After the sun's remove.

I see them walking in an air of glory,
Whose light doth trample on my days:
My days, which are at best but dull and hoary,
Mere glimmering and decays.

O holy hope! and high humility,
High as the Heavens above!
These are your walks, and you have showed them me
To kindle my cold love,

Dear, beauteous death! the jewel of the just,
Shining nowhere, but in the dark;
What mysteries do lie beyond thy dust;
Could man outlook that mark!

He that hath found some fledged bird's nest, may know
At first sight, if the bird be flown;
But what fair well,† or grove he sings in now,
That is to him unknown.

And yet, as Angels in some brighter dreams
Call to the soul, when man doth sleep:
So some strange thoughts transcend our wonted themes,
And into glory peep.

well the vicinity of a spring

If a star were confined into a tomb
Her captive flames must needs burn there;
But when the hand that locked her up, gives room,
She'll shine through all the sphere.

O Father of eternal life, and all
Created glories under thee!
Resume thy spirit from this world of thrall
Into true liberty.

Either disperse these mists, which blot and fill
My perspective* (still) as they pass, telescope
Or else remove me hence unto that hill,
Where I shall need no glass.

1655

THE NIGHT

John iii 2

Through that pure Virgin-shrine,†
That sacred veil drawn o'er thy glorious noon
That men might look and live as glow-worms shine,
And face the moon:
Wise Nicodemus† saw such light
As made him know his God by night.†

Most blest believer he!
Who in that land of darkness and blind eyes
Thy long expected healing wings could see,
When thou didst rise,
And what can never more be done,
Did at mid-night speak with the Sun!

O who will tell me, where
He found thee at that dead and silent hour!
What hallowed solitary ground did bear
So rare a flower,
Within whose sacred leaves did lie
The fulness of the Deity.

Virgin-shrine the night sky
Wise Nicodemus . . . night a Pharisee named Nicodemus came to Jesus by night (John 3.1–2)

No mercy-seat of gold,
No dead and dusty Cherub, nor carved stone,
But his own living works did my Lord hold
And lodge alone;
Where trees and herbs did watch and peep
And wonder, while the Jews did sleep.

Dear night! this world's defeat;
The stop to busy fools; care's check and curb;
The day of Spirits; my soul's calm retreat
Which none disturb!
Christ's progress,† and his prayer time;
The hours to which high heaven doth chime.

God's silent, searching flight:
When my Lord's head is filled with dew, and all
His locks are wet with the clear drops of night;
His still, soft call;
His knocking time; the soul's dumb watch,
When Spirits their fair kindred catch.

Were all my loud, evil days
Calm and unhaunted as is thy dark tent,* tabernacle
Whose peace but by some Angel's wing or voice
Is seldom rent;
Then I in Heaven all the long year
Would keep, and never wander here.

But living where the sun
Doth all things wake, and where all mix and tire
Themselves and others, I consent and run
To every mire,
And by this world's ill-guiding light,
Err more than I can do by night.

There is in God (some say)
A deep, but dazzling darkness; as men here
Say it is late and dusky, because they
See not all clear;
O for that night! where I in him
Might live invisible and dim.

1655

progress a royal journey, in this case to 'a solitary place' (Mark 1.35) or the Mount of Olives (Luke 21.37)

Margaret Cavendish, Duchess of Newcastle

1624?–74

Margaret Lucas was born at St John's, near Colchester; she was the youngest child of Sir Thomas Lucas, a wealthy landowner who died shortly after his daughter was born. She was educated at home, and eventually joined the court as a maid-of-honour to Queen Henrietta-Maria, whom she accompanied into exile in Paris in 1643. Two years later she married William Cavendish, Marquis of Newcastle; they lived in reduced circumstances in Paris, Rotterdam and Antwerp until the Restoration in 1660, when they returned to England. In 1665 her husband was created Duke of Newcastle, and Margaret accordingly became Duchess of Newcastle. She died in 1674, and was buried in Westminster Abbey.

Margaret Cavendish wrote a large number of philosophical and scientific poems, a number of plays, and a biography of her husband. She was regarded as a figure of fun by the courtiers of Charles II, partly because she was a woman with literary ambitions, and partly because her poems and her biography of her husband were thought to be very eccentric. The extract printed here is taken from *Poems and Fancies* (1653).

From POEMS AND FANCIES

To All Writing Ladies

It is to be observed, that there is a secret working by Nature, as to cast an influence upon the minds of men. Like as in contagions, when as the air is corrupted, it produces several diseases; so several distempers of the mind, by the inflammations of the spirits. And as in healthful ages, bodies are purified, so wits are refined; yet it seems to me as if there were several invisible spirits that have several but visible powers, to work in several ages upon the minds of men. For in many ages men will be affected and disaffected alike, as in some ages so strongly and superstitiously devout that they make many gods, and in another age so atheistical as they believe in no god at all, and live to those principles. Some ages again have such strong faiths, that they will not only die in their several opinions, but they will massacre, and cut one another's throats, because their opinions are different. In some ages all men seek absolute power, and every man would be emperor of the world, which makes civil wars; for their ambition makes them restless, and their restlessness makes them seek change. Then in another age all live peaceable, and so obedient that the very governors rule with obedient power. In some ages again, all run after imitation like a company of apes, as to imitate such a poet, to be of such a philosopher's opinion. Some ages mixed, as moralists, poets, philosophers and the like; and in some ages again, all affect singularity, and they are thought the wisest that can have the most extravagant opinions. In some ages learning flourisheth in arts and sciences; other ages so dull, as they lose what former ages had taught. And in some ages it seems as if there were a commonwealth of those governing spirits, where most rule at one time. Some ages, as in aristocracy, when some part did rule; and in other ages a pure monarchy, when but one rules; and in some ages, it seems as if all those spirits were at defiance who should have most power, which makes them in confusion and war; so confused are some ages, and it seems as if there were spirits of the feminine gender, as also the masculine. There will be many heroic women in some ages, in others very prophetical; in some ages very pious and devout, for our sex is wonderfully addicted to the spirits. But this age hath produced many effeminate writers, as well as preachers, and many effeminate rulers, as well as actors. And if it be an age when the effeminate spirits rule, as most visible they do in every kingdom, let us take the advantage and make the best of their time, for fear their reign should not last long, whether it be in the Amazonian† government, or in the politic† commonwealth, or in flourishing monarchy, or in schools of divinity, or in lectures of philosophy, or in witty poetry, or anything that may bring honour to our sex; for they are poor dejected spirits that are not ambitious of fame. And though we be inferior to men, let us show ourselves a degree above beasts, and not eat and drink and sleep away our time as they do, and live only to the sense, not to the reason, and so turn into forgotten dust. But let us strive to build us tombs while we live, of noble, honourable and good activities, at least harmless:

That though our bodies die,
Our names may live to after memory.

1653

Amazonian the Amazons were a mythical race of warrior women who tolerated men only as breeding stock

politic constitutional

Thomas Traherne

1637–74

Thomas Traherne was born in Hereford, the son of a shoemaker. His parents seem to have died shortly after his birth; he was raised by a wealthy relative, and educated at Brasenose College, Oxford. He was appointed rector of Credenhill (Herefordshire) in 1657, but did not take up the post until 1661; he had been ordained in 1660. In 1669 he was appointed chaplain to Sir Orlando Bridgeman, Lord Keeper of the Great Seal, and three years later retired to Bridgeman's home in Teddington.

Traherne's only publication during his lifetime was a scholarly anti-Catholic work called *Roman Forgeries*, and just before he died he prepared *Christian Ethics* for the press. The manuscript of his poems and of the prose *Centuries of Meditations* was found on a street bookstall in London in the winter of 1896–7. The central theme of his poems and of the *Centuries* is the need for adults to recover the simple faith and perceptions of childhood.

WONDER

How like an angel came I down!
How bright are all things here!
When first among his works I did appear
O how their glory me did crown?
The world resembled his eternity,
In which my soul did walk,
And every thing that I did see,
Did with me talk.

The skies in their magnificence,
The lively, lovely air,
Oh how divine, how soft, how sweet, how fair!
The stars did entertain my sense,
And all the works of God so bright and pure,
So rich and great did seem,
As if they ever must endure,
In my esteem.

A native health and innocence
Within my bones did grow,
And while my God did all his glories show,
I felt a vigour in my sense
That was all spirit. I within did flow
With seas of life, like wine;
I nothing in the world did know,
But 'twas divine.

Harsh raggèd objects were concealed,
Oppressions, tears and cries,
Sins, griefs, complaints, dissensions, weeping eyes
Were hid, and only things revealed
Which heavenly spirits and the angels prize.
The state of innocence
And bliss, not trades and poverties,
Did fill my sense.

The streets were paved with golden stones,
The boys and girls were mine,
Oh how did all their lovely faces shine!
The sons of men were holy ones!
In joy and beauty, then appeared to me,
And every thing which here I found,
While like an angel I did see,
Adorned the ground.

Rich diamond and pearl and gold
In every place was seen.
Rare splendours, yellow, blue, red, white and green,
Mine eyes did everywhere behold,
Great wonders clothed with glory did appear,
Amazement was my bliss.
That and my wealth was everywhere;
No joy to this!

Cursed and devised proprieties,
With envy, avarice,
And fraud, those friends that spoil even paradise,
Fled from the splendour of mine eyes.
And so did hedges, ditches, limits, bounds,
I dreamt not aught of those,
But wandered over all men's grounds,
And found repose.

Proprieties themselves were mine,
And hedges ornaments,
Walls, boxes, coffers and their rich contents
Did not divide my joys, but all combine.
Clothes, ribbons, jewels, laces I esteemed,
My joys by others worn;
For me they all to wear them seemed
When I was born.

1903

From CENTURIES OF MEDITATIONS

[*A Vision of Heaven*]

The corn was orient and immortal wheat which never should be reaped nor was ever sown. I thought it had stood from everlasting to everlasting. The dust and stones of the street were as precious as gold; the gates were at first the end of the world. The green trees when I saw them first through one of the gates transported and ravished me; their sweetness and unusual beauty made my heart to leap, and almost mad with ecstasy, they were such strange and wonderful things. The men! O what venerable and reverend creatures did the aged seem! Immortal cherubims! And young men glittering and sparkling angels, and maids, strange seraphic pieces of life and beauty! Boys and girls tumbling in the streets were moving jewels; I knew not that they were born or should die. But all things abided eternally as they were in their proper places. Eternity was manifest in the light of the day, and something infinite behind everything appeared, which talked with my expectation and moved my desire. The city seemed to stand in Eden or to be built in heaven. The streets were mine, the temple was mine, the people were mine, their clothes and gold and silver were mine, as much as their sparkling eyes, fair skins and ruddy faces. The skies were mine, and so were the sun and moon and stars, and all the world was mine; and I the only spectator and enjoyer of it. I knew no churlish proprieties, not bounds nor divisions; but all the proprieties and divisions were mine, all treasures and possessors of them. So that with much ado I was corrupted, and made to learn the dirty devices of this world, which now I unlearn, and become, as it were, a little child again that I may enter into the kingdom of God.

1908

Ballads

A ballad is a narrative song, normally characterised by the recitation in simple language of a story which is presented through dialogue and described action. Traditionally the ballad was composed anonymously and passed on from one singer to another; singers often adapted both the dialect and the narrative details of ballads, so they tend to survive in several different versions. The process of collecting and publishing ballads began in the late sixteenth century. Some of the ballads collected in the next hundred years were medieval in origin, but they were printed in a form which was then contemporary. Printing inevitably inhibits further development, because the oral mode of transmission, which allows for continuous development of the ballad, gives way to the fixity of print. Eventually the printed form of ballads encouraged the composition of literary ballads, poems which imitate the conventions of authentic ballads; Coleridge's *Rime of the Ancient Mariner* and Wilde's *Ballad of Reading Gaol* are among the best examples of literary ballads.

The three ballads printed here may all be medieval in origin, but the language of the surviving versions places them in the period covered by this volume. The ballad of 'Dives and Lazarus' was first registered for printing in 1558; the ballad of 'Little Musgrave and Lady Barnard' is quoted in early seventeenth-century plays, but was not printed until 1658. 'Robin Hood and Little John' was first printed in an undated late seventeenth-century broadsheet.

DIVES AND LAZARUS†

As it fell out upon a day,
Rich Dives he made a feast,
And he invited all his friends,
And gentry of the best.

Then Lazarus laid him down and down,
And down at Dives's door:
'Some meat, some drink, brother Dives,
Bestow upon the poor.'

'Thou art none of my brother, Lazarus,
That lies begging at my door;
No meat nor drink will I give thee,
Nor bestow upon the poor.'

Then Lazarus laid him down and down,
And down at Dives's wall:
'Some meat, some drink, brother Dives.
Or with hunger starve I shall.'

'Thou art none of my brother, Lazarus,
That lies begging at my wall;
No meat nor drink will I give thee,
But with hunger starve you shall.'

Then Lazarus laid him down and down,
And down at Dives's gate:
'Some meat, some drink, brother Dives,
For Jesus Christ his sake.'

'Thou art none of my brother, Lazarus,
That lies begging at my gate;
No meat nor drink will I give thee,
For Jesus Christ his sake.'

Dives and Lazarus the ultimate source of the ballad is the parable recorded in Luke 16.19–31. In the parable the rich man is not named, but when the New Testament was translated from Greek into Latin, the man was described as a certain '*dives*' (the Latin word for 'rich man'), and eventually 'Dives' came to be thought of as a proper name. In this ballad both 'Lazarus' and 'Dives' are pronounced as two-syllable words

Then Dives sent out his merry men,
To whip poor Lazarus away;
They had no power to strike a stroke,
But flung their whips away.

Then Dives sent out his hungry dogs,
To bite him as he lay;
They had no power to bite at all,
But licked his sores away.

As it fell out upon a day,
Poor Lazarus sickened and died;
Then came two angels out of heaven
His soul therein to guide.

'Rise up, rise up, brother Lazarus,
And go along with me;
For you've a place prepared in heaven,
To sit on an angel's knee.'

As it fell out upon a day,
Rich Dives sickened and died;
Then came two serpents out of hell,
His soul therein to guide.

'Rise up, rise up, brother Dives,
And go with us to see
A dismal place, prepared in hell,
From which thou canst not flee.'

Then Dives looked up with his eyes,
And saw poor Lazarus blest:
'Give me one drop of water, brother Lazarus,
To quench my flaming thirst.

'Oh had I as many years to abide
As there are blades of grass,
Then there would be an end, but now
Hell's pains will ne'er be past.

'Oh was I now but alive again,
The space of one half hour!
Oh that I had my peace secure!
Then the devil should have no power.'

1558

LITTLE MUSGRAVE AND LADY BARNARD†

As it fell one holy-day, hey down†
As many be in the year,
When young men and maids together did go,
Their mattins* and mass to hear, — morning prayers

Little Musgrave came to the church-door;
The priest was at private mass;
But he had more mind of the fair women
Then he had of our lady's* grace. — the Virgin Mary

The one of them was clad in green,
Another was clad in pall,* — rich material
And then came in my lord Barnard's wife,
The fairest amongst them all.

She cast an eye on Little Musgrave,
As bright as the summer sun;
And then bethought this Little Musgrave,
'This lady's heart have I won.'

Quoth she, 'I have loved thee, Little Musgrave,
Full long and many a day';
'So have I loved you, fair lady,
Yet never word durst* I say.' — dared

'I have a bower at Buckelsfordbery,
Full daintily it is dight;* — decorated
It thou wilt wend thither, thou Little Musgrave,
Thou's lig* in mine arms all night.' — you shall lie

Quoth he, 'I thank ye, fair lady,
This kindness thou showest to me;
But whether it be to my weal* or woe, — happiness
This night I will lig with thee.'

Little Musgrave and Lady Barnard this ballad survives in at least fifteen different versions, in some of which Lady Barnard (or Barclay) commits suicide; this version was printed in a broadsheet in 1658. The origins of the names and events are not known

hey down a 'down' is the subject of a ballad, and 'hey' is a word interpolated into ballads to indicate rhythm; the phrase is intended to introduce the ballad, but does not have a precise meaning

With that he heard, a little tiny page,
  By his lady's coach as he ran:
'Although I am my lady's foot-page
  Yet I am lord Barnard's man.

'My lord Barnard shall know of this,
  Whether I sink or swim;'
And ever where the bridges were broke
  He laid him down to swim.

'Asleep or wake, thou lord Barnard,
  As thou art a man of life,
For Little Musgrave is at Buckelsfordbery,
  A bed with thy own wedded wife.'

'If this be true, thou little tiny page,
  This thing thou tellest to me,
Then all the land in Buckelsfordbery
  I freely will give to thee.

'But if it be a lie, thou little tiny page,
  This thing thou tellest to me,
On the highest tree in Buckelsfordbery
  Then hanged shalt thou be.'

He callèd up his merry men all:
  'Come saddle me my steed;
This night must I to Buckelsfordbery,
  For I never had greater need.'

And some of them whistled, and some of them sung,
  And some these words did say,
And ever when my lord Barnard's horn blew,
  'Away, Musgrave, away!'

'Methinks I hear the thrushel-cock* song-thrush
  Methinks I hear the jay;
Methinks I hear my lord Barnard,
  And I would I were away.'

'Lie still, lie still, thou Little Musgrave,
  And huggle* me from the cold; hug
'Tis nothing but a shepherd's boy;
  A driving his sheep to the fold.

'Is not thy hawk upon a perch?
Thy steed eats oats and hay;
And thou a fair lady in thine arms
And wouldst thou be away?'

With that my lord Barnard came to the door,
And lit a stone upon;
He pluckèd out three silver keys,
And he opened the doors each one.

He lifted up the coverlet,
He lifted up the sheet:
'How now, how now, thou Little Musgrave,
Doest thou find my lady sweet?'

'I find her sweet,' quoth Little Musgrave
'The more 'tis to my pain;
I would gladly give three hundred pounds
That I were on yonder plain.'

'Arise, arise, thou Little Musgrave,
And put thy clothès on;
It shall nere be said in my country
I have killed a naked man.

'I have two swords in one scabberd,
Full dear they cost my purse;
And thou shalt have the best of them,
And I will have the worse.'

The first stroke that Little Musgrave stroke,
He hurt lord Barnard sore;
The next stroke that lord Barnard stroke,
Little Musgrave nere* struck more. never

With that bespake this fair lady,
In bed whereas she lay:
'Although thou 'rt dead, thou Little Musgrave,
Yet I for thee will pray.

'And wish well to thy soul will I,
So long as I have life;
So will I not for thee, Barnard,
Although I am thy wedded wife.'

He cut her paps from off her breast;
Great pity it was to see
That some drops of this lady's heart's blood
Ran trickling down her knee.

'Woe worth* you, woe worth, my merry men all. happen to
You were nere born for my good;
Why did you not offer to stay my hand,
When you see me wax so wood?†

'For I have slain the bravest sir knight
That ever rode on steed;
So have I done the fairest lady
That ever did woman's deed.

'A grave, a grave,' lord Barnard cried,
'To put these lovers in;
But lay my lady on the upper hand,
For she came of the better kin.'* family

1658

ROBIN HOOD AND LITTLE JOHN†

When Robin Hood was about twenty years old,
With a hey down down and a down†
He happened to meet Little John,
A jolly brisk blade,† right for the trade,†
For he was a lusty young man.

Though he was called Little, his limbs they were large,
And his stature was seven foot high;
Wherever he came, they quaked at his name,
For soon he would make them to fly.

wax so wood become so violently angry
Robin Hood and Little John Robin Hood is the most enduring creation of the ballad tradition. He is the subject of a late medieval 'gest' (popular epic), and of a large cycle of medieval ballads. This ballad of 'Robin Hood and Little John' is a seventeenth-century version of an earlier ballad
With a hey . . . down this extra line serves to establish the metre of the ballad
jolly brisk blade handsome athletic fellow
trade way of life

How they came acquainted, I'll tell you in brief,
If you will but listen a while;
For this very jest,* amongst all the rest, tale
I think it may cause you to smile.

Bold Robin Hood said to his jolly bowmen
'Pray tarry you here in this grove;
And see that you all observe well my call,
While through the forest I rove.'

'We have had no sport for these fourteen long days,
Therefore now abroad will I go;
Now should I be beat, and cannot retreat,
My horn I will presently blow.'

Then did he shake hands with his merry men all,
And bid them at present good b'w'ye;†
Then, as near a brook his journey he took,
A stranger he chanced to espy.* see

They happened to meet on a long narrow bridge,
And neither of them would give way;
Quoth bold Robin Hood, and sturdily stood
'I'll show you right Nottingham play.'

With that from his quiver an arrow he drew,
A broad arrow with a goose-wing:
The stranger replied, 'I'll liquor thy hide,†
If thou offerst to touch the string.'

Quoth bold Robin Hood, 'Thou dost prate like an ass,
For were I to bend but my bow,
I could sent a dart quite through thy proud heart,
Before thou couldst strike me one blow.'

'Thou talkst like a coward,' the stranger replied;
'Well armed with a long bow you stand,
To shoot at my breast, while I, I protest,
Have nought but a staff in my hand.'

---

good b'w'ye goodbye (literally 'God be with you')

liquor thy hide soak your skin (i.e. throw you into the water)

'The name of a coward,' quoth Robin, 'I scorn,
   Wherefore my long bow I'll lay by:
And now, for thy sake, a staff will I take,
   The truth of thy manhood to try.'

Then Robin Hood stepped to a thicket of trees,
   And chose him a staff of ground-oak;†
Now this being done, away he did run
   To the stranger, and merrily spoke;

'Lo! see my staff, it is lusty and tough,
   Now here on the bridge we will play;
Whoever falls in, the other shall win
   The battle, and so we 'll away.'

'With all my whole heart,' the stranger replied;
   'I scorn in the last to give out;'
This said, they fell to 't without more dispute,
   And their staffs they did flourish about.

And first Robin he gave the stranger a bang,
   So hard that it made his bones ring:
The stranger he said, 'This must be repaid,
   I'll give you as good as you bring.'

'So long as I'm able to handle my staff,
   To die in your debt, friend, I scorn:
Then to it each goes, and followed their blows,
   And if they had been threshing of corn.

The stranger gave Robin a crack on the crown,
   Which causèd the blood to appear;
Then Robin, enraged, more fiercely engaged,
   And followed his blows more severe.

So thick and so fast did he lay it on him,
   With a passionate fury and ire,
At every stroke, he made him to smoke,
   As if he had been all on fire.

ground-oak   an oak sapling

O then into fury the stranger he grew,
And gave him a damnable look,
And with it a blow that laid him full low,
And tumbled him into the brook.

'I prithee, good fellow, O where art thou now?'
The stranger, in laughter, he cried;
Quoth bold Robin Hood, 'Good faith, in the flood,
And floating along with the tide.'

'I needs must acknowledge thou art a brave soul;
With thee I'll no longer contend;
For needs must I say, thou hast got the day,
Our battle shall be at an end.'

Then unto the bank he did presently wade,
And pulled himself out by a thorn;
Which done, at the last, he blowed a loud blast
Straightway on his fine bugle-horn.

The echo of which through the valleys did fly,
At which his stout bowmen appeared,
All clothèd in green, most gay to be seen;
So up to their master they steered.

'O what's the matter?' quoth William Stutely;†
'Good master, you are wet to the skin:'
'No matter,' quoth he; 'the lad which you see,
In fighting, hath tumbled me in'.

'He shall not go scot-free,' the others replied;
So straight they were seizing him there,
To duck him likewise; but Robin Hood cries,
'He is a stout fellow, forbear.'

'There's no one shall wrong thee, friend, be not afraid;
These bowmen upon me do wait;
There's threescore and nine; if thou wilt be mine,
Thou shalt have my livery straight.'

William Stutely one of the legendary followers of Robin Hood

'And other accoutrements fit for a man;
  Speak up, jolly blade, never fear;
I'll teach you also the use of the bow,
  To shoot at the fat fallow-deer.'

'O here is my hand,' the stranger replied,
  'I'll serve you with all my whole heart;
My name is John Little, a man of good mettle;* courage
  Nere doubt me, for I'll play my part.'

'His name shall be altered,' quoth William Stutely,
  'And I will his godfather be;
Prepare then a feast, and none of the least,
  For we will be merry,' quoth he.

They presently fetched in a brace of fat does,
  With humming strong liquor likewise;
They loved what was good; so, in the greenwood,
  This pretty sweet babe they baptize.

He was, I must tell you, but seven foot high,
  And, maybe, an ell in the waist;†
A pretty sweet lad; much feasting they had;
  Bold Robin the christening graced.

With all his bowmen, which stood in a ring,
  And were of the Nottingham breed;
Brave Stutely comes then, with seven yeomen,
  And did in this manner proceed.

'This infant was called John Little,' quoth he,
  'Which name shall be changèd anon;
The words we'll transpose, so wherever he goes,
  His name shall be called Little John.'

They all with a shout made the elements ring.
  So soon as the office was ore;†
To feasting they went, with true merriment.
  And tippled strong liquor galore.* in abundance

ell in the waist an English ell was about 45 inches, which is the measure of Little John's girth

office was ore ceremony was finished

Then Robin he took the pretty sweet babe,
And clothed him from top to the toe
In garments of green, most gay to be seen,
And gave him a curious* long bow. artfully made

'Thou shalt be an archer as well as the best,
And range in the greenwood with us;
Where we'll not want gold nor silver, behold,
While bishops have ought* in their purse. anything

'We live here like squires, or lords of renown,
Without ere* a foot of free land; even
We feast on good cheer, with wine, ale, and beer,
And everything at our command.'

Then music and dancing did finish the day;
At length, when the sun waxèd low,
Then all the whole train* the grove did refrain,† retinue
And unto their caves they did go.

And so ever after, as long as he lived,
Although he was proper and tall,
Yet nevertheless, the truth to express,
Still Little John they did him call.

grove did refrain the woods echoed the music and dancing

Characters

A 'character' is a short portrait in prose. This literary form became very popular in the seventeenth century, both in historical writings and in treatises designed to illustrate various virtues and vices by reference to the lives of great men. Of the four characters printed here, the first is Thomas Fuller's account of Sir Francis Bacon, the second and third are descriptions of Ben Jonson and Oliver Cromwell by Lord Clarendon, and the fourth is Richard Baxter's portrait of General Fairfax.

THOMAS FULLER ON SIR FRANCIS BACON†

None can character him to the life, save himself. He was in parts more than a man, who in any liberal profession, might be whatsoever he would himself. A great honourer of ancient authors, yet a great deviser of new ways in learning. Privy Counsellor, as to King James, so to Nature itself, diving into many of her abstruse mysteries. New conclusions he would dig out with mattocks† of gold and silver, not caring what his experience cost him, expending on the trials of Nature, all and more than he got by trials at the Bar, posterity being the better for his, though he the worse for his own dear experiments. He and his servants had all in common, the men never wanting what their master had, and thus what came flowing into him, was sent flying away from him, who in giving of rewards knew no bounds but the bottom of his own purse. Wherefore when King James heard that he had given ten pounds to an underkeeper,† by whom he had sent him a buck, the King said merrily 'I and he shall both die beggars', which was commendable prodigality in a subject. He lived many years after, and in his books will ever

Fuller on Bacon Thomas Fuller (1608–61) was the author of many topographical, historical and theological works, the best-known of which is his *History of the Worthies of England*. His 'character' of Bacon is contained in his *Church History of Britain* (1655)

mattocks a mattock is a tool for digging hard ground

underkeeper assistant gamekeeper

survive, in the reading whereof modest men commend him in what they do, condemn themselves in what they do not understand, as believing the fault in their own eyes, and not in the object.

1655

LORD CLARENDON ON BEN JONSON†

Ben Jonson's name can never be forgotten, having by his very good learning, and the severity of his nature, and manners, very much reformed the stage and indeed the English poetry itself. His natural advantages were judgement to order and govern fancy, rather than excess of fancy, his productions being slow and upon deliberation, yet then abounding with great wit and fancy, and will live accordingly; and surely as he did exceedingly exalt the English language, in eloquence, propriety, and masculine expressions, so he was the best judge of, and fittest to prescribe rules to poetry and poets, of any man who had lived with or before him, or since, if Mr Cowley† had not made a flight beyond all men, with that modesty yet to owe much of his to the example and learning of Ben Jonson. His conversation was very good and with the men of most note, and he had for many years a kindness for Mr Hyde,† till he found he betook himself to business, which he believed ought never to be preferred before his company. He lived to be very old, and till the palsy made a deep impression upon his body and his mind.

1759

LORD CLARENDON ON OLIVER CROMWELL†

He was not a man of blood, and totally declined Machiavel's† method, which prescribes upon any alteration of a government, as a thing absolutely necessary, to cut off the heads of those and extirpate their families, who are friends to the old, and it was confidently reported

Clarendon on Jonson Edward Hyde, Earl of Clarendon (1609–74), was a Royalist statesman and historian who followed Prince Charles into exile and after the Restoration became Lord Chancellor. His remarks on Ben Jonson appear in his autobiography, which was first published in 1759

Cowley the poet Abraham Cowley

Mr Hyde Clarendon is referring to himself

Clarendon on Cromwell Oliver Cromwell (1599–1658), soldier and statesman, was Lord Protector from 1653 to 1658. Clarendon's character sketch was first printed in his *History of the Rebellion* (1704)

Machiavel the advice derives from Machiavelli's *The Prince*, ch. 7

that in the Council of Officers[†] it was more than once proposed that there might be a general massacre of all the royal party, as the only expedient to secure the government, but Cromwell would never consent to it, it may be out of too much contempt of his enemies. In a word, as he had all the wickednesses against which damnation is denounced and for which hellfire is prepared, so he had some virtues, which have caused the memory of some men in all ages to be celebrated, and he will be looked on by posterity as a brave bad man.

1704

RICHARD BAXTER ON SIR THOMAS FAIRFAX[†]

For general they chose Sir Thomas Fairfax (son of the Lord Ferdinando Fairfax), who had been in the wars beyond sea,[†] and had fought valiantly in Yorkshire for parliament, though he was overpowered by the Earl of Newcastle's[†] numbers. This man was chosen because they supposed to find him a man of no quickness of parts, of no elocution, of no suspicious plotting wit, and therefore one that Cromwell could make use of at his pleasure. And he was acceptable to sober men, because he was religious, faithful, valiant and of a grave, sober and resolved disposition, very fit for execution[†] and neither too great nor too cunning to be commanded by the parliament.

1696

Council of Officers refers to the executive body of government during the Interregnum

Baxter on Fairfax Richard Baxter (1615–91) was a Puritan minister who sided with Parliament during the Civil War; his description of Sir Thomas Fairfax (1612–71), the parliamentarian general, was published in his autobiography, *Reliquiae Baxterianae*

beyond sea Fairfax had served in the Netherlands from 1629 to 1631

Earl of Newcastle Charles I's northern commander, who overran Yorkshire in June 1643

execution the fulfilling of his duties

The English Bible

The Protestant belief that the Bible should be available to all Christians in their native languages occasioned many new translations of the Bible into English, the most famous of which is the Authorised or King James Version, which was published in 1611. The Geneva Bible was published in 1559 (Psalms) and 1560 (complete Bible) for the benefit of Protestants who had escaped from the persecutions of Queen Mary; its marginal commentary is Calvinist in bias. The Church of England attempted to counteract the influence of the Geneva Bible by publishing the Bishops' Bible (1568), on which the Authorised Version was largely based. The Roman Catholics responded with an English New Testament published at Rheims (1582) and an English Old Testament published at Douai (1609–10). Thomas Sternhold published a versified version of nineteen Psalms in 1547; this was expanded to thirty-seven Psalms in 1549. In 1556 a third edition appeared with seven further Psalms by John Hopkins. In the next hundred years this edition was republished more than three hundred times.

THE TWENTY-THIRD PSALM

The Lord is my shepherd; I shall not want. He maketh me to lie down in green pastures; he leadeth me beside the still waters. He restoreth my soul; he leadeth me in the paths of righteousness for his name's sake. Yea, though I walk through the valley of the shadow of death, I will fear no evil, for thou art with me; thy rod and thy staff they comfort me. Thou preparest a table before me in the presence of mine enemies. Thou anointest my head with oil. My cup runneth over. Surely goodness and mercy shall follow me all the days of my life, and I will dwell in the house of the Lord forever.

(Authorised or 'King James' Version) 1611

My shepherd is the living Lord; nothing, therefore, I need.
In pastures fair, with waters calm, he set me for to feed.
He did convert and glad my soul, and brought my mind in frame,
To walk in paths of righteousness, for his most holy name.

Yea though I walk in vale of death, yet will I fear none ill;
Thy rod, thy staff, doth comfort me, and thou art with me still.
And in the presence of my foes, my table thou hast spread;
Thou shalt, O Lord, fill full my cup, and eke anoint my head.
Through all my life thy favour is so frankly showed to me,
That in God's house for evermore my dwelling place shall be.

(Sternhold and Hopkins) 1549

The Lord is my shepherd; I shall not want. He maketh me to rest in green pasture, and leadeth me by the still waters. He restoreth my soul and leadeth me in the paths of righteousness for his name's sake. Yea, though I should walk through the valley of the shadow of death, I will fear no evil, for thou art with me; thy rod and thy staff they comfort me. Thou dost prepare a table before me in the sight of mine adversaries. Thou dost anoint mine head with oil, and my cup runneth over. Doubtless kindness and mercy shall follow me all the days of my life, and I shall remain a long season in the house of the Lord.

(Geneva Bible) 1559

God is my shepherd, therefore I can lack nothing; he will cause me to repose myself in pasture full of grass, and he will lead me unto calm waters. He will convert my soul; he will bring me forth into the paths of righteousness for his name's sake. Yea, though I walk through the valley of the shadow of death, I will fear no evil, for thou art with me; thy rod and thy staff be the things that do comfort me. Thou wilt prepare a table before me in the presence of mine adversaries; thou hast anointed my head with oil, and my cup shall be brimful. Truly felicity and mercy shall follow me all the days of my life, and I will dwell in the house of God for a long time.

(Bishops' Bible) 1568

Our Lord ruleth me, and nothing shall be wanting to me; in place of pasture there hath he placed me. Upon the water of reflection he hath brought me up; he hath converted my soul. He hath conducted me upon the paths of justice, for his name. For although I shall walk in the midst of the shadow of death, I will not fear evils, because thou art with me; thy rod and thy staff, they have comforted me. Thou hast prepared in my sight a table against them that trouble me. Thou hast fatted my head with oil, and my chalice inebriating how goodly it is. And thy mercy shall follow me all the days of my life, and that I may dwell in the house of the Lord in longitude of days.

(Douai Bible) 1609–10

Further Reading

Anne Barton, *Ben Jonson, Dramatist* (Cambridge University Press, 1977)

Norman Blake, *Shakespeare's Language* (Macmillan, London, 1983)

D. Bush, *English Literature in the Earlier Seventeenth Century* (revised edition, Oxford University Press, 1962)

D. Bush, *Mythology and the Renaissance Tradition in English Poetry* (Pageant Books, New York, 1957)

John Carey, *John Donne: Life, Mind and Art* (Faber, London, 1981)

Chris Coles, *How to Study a Renaissance Play: Marlowe, Jonson, Webster* (Macmillan, London, 1986)

E. R. Curtius, *European Literature and the Latin Middle Ages*, trans. W. R. Trask (RKP, London, 1948)

Anthony Dawson, *Watching Shakespeare: A Playgoers' Guide* (Macmillan, London, 1987)

A. G. Dickens (ed.), *Background to the English Renaissance* (Gray-Mills, London, 1974)

Margaret Drabble, *The Oxford Companion to English Literature* (Oxford University Press, 1985)

G. R. Elton (ed.), *Renaissance and Reformation, 1300–1648* (Macmillan, third edition, 1976)

Alastair Fowler, *A History of English Literature* (Blackwell, Oxford, 1987)

Christopher Hill, *Milton and the English Revolution* (Faber, London, 1977)

Emrys Jones, *The Origins of Shakespeare* (Oxford University Press, 1977)

Bruce King, *Seventeenth-Century English Literature* (Macmillan, London, 1985)

C. S. Lewis, *English Literature in the Sixteenth Century excluding Drama* (Oxford University Press, 1954)

C. S. Lewis, *The Discarded Image: An Introduction to Medieval and Renaissance Literature* (Cambridge University Press, 1964)

Arthur Lovejoy, *The Great Chain of Being* (Harvard University Press, Cambridge, Mass., 1936)

Anthony Low, *Love's Architecture: Devotional Modes in Seventeenth-Century English Poetry* (New York University Press, 1978)

John Peck and Martin Coyle, *How to Study a Shakespeare Play* (Macmillan, London, 1985)

Isabel Rivers, *Classical and Christian Ideas in English Renaissance Poetry: A Students' Guide* (Allen & Unwin, London, 1979)

Murray Roston, *Sixteenth-Century English Literature* (Macmillan, London, 1982)

Michael Scott, *Renaissance Drama and a Modern Audience* (Macmillan, London, 1982)

E. N. Williams, *Penguin Dictionary of English and European History 1485–1789* (Harmondsworth, 1980)
E. Wind, *Pagan Mysteries in the Renaissance* (Faber, London, 1958)

Index of First Lines

Index of Authors

Source List

Lancelot Andrewes: *Sermons*, ed. G. M. Story (OUP, 1967); **Francis Bacon:** *Selection of Writings*, ed. Sidney Warhaft (Macmillan of Canada, 1965); **Richard Barnfield:** edited from original publication; **Beaumont and Fletcher:** *The Maid's Tragedy*, ed. H. B. Norland, Regent's Renaissance Drama Series (Edward Arnold, 1968); **Nicholas Breton:** *Works in Verse and Prose*, ed. A. B. Grosart (1879); **Sir Thomas Browne:** *The Major Works*, ed. C. A. Patrides (Penguin English Library, 1977); **Thomas Campion:** *The Works of Thomas Campion*, ed. A. H. Bullen (1889); **Thomas Carew:** edited from 1640 original; **Margaret Cavendish:** from original edition; **George Chapman:** edited from original text; **Abraham Cowley:** *English Writings*, ed. A. R. Waller (CUP, 1906); **Richard Crashaw:** *Poetical Works*, ed. L. C. Martin (OUP, 1927); **Samuel Daniel:** *Delia*, edited from original; **John Donne:** *Complete English Poems*, ed. A. J. Smith (Penguin, 1971); **John Donne:** *Selected Poems*, ed. Neil Rhodes (Penguin, 1987); **Michael Drayton:** *Poems of Michael Drayton*, ed. John Buxton (Routledge, 1953); **William Drummond:** *Poems and Prose*, ed. R. H. Macdonald (Scottish Academic Press, 1976); **George Gascoigne:** *The Green Knight*, ed. R. Pooley (Carcanet, 1982); **Arthur Golding:** *Shakespeare's Ovid*, ed. W. H. P. Rouse (facsimile of 1904 edition) (Centaur Press, 1961); **Sir Fulke Greville:** *Selected Writings of Fulke Greville*, ed. Joan Rees (Athlone Press, 1973); **Robert Greene:** edited from original text; **Henry VIII and Queen Elizabeth:** *Poetry of the English Renaissance*, ed. J. W. Hebel and H. M. Hudson (Appleton-Century-Crofts, NY, 1929); **George Herbert:** *Poetical Works*, ed. Gillfillan (1853); **George Herbert:** *Works of George Herbert*, ed. F. E. Hutchinson (OUP, 1941); **Robert Herrick:** *Poetical Works*, ed. L. C. Martin (OUP, 1956); **Richard Hooker:** *The Works of Richard Hooker*, ed. Gerald Hammond (OUP, 1865); **Henry Howard, Earl of Surrey:** *Selected Poems*, ed. D. Keene, Fyfield Books (Carcanet, 1985); **Lucy Hutchinson:** *Memoirs of Colonel Hutchinson* (Bohn, 1854); **King James:** *Counterblast to Tobacco*, edited from original text; **Ben Jonson:** *Three Comedies*, ed. M. Jamieson (Penguin English Library, 1966); **Ben Jonson:** *Complete Poems*, ed. G. Parfitt (Penguin English Poets, 1975); **Ben Jonson:** *Volpone*, ed. Philip Brockbank, New Mermaids (Ernest Benn, 1968); **Ben Jonson:**

Alchemist, ed. Douglas Brown, New Mermaids (Ernest Benn, 1966); **Ben Jonson:** *Bartholomew Fair*, ed. E. P. Horsman, Revels Plays (Methuen, 1960); **Henry King:** *The Poems of Bishop Henry King*, ed. Margaret Crum (OUP, 1965); **Thomas Lodge:** edited from original text; **Richard Lovelace:** edited from 1649 original; **John Lyly:** *Euphues*, ed. E. Arber (Murray & Son, 1868); **Christopher Marlowe:** *Complete Plays and Poems*, ed. Pendry and Maxwell, Everyman (J. M. Dent, 1976); **Andrew Marvell:** *Complete Poems*, ed. E. S. Donno (Penguin, 1972); **Thomas Middleton:** edited from original text; **John Milton:** *The Poems*, ed. J. Carey and A. Fowler (Longman's Annotated English Poets, 1986); **John Milton:** *Prose Writings*, ed. K. M. Burton, Everyman (J. M. Dent, 1958); **Thomas Nashe:** *The Unfortunate Traveller and Other Works*, ed. J. B. Steane (Penguin English Library, 1972); **George Peele:** edited from original text; **Francis Quarles:** *Works of Quarles*, ed. A. Grosart (1880–1); **Sir Walter Ralegh:** *Selected Writings*, ed. G. Hammond (Penguin Classics, 1986); **William Shakespeare:** edition used, The Macmillan Shakespeare: *Richard III*, ed. R. Adams; *Romeo and Juliet*, ed. J. Gibson; *The Taming of the Shrew*, ed. R. Hood; *A Midsummer Night's Dream*, ed. N. Sanders; *Richard II*, ed. R. Adams; *The Merchant of Venice*, ed. C. Parry; *Henry IVth Part I*, ed. P. Hollindale; *Henry IVth Part II*, ed. T. Parr; *Much Ado About Nothing*, ed. J. McKeith; *Henry V*, ed. B. Phythian; *Julius Caesar*, ed. D. R. Elloway; *As You Like It*, ed. P. Hollindale; *Twelfth Night*, ed. E. A. J. Honinghmann; *Hamlet*, ed. N. Alexander; *Othello*, ed. C. Hilton and R. T. Jones; *King Lear*, ed. P. Edwards; *Macbeth*, ed. D. R. Elloway; *Antony and Cleopatra*, ed. J. McKeith and R. Adams; *Coriolanus*, ed T. Parr; *The Winter's Tale*, ed. C. Parry; *The Tempest*, ed. A. C. Spearing; **Sir John Suckling:** *The Works of Sir John Suckling*, ed. A. Hamilton Thompson (Routledge, 1910); **Sir Philip Sidney:** *Arcadia*, ed. M. Evans (Penguin, 1977); **Sir Philip Sidney:** *An Apology for Poetry*, ed. G. Shepherd (Thomas Nelson/Manchester University Press, 1965); **Sir Philip Sidney:** *The Poems of Sir Philip Sidney*, ed. W. A. Ringler (OUP, 1962); **Edmund Spenser:** *Books I and II of the Faerie Queene, The Mutability Cantos and Selections from the Minor Poetry*, ed. R. Kellogg and O. Steele (Odyssey Press, NY, 1965); **Chidiock Tichborne:** *An Anthology of 16th Century Poetry*, ed. R. Hamilton and S. de Lancey, Nottigham Drama Texts (Nottingham University Press, 1981); **Cyril Tourneur:** *Revenger's Tragedy*, ed. Brian Gibbons, New Mermaids (Ernest Benn, 1967); **Thomas Traherne:** *Poems, Centuries and Thanksgivings*, ed. Anne Ridler (OUP, 1966); **Henry Vaughan:**

Complete Poems, ed. A. Rudram (Penguin English Poets, 1976); **Edmund Waller:** *Poetical Works* (1857); **Izaak Walton:** *The Complete Angler* (Penguin, 1939); **Izaak Walton:** *Izaak Walton's Lives* (T. Nelson & Son); **John Webster:** *Three Plays*, ed. D. Gunby (Penguin, 1972); **Sir Thomas Wyatt:** *Collected Poems*, ed. J. Daalder (OUP, 1975).

Additional Source Books

Mirror for Magistrates, ed. L. B. Campbell (CUP, 1938); *English and Scottish Ballads*, ed. F. J. Child (George Harrap, 1904); *Characters from the History and Memoirs of the Sixteenth Century*, ed. David Nichol Smith (OUP, 1920); *Bible: 23rd Psalm*, from 17th century edition.